ACTIVE
TREATMENT OF
DEPRESSION

Also by Richard O'Connor

Undoing Depression: What Therapy Doesn't Teach You and
Medication Can't Give You

A NORTON PROFESSIONAL BOOK

ACTIVE
TREATMENT OF
DEPRESSION

Richard O'Connor, M.S.W., Ph.D.

W.W. Norton & Company
New York • London

For information about permission to reproduce selections
from this book, write to
Permissions, W. W. Norton & Company, Inc.,
500 Fifth Avenue, New York, NY 10110

The text of this book is composed in Electra
Composition by PRD Group
Manufacturing by Haddon Craftsmen

Library of Congress Cataloging-in-Publication Data

O'Connor, Richard.
   Active treatment of depression/Richard O'Connor
      p.   cm.
   "A Norton professional book."
   Includes bibliographical references and index.
   ISBN 0-393-70322-3
   1. Depression, Mental—Treatment.   2. Depression, Mental—Patients—Counseling of.
   I. Title.

RC537.O323   2000
616.85'2706—dc21   00-064724

W. W. Norton & Company, Inc., 500 Fifth Avenue, New York, N.Y. 10110
www.wwnorton.com
W. W. Norton & Company Ltd., 10 Coptic Street, London WC1A 1PU

1 2 3 4 5 6 7 8 9 0

Contents

Acknowledgments

I AM MOST IN DEBT to my patients, especially those who were brave enough to let me use bits and pieces of their stories here; but equally to all my patients and group members who have let me share part of their lives. Also to visitors to my Web site and others who have told me of their experiences being treated for depression. One thing I continually note about depression is that patients, for all the "self absorption" that is supposed to accompany the disease, are always happy to see that their own experience can make someone else's life a little easier.

The major intellectual sources for this book should be fairly obvious from the references, but I want to emphasize some authors whose work I have found especially inspiring and stimulating. These include Irwin Hoffman, Paul Lippmann, David Karp, Darlene Ehrenberg, Paul Wachtel, Martin Seligman, and George Vaillant. To William Styron I owe special thanks for his courage and example.

The staff of the Surgeon General's Office were kind enough to let me participate in a small way in the development of the Surgeon General's Report on Mental Health, an experience that taught me a great deal about how depression is perceived in the wider world. The Carter Center in Atlanta, long concerned about addressing mental health as a public health issue, merits the gratitude of all for their leadership. Representative Nancy Johnson got me into the White House Conference on Mental Health, a wonderful experience.

Members of the Mood Disorders Support Group/New York have allowed me to learn from them, and I am very grateful. They have a powerful model for self-help, and I hope that someday groups like theirs will take root all across the country.

The Austin Riggs Center and particularly Rachel Vigneron in the library were extremely helpful and accessible, a great resource for those of us far from a university. Jim Levine, who has been my agent through two books now, has been instrumental in helping me focus. And Susan Munro and Regina Ardini at Norton have been very wise and helpful in making this book as coherent as it is.

My now-adult children, Sarah and Michael, have been a constant source of inspiration to me, and it's been an amazing journey to see maturity, judgment, and joy develop firsthand. Most of all, I am grateful to my wife, Robin, for working so hard to keep me relatively sane and happy, and for always believing in me. You can't get along without that.

Introduction

INTRODUCTIONS ARE WRITTEN when books are completed. As I approach the end of this one, I suspect I understand one of the reasons why Freud never wrote his promised book on technique: It's a very difficult task. To propose rules about what to say when in psychotherapy can seem to be an exercise in either hubris or ignorance. How to respond to a given patient in a given hour depends on so many factors—tact and timing, the patient's diagnosis, the context of the relationship so far, short-term tactical needs vs. long-term strategic goals, the therapist's personality, the therapist's emotional reaction to the patient in the moment, and so on ad infinitum—that there are potentially thousands of "correct" or helpful interventions. In addition, one of the therapist's most powerful tools is his own unconscious; his associations to the patient's material can often advance the therapy even when he is uncertain exactly where they will lead. So it can seem like a forlorn hope to try to write a prescriptive book. But I am trying, despite all these caveats, because people with depression need a different approach to treatment than what standard practice is today.

This is a book for mental health professionals who treat patients with depression. I am a therapist who suffers from depression myself. I have tried to write something that will be practical and helpful to therapists, physicians, and pharmacologists who are trying to help patients who do not respond quickly or easily to the standard prescribed treatments. Unfortunately, research is confirming that these are the majority of people suffering from depression. As I did the literature review for this book, I found myself more and more concerned that most care for depression is superficial, inadequate, and based on false information. Many assumptions commonly held in the professional community— that newer antidepressants are reliably safe and effective, that short-term cognitive and interpersonal psychotherapy help most patients, that many people with depression can be effectively treated in primary care, that most patients can recover from an episode of depression without lasting damage—on close examination turn out not to be true at all. And practice based on these assumptions is not only inadequate for treatment of depression, it can also actually exacerbate the disease.

Most therapists and psychopharmacologists can help a patient recover from a single episode of depression, but our relapse rate is far too high: Patients who have one episode of major depression are 50 percent likely to have another; patients who have three episodes are ninety percent likely to have more (Thase, 1999). And, if we are honest with ourselves, we will also admit that our batting average is not so good either; for every patient we can help, we probably see two whom we can't. *Active Treatment of Depression* suggests that we accept the idea that depression is a chronic disease, and that we help our patients plan their lives accordingly. Medications are usually helpful and often will be a part of the patient's life for some time to come, but rarely can they prevent future episodes and help the patient resolve the problems that led to trouble in the first place. Patients must learn, practice, and plan to reinforce more adaptive ways of functioning—they must change how they deal with emotions, they must identify and challenge depressed thinking habits, they must change how they work, play, take care of themselves, cope with stress and loss, and interact with others. And therapists must be ready to give hope, to reduce shame, to be mentor, coach, cheerleader, idealized object, playmate, nurturer, *nudge*—many different roles. In doing so, inevitably, we must challenge many of our assumptions about the use of the self in psychotherapy.

The ugly fact is that too much of treatment for depression only reinforces the disease. Any experienced therapist has encountered patients who have been damaged by previous treatment, sometimes by highly qualified practitioners. Analytic therapy has reinforced depression in some who become mired in rumination. Directive treatment has demoralized and shamed patients by sadistically attacking their defenses. Medication, even when effective, can reinforce passivity. ECT can do the same. Yet all of these approaches also can be beneficial, with the right patient at the right time. How do we understand this?

I urge the reader to accept the fact that no single theory can yet explain this complex condition that affects more than 20 percent of the population. In fact, trying to understand depression exclusively from a single perspective—for instance, a cognitive-behavioral, psychodynamic, or a biochemical point of view— will necessarily limit our understanding and our ability to help our patients. Rather, we must be willing to take the best knowledge from many different points of view and shape it into practice guidelines. In doing so, we must also practice "active treatment" because many of our customary ways of operating are counterproductive with depression. We must find ways of lending hope, of engaging the patient's emotions, of mitigating the effects of the patient's shame, of helping the patient see the connections between what happens in his life and how he feels inside. We must engage family members as helpers, advocate for medication, and actively plan for how the patient can continue to recover when treatment ends.

Our field is fragmented and divided. It would be foolish to try to write a book on a subject as broad as depression without creating disagreement and controversy. As a patient advocate, I want to challenge assumptions and shake up the way we normally do business. In doing so I have tried to be fair, complete, and objective, but it's quite possible that I have in places not presented a perfect understanding of why some people might hold a position I am in disagreement with. When this happens, I hope that the reader will not hold my error against me immoderately but judge it in the overall context of the message in this book. I think that this will be good for the reader; one of the most destructive problems in the mental health professions — probably in all professions — is that we tend only to read that which confirms our pre-existing beliefs.

I also hope that the reader will consider the nature of the problem we're trying to address. Depression is more difficult to treat than we want to acknowledge. Everyone believes that research has proven that cognitive behavioral therapy, interpersonal psychotherapy, and medication are demonstrably and equally effective in treating depression. But that was at three months after treatment. At eighteen months, not a single one of the patients, no matter what treatment they'd received, was any better off than the control group (Shea et al., 1992). In order to truly help people who are suffering with this venomous and insidious condition, we have to be willing to challenge some of the assumptions we hold dear. I hope the reader will bring an open mind. I have attempted to present a reasonably thorough and objective review of the current state of knowledge, and I hope that the result is both reliable and provocative.

Much of what is to follow is rather prescriptive. I don't want to gloss over the individual differences between patients and between therapists. Any therapeutic dyad is a highly unique entity. Each therapist is — or should be — struggling with his own uncertainty, how to help this patient in this situation given the limits of his professional knowledge, his incomplete understanding of the patient, the constraints of the therapeutic relationship, and individual biases and anxieties. I'm trying to give advice to the therapist based on my own perspective about depression, advice that hopefully informs and enlightens without ignoring the uniqueness of the patient-therapist situation and without ignoring the complex, unfathomable, potential of human existence. I do not believe it is helpful for our profession to pursue the belief that there is one, and only one, technically correct intervention at any given point in time in a therapeutic relationship. Rather, there are infinite interventions, some more helpful than others. But even the most helpful interventions have the effect of constraining the future dialogue, of co-constructing a reality that will have an impact on the future that is impossible to predict with reliability. When the patient has depression, that new, constructed reality must provide a different perspective: hope, alternatives, openings, even wisdom and power. To settle for less is to sell the patient short.

The plan of the book is as follows: The next three chapters present three perspectives on what we know about depression. Chapter 1 describes what it's like to live with depression—the effects, the stigma, the difficulty getting treatment—which I think will unfortunately be new information to many therapists and psychiatrists. Chapter 2 introduces what I refer to as the "common-sense" model of depression, a model that emphasizes the multiple systems involved in the illness and the functional autonomy of the disease. Depression is, perhaps foremost among other things, a vicious circle that generates the conditions that sustain it, and the therapist and patient need to consider all the systems involved in this process if treatment is to be successful. Chapter 3 describes the "skills of depression"—the things we get good at that we should not be so good at, like stuffing feelings, depressed logic, victimizing, passive aggression, and recruiting accomplices. These are skills of depression in that we have learned them in a vain effort to save ourselves pain, by keeping us out of the feared situation—out of intimacy, or conflict, or the demand to perform. But they backfire on us and only reinforce the depressed state. Part of any therapy is to help the patient take these skills and reapply them in newer, more adaptive, ways.

The balance of the book is a review of principles of active treatment. Chapter 4, "A Biopsychosocial Assessment," presents a framework for conducting a systematic assessment of the individual patient who may be suffering from depression, an assessment that leads to a therapeutic focus. It also discusses issues involved in management of the suicidal patient. Chapter 5 focuses on the necessity of engaging the patient's emotions in the treatment process, a special problem with depressed patients, who are trying with all their might not to feel anything at all. Chapter 6, "Grief, Entitlement, Rage, and Hope," reviews psychodynamic thinking about depression, discusses the concept of "resistance" to treatment and what it means with this unique condition, and presents some of the reasons why depression manifests itself differently in men and women. Then, Chapter 7 reviews the appropriate use, limitations, and advantages of antidepressant medication.

Chapter 8, "Use Yourself Wisely," focuses on the role of the therapist's self in the treatment of depression. Treating patients with depression is hard work, and the therapist must make sure he is in good mental shape in order to bear the strain. At the same time, there are great rewards in our work, which if we appreciate them can contribute greatly toward keeping us fit. This chapter also talks about "the therapist's use of self" in the other sense of the phrase—use of the self as a therapeutic tool—specifically, playfulness and self-revelation. It concludes with a discussion of depression among therapists and what we can and should do about it.

The next chapter, "Maintain a Therapeutic Focus," presents some ideas about the concept of a central issue in depression—one that is manifested in the first episode, the immediate precipitant, and the transference. Chapter 10 discusses how the therapist understands and interacts with the patient's interpersonal world—too often a stable, dysfunctional world that reinforces the depressed state. It contains a review of interpersonal psychotherapy for depression, one of the newer widely accepted treatment methods. Chapter 11 focuses on the patient's cognitive processes, how they contribute to and in turn are affected by his emotional state. Principles of cognitive-behavioral therapy are reviewed, with a discussion of what it takes to be a good enough cognitive therapist.

Self-care is the topic of Chapter 12. Depression is an illness, and the patient has to learn to take adequate care of himself; not just physical and emotional care but also prevention of further damage to self and people he loves through impulsive or destructive activity. Chapter 13, "Practice, Practice, Practice," reviews a set of twelve "aphorisms of depression," which I suggest be introduced to the patient early in the treatment and reviewed frequently as treatment progresses. Some of these are rather bald confrontations of resistances ("There is a part of me that doesn't want to get well") that can disarm defenses when presented matter-of-factly as symptoms of the disease. Others are more simply reminders of the principles of recovery ("I need to practice detachment"). The final chapter discusses issues of termination with the depressed patient, including the likelihood of recurrence of the disease and the patient's need for continuing care. It ends with a model of a self-help group for depression which I have found popular with patients and personally rewarding.

This book does not address bipolar disorder, for two reasons. One is that I have not treated enough bipolar patients to talk intelligently about the subject; the other is that I tend to agree with the belief that bipolar disorder is a different species than simple depression. While major depression, dysthymia, and a depressed adjustment reaction may be points on a continuum, it seems most useful at present to view manic depression as inherently different. Much of what I have to say here may be useful for working with bipolar patients in a depressed state, but I make no claim to have any particular insight on this condition.

For reasons of space, I've also had to omit discussion of depression among the young and the old. This is a decision I've taken with regret, because if depression is an epidemic it seems to be most acutely so at the ends of the age spectrum. I am hopeful that better understanding of the genesis of depression among young people will result in changes in our social structure that can reduce the impact of the disease, but exploration of that subject will have to wait for another occasion. And it seems to me also that much of the rise in depression among the aging has to do with social change that has made it more difficult to find meaning and fulfillment in life, a process that begins far earlier and only becomes manifest as we age. But these topics will have to wait for another time.

The sensitive topics of gender and disability merit a few words. I have made a decision in this book to stick with the masculine pronoun rather than try to alternate he and she, him and her, or other strategies I've seen used to try to overcome a gender bias in language. I do this because all these other strategies, to my ear, end up sounding labored and distracting. I hope that the reader who is attuned to these issues will give me the benefit of the doubt and not assume I am unconsciously sexist.

I've used the word "patient" rather than "client" or "consumer" for much the same reason: just to be consistent and stick with generally accepted terminology.

I certainly am aware that being considered a patient can convey all sorts of messages about one's competency, but I hope that the tone of the book conveys the great respect I feel for people who suffer with depression.

Even more of a problem is what to call someone who has depression. There is more than a suggestion of dismissal in some writing that uses the term "depressive" as a label, and I've tried to avoid that use. But sometimes it just gets too awkward to keep referring to "the depressed person," and I've used shorthand. Similarly with referring to the depressed person as a victim or sufferer; although the individual suffers, he's much more than those labels imply.

There is also the matter of my self-consciousness about my own depression. In some situations I'm afraid I will confuse the reader because I will use the word "we" to refer to the community of therapists, while at other times I use it to refer to people with depression. I hope it is clear from the context which usage is intended.

In *Undoing Depression* I wrote about my own experience with the disease in order to provide some guidelines for self-help and recovery to the millions of people who are unable to get adequate care. This is, on the surface, much less of a personal book; my story as someone with depression is not particularly interesting or relevant to the professional reader, except specifically in some areas where I have some experience about patients' reaction to the therapist's depression. Nevertheless, this book cannot not be personal, in that my opinions about what the depressed patient needs from the therapist are inevitably informed by my identification with the patient. I don't think I'm alone in this. I believe that most of the best theorists and therapists have a deeper understanding of the patient's needs because of their own experience with the same struggles. As I do workshops and consultations I am moved by the increasing number of professionals who are willing to acknowledge that they get depressed too. Unfortunately, these are still the minority. As professionals, we too often seem to be no more able than the general public to come to grips with the stigma of depression. I hope that this book will help change that.

ACTIVE
TREATMENT OF
DEPRESSION

What is Depression?

THREE MONTHS AGO, 24-year-old Jessica was hospitalized after an abortive suicide attempt. Today, she sits in my office, the picture of despair. Tense and
worried, she has intrusive thoughts of hurting herself or of other impulsive actions,
which she tries desperately to control. She feels guilty and inadequate, hopeless
and helpless. Despite medication, she wakes up every morning at 5 A.M. after a
few hours of sleep. She's lost 20 pounds. She's had to reduce her responsibilities
at work, where she cannot concentrate or make decisions. She constantly asks others for reassurance. Although she goes through the motions of living, she's unable
to enjoy any activity. This all seemed to come out of the blue. Jessica had a fight
with her mother and decided it was time to leave the nest. She confidently made
plans to find her own place until early one morning the impulse to hurt herself—
for no reason that she can understand—suddenly overcame her and she slashed
her wrists.

Roger is a man in his fifties who works in an autobody shop. Roger joined AA and
quit drinking about two years ago, and it's made his life smoother but not much
happier. He works steadily and does everything he can to support his wife and children, but takes no pleasure in it. He never has any energy or shows any excitement.
He's quiet and unassertive, and gets picked on at work. His rotten self-esteem is
made worse by his virtual illiteracy, a result of undiagnosed dyslexia. This also
makes him rely on his wife to make all the important decisions about the family.
Roger has been unhappy and in the background almost all his life, since his mother
died when he was 9. He started drinking and drugging in his early teens, but when
he was a young man it was important to him to have a family and be a responsible adult; he's done the best he could, just never enjoyed it.

These are the two principal subtypes of depression. Jessica is diagnosed with
major depression. The formal criteria as spelled out in the *Diagnostic and
Statistical Manual of Mental Disorders*, 4th ed. (DSM-IV; American Psychiatric

Association, 1994) for her diagnosis include a depressed mood or a loss of interest or pleasure in ordinary activities most of the day and nearly every day for at least two weeks, accompanied by at least four of the following symptoms:

1. significant weight loss when not dieting, weight gain, or change in appetite
2. insomnia or hypersomnia nearly every day
3. psychomotor agitation or retardation (activity level slows down or increases)
4. fatigue or loss of energy
5. feelings of worthlessness or excessive guilt
6. diminished ability to think, concentrate, or make decisions
7. recurrent thoughts of death or suicide, suicidal ideation, or a suicidal plan or attempt

Roger's diagnosis is dysthymia. In the *DSM-IV*, the essential criterion for this diagnosis is a depressed mood for most of the day, for more days than not, for a period of at least two years. In addition, there must be at least two of the following symptoms while feeling depressed:

1. poor appetite or overeating
2. insomnia or hypersomnia
3. low energy or fatigue
4. low self-esteem
5. poor concentration or difficulty making decisions
6. feelings of hopelessness

Strictly speaking, almost all the new developments in psychopharmacology for depression apply to Jessica but not to Roger. Major depression has the advantage of being researchable. It is usually characterized by rapid onset, and most patients can be expected to get better within a reasonable amount of time. But we conveniently ignore the fact that most people like Jessica are permanently damaged by their experience with depression, and are likely to have more episodes as their life goes on. As far as Roger is concerned, no one wants to fund research lasting the amount of time to treat dysthymia adequately. But that doesn't stop Roger's doctor from prescribing the same type of antidepressants for him. In fact, they seem to be working better for Roger than for Jessica right now.

There is room for a great deal of discussion, some of which we will explore, about whether Roger and Jessica have two different but related diseases, or two manifestations of the same process. Whichever position we take, it's important to recognize that for both Roger and Jessica depression represents at least four things all at the same time: an adaptation, an illness, a communication, and a vicious circle. I make no apologies for this state of affairs; if light can be both a wave and a particle and an electron can be in two places at once, we can surely think of something as complex as depression as having several coexisting manifestations. In fact, we can avoid a lot of argument and misunderstanding about depression if we make it clear which aspect we are talking about. In order to treat depression successfully, we must keep all aspects in mind, but may want to emphasize one or another at any given time depending on the needs of the patient.

Depression as adaptation. When a hungry infant's cries elicit no response, eventually the child will retreat into a state that looks like depression: withdrawn, self-absorbed, and self-soothing. This state serves several purposes: The infant is saving his resources for another occasion when the environment may be more responsive, putting a limit on his own distress, and reducing the risk of alienating his environment.

Likewise, depression in an adult is an adaptation to a nonresponsive environment. When we lose someone who loves us, grief is the natural result. When we don't believe we can replace that love, we become depressed. We stop trying to achieve what we think is impossible. If we become severely depressed, we are likely to suffer further rejection and outright discrimination, to which ironically our only response seems to be adoption of a depressed identity. Depression becomes a solution to a problem for us. Instead of continuing to seek love, justice, or whatever we feel deprived of, we lower our expectations and focus on trying to prevent further disappointment and hurt.

Depression as illness. Depression is highly analogous to a systemic disease like a fever or an endocrine malfunction. It affects our entire being and experience. We don't merely have trouble sleeping or guilty thoughts or lack of energy or a feeling of pessimism and hopelessness, we have all at the same time; it's a predictable syndrome in which the symptoms accompany each other. We function at a less effective rate physically, intellectually, emotionally, socially. There is good reason to believe that something is going haywire in our brains that mediates all these effects, something that can often be helped by medication.

Recognizing that one is ill is the first step in recovery. When we know that we are sick, we start listening to professional advice, we take better care of ourselves, we give ourselves a moratorium from striving. Much of the difficulty with depression is that it is often very difficult for the patient to recognize his illness. Much of the hope for prevention and improved treatment comes from improved general awareness of the disease aspects of depression.

Depression as communication. Psychiatric symptoms can be understood as a disguised attempt at expressing feelings, a communication from the sufferer to others in his life. The disguise can be necessary for a variety of reasons—the nature of the relationship may make open expression of needs undesirable, or we may not want to consciously acknowledge our feelings. Our defense mechanisms work to keep the feeling out of conscious awareness, but the other person usually responds to the feeling. When someone close to us "forgets" our birthday, we feel justified in being angry because we assume that the forgetting is a communication.

Depression, at one time or another, can express all these messages and many
more: *Take care of me. Give me a little slack. You can't help me. Don't leave me.
Give me some extra attention. No one understands me. I can't take it anymore.
I hate myself. You don't really love me.* Therapy can be directed toward twin goals:
helping the patient become more aware of needs and feelings that he keeps out
of awareness but nevertheless communicates to others, and helping him get those
needs met in ways that are less likely to backfire and do not continue to reinforce the illness aspect of depression.

Depression as vicious circle. An acute illness will remit when the disease has
run its course. We can leave behind a particular adaptation when the external
stress is removed. But depression is a self-reinforcing cycle, a functional autonomy that does not end because the conditions that brought it about are
relieved. The neurochemistry in the brain doesn't reliably repair itself when
good things happen to us. A continually depressed mood means that we only
see things that confirm our depression. We think depressed thoughts and we act
in self-destructive ways, and we do real damage to ourselves and those we love.
All our experience confirms that we are right to be depressed. We cannot lift
ourselves up by our bootstraps or snap out of it, because depression feeds itself.

The result is that depression is at the same time a disease and a social problem, an understandable reaction to stress and a self-destructive state. In this initial
chapter I am going to focus on depression as a social problem: how our society
conceives of it now, how we respond to it, how we try to treat it. As we then
move on to discuss direct treatment, the rest of the book will speak to the other
aspects of depression.

THE CRISIS IN CARE FOR DEPRESSION

Depression is second only to heart disease in its health impact worldwide. This
surprising news comes not from any mental health advocacy group, but from the
World Bank and World Health Organization (Murray & Lopez, 1996), which
measured the lost years of healthy life due to disease. In the United States in
1990, the cost of treatment of depression, increased mortality, and loss of productivity was estimated at $44 billion a year, higher than any disease but heart
disease, greater than the effect of cancer, of AIDS, of lung disease, MS, or any
other single disease entity (Greenberg, Stiglin, Finkelstein, & Berndt, 1993).
Nationally, there are approximately 30,000 suicides annually, as compared to
20,000 homicides (American Association of Suicidology, 1997). One person in
five will suffer an episode of major depression during his or her lifetime, and one
person in five is suffering from some form of depression at any given moment
(Agency for Health Care Policy and Research [AHCPR], 1993). Health econo-
mists equate the disability caused by major depression with that of blindness or
paraplegia (Murray & Lopez, 1996). And the impact will only get worse: For each
group born since 1900, the age of onset of depression has gotten younger, and

the lifetime risk has increased. If current trends continue, the average age of onset for children born in the year 2000 will be 20 years old (Thase, 1999).

If all this is true, if depression is indeed our second biggest public health problem, if it affects 20 percent of the population, costs us so much, and is only getting worse, you may be asking yourself, Where's the big national foundation leading the battle against depression? Where's Jerry Lewis and Ronald McDonald? But if you understand depression, these questions answer themselves. People with depression are ashamed of their disease. This is partly a reflection of public attitude, but also partly a manifestation of the disease itself; we blame ourselves for being weak or lacking character instead of accepting that we have an illness, instead of realizing that our self-blame is a symptom of the disease. And feeling that way, we don't step forward and challenge unthinking people who reinforce those negative stereotypes. So we stay hidden away, feeling miserable and blaming ourselves for our own misery.

This is a dirty little secret of mental health economics: If you're depressed, you don't think you're worth the cost of treatment. You feel guilty enough about being unproductive and unreliable; most likely your family members have been telling you to snap out of it and you believe you should. You're not likely to shell out a hundred dollars an hour to see a therapist, and if your insurance won't pay you're not likely to put up a fight. Yet your therapist wants to get paid, hospitals will bill you whether you get better or not, and HMOs require you to be very determined before they will pay their share. They will play on your own guilt about your condition to make it difficult for you to get anything more than the absolute minimum treatment. They count on discouraging you from pursuing your claims in order to save themselves money; and, in doing so, they reinforce your depression. Meanwhile, publicly funded mental health services dismiss the depressed as the "worried well," focusing their resources on patients with schizophrenia. And though there's a lot of talk about "parity" for mental health services, it's just talk. Most managed care plans find ways of drastically restricting coverage for outpatient care. The myth is that depression can be treated successfully by medication alone; but, as we shall see, that is only a myth, and a cruel one that reinforces patients' ideas that there is something wrong with them if they do not recover in the prescribed manner.

Suppose you had cancer and required regular chemotherapy, or kidney disease and required dialysis, or pulmonary disease and required oxygen and physical therapy; or that your child had an accident and required surgery—what would happen if there were an annual cap on benefits for these conditions? What would happen if there were a copay of 50 percent on these benefits? You know what would happen—we'd have a revolution. But we seem to take it for granted that there should be caps and copays on mental health services—which is our way of reinforcing the message that the victim is to blame for his own disease. We're begging for parity when we should be demanding equality.

While there seems to be greater recognition of depression as a public health problem, there is also more of an emphasis on treating it medically, and psychotherapy seems in danger of becoming obsolete. *U.S. News* recently ran a cover story on the continued increase and greater recognition of depression (Schrof & Schultz, 1999). The banner on the magazine cover reads "Depression is on the Rise, Despite Prozac and Other Drugs. But New Treatments Could Help Millions." When you look inside, you see that the new treatments are additional medications and magnetic stimulation of the brain. Psychotherapy isn't mentioned. Managed care has made adequate psychotherapy very difficult for most Americans to get, but no one seems to mind too much because the answer to our problems is expected to come from a pill, from lights, from magnets. If in the fifties America had a love affair with Freud, in the nineties we tossed him aside. Yet, though we keep pinning our hopes on medications, very few people who are actually taking the pills feel they're a panacea. "Prozac poop-out" (Slater, 1998) is in the news. The National Depressive and Manic-Depressive Association (1999), surveying visitors to its Web site, found that a majority reported troublesome medication side effects and only modest improvement in their condition; more than two-thirds were not satisfied with their relationship with their provider. The popular press (Fox, 1998) and serious research (e.g., Judd et al., 1998a; Keller & Hanks, 1994; Solomon et al., 2000; Thase, 1999) are increasingly recognizing that depression is a very debilitating, long-term illness that can't be treated successfully by a prescription or by a twelve-week psychotherapy trial, but serious discussion of alternatives is almost nonexistent.

In 1998, more than 130 million prescriptions for antidepressants were written in the United States, and Prozac, Paxil, and Zoloft were among the six best-selling drugs of any kind (Moore, 1999). By some estimates one out of ten Americans has tried one of the new antidepressants (Glenmullen, 2000). Seventy percent of antidepressant prescriptions are written by general practice MDs (Yapko, 1997a). This extraordinary popularity comes about chiefly because of marketing of the newer medications by the pharmaceutical industry, the economics of health care, and the stigma of depression (Kirkpatrick, 2000). Research shows that selective serotonin reuptake inhibitors (SSRIs) and other new medications are in fact no more effective than the older antidepressants, and despite their reputed lower side effect profile, the dropout rates are similar for both treatments (AHCPR, 1999a). MDs in general practice have been encouraged to believe that it's more acceptable to patients who present with depression to give them a pill rather than refer them to a specialist. Meanwhile, studies comparing the effectiveness of newer antidepressants with psychotherapy, or researching the effects of the two combined are few and far between (Keller et al., 2000). Only a few projects have studied the effects of combined psychotherapy and pharmacotherapy (see Thase et al., 1997, for a review). The Surgeon General's Report to the Nation on Mental Health apologizes for the brevity of its review of psychotherapy for mood disorders, noting that psychosocial interventions "are much less studied than the pharmacotherapies" (U. S. Department of Health and Human Services, 1999, p. 265). It's as if psychotherapy has become irrelevant.

This is despite the fact that we have known for a long time that psychotherapy is more effective than medication alone at preventing relapse (Blackburn, Eunson, & Bishop, 1986; Evans et al., 1992; Fava, Rafanelli, Grandi, Conti, & Belluardo, 1998).

It seems reasonable to ask, if the new antidepressants really are effective, shouldn't we see some decline in the suicide rate by now? Perhaps we are not because the actual effects of the drugs have been magnified by the way we conduct research. There are some serious problems with the generally accepted research that documents the efficacy of antidepressant medications, both the newer SSRIs and the older tricyclics (Antonuccio, Danton, DeNelsky, Greenberg, & Gordon, 1999; Moore, 1999). Pharmaceutical manufacturers support, authors submit, and journals publish articles that demonstrate a positive effect of treatment more readily than those that do not disprove the null hypothesis. Thus, meta-analyses that report 19 of 21 studies show that medication X is more effective than a placebo may present a distorted picture; there may have been 15 studies that failed to show the effect of treatment but didn't get published. Further, placebo responses to depression are generally high; up to 60 percent of patients improve on placebo alone. Efforts to control for these effects bias the investigation in favor of the active agent, by including a pretreatment "washout" phase in which all patients are taken off their active medication and given a placebo; those who have a positive placebo response during this phase are then eliminated from the study (Brown, 1994). The sample is thus skewed from the outset by excluding those who are the most active placebo responders, but even so almost as many people in antidepressant trials respond to placebo as to the active agent (Talbot, 2000; Thase & Howland, 1995). Most studies also exclude from the data all subjects who drop out before the conclusion of treatment, skewing the sample further by eliminating many who may be dissatisfied or experiencing negative side effects. Finally, the double-blind procedure itself is open to question when patients and clinicians can generally determine whether the subject is receiving active treatment or a placebo on the basis of the side effects. There are relatively few studies that use an active placebo mimicking the side effects of medication.

Most troubling of all, perhaps, is the appearance of conflict of interest among researchers who receive financial support from pharmaceutical companies. For instance, it was recently disclosed that Dr. Martin Keller of Brown University, whose studies are cited several times in this book, received over $550,000 in consulting fees—not research support, but personal income—from drug companies in 1998 (Bass, 1999). Despite professional journals' expectation that authors disclose conflicts of interest, Dr. Keller did not disclose the extent of his financial ties to drug companies. Payments on that scale inevitably raise the suspicion of bias, and we can only regret that a respected researcher has put himself in a position where his results can be questioned. Dr. Keller is the principal author of a major new study (Keller et al., 2000) demonstrating that combined treatment with Serzone and cognitive-behavioral analysis psychotherapy (McCullough,

2000) is markedly more effective than either alone, a result that supports a principle thesis of this book; unfortunately, as a result of drug industry influence, that support feels suspect to me.

Although for the purposes of conducting treatment with patients in the real world of today we need to assume that antidepressant medications can often be effective, these issues seem to me to introduce enough doubt to question whether the difference between the typical 40 percent improvement rate with placebo and 60 percent with the active agent is really meaningful. In any case it seems remarkable how easily and wholeheartedly our society has swallowed the idea of antidepressant efficacy. I think the only reason for this is that there *is* indeed an epidemic of depression, and the pills have come along at the right time to help reassure us all.

Misdirected Science

Market research suggests that most Americans, after decades of tobacco wars, marijuana scares, and debate about global warming, believe science is bought and paid for, so subject to the influence of the sponsors of the research that it has lost its objectivity (Lake Snell Perry & Assoc., 1999). If the public understood depression research, that same skepticism would only be reinforced. Politics, economics, turf, and the absence of independent thinking combine to prevent us from creative, meaningful work.

At the White House Conference on Mental Health in June 1999, Steven Hyman, the director of the National Institute of Mental Health, was interrupted twice with applause during his brief presentation. On both occasions he had alluded to the value of psychotherapy for the treatment of mental illness. The audience was moved to applause by surprise and relief. For far too long, NIMH has focused almost exclusively on research into the biochemical aspects of mental illness, ignoring other influences such as the well-known fact that the best single predictor of mental illness is poverty (Shore, 1994). This position has been politically popular: It supports the pharmaceutical industry, which has had a very close relationship with NIMH, and it is supported by the most vocal advocates for the mentally ill, who insist that these conditions are "no-fault brain diseases." But it has come at the cost of trivializing research, inhibiting research into effective psychotherapy, and making the idea of prevention a taboo subject.

NIMH, of course, is only a reflection of our society. There is a gee-whiz mentality about American culture that seems to favor technology over people. A recent lead editorial in *Archives of General Psychiatry*—an AMA publication—proudly trumpets that we are "beginning to see the light" in light therapy for seasonal affective disorder (Wirz-Justice, 1998). In other words, some researchers have finally published articles that seem to establish that light therapy is more effective than a placebo. From reading the popular press, you would never have suspected that there was any question about the effectiveness of light therapy, but apparently researchers have never been able to demonstrate its efficacy. When you read the first article (Eastman, Young, Fogg, Liu, & Meaden, 1998), on first blush it's hard to see the heralded effects. Members of both treated and placebo groups report less depression as time goes on; the mean scores on a depression rating scale for both groups over time (only four weeks in this study) are substantially the same. But the eager researchers do some number crunching and discover that of those who had the greatest improvement, substantially more were in the treated group. Of course if the mean scores were the same this implies that the treated group also had substantially more who had little or no improvement, as is indeed the case, though the authors gloss over that fact. In the second study, there are two placebo conditions, and light therapy proves to be better than one of them (Terman, Terman, & Ross, 1998). I leave it up to the reader and to further research to determine if these studies will ever have an impact on actually helping patients, but I do note that this seems to be the best technology can do, after at least fifteen years and millions of American research dollars, trying to show that light therapy does something for depression.

Meanwhile, in almost the same month, the *British Journal of Psychiatry* published studies demonstrating that sending an interested and well-meaning volunteer out to visit the depressed in their homes once a week for an hour helps them feel significantly less depressed (Harris, Brown, & Robinson, 1999a, 1999b). No fancy statistical analysis—the results are obvious. In the treated group, 65 percent attained remission of symptoms, as opposed to 39 percent of the control group. But no one is investigating such ideas in the United States. You couldn't get that paper published here. Maybe it's because no one can make a buck off volunteers.

At the same time, there is growing evidence that the distinctions drawn in the *DSM-IV* between major depression, dysthymia, and "depressive disorder not otherwise specified" (a wastebasket diagnosis with an estimated prevalence of 14 percent of the population at any given time) distort our understanding of what is in reality a single disease that has different manifestations at different points in our lives. A twelve-year follow-up of 431 patients who had sought treatment for a major depressive episode found that although subsequent episodes occupied only about 15 percent of the patients' lives, still only 41 percent of their time was spent symptom-free (Judd et al., 1998a). The rest of the time was spent in states comparable to dysthymia (27 percent) and in subthreshold depression (17 percent). This is despite the fact that patients were being treated with medication or psychotherapy in 62 percent of the weeks. Remaining in subthreshold depression was a powerful predictor of relapse into major depression (Judd et al., 1998b), suggesting that simply no longer meeting all the criteria for major depression is a very poor definition of recovery. Patients who had presented with their first lifetime episode of major depression had a higher proportion of time (54 percent) symptom-free, suggesting that adequate treatment early in the illness can prevent some suffering. We need to be preparing the public and the health insurance industry for the idea that depression is a chronic disease that waxes and wanes over a lifetime, especially if inadequately treated.

Assuming that dysthymia and major depression are distinct diseases leads to some strange conclusions. In an outstanding application of circular reasoning, some researchers argue with a straight face that the fact that dysthymia in children has an earlier onset than major depression means it is a distinct entity (Kovacs, Akiskal, Gatsonis, & Parrone, 1994), apparently without considering that it's simply easier to meet the criteria for dysthymia; the diagnosis is less restrictive. Symptoms develop gradually, and a child is more likely to "qualify" for dysthymia earlier in development than for major depression, just as some children's bronchial infections develop into pneumonia while others do not. Still other researchers advocate for the concept of "double" depression (Keller, Hirschfeld, & Hanks, 1997)—dysthymia and major depression—giving the idea that there are separate disease processes at work and an individual has been unlucky enough to catch both, rather than simply stating that a person who has been depressed for some time has recently gotten worse.

In all this flurry of research, we rarely mention that most patients who suffer from depression have poor outcomes in the long run. Clinical trials generally run for two to three months, with "recovery" measured at the end of treatment and little if any follow-up conducted; but this is like arguing that ice is a cure for fever. Adequate treatment for depression increases the likelihood of complete recovery, but most patients still remain vulnerable. The best predictor of chronic outcome is the duration of the initial episode, from before treatment begins until the patient recovers; thus early detection and effective treatment should be a priority (Angst, 1999). Recurrence becomes more likely over time; three-quarters of patients can expect to have another episode within five years (Lavori, Keller, Mueller, & Scheftner, 1994). The major risk factors for recurrence are psychosocial: the patient's level of neuroticism and lack of self-confidence, areas that are much more likely to be improved by psychotherapy than by medication (Angst, 1999).

The very limited amount of research on psychotherapy still being conducted largely focuses on applications of interpersonal psychotherapy or cognitive-behavioral therapy (see chapters 10 and 11), which have the reputation of having been demonstrated to be effective treatments for depression. Little research is going into investigating the question of what makes these approaches effective, although their theoretical base is limited and certainly needs greater elucidation (cf. Jacobson & Gortner, 2000). Generally what research there is shows that psychotherapy and medication have different effects on the course of treatment of depression (Klerman, 1993; Klerman, Weissman, & Markowitz, 1994). Medication reduces symptoms, and therapy helps improve social functioning and interpersonal relations. Medication has its effect within a few weeks, while psychotherapy usually takes months. There has been virtually no evidence that psychotherapy and medication have any negative effect on each other, despite the fears of many practitioners on both sides; but partly because of the polarity in the field, there has been little systematic attempt to understand how they complement each other.

No one seems to be working on an integrative model that would attempt to describe how to use pharmacology and psychotherapy most effectively together, despite some promising clinical applications (e.g., Schuchter, Downs, & Zisook, 1996). "Separatist tendencies and fragmentation of the field have occurred throughout the history of psychiatry and are largely reflective of a complex evolution of disparate belief systems, social trends, and hidden biases about the nature of man, the origin of his psychopathology, and how he can be healed" (Karasu, 1993, p. 11). The separatist tendencies continue, driven by prestige, turf, money, and closed-system thinking; practitioners who seek a holistic model to help their depressed patients are left to their own devices. Luhrmann (2000), after a thoughtful, observant analysis of the development of the split between the biomedical and psychodynamic camps in psychiatry, presents a devastating vision of the future in which patients are reduced to chemistry and knowledge about such things as personality, stress, or how to get the patient to take the pill, will be lost to psychiatry forever.

Likewise, there is precious little research going on about how we can prevent depression or other serious mental illnesses. British research shows the effects of childhood experience on development of adult depression. In a study of 1,142 children who were followed from birth to age 33, it was found that factors like poor mothering, poor physical care, parental conflict, overcrowding, and social dependence were all highly linked with development of adult depression (Sadowski, Ugarte, Kolvin, Kaplan, & Barnes, 1999). Findings like these are unpopular in the United States; the emphasis on mental illness as "brain disease" suggests that developmental factors and the social environment are not to be looked into. At a recent conference, the director of a major national mental health foundation told me she does not believe mental illness can be prevented. Yet adult patients keep coming into our offices, telling us that their depression feels as if it's related to past experiences of trauma and deprivation. Are we not to believe them? Are there not ways to help people improve their parenting so that their children will be less vulnerable to depression? Or ways to structure our society so that we all have less chance of becoming depressed?

Meaningless Research = Bad Policy

From the "Medicare Provider News":

> Patients with Major depressive disorders . . . require treatment with medications *with or without psychotherapy*. . . . Providers who's [sic] license does not allow them to prescribe medications . . . must refer the patient to a psychiatrist for evaluation and treatment with medication *before continuing any further psychotherapy*. . . . Psychotherapy is not a treatment that is required or rendered on

an ongoing basis or indefinitely in every patient. . . . severe depression or schizophrenic conditions (while being treated with medications) may require 15 to 20
sessions. (Health Care Financing Administration, 1999)

The implications of this sort of policy being applied to all Medicare patients
boggle the mind. What if the patient doesn't want medication? What if medications have had significant side effects with this patient? What if this patient
is among those who do not respond to medication? What if the patient is anxious
or suspicious and referring him to a psychiatrist means he will drop out of treatment? What if severe depression does not remit after 15 to 20 sessions? And what
does it mean to put severe depression and schizophrenic conditions on the same
footing?

A policy like this sends a clear message to patients that there is something
wrong with them if they don't want to take medication, or if they do not respond. It reinforces the guilt and self-blame that people with depression suffer
from already. It is clearly discriminatory and should be illegal.

Depression rarely occurs alone. There is enormous overlap with other emotional problems, but this ugly fact gets in the way of "clean" research. The NIMH
Epidemiologic Catchment Area study found that 75 percent of people who have
had a major depressive episode also had a history of some other psychiatric disorder (Robins & Regier, 1991). Analysis of data from the National Comorbidity
Study (Kessler et al., 1994; Kessler et al., 1996) revealed that major depression
developed secondarily to other psychiatric disorders in 62 percent of all cases.
Among those who had suffered a major depressive episode within the past year,
51 percent had also suffered an anxiety disorder during the same time, 4 percent had experienced dysthymia, and 18.5 percent had also suffered a substance
abuse disorder. Co-occurring anxiety disorder and dysthymia were both predictive of poor outcome for major depressive disorder. The WHO study (Goldberg,
1996) found a remarkably similar comorbidity between depression and anxiety:
68 percent.

Yet FDA trials require pharmaceutical manufacturers to focus on the effects
on a single "disease" at a time. Researchers know, but clinicians, insurers, and
legislators forget, that there are several equally respectable explanations for the
co-occurrence of depression and other mental illnesses. It could be that when
a person has been excessively anxious for some time, feeling unable to cope with
life, depression is a natural result. It could also be that vulnerable people react
to stress differently, and that what our diagnostic systems classify as anxiety and
depression are manifestations of the same process. It could be that alcoholism
leads to depression, or that depression leads to alcoholism, or that both drinking excessively and depression are the same person's unsuccessful attempts to
cope with life. If we have a diagnostic system that allows 26 different kinds of
depression, as the ICD-9 does, we will observe 26 different kinds of depression,
and we may think they are all different animals, but we would be foolish to do
so. If we want to study "pure" depression and not measure the impact of our

treatment on the patient's anxiety, substance abuse, or problems in living, we may be tempted to do so because it's easier to draw statistical conclusions, but we won't be helping patients much.

In the end, we must keep in mind some simple facts. People often want psychotherapy. Life is hard and we need all the help we can get. But training in psychotherapy rarely benefits from the results of empirical research, because the research isn't being focused on real-world issues. Turf, money, and politics have driven American science away from a meaningful investigation of how best to help our patients cope with real problems. People with depression can't overcome their symptoms without solving their problems; in my experience, most of them don't even want to.

LIVING WITH DEPRESSION
IN THE REAL WORLD

Stigma

Look for a minute at how we think about chronic fatigue syndrome, a complex illness for which no physiological basis has yet been found, but which seems to be on the increase and certainly captures much media attention (see chapter 12 for a more thorough discussion of this condition). Though most scientific studies of chronic fatigue syndrome refer to psychological causes, most news accounts refer to physiological causes. Many news stories are slanted in such a way that the scientist who talks about psychology is painted as dismissive, patronizing, or protecting his turf, wasting time and research funds, while the magic bullet for chronic fatigue syndrome is out there somewhere waiting to be found. Patients feel like an oppressed minority. And too many physicians reinforce the idea that it insults the patient to suggest that his problems are in his head. "Professor Arthur Kleinman, from the departments of anthropology and social medicine at Harvard . . . believes that chronic fatigue syndrome should be treated by a physician, not a psychiatrist, to maintain the patient's self-respect" (Showalter, 1997). These reactions and attitudes reflect the values of our culture, that psychological distress is less real than physical distress, that to be told your symptoms are due to stress is to be told you're weak or malingering. The implication at the bottom, which many of us still believe, is that you should be able to pull yourself out of mental illness if you really want to. The patient with chronic fatigue syndrome believes he's being insulted when perhaps his doctors are really trying to help him.

We can see the effects of stigma operating in managed care. Expecting patients to get a referral for mental health services from a "gatekeeper"—a primary care physician—is an effective way of limiting access. When patients are switched from a gatekeeper plan to a "carve-out" plan, wherein they call a special telephone number to get a referral, the change has the effect of doubling utilization of mental health and substance abuse services (Sturm, 1997). In other words, people find it much easier to ask for help when they don't have to go through their family doctor. Most people know that what they are feeling—depression, anxiety, confusion, conflict—is about what is happening in their lives, not about their biochemistry, and they do not particularly wish to confide in their physician in order to get the help they need.

Another subtle manifestation of stigma is the continuing enthusiasm among personality researchers for the diagnosis of "depressive personality disorder," or DPD (Millon & Kotik-Harper, 1995), which is in the *DSM-IV* as a classification requiring further study. This diagnosis refers to people who suffer from a chronic low-grade depression that is difficult to treat, with the implication that something in their personality causes them to get into situations of rejection or punishment. A careful study (Klein & Shih, 1998) of DPD among 400 patients with mood disorders and their first-degree relatives found a high degree of overlap with dysthymia (80 percent of participants with DPD had dysthymia, and 73 percent of those with dysthymia had DPD). Further, only 49 percent of participants initially diagnosed with DPD retained it at a 31-month follow-up. Of course, in order to have real meaning, a construct such as DPD should be independent of diagnoses like dysthymia, and should be stable over time. Another recent study—which most clearly succeeds in demonstrating the ability of researchers to apply muddy reasoning under the pressure to publish or perish—compared a small group of patients who tested positive for this supposed disorder to others who had similar histories of longstanding depression without the hypothesized personality traits (Lyoo, Gunderson, & Phillips, 1998). It was found, not surprisingly, that those who fit the profile for DPD scored higher on measures for harm avoidance and neuroticism, and lower on scales of novelty seeking and extraversion, than the other depressed patients. That this is not surprising is because those with DPD are by definition expected to be inhibited and constricted. This kind of finding could be dismissed as an irrelevant academic exercise except for the familiar reification process in science. If depressive personality disorder does become an accepted diagnosis, health insurance won't pay for treating it, and thousands of depressed individuals will be unable to get help.

Here's why: The rigorous and respected experts who organized the *DSM-III* and *DSM-IV* took a strictly phenomenological approach to classification; while they hoped that use of their very objective definitions for different syndromes would lead eventually to identification of underlying mechanisms, they never intended that the manual would be interpreted to suggest that one disorder is more treatable, or is due to different causes, than another. Imagine their surprise to find that Congress has legislated that major depressive disorder is a biologically based mental illness and dysthymia is not. Thus major depression is covered by our existing "parity" law, while insurance companies remain free to restrict coverage to patients suffering from dysthymia, as if the two entities are as distinct as reconstruction of a cleft palate or a nose job. And if dysthymia is discriminated against, what will happen to depressive personality disorder? As it is now, no insurance company will pay for treatment of any personality disorder. Many patients with depression who do not respond quickly to standard treatment are likely to get dismissed as having a personality disorder—in other words, told they're both beyond help and that it's their own character that's to blame.

Health Insurance Reimbursement

Many years ago psychotherapists made a devil's bargain with the health insurance industry, and today the chickens have come home to roost. In an effort to get health insurance reimbursement for our patients, we agreed that they had to have a specific disease, like major depression or anxiety disorder. But our treatment was generally not addressed at the disease, it was directed at the whole person; that's how psychotherapy works. And we swept under the carpet the difficult issues of just how much care is legitimate to expect a third party to pay for, just how much of our work with a particular patient is directed at self-improvement rather than fixing a specific problem, and at what point self-improvement becomes elective. We all could afford to ignore these issues until the health care system started to go bankrupt. Then, the insurance industry stepped in to control costs through various means we refer to collectively as managed care, and psychotherapists have been on the defensive ever since, as if we got caught with our hands in the cookie jar.

After all, the purpose of health insurance is to pay the cost of treatment if you get sick. In most cases, sickness can be objectively determined through blood tests, X rays, MRIs, and the like. If you have an infection, there are germs; if you have cancer, there are mutated cells; if you have heart disease, your blood pressure and cholesterol change. There is usually an empirically validated or at least consensus-based treatment for such sicknesses. And—most important from the insurer's point of view—there is a predictable course to the sickness, with proof that treatment alters the course. If it couldn't be shown that treatment alters the course of the illness or at least diminishes the symptoms, no one would expect insurance to pay for treatment. This is the doctrine of medical necessity (Bennett, 1996).

But these elements—an objectively verifiable disease, with a predictable course and an empirically validated treatment—are hard to establish when it comes to mental illness. Even schizophrenia and manic depression, widely accepted as having a "biological" basis, still can't be verified by any objective test, although there is a course and a treatment. With depression and anxiety disorders, when so much of the diagnosis is based on the patient's own subjective experience, the diagnostic picture is less clear still, the course is unpredictable, and we are just beginning to have empirically validated treatments.

So why should I expect my insurance company to pay for my therapy? I've been seeing my present therapist for four years, usually every other week. What proof do I have that it's helping my depression? Indeed, could I even prove to my insurance company that I *have* depression? I go to work every day, I'm not suicidal, I'm productive, I vote, I even have fun sometimes. In fact, sometimes I even have fun in my psychotherapy. Should Blue Cross pay for me to have fun?

The image of Woody Allen whining on the couch, narcissistic and self-righteous, comes to mind. Did health insurance really pay for everyone to have analysis four or five times a week for years? No wonder there's a backlash. We can't have that.

Actually, we never did have that. Insurance paid for very few analyses. Where health insurance was abused was in inpatient treatment, which until 1989 accounted for more than 80 percent of all mental health care expense (Borenstein, 1996). When insurance paid for 28 days of hospital stay per year, hospitals planned their programs around a 28-day stay, regardless of whether it was in the patient's best interests or not. For example, in 1981 all employees covered by the Blue Cross federal employee plan who were treated as inpatients stayed an average of 27.5 days; an amazing coincidence, or an example of "fiscogenic" treatment (Fiedler & Wight, 1989).

My answer to Blue Cross is that it should pay for my outpatient mental health care, within limits that we should be able to negotiate like rational people. To destigmatize mental illness and encourage people to get help before problems become unmanageable, some level of outpatient care should be available to everyone without oversight of any sort. We can negotiate around copayments, caps, frequency of treatment, etc. if treatment lasts longer than the eight sessions that most people find sufficient. We need much greater awareness that mental disorders are real. The doctrine of medical necessity is misapplied; treatment may not be necessary but advisable, both for the individual patient and for society as a whole.

At the same time, I think any honest psychotherapist will admit that many of his patients are in the position where treatment is optional. Yes, they would probably be worse off without it, but could we prove that to the insurance company? We need to get off the defensive. It doesn't help matters much to have serious researchers demonstrate that both medication and psychotherapy are more effective in treating depression than standard medical practice, yet apologize that they cost more (Lave, Frank, Schulberg, & Kamlet, 1998; Von Korff et al., 1998). Of course they cost more! Treating anything costs more than not treating it. That's why we have health insurance.

The now-famous *Consumer Reports* survey (1995) of readers' experience with psychotherapy and the mental health system, while it has its methodological drawbacks (Seligman, 1995), demonstrated several important points:

- Most patients who saw a mental health professional reported significant improvement and a high degree of satisfaction.
- Patients who were seen by psychiatrists, social workers, and psychologists all improved equally.

- There were no differences between specific modalities of therapy.
- Long-term therapy was more effective than short-term therapy.
- People whose choice of therapists or length of treatment was limited by managed care did worse.
- People who went to AA improved even more than the patients in psychotherapy.

While this is strong evidence for the value and utility of psychotherapy and self-help, unfortunately it has little to say about the impact of treatment on specific diseases, the issue we are forced to address by the medical model. It's very difficult to prove the efficacy of psychotherapy with a specific disease to the degree of precision and control that the FDA, the medical profession, and the general public expects. The reason is that what I do with patient A is going to be very different from what I do with patient B, even though they have the same diagnoses—and what therapist X does with these two patients is going to be different from what I do. So if we want to study the effects of psychotherapy on a group of 200 patients with depression (and the more patients the better so that our results can achieve statistical significance), we quickly find that we're comparing apples to oranges to bananas, because the course of therapy of each of these 200 patients is unique. And, in fact, over all 200, maybe no more get better than if they were not treated at all; but the effect of therapy may be that some of them get *a lot* better. The near-impossibility of conducting studies assessing the effectiveness of long-term treatment gets twisted and used by the managed care industry to conclude that long-term therapy is not effective or necessary.

That is precisely why cognitive-behavioral therapy and interpersonal psychotherapy are usually touted as the treatments of choice for depression. The approaches are so specific that they give the practitioner a guidebook for what to do, so that they *are* researchable, and have been demonstrated to have some impact. As I hope to make clear, though any good practitioner should be familiar with both of these approaches and prepared to use their methods when appropriate, in my belief they don't go far enough to be of lasting benefit to most patients. Their research base, though deep, is narrow, because their proponents are generally unwilling to examine aspects of successful treatment that don't fit their theoretical model.

Let's look more closely at how the present system reinforces the patient's tendency to blame himself. Managed care is touted as a "free-market" institution. If a plan does not provide quality care, so the argument goes, it will lose customers and eventually either have to improve its services or go under. The competitive forces of the marketplace, in other words, are thought to ensure continual improvement in quality. But people with depression may lack the energy and assertive skills needed to advocate for themselves, to go to the time and trouble of complaining or switching plans; they may just assume that there is nothing they can do about their dissatisfaction. A study by Druss, Schlesinger, Thomas, and Allen (1999) seems to support this. Analysis of data from a survey of 20,000 employees at major corporations, who did have the capability of switching plans without penalty, found that enrollees who had a high level of depressive symptoms were significantly less likely to switch plans. A high level of symptoms of any kind—physical or psychological—was associated with greater dissatisfaction; but the enrollees whose complaints were primarily physical were much more likely to actually make the change to a different plan.

Another study, by Druss and Rosenheck (1998), suggests that people with mental disorders may actually be correct in assuming that they are powerless to change their situation vis-à-vis managed care. A survey of over 75,000 individuals found that, while people with mental disorders were no more likely to be uninsured or to go without a primary provider than those without mental disorders, those with mental disorders were twice as likely to report having been denied coverage because of a preexisting condition, or to report staying in a job because of fear of losing benefits.

Is it going too far to argue that, if the industry counts on factors like stigma, ignorance, and poverty to prevent people from getting their needs met, that is discrimination? We've all known for years that mental health consumers are poor advocates for themselves. In the National Comorbidity Study, only one in five respondents who had had a mental health need in the past year had gotten any help at all, and only one in nine had gained access to mental health services (Kessler et al., 1994). The managed care industry uses low utilization and the low rate of complaints about managed mental health care to rationalize cuts in services and to suggest that professionals who advocate for their clients are only motivated by self-interest (Goleman, 1996). It's rather like the schoolyard bully who can count on his victims not to defend themselves.

A popular response to the difficulty of funding treatment for depression by specialists has been to attempt to treat it in primary care. The NIMH Depression Awareness, Recognition, and Treatment (D/ART) campaign, begun in 1988, was a highly visible effort to educate the public and health care providers about the incidence and treatability of depression. Incredibly enough, no study of the campaign's effectiveness was ever completed (Magruder & Norquist, 1999). NIMH has also sponsored extensive research to investigate how depression can be treated more effectively by the primary care physician. "Enhanced acute-phase treatment," consisting of physician training, patient education, and consultation between physicians and mental health specialists, has been shown to improve compliance with medication regimes and better outcomes shortly after treatment (Katon et al., 1995; Katon et al., 1996). However, at 19 months the effects disappeared; both the treated and untreated groups scored the same on several measures of depression, and were likewise indistinguishable on continuation of medication (Lin et al., 1999). Another study of physicians who participated in a special four-hour training seminar on practice guidelines for depression found that their sensitivity to depressive symptoms was no better than a control group, despite the participants' belief that the seminar was effective in changing their practice (Thompson, 2000). Most primary care physicians have minimal training in providing mental health care and very limited time to work with each patient; those who participate in research studies like these are likely to be a self-selected subgroup with a special interest in mental health; yet their results are no better than this.

Parity

The issue of "parity" for mental health benefits, which many people thought was settled at least for the eight "biologically-based" conditions, hasn't gone away at all. In several states and in Medicare regulations, eight conditions including major depression were declared to be "biologically-based" mental illnesses, therefore to be treated exactly the same as physical illnesses—no higher deductibles or copayments. But as of 1999, the Clinton administration hadn't issued the regulations required to enforce the law passed the previous year, and seemed to be waffling on whether it intended to enforce the law at all. Meanwhile, the insurance companies found that they could get around the law by placing no restrictions on cost, but by limiting the number of outpatient sessions or inpatient days. It strains credulity to think that Congress, if it really wanted to guarantee parity, could have overlooked that loophole.

A woman contacted the nonprofit clinic where I worked to arrange follow-up care for her adolescent daughter, who was being discharged from a psychiatric hospital after a bizarre runaway episode. But let's focus now on the mother, not the child.

Sheila is a witty, sensitive, intelligent woman in her 30s. If she were your neighbor you would like her. She works hard, pays her bills, in general is an upstanding citizen. She is a single mother, having been divorced from her husband a few years ago.

She is the daughter of alcoholic parents. Her father was physically and emotionally abusive to her; Sheila was beaten frequently, and made to feel that she was ugly, bad, useless, incompetent, and to blame for all the family problems. You would not have known any of this if you lived next door to them. The family was successful economically, liked and respected in the community. Sheila got out of the home as soon as she could by marrying the first man who asked her.

But by the time their child was born, Sheila's husband had begun beating her. She became an example of the cycle of abuse, which is hard to understand but is seen a lot, where women who have been abused as children find themselves in abusive marriages. She put up with it for a few years, then got away with her daughter. She made good use of women's services, and seemed to land on her feet.

However, by the time she contacted us there was more trouble. Her daughter was out of control. As we explored, we found that not only did the daughter run away from home repeatedly, but she was also defiant, belligerent, and physically aggressive toward her mother. Sheila was intimidated and felt helpless to do anything about it. In fact, she had a major depression: She couldn't sleep or eat right, felt hopeless, guilty, and ashamed all the time, couldn't concentrate, had thoughts of suicide—all the symptoms. She was surprised to hear that, from our point of view, she had an illness; her state felt normal to her. But depression is a disease that often goes unrecognized, even by those who have it.

So here we are: abused by her father, her husband, now by her child. Our patient was aware of the irony; it was another stick she would beat herself up with. "Why can't I just snap out of it?" she asked. "Why can't I just take charge of my life?" Our answer—that she had a disease called depression which she couldn't cure by herself—didn't entirely satisfy her. Like most of those who suffer with the disease, Sheila agreed with the conventional wisdom that depression is a sign of moral weakness or lack of character.

This is another aspect of Sheila's problems. Imagine that every time you went to the doctor you were made to feel guilty. Imagine that we as a society assumed that there is a state called "health," which is "normal" and that being ill is deviant, weak, shameful, or your own fault. Because that is exactly how Sheila, and in fact all our patients, are made to feel. Wouldn't it be crazy if you had to feel that you were somehow to blame if you caught pneumonia, broke a leg, or developed a degenerative disease? Isn't it crazy now that people with depression or posttraumatic stress disorder or schizophrenia have to feel that way?

Now let's ask: How does Sheila pay for getting the help she needs?

First of all, it's necessary to recognize that *she* has to pay for it. The agency had a state grant that helped us pay for services to her children, but there was no state grant for adult mental health services. If Sheila had a substance abuse problem, or were chronically mentally ill, there would also be state funds to help her out, but states have cut back on subsidies for people with acute mental health needs, who are dismissed as "the worried well." So Sheila was on her own.

Now, Sheila's employer was using a managed care plan. This meant they would reimburse the agency following their usual practice for mental health services: 50 percent of the cost of each office visit, to a maximum of $1,000 annually. This is a rather standard benefit plan. At the commercial rate of $120 per hour for individual psychotherapy, they would pay $60 per visit. At that rate her benefits for the year would be exhausted after 17 treatment hours, four months of once-a-week treatment. Plus, she was expected to pay the copay of $60 per visit.

We worked out a plan with Sheila for psychotherapy every other week, and attendance at our free self-help group on depression. She paid the minimum fee out of pocket, and the agency accepted what her insurance paid. The agency continued to treat her after her insurance benefits were exhausted, relying on its own fundraising to do so. It would have been preferable for her to be seen weekly until she was better, but she didn't want to do that, even when we offered to reduce her fee further. In addition, she saw our psychiatrist about every other month. Her medication cost $8 a day—$3,000 a year—thank God her insurance only required a copay of $10 on each prescription. She made about $15 an hour on her job—that's a gross of $30,000 per year—could anyone expect her to pay 10 percent of her gross pay for medication?

Sheila paid the clinic about $900 a year for her counseling, and her insurance paid another $1,000. But it cost something like $3,800 to provide her with the group weekly and individual counseling every other week and her psychiatrist visit. The agency did its best to be efficient and cost-effective, but realistically Sheila would require perhaps a year or two of professional help before she could recover.

Sheila was very fortunate to live in a community that made it possible for a clinic like ours to come up with the $1,900 in additional funds that it took to help her get back on her feet. Most people in the United States don't have that kind of resource.

But, personally, I had become burned out with organizing fundraisers, coaxing our board members to ask their friends for contributions, and going hat in hand to the United Way year after year. They were all tired of hearing from me, too. Isn't it time we face up to the problem? Can anyone provide an argument on any ground—economic, moral, therapeutic—to explain why we don't embrace Sheila's problems as part of the social contract? Even in the crassest financial terms, it just makes sense to help keep Sheila working so that she continues to pay into Social Security rather than draw on it, help her function as a mother to keep her daughter in school and out of trouble and the hospital again.

How did we get into a situation where "parity" is even a subject of discussion?

Among all the other things that depression is, it is a perfectly reasonable response to the way our society treats the individual who has it. People with mental illnesses are discriminated against by our healthcare system. People with depression have their feelings of guilt and inadequacy reinforced by this discrimination. Touting medication as a panacea for what are actually reactions to complex living problems reinforces the stigma when the medication doesn't live up to expectations. Any improvement we want to make in direct treatment of depression must take these harsh realities into consideration. We need to advocate for our patient and we need to help him understand what the system is doing to him. And we have a responsibility as citizens and as professionals to address these issues on a larger scale as well. Our failure to do so puts us in an indefensible position when we are trying to help an individual patient recover.

CHAPTER 2

The Disease that
Causes Itself

W HAT IS THE MOST USEFUL way of understanding depression in order to help
patients recover quickly and with as little lasting damage as possible? Do
we define it as a physiological disease, a personality trait, or a reaction to stress?
Is it in our genes, our childhood experience, our high rate of serotonin reuptake, our anger turned inward, our low self-esteem, our experience with loss, our
deprivation of sunlight, our moral character? What is the role of how society
treats people who are down and out? Most current thinking treats depression as
an entity, as something that the patient has, something that he carries with him
from one situation to another. And yet most depression makes sense, once you
get to understand the situation fully. Sometimes I think of "The Truman Show,"
and wonder, if my patients could just have a few solid weeks where everything
went exactly their way, where everyone loved them, no one disappointed or
rejected or criticized them—wouldn't their depression go away? In most cases I
think it would. What does this notion do to the disease concept?

Here's a radical thought: What if we can't answer these questions? Maybe
we're in a place right now in the history of science where we're just not sophisticated enough to have a model that explains both heredity and environment.
Maybe, in fact, we never will be able to fully answer these questions. Maybe
we'll find that we have the equivalent of Heisenberg's uncertainty principle in
physics: that we'll eventually be able to explain the behavior of a mass of elec-
trons, of the "average" electron, but if we focus too closely on a single electron,
a single case, it moves away from us, it eludes us.

We need to accept that at this point we don't have a theory that fully explains
depression, and we may be a long way from getting one. There are biochemical mechanisms involved. There is often a history of loss or trauma. There are
characteristic patterns of thinking, behaving, relating to others, and viewing the

self that perpetuate the symptoms. No single perspective—psychiatric, psychological, or sociological—can explain all these phenomena.

Nor do we have a comprehensive, coherent theory for treatment of depression. Medication is usually effective, but it often takes many tries to find just the right medication for the individual patient. A few specific psychotherapy models have been demonstrated to be effective. Most well-trained therapists find that they can help many of their depressed patients, but not all or even most, and no one can predict what will make the difference with an individual patient. Situational factors—stress, family support, economic hardship—are generally accepted as important elements in causation and recovery, but these effects are not well understood or addressed systematically.

And there is a wide variety in how patients present themselves. Some are obviously, classically, "depressed." But many appear anxious, many are angry, many are abusing substances, many present with chronic pain conditions or other illnesses. Depression seems to affect men and women in very different ways. The presentation in children and the elderly is just beginning to be understood. Even among adults, some people experience depression as a dramatic change from a previously better state of functioning, but for many if not most, the depression has developed gradually and insidiously to the point where it feels "normal" to the patient and it takes an external crisis for him to seek help. These differences make it very difficult to develop a therapy model that can help professionals engage and effectively treat most patients.

Indeed, it is difficult even to conceive of a theory that could explain chemical changes in the brain, changes in cognition and emotions, differences in men and women, the role of loss, the role of family support, the effect of sunlight, and all the other phenomena associated with depression. For all these reasons, it makes sense now to put forward a guide to treatment of depression that avoids the blinders of a constricting theory. Rather than take a narrow theoretical perspective and try to shoehorn observations into fitting the theory's assumptions, I hope to describe a synthesis of the best of our knowledge about depression from different points of view, and to put it into a form that is immediately applicable to practice.

This synthesis is summarized in Figure 2.1, which I refer to as the "common sense" model of depression. In this model, the parts of the system, the factors that create a vulnerability, the stresses that precipitate an episode, and the elements of the patient's life that mediate depression in the present, should be familiar to all readers. The major contribution of the model beyond its value as an organizational tool is its emphasis on functional autonomy and circular causality, so that factors like depressed thinking, neurochemical changes, and distressed relationships are seen as both symptoms and causes at the same time. Like so many others, this is a stress-diathesis model (cf. Abramson, Seligman, & Teasdale, 1978; Beck, 1967; Coyne, 1999; Klein & Wender, 1993; Lewinsohn, Hoberman, Teri, & Hautzinger, 1985; Nemeroff, 1998; Pyszczynski & Greenberg, 1987; Rado, 1928/1994). It assumes that the potential depressive has a vulnerabil-

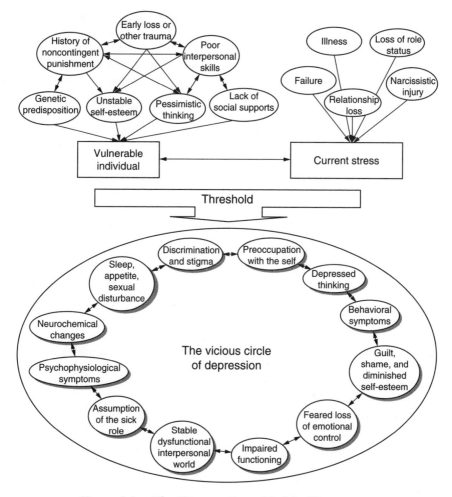

Figure 2.1. *The Common Sense Model of Depression*

ity (diathesis) to depression. This vulnerability results in a unique individual threshold level of stress, beyond which a depressive episode is inevitable. When a current stress is sufficient to push the patient beyond the threshold, depression is the result. Unless there is a rapid recovery, depression goes on to develop a *functional autonomy*, implying that the patient can't be expected to recover through normal life experiences.

Depression is inherently circular. Observers from many different points of view have commented on the irony of depression, the fact that the sufferer's behavior so often has unintended negative consequences that perpetuate the depression (e.g., Lewinsohn, 1974; Rado, 1928/1994; Wachtel, 1993). Once we have crossed over the threshold into a depressive cycle, the door slams shut behind us. We can't return to a state of health merely by an act of will because we are caught in a process that repeats itself over and over; a vicious circle that creates the conditions that sustain it. The ways we adopt to seek love drive others away; the ways we have of chasing success guarantee our failure. We actually generate disappointing experiences; we generate rejection and low self-esteem; we generate experiences that reinforce our sense of hopelessness.

Many factors can play a role in contributing to an individual's vulnerability to depression, just as many stressors can hypothetically contribute to reaching the threshold. The vulnerability factors and stressors that I enumerate are not meant to be an exhaustive list, nor is any particular item or combination of items assumed to be either necessary or sufficient to "cause" depression. Likewise, I have listed a number of mediating variables that contribute to the circularity of depression once it's begun. Others might easily emphasize different factors, or view these same elements through different lenses, giving them different labels. To me, at this point in time, however, these factors seem to comprise the most important elements in the functional autonomy of depression. The list is complete enough to serve as a basis for understanding the patient's problem systematically and planning treatment, and as a way of anticipating and beginning to address issues that will arise in the treatment relationship.

The mediating variables, the factors that sustain the depression, exist in a complex network of relationships in which they are continually causing and being caused by each other. The circularity depicted in the diagram is an over-simplification. A preoccupation with the self exists in a reciprocal relationship not only with depressed thinking habits and sleep, appetite, and sexual disturbance, but also with one's overall functioning, the likelihood of satisfactory social and interpersonal interactions, a tendency to somatize, etc. Similarly, changes in catecholamine levels that have been observed in animal studies of depression and are assumed to be parallel with human depression are affected both by early trauma and by current stress, and in turn affect the individual's overall functioning, social status, and activity level (Suomi, 1991).

In a similar manner, the elements that contribute to vulnerability and the elements that serve as stressors do not exist independently of each other. A genetic predisposition to depression is not only a vulnerability factor in itself, it may also contribute to a childhood history of noncontingent punishment, a feeling of unlovability, and a characteristic pessimistic thinking pattern. Depressed children may elicit rejecting behavior from their parents. A stressful event may have characteristics of several different known types of stressors; an illness may lead to employment difficulties and relationship problems, each of which is also a narcissistic injury.

In this model, the functional autonomy of depression is maintained by the mediating variables—depressed thinking, behavioral symptoms, neurochemical changes—which are caused by and cause each other. In using the model as a therapeutic tool, I find that it's quite helpful to patients to emphasize the circularity of depression and the fact that change in any of the mediating variables has the potential to break the circle. However, I find that discussion of these mediating variables is at too high a level of abstraction to be directly helpful to patients in directly changing their behavior, and I generally prefer to talk about the "skills of depression." As the next chapter explains, these skills are rather specific patterns of behavior, thinking, or social interaction, some of which are practiced by all depressed patients. From the standpoint of model building, the skills of depression can be understood as concrete manifestations of the variables that mediate depression.

PREDISPOSING FACTORS

Vulnerabilities

Genetic Predisposition It's generally recognized that there is some inheritable component to depression, over and above the effects of living with depressed parents. When one identical twin has an affective disorder, his twin will have the same disorder 67 percent of the time; the ratio is only 20 percent for fraternal twins (Bertelsen, Harvald, & Hauge, 1977). Of course, this observation raises the question of why a third of the identical twins, with exactly the same genetics and raised in the same environment, did not develop depression—but at this point the fact that our genetic endowment plays some role in vulnerability to depression is strongly substantiated.

History of Noncontingent Punishment We want to believe in a world where, in the end, virtue is rewarded and evil is punished. In fact, we can make a case that, on average, that's the way the world works. A child's natural behavior elicits appropriate comforting, affection, and guidance from the parents, and the child grows up with a sense of basic trust. In the adult world of work and relationships, acting in accordance with experience and conventional wisdom is more likely to be rewarded than acting selfishly or impulsively. But if a child has been raised in an atmosphere where parental attention, criticism, love, or abuse are meted out in an arbitrary way—say by alcoholic parents—it's hard to maintain basic trust. Or if an adult has been arbitrarily discriminated against or taken advantage of, the expectation of life's ultimate fairness begins to seem naïve. Without such beliefs, it's difficult to live up to one's responsibilities in the face of adversity. Bitterness, cynicism, avoidance, hopelessness may be the result.

This is the "learned helplessness" model of depression (Abramson et al., 1978). Dogs, put in experimental situations in which they are physically restrained from escaping from a shock, often stop trying to escape even after they can see that the restraints are gone. After a few seconds of anxiety, they lie down and whine. Further, the dogs maintain this response when exposed to other noxious stimuli in other experimental situations. It is as if these dogs have learned the belief that nothing they can do will prevent punishment. Of course, their physical health and their overall disposition suffers as well. The same observations have been made for rats, cats, and humans (Seligman, 1990).

Note that I mean punishment here in the strict behavioral sense: Punishment can be either the application of an aversive stimulus or the withdrawal of a pleasurable stimulus. Threat of loss of love can be just as powerful a teacher of learned helplessness as corporal punishment.

Poor Interpersonal Skills Shyness and social phobia are highly linked with depression. Shy people have difficulty establishing supportive and intimate interpersonal relationships; their history of failures and embarrassments with others leads to social isolation and loneliness. Many patients complain of their inability to make small talk. Their feeling of isolation and embarrassment in social gatherings leads them to avoid such settings, resulting in reduced opportunities for relationships. Libet and Lewinsohn (1973) verified that subjects who are more depressed tend to emit less behavior of any kind in social situations. The lack of meaningful relationships directly contributes to depression, and repeated episodes of embarrassment, anxiety, and shame lead to dysphoric affect and diminished self-esteem (Dill & Anderson, 1999).

Lack of Social Supports Isolation is not only a matter of social skills. Many depressed people are isolated by circumstances. My groups are filled with people who do not have siblings, who work in jobs that provide little or no social contact, who are divorced, estranged from their families, and/or live out in the middle of nowhere. Poverty makes things worse; they don't have money to spend on social activities, can't spend money on clothes or cosmetics to make themselves more attractive, sometimes can barely afford the gas to make their cars run. The result is that they spend a great deal of time alone, or in stable relationships usually with people who are just as distressed as they are. I have contact with a great many people who have found that AA is a reliable outlet where they know they will not be judged and where they can find some degree of intimacy; they often continue to attend regularly even when it's been years since they've had the desire for a drink.

Contemporary culture—the breakdown of the family, the loss of a sense of community, the instability of careers—has a significant impact on vulnerability to depression, and perhaps is responsible for its increasing incidence.

Unstable Self-Esteem Clearly, most people with depression lack resilience in self-esteem. It's natural to be downcast by rejection and buoyed by affirmation, but a hallmark of depression is that rejection seems to hurt more and have more lasting effects, while good things only result in a fleeting pleasant feeling, if any at all. In *Undoing Depression* I used the analogy of a car's oil system. Oil serves as a lubricant to the engine; by reducing friction between moving parts, it helps the engine run smoothly and efficiently. The oil needs to be changed at regular intervals because it accumulates dirt, but for the most part when the engine works well the oil system requires little maintenance. But when there is a leak in the system, like a cracked oil pan or blown gasket, the oil runs out or burns up and we have to keep replenishing the supply. The depression-resistant person has the equivalent of a good tight oil system; he can function well in life with only occasional support from others, and isn't thrown for a loop by loss or reversal. But the person with depression has a "crack in the pan"—a leaky oil system—and needs more or less continual affirmation, love, or success to function.

The unstable self-esteem of depression, of course, can be explained cognitively, interpersonally, or psychodynamically, depending on one's predilection. It may be a result of disruption of attachment in infancy or childhood or it may be an effect of later trauma. There is also reason to think it may be to some extent innate (Kramer, 1993). Whatever the reason, the effect is the same: Because of their unstable self-esteem, people with depression are prone to difficulty in interpersonal relationships, have fewer inner resources and are thus more likely to give up in the face of adversity, and of course are vulnerable to changes in mood that seem to be precipitated by experiences that others might shrug off.

Pessimistic Thinking The work of Beck and others writing from a cognitive-behavioral perspective has convincingly demonstrated that people with depression employ characteristic methods of thinking that contribute to the maintenance of the disease. Among these are a distorted perception of the self and others (seeing oneself as damaged); characteristic logical errors (e.g., perfectionism); characteristic false beliefs (if I'm not universally liked I'm worthless); and a negative attributional style (assuming that bad things are permanent and pervasive while good things are only temporary). It has been difficult to establish a linear causal connection between pessimistic thinking and depression—that children who think pessimistically grow up to be more vulnerable to depression—but the reciprocal nature of the relationship is clear. (Haines, Metalsky, Cardamone, and Joiner [1999] provide a good summary of current research.) It seems safe to assume that children who grow up with a history of noncontingent punishment learn pessimistic thinking, that pessimistic thinking contributes to poor interpersonal skills, that poor interpersonal skills contribute to unstable self esteem, and so on in a vicious circle of vulnerabilities.

Early Loss and Other Trauma There has been a common presumption that childhood loss of a parent may predispose an individual to depression, but this has been difficult to verify empirically. Brown and Harris (1978), in a landmark study of social origins of depression, found that the loss of mother before age 11 resulted in a vulnerability. But Lewinsohn and colleagues (1994), in a study of 60-some psychosocial risk factors associated with adolescent depression, found that death of a parent in childhood was not linked with depression, though 45 of the other variables were. The impact of other childhood trauma is likewise poorly understood, though most researchers conclude that a link with adult depression is highly probable (Kaelber, Moul, & Farmer, 1995). In animals, early maternal deprivation has been shown to produce both changes in behavior and changes in brain chemistry analogous to human depression; treatment of such animals with Paxil has been shown to reverse both processes (Nemeroff, 1998). We now recognize that many "personality disorders" are highly associated with trauma and abuse in childhood. Personality disorders that are manifested by self-destructive behavior, self-defeating behavior, avoidance, social isolation, and substance abuse are of course likely to be associated with depression.

There is increasing recognition that childhood sexual abuse increases vulnerability to adult-onset depression, though the mechanisms are poorly understood. A review of the literature (Weiss, Longhurst, & Mazure, 1999) identified 21 studies of women and three of men, almost all of which found a close relationship between childhood sexual abuse and adult depression. There was a suggestion that greater severity, frequency, and duration of abuse increases the likelihood of depression. The Adverse Childhood Experiences study (Felitti et al., 1998) found a strong relationship not only between childhood abuse experience and depression, but also for alcoholism, drug abuse, suicide attempt, sexually transmitted disease, smoking, and such surprises as heart disease and fractures.

Stresses

Anecdotally and logically it has always made sense to believe that depressive episodes are triggered by recent stressful life events, but it proved difficult to demonstrate the connection empirically (see Kaelber et al., 1995, for a review). Now new research is validating this connection for the first time. A survey of approximately 2,000 twins with no identified mental health problems (Kendler, Karkowski, & Prescott, 1999) found that stressful life events were highly correlated with subsequent onset of major depressive episodes. Events such as assault, divorce, financial problems, marital problems, interpersonal conflict, death or serious illness were all demonstrated to predict depression. Use of twins allowed the researchers to control for the observation that some individuals are apparently genetically prone to live a stressful life. Though this was borne out in the study (twins varied with each other in terms of number of stressful events), the actual occurrence of an event was associated with depression regardless.

Similarly, it has been difficult to demonstrate that long-term low socioeconomic status increases the incidence of depression, because there are so many variables confounded with low SES—divorce, poor physical health, inadequate parenting, violence, substance abuse. Nevertheless, most recent studies conclude that low SES by itself does indeed increase risk of depression (Kaelber et al., 1995). Interesting research conducted in Israel suggests that, while mental illnesses like schizophrenia seem to *result in* lower SES, depression in women and antisocial personality and substance use in men are at least in part *an effect* of low SES (Dohrenwend et al., 1992). And the National Comorbidity Survey (Kessler et al., 1994), investigating the incidence, risk factors, and comorbidity of mental illness in the United States, found that while the risk for most mental disorders was reduced by greater affluence, as if greater wealth was able to soothe or protect us from anxiety disorders by insulating us from stress, this effect was less so for affective disorders than for others.

Illness Hard research documents that cancer and migraine are consistently associated with depression; myocardial infarction, stroke, epilepsy, Huntington's disease, MS, and Parkinson's are likely to be associated; and diabetes, lupus, and rheumatoid arthritis are possibly associated (Stevens, Merikangas, & Merikangas, 1995). These are illnesses that seem to be more strongly associated with depression than the effects of the illness (pain, disability, anxiety, etc.) alone would predict. But any major illness has the potential to set off a depressive cycle because of the associated stress. The lack of energy and difficulty concentrating, the increased preoccupation with the self, the whole new set of problems and decisions associated with getting adequate information and care, the concern over long-term consequences, the brush with death—in an individual who is already vulnerable to depression, these are more than sufficient to precipitate an episode. Some illnesses apparently trigger changes on a biological level that are associated with depression, but the psychosocial changes associated with any illness can increase susceptibility.

Failure

> A man wears a Rolex not because it tells time more accurately than a $14.95 Timex but because, like a penis shield, it signifies an advanced degree of manhood. . . . [But] within the last decade someone has upped the ante on the tokens required for manhood. A generation ago providing for one's family was the only economic requirement. Nowadays . . . if your work allows you only to survive you are judged to be not much of a man. To be poor in a consumer society is to have failed the manhood test. (Keen, 1991, p. 53)

American culture puts an exceptionally high value on success, and also defines success in highly mercenary and individualistic terms. These standards are not permanent or universal, but defined by the culture of the times. Before 1700 in America, a man was measured by how he fit in the community. He was expected to conform, and to see to it that his family did as well. There was an emphasis on duty, responsibility, and on controlling desire and impulse. "The ideal man, then, was pleasant, mild-mannered, and devoted to the good of the community. He performed his duties faithfully, governed his passions rationally, submitted to his fate and to his place in society, and treated his dependents with firm but affectionate wisdom" (Rotundo, 1993).

After the Revolution and the opening of the West, self-interest and individual initiative came to be more respected as manly virtues. The individual, not the community or even the family, came to be seen as the basic unit of society, and each individual was expected to find his proper place in the world through his own efforts.

These values not only have the effect of overemphasizing material success, so that those who are unfortunate enough not to be rich consider themselves failures, but they also reinforce traits like defining relationships in terms of competition rather than mutual aid, keeping vulnerabilities hidden, and resolving conflict through intimidation. All of these attitudes promote social isolation and denial of one's own interpersonal needs, further increasing vulnerability to depression.

Women are equally affected by the trap of shallow values. Until the sexual revolution, a woman was largely defined by the success of her man and her marriage; divorce automatically meant failure as a woman. Putting all of one's eggs in one basket—having fewer arenas in which to engage in activities that could lead to a sense of mastery—may have contributed to women's greater vulnerability to depression. Now women are subject to the same pressures to succeed as individuals that men are, and it remains to be seen if perhaps they can have an influence on redefining success in more humane terms, or will just be caught in the short-sighted value trap that our consumer culture maintains.

Loss of Relationship Loss of a deeply significant loved one through death, separation, illness, or other circumstances is perhaps the most common stress leading to depression. We all recognize that the experience of grief is very much like that of depression, and there is reason to conceive of depression as a refusal to accept a loss, a getting stuck in the early stages of grief. It is conceivable that the feelings associated with grief—sad mood, anhedonia, lethargy, crying, difficulty sleeping, concentrating, etc.—precipitate a depressive episode through a kind of kindling process (see Klein & Wender, 1993; Post, Uhde, Putnam, Ballenger, & Berrettini, 1982) in which these feelings precipitate other feelings associated with hopelessness and self-blame. Further, the loss of the relationship entails the loss of important sources of love, affirmation, and self-esteem for the patient. The more constricted the patient's interpersonal world, the more dependent he is on the lost relationship for a good feeling about the self, and the greater his vulnerability to depression.

Loss of Role Status Other things than relationships with individuals can serve important sustaining functions for us that, when threatened or lost, can precipitate depression. Achievement in one's career or financial success are familiar examples. The individual who has suffered a significant reversal not only suffers whatever degree of shame is dictated by his own value system, he also frequently loses his social support system. In divorce, a great deal of the acrimony comes from a power struggle over who is to be seen as the "winner"—the one who did the leaving, who ends up better off financially and emotionally (cf. Wallerstein & Blakeslee, 1989). The spouse who is forced to accept the role of the "loser" often takes on a depressed identity, feeling hopeless and full of shame; the loser is also more likely to lose more of the social support system, not only friends but also to some extent the children, than the winner. In adolescence, of course, a great deal of the extreme vulnerability to depression comes from the exaggerated value of having a status, so that not making the team or being rejected by a more popular girl can precipitate a crisis.

Narcissistic Injury Even though all the stressors listed above are, of course, narcissistic injuries, I list this as a separate category as well because I find myself in strong agreement with the argument that some depressions are a response to shaming experiences, and that such experiences can be highly unique to the individual and his context. It is a blow to the self that precipitates depression. But some blows are too subtle or too unique to be characterized as object loss, or loss of role.

Some self psychologists distinguish between two effects of narcissistic object loss. Fragmentation is a primitive state resembling psychosis; an individual becomes vulnerable to fragmentation anxiety through repeated traumatic failure of the parent or other selfobject to accept a child's grandiosity. Depletion or enfeeblement, on the other hand, is thought to result from failure of the self-object to provide an adequate model for idealization, leading to feelings of emptiness, depression, and shame (Morrison, 1989). Many of the skills of depression can be understood as attempts to avoid or reconstitute from experiences of depletion anxiety.

It is important to include this concept as a potential stressor because the therapist must be sensitive to, and have a way of understanding, the unique meanings of narcissistic injuries to different patients. It's easy for us to empathize with the grieving widow or the depressed man who has been forced into retirement. It's more difficult for us to understand the young woman who seems to invite rejection by expecting her boyfriend to be perfect, or the empty depression of the alcoholic who is newly sober. Yet, that hoped-for perfect boyfriend or the soothing qualities of alcohol may have been vital in staving off depression.

THE VICIOUS CIRCLE OF DEPRESSION

Preoccupation with the Self

Choosing where to start in a circular process is by nature arbitrary. I start here because this factor seems to develop rather early in most depressions, but specifically want to make clear that I do not mean to imply that this factor is primary in "causing" depression. All of these factors maintain depression, playing relatively more or less salient roles with a particular individual, but none is by definition more important than others.

There is a striking parallel between some features of depression and the effects of experimental studies of self-directed attention (Musson & Alloy, 1988). Subjects are asked to perform tasks in front of a mirror or a television camera, or after hearing a tape of themselves. Compared to controls, subjects under such conditions experience intensified emotional experience, lowered self-esteem, higher standards for their own performance, increased tendency to assume responsibility, and increased accuracy of self reports—just like depressives. Depressive self-absorption may account for much of "depressive realism" (see Chapter 3), in that we are all more likely to be accurate in our estimations of what we pay attention to. Nondepressives, who are presumably not so self-conscious, will be more likely to have a distorted (optimistic) view of themselves.

Historically, the melancholic has always been observed to be self-absorbed. Clinically, many of our depressed patients are aware that they have no energy left over for others; many have been informed by family and friends that their self-absorption is annoying and unattractive. Pyszczynski and Greenberg (1987) put forward a complete theory of depression built around this phenomenon: For complex social, environmental, and genetic reasons, the potential depressive experiences his first depressive episode after an object loss. The lost object was a principal source of security, identity, and self-worth, and there are few substitutes available. The individual is unable to accept the loss and move on to other alternatives. This leads to a preoccupation with the self and the virtually constant sense of being helpless and forlorn. The preoccupation with the self leads inevitably to self-blame and damage to self-esteem. Negative events are likely to continue to occur, because attention is not focused on the outside world; and because of the excessive attention to the self, new negative events are interpreted as confirming self-blame and helplessness. Positive events are likely to be viewed as distractions from the primary task, which is to regain the lost object. At this point, the individual may be said to have taken on a depressive self-focusing style. Success and happiness are pushed aside out of experience; failure, negative affect, and self-blame are the only things paid attention to.

The negative self-image that evolves out of repeated experience with the depressive self-focusing style may begin to have some benefits for the depressed individual. It provides relief from efforts to feel better, a simple explanation for complex events, and a defense against the reality principle. "I'm a loser," for some people, is easier to accept than "life is unfair." Most important, the individual can stop trying to be successful and concentrate on preparing for future disappointment by expecting the worst. Hope and a sense of competence, value, or lovability become stressful feelings to be avoided. The depressive self-focusing style supports the individual's attempts to maintain a negative self-image by magnifying the consequences of failures and minimizing the effects of successes.

One important implication of such a model is that therapy that supports self-focusing may be contraindicated for depression. Therapy can become an endless litany of complaints and self-pity. Skilled analysts or dynamic therapists are likely to be able to avoid this common pitfall, but a more active approach may circumvent it altogether.

Depressed Thinking

Mood pervades our consciousness. We tend to remember and focus on things that are congruent with our present mood (Hartlage, Arduino, & Alloy, 1998). When we are feeling sad, sad things come into our mind unbidden, and good things slip away. We think depressed thoughts.

Many patients experience a rueful recognition of themselves when they begin to learn the tenets of cognitive therapy for depression. Beck put forward the original cognitive theory of depression in 1967 and there has been little need to change it since, because it is so accurate (cf. Sacco & Beck, 1995). People with depression experience themselves as unworthy, inept, and undesirable. They expect the worst, and they distort their experience so that the worst is perceived. They have a pattern of negative automatic thoughts which is so familiar that it seems normal: *You're such a loser. Why do you even try? You sure screwed that up. No one likes you. You'll never finish, why bother starting?* There is also a pattern of "depressogenic assumptions" (Beck, 1976), impossible to fulfill, that means the individual will be perennially disappointed, embarrassed, or hurt: *In order to be happy, I have to be liked by everyone. I have to succeed at everything. I can't live without (person or thing).*

Other cognitive researchers have noted the negative attributional style of people with depression: Good things are assumed to be temporary, limited in scope, and caused by chance, while bad things are assumed to be permanent, pervasive, and due to one's own actions. It is a distortion of perception that can be reliably demonstrated to accompany depression, leading to passivity and negative expectations.

Beliefs like these are manifested by, or perhaps are manifestations of, emotions and behavior. Negative automatic thoughts are the voice of shame and self-blame. Depressogenic assumptions result in, or may be rationalizations for, lack of decisive action. Although Beck and others assert the primacy of cognition, and have convincingly demonstrated that therapy aimed at changing cognition can help resolve a depressed episode, to me it seems unproductive to emphasize one aspect of depression at the expense of others.

Behavioral Symptoms

Certain patterns of overt behavior are characteristic of depression. Suicide is the extreme example. Self-destructive behavior and self-defeating behavior are very familiar. Drug and alcohol abuse frequently are both self-destructive and temporarily soothing to a depressed psyche. Procrastination, disorganization, and passive aggression manifest themselves in many depressed patients. Social withdrawal, shyness, and unassertiveness may be considered an absence or a repression of behavior, depending on one's theoretical perspective. Likewise, lethargy and passivity may be viewed as an absence or a constraint. Violence is an all-too-common result of depression.

Obviously, behavioral patterns like these have ramifications throughout the vicious circle of depression. They reinforce depressed thinking and provide ammunition for feelings of guilt and shame. They are evidence that one is not in control. They have important sequelae for the individual's future functioning, resulting in, for example, educational, interpersonal, and employment deficits, which lead to developmental arrests. They drive away potential objects who are mature and well-functioning and attract others who are equally dysfunctional. Lack of self-care or overt abuse of the body will have physiological consequences.

Guilt, Shame, and Diminished Self-Esteem

In the *DSM-IV*, feelings of worthlessness or guilt are primary indicia of major depression, and low self-esteem, of dysthymia. Guilt and shame are, of course, not necessarily manifestations of disease; they are important regulators of behavior, serving as aversive stimuli when we transgress. But a pervasive sense of guilt, inadequacy, unworthiness, or unlovability that is not alleviated by good works, love, reassurance, or forgiveness is almost pathognomic of depression. As we will discuss later, guilt is usually occasioned by actions or intentions, while shame is a more basic feeling having to do with our core identity. Blaming others is guilt projected, a defense that may be effective in the present but leads to isolation and paranoia in the long run; contempt is shame projected, which has the same results.

The role of aggression in depression has been endlessly debated, ever since the formulation by Abraham (1927/1979) that depression has to do with the aggressive drive turned inward on the self. Now that we understand aggression to be a response to shame, not a drive at all, we can stop worrying about the primacy of the drives and the possibility of symptom substitution. When we can help our patients gain cognitive or behavioral control in situations that are likely to lead to guilt or shame, we no longer have to be concerned that we are providing mere palliative care.

In depression, feelings of guilt and shame seem less likely to be tied to specific events or traits and more to do with the whole person; they pervade the sense of self. Unable to be assuaged by amends or contrition, they reinforce a sense of hopelessness and helplessness. They form the content of automatic negative thoughts and distort perception. They become the stick we use to beat ourselves up with. They make assumption of the sick role more attractive, as a way out of what seems to be an impossible situation.

I discussed above the concept of low self-esteem as a vulnerability factor in depression. If healthy self-esteem is the ability to regard oneself with a certain basic affection, objectivity, and forgiveness, its absence perpetuates depression by making the individual dependent on outside sources for those feelings. Those outside sources—people, achievements, money—are notoriously more fickle than the self, and they notoriously don't solve the problem. The love you receive from others is not going to be able to make you like yourself.

Feared Loss of Emotional Control

A powerful aspect of depression, frequently overlooked in the professional literature but emphasized again and again by patients (see Cronkite, 1994; Karp, 1996; Slater, 1998; Styron, 1990), is the fear that one is losing one's mind, a fear that increases in intensity as the depression worsens, often becoming the dominant theme in the patient's thoughts. This fear cannot be discussed openly because of the patient's own shame and his reasonable concern about the reactions of others. In some cases, it is a major motivation for suicide; in other cases, it is acted out by behavior that results in a crisis psychiatric admission. There are often episodes of panic associated with developing depression—racing thoughts, increased motor activity, shortness of breath, ringing in the ears. Feelings of depersonalization, déjà vu, and jamais vu are common. Intense mood swings, crying jags, insomnia, and inappropriate laughter feed the fear, which is of some nameless, cataclysmic, and permanent change to the self. Sometimes rather than insanity the fear is of a dread disease affecting the brain, a violent outburst, exploding, floating away like a balloon, dissolving into a puddle on the floor, or simply being unable to get out of bed.

The fear is fed by the awareness that you are not seeing things as they are or as they used to be, that your friends are looking at you strangely, that you can't seem to do anything right or get anything done, and that you can't keep yourself from being irritable or crying. Popular stereotypes of mental illness as a permanent crippler resulting in violence and homelessness also add to the fear.

As Karp (1996) points out, the mere experience of this kind of fear results in lasting change to the self. We never again will feel omnipotent or invulnerable; we are shaken to the core. I call it a loss of gyroscopic stability, the confidence that though we can be buffeted by events we have a natural momentum that will automatically restore us to our course. Ideally this loss of innocence will set forces in motion that can lead to greater wisdom, increased empathy, an appreciation of life. But it can also result in a permanent loss of self-confidence, behavioral inhibitions, generalized anxiety disorder, substance abuse, and depressed thinking patterns.

Impaired Functioning

Depression is accompanied by impaired cognitive functioning—difficulty concentrating, making decisions, remembering, and learning new information—and impaired behavioral and interpersonal functioning. These can have permanent and lasting consequences, referred to as "collateral damage" (Schuchter et al., 1996). "It is bad enough that the depressed person feels terrible, but worse still that the depression can ruin his or her life" (p. 86). The damage can come about from the consequences of bad decisions made under the duress of symptoms, from tunnel vision that restricts the ability to see alternatives, from the lethargy and pessimism that inhibit opportunity, from destructive or self-destructive habits—like irritability or procrastination—that interfere with desired outcomes. The earlier the onset of depression, the greater the possibility of permanent damage. Childhood depression can lead to inability to participate successfully in school; depression in adolescence to dangerous or self-destructive decisions; in early adulthood, to inability to develop a career or form a lasting relationship.

Effects like these, of course, tend to confirm the depressive's self-blame and negative cognitive set, and reinforce feelings of bitterness and estrangement. Helping the patient come to terms with the present results of damage done in the past calls for great skill and tact on the therapist's part.

Yet, one of the most dazzling ironies of depression is that so many patients don't realize they have it. It can develop so gradually and insidiously that the depressed state feels normal. Studies of patients with depression of approximately 20 years' duration routinely find that the majority of patients have had no prior treatment, and of those who have had treatment, only about a third have had an adequate medication trial (Hirschfeld et al., 1997). The experience at clinics where I've worked is quite common: People usually seek help because of an external crisis in their lives. They feel that their marriage, family, or employment is in jeopardy. They don't seek help complaining of symptoms of depression—because they realize they've stopped enjoying life, or because they have insomnia, or because they have intrusive thoughts of death; they think that these symptoms are a result of the external stress they're experiencing. Yet, the stress is at least in part caused by their own diminished capability.

Development of a Stable, Dysfunctional
Interpersonal World

It's not unusual for the patient recovering from depression to realize that, in some ways, people around him counted on his depressed behavior and resent changes in the routine. A mother of five, who never let anyone know how she was feeling but one day tried to gas herself in the garage, realized when she got home from the hospital that her husband and children expected her to step right back into the role of domestic manager, fetching, cooking, and cleaning up after everyone. When she tried to take a part-time job, there was a lot of talk about how she was inconveniencing everyone. When she tried to talk about her feelings, no one would listen.

People with depression often become mired in relationships that reinforce the depression. The patient is expected to be self-sacrificing, hard-working, and uncomplaining, to be attentive to the needs and interests of others, to avoid the limelight and be satisfied with the smallest piece of the pie. How much of this phenomenon is due to selection (people who don't like being around depression drop out of the patient's life) and how much is due to others' adaptation to the patient's dysfunctional habits is a question to be addressed individually.

Sometimes the stability in the patient's interpersonal world comes not from the same cast of characters, but from the repeated pattern of interaction. Some depressed people are always falling in love with people who can be predicted to reject them. Some seem to induce sadistic behavior in bosses and coworkers. But whether the stability comes from unbroken dysfunctional relationships or repetitions of the same self-destructive scenario, the patient's problems are not simply in his head. They have a real life, with real consequences. It is quite likely that his efforts to change will result in some of the consequences he fears most: the loss of relationships that although often miserable at least have been predictable. If not this extreme, still we must expect that the process of change will be painful and difficult, in part because life will not immediately reward the change. It is obviously incumbent on the therapist to do what he can to smooth the way.

Assumption of the Sick Role

The notion of the "sick role" was put forward by the sociologist Talcott Parsons many years ago (Parsons, 1951; see also Karp, 1996). Society allows the individual who is experiencing an illness to withdraw temporarily from normal expectations and responsibilities without sanction. The nature and extent of the illness determine how much and how long this deviation from social norms will be permitted. In order to continue to merit this special status, the patient is expected to do everything he can to facilitate his own recovery. "However difficult or deadly one's illness, sick people have only so many 'sympathy credits' they can use to legitimate total immersion in the sick role" (Karp, p. 106). If the patient is not seen to be doing everything he can to help himself, family and friends get angry, feel manipulated, and ultimately reject the patient, who is perceived as "milking" his disease.

When it comes to depression, this formulation has unique issues. Depressed patients frequently express the wish that their illness had some outward physical manifestation, like a cast on the leg, that would remind everyone, including themselves, that they have a "real" illness. Given society's still-suspicious attitude about the validity of depression, family and friends who are impatient, selfish, or merely ignorant will find plenty of support for their resistance to extending the benefits of the sick role to the patient. Given also that it is difficult for others to effectively gauge the extent to which the patient is indeed trying to help himself—staying busy and looking cheerful is not always the best thing for the patient—sympathy credits are likely to be in short supply. Marketing of the new antidepressant drugs has ironically made things worse for the patient who doesn't respond, because the message is clearly that *something* should do the trick. Finally, the very nature of the disease, which implies lethargy, self-absorption, and pessimism, makes it difficult even for the patient to feel sympathetic for himself.

But if depression lasts long enough, the patient will assume a special depressed version of the sick role. Both the patient and his family will no longer expect him to function as an adult in our society, but the suspicion that the illness is not quite real never disappears. It may be given a name—depression, nervous breakdown, delicate, weak, funny, not quite right. Depressed patients often develop chronic pain conditions or other states that are more readily recognized as true diseases; or turn to alcohol or self-medication to get them through the day. The bottom line is that at this point both the patient and his loved ones have given up on him. It is a devastating outcome, a waste of a life.

Physiological Symptoms

The relationship between depression and physical health is close, complex, and not well understood. Western medical traditions, with their grounding in mind-body dualism and emphasis on the experimental method, have contributed to the confusion. There is reason to believe that some conditions like fibromyalgia and chronic fatigue syndrome may be psychophysiological problems—in my view, manifestations of depression (see chapter 12). Other diseases that are seen as exclusively physiological—like cancer, stroke, and MS—carry with them a high risk of depression. And depression may contribute to disease—years of stress, insomnia, and hypervigilance take a toll on endocrine systems and neurotransmitter production (Sapolsky, 1998). The depressive's lack of good self-care habits contributes to increased risk. Excessive self-focusing may lead to preoccupation with and treatment for ailments that others might dismiss. Physical disease may result in changes in the nervous system that precipitate depression. Depression's effect on the nervous system may trigger endocrine changes.

In the end, depression shortens the lifespan, even if the sufferer doesn't commit suicide, and increases the risk of other medical problems. Patients with depression visit their MDs more frequently, are operated on more frequently, and have more nonpsychiatric emergency-room visits than the general population (Herrmann et al., 1998). Chronic pain, gastrointestinal problems, migraine, menstrual discomfort and dysphoria, weight control issues, all increase greatly the suffering of depression. They also compound the effects of the disease, further restricting activity, nutrition, and self care, and reinforcing the depressive's idea of himself as out of control, bad, or weak.

Neurochemical Changes

Researchers have documented many changes in the nervous system that accompany depression: changes in concentration of neurotransmitters in the urine, blood, and cerebrospinal fluid; changes in brain function and perhaps structure documented by neuroimaging techniques; and other neurochemical abnormalities (U. S. Department of Health and Human Services, 1999). Generally, the hope that a single factor would account for depression—for instance, the "catecholamine hypothesis" emphasizing the action of serotonin— has had to be abandoned, so that researchers are still trying to understand the interplay among neurochemical factors and their interaction with psychosocial risk factors. We simply don't know if the frequently observed deficiency of serotonin in the synapses of depressed patients is a cause or an effect of depression. In any case, antidepressants that address serotonin levels and other neurotransmitters are often helpful with many patients. Changes in the brain and nervous system associated with depression are powerful factors in its functional autonomy; they may be especially responsible for the disturbed sleep, persistent anhedonia, low self-esteem, and intrusive negative thought patterns of depression.

Based on the high recurrence rate of depression, some observers have suggested a "kindling" model, which implies that a depressive episode leaves a "scar" in brain tissue that lowers the threshold required to precipitate another episode (Post et al., 1982). There is evidence that people with recurrent depression do have more pronounced abnormalities of adrenocortical regulation and sleep neurophysiology than people suffering a single episode (Thase, 1999). However, it's important to recognize that the "scar" can be healed. "The capacity for experience-dependent plastic changes in the nervous system remains in place throughout the lifespan" (Schore, 1997). This continuing plasticity is most pronounced in those areas of the brain that have to do with memory and regulation of emotion. Successful psychotherapy has been shown through PET scanning to result in significant changes in just those same areas of the brain (Schwartz, Stoessel, Baxter, Martin, & Phelps, 1996).

Vegetative Signs

Disturbed sleep—either difficulty falling asleep or early morning awakening, or sometimes both—is a hallmark of depression. (Some patients suffer from the opposite, hypersomnia, rarely ever able to fully awaken.) Sleep patterns of people with depression typically show that REM sleep is more intense and of more rapid onset and longer duration than normal. Successful use of some but not all antidepressant medication typically returns REM sleep to normal, although interestingly enough successful psychotherapy does not seem to have the same effect (Thase & Howland, 1995).

Disturbances of appetite are also expected. Loss of appetite is the most common symptom, sometimes leading to substantial weight loss. A substantial minority of patients gain weight when depressed, and many patients on the newer antidepressants report great difficulty losing weight despite remission of depression. The relationship between depressed appetite disturbances and the patient's damaged self-image and sense of powerlessness because of ineffectual efforts to lose weight is reciprocal. There is a close association between anorexia and bulimia and depression.

Other common vegetative signs of depression include decreased energy or fatigue, psychomotor agitation or retardation, and anhedonia. All of these indicators of depression are powerful reinforcers of the patient's sense of being out of control. They also can have unpleasant consequences—loss of employment, inability to take advantage of opportunities, cognitive and emotional dysfunction. But frequently these vegetative signs are the most disturbing symptoms to the patient, and because they "feel" physical they are often enough to overcome resistance to trying antidepressant medication.

Discrimination and Stigma

> Depression is a pernicious illness associated with episodes of long duration, high rates of chronicity, relapse, and recurrence, psychosocial and physical impairment, and mortality and morbidity—with a 15% risk of death from suicide in patients with more severe forms of depression. Despite these facts, . . . patients with depression are being seriously undertreated, even though effective treatments have been available for more than 35 years. . . . The vast majority of patients with chronic depression are misdiagnosed, receive inappropriate or inadequate treatment, or are given no treatment at all. (Hirschfeld et al., 1997, p. 333)

In 1993 *Parade* magazine conducted a now-classic survey of public attitudes about depression (Clements, 1993). Despite all the effort that has gone into education, and despite the beginning wave of publicity about Prozac which strongly supported the disease model, the survey found that 43 percent of respondents viewed depression as a "sign of personal or emotional weakness." These people were significantly less likely to seek professional help than the rest of the sample. Another third would not tell their friends if a spouse or child were receiving treatment. Those who held the most stigmatized attitudes about depression were actually more likely to report that they have experienced depression or "feel really depressed" about once a month. Younger people were more knowledgeable about the symptoms of depression, but they were also more likely (55 percent) to view it as a sign of weakness—this chiefly due to the harsh attitudes young men expressed about depression and about seeking help.

People with depression are ashamed of their own disease; and though we've tried for years to educate the public and destigmatize the illness, our efforts have largely been in vain. Perhaps this is because of "depressive realism"—the uncomfortable tendency of depressed people to see the objective truth, without the comforting illusions that most of us rely on to get through life. Because the objective truth is that our society, including the healthcare field, continues to play on the depressed person's self-blame to the point where depression often appears to be a perfectly legitimate and rational response to the way the individual is being treated by society. "I get the message; I'm a loser, I'm wasting everyone's time, I'm just in the way."

Janey, 32, five feet and 100 pounds, was physically abused by her husband for years. She's had a broken jaw and internal injuries so severe that her endocrine system barely functions. Nerve damage in her back means that periodically without warning she loses the functioning of her legs.

She left her husband five years ago, joined AA, and has been sober since, caring for her four children with the help of her mother and a new man in her life who seems to be kind and decent. Recently, however, she became so distraught after a fight with a relative that she slashed her wrists. Taken to the hospital, she was told that she would have to pay for the costs of getting stitched up—that her state insurance did not cover self-inflicted injuries. (I was told later that this was not the state's policy and must have been the hospital's attempt to collect something in cash.)

I asked her what she thought the message to her was. She laughed: "Next time, I should use a gun. I'm just white trash to these people; they just wish I'd die and not bother them."

Depression is not merely a result of neurochemistry, genetics, stress, early loss, a punitive superego, or any of the other factors that have been proposed over the years. It is also a result of how society treats the patient. I feel strongly that it's not only helpful to the treatment to acknowledge that fact, it's destructive to ignore it. If we don't acknowledge stigma and discrimination when our patients experience it, we are in essence telling them they are merely imagining it.

AVENUES FOR INTERVENTION

At this point, the reader may be daunted by the litany of complications and manifestations of depression, all interacting with each other and reinforcing each other. It is a true vicious circle, a self-reinforcing system that can seem impossible to break; but this same circularity, from a slightly different perspective, provides the key to its own solution.

Everyone knows how hard it can be to escape from a vicious circle. What we usually overlook, however, is a very important and optimistic implication of circularity: In a vicious circle, we can intervene anywhere. We don't have to waste time establishing the "real" cause of the problem. When we assume a model of linear causality, we also assume we need to find the real or primary cause, because if we only fix a problem that is merely a secondary effect of the primary cause, other unforeseen and perhaps worse problems will ensue. That way of thinking about depression has been pursued for decades, and we are no closer to finding agreement on the "real" cause. But abandoning linear causality gives us tremendous freedom. All it takes, theoretically, to stop a vicious circle is for one element in the chain to break down. We can choose where we intervene based on factors like economy, ease of access, lack of resistance, or synergistic effects rather than being forced to pursue a single course of action. Instead of forcing our patients to adapt to our method, we can adapt the method to the patient.

Annie doesn't look or sound depressed. She calls from her office to make an initial appointment, and sounds dynamic and energetic, like a good salesperson. When she arrives, she seems the picture of health: tall, dressed professionally and well-groomed, good eye contact. But she's badly stuck. She takes no pleasure in life at all and fears that she's losing her mind. She and her live-in boyfriend are on the outs, fighting and bickering. She hates her job, but can't get it together to leave. She goes home from work, has two beers and a little dinner, and goes to bed, where she sleeps fitfully. Sometimes she doesn't even take her dog for a walk. It's been like this for more than a year.

Annie recognizes that she has depression, and also recognizes that she has good reason to feel this way. She is the youngest child of a large family. Her mother developed a fatal disease while pregnant with Annie, and died when Annie was five. Some of her fondest memories are of sleeping curled up on the floor by her mother's sickbed. As her mother's disease progressed, and her speech became slurred, Annie became the only one in the family who could understand what she was saying. Her mother's death was a devastating loss for her.

After her mother's death, Annie's father became depressed, withdrawn, and preoccupied with his own loss. Annie was cared for largely by her older sister, who did an adequate but far from perfect job. Annie has painful memories of being teased at school because the hem of her dress was stapled together, or because she had a bad haircut, or because her clothes were obvious hand-me-downs. One bright light was her brother, the family's star—an athlete, successful in everything he tried, handsome, charming, and popular—Annie felt good just to be around him. Eventually her father remarried. Again, Annie's stepmother was adequate but not perfect. Annie had a full-fledged adolescent rebellion that left deep wounds in her relationship with her father. She went away to college and supported herself completely, never taking a dime from her family, although it took her seven years to get her college degree.

Then tragedy struck again. Annie's brother developed cancer. Treatment was ineffective. His personality changed, becoming self-absorbed and callous. After more than a year of treatment, a bone-marrow transplant was the last resort. Annie was the closest match. She went through the harrowing donation process, but it was futile, and her brother died.

Now, five years later, Annie has found her way to my office, and I have a dilemma, because Annie's depression is not only in the past but also in the present. She works for an employment service, where she is the star employee and the owner's favorite. She generates more business than anyone else, and her accounts all love her. But she hates the work. She wears a mask of efficiency and profes-

sionalism all day, while she is deeply distressed at the fate she knows will meet the people she places in jobs. She sees them as victims, undereducated, underskilled, nearly unemployable, but hopeful, trying, wanting to better themselves. She knows it's not going to happen. The accounts will underpay them, deny them benefits, lead them on with a promise of a permanent job, then let them go at the least provocation. It is, in Annie's words, a "shitty job getting people shittier jobs." And Annie feels like a hypocrite, a liar, a manipulator.

While Annie clearly sees the connection between her depression and her relationship with her mother and the death of her brother, she doesn't seem to see the connection with her job—yet she punishes herself every day going to work. If my questions and encouragement can get her to consider other options, and that leads to some immediate relief, isn't that the correct, empathic, professional direction to take? There is still a balance; she needs to grieve, to talk about her mother and brother. I will lose this patient who has summoned up tremendous courage to let her guard down if I give her the idea that her feelings are unimportant or that the solution to her problem is simple. But if I don't help her to see the connection between her depression and the pain she gives herself every day in this job, I believe she will continue to suffer needlessly.

Stubbornly self-reliant, Annie refuses to consider medications and will only see me when she's got the cash to pay for a session, about once a month. She also refuses to feel sorry for herself. We try to work the balance. We talk about her father, her brother, and her boyfriend, and her feelings for all of them are more complicated than they first seemed. We don't talk about her mother much, but we do talk through those painful memories of childhood, adolescence, and college, when Annie felt more than anything else like an orphan. Annie befriends a little girl in her neighborhood who seems somewhat needy and neglected, and she allows herself to feel good about the girl's obvious adoration of her. When her boyfriend hears of a possible job opening with a reliable employer, Annie applies. With my encouragement, she opts for shorter hours and the chance to attend professional school part-time. Her symptoms—the lethargy, emotional withdrawal, anhedonia—are substantially reduced.

What do we really know about how people recover from depression, anxiety, and other psychological problems? I believe that most honest theorists, whether psychologically or biologically oriented, will admit that very little is known for certain. One way seems to be through the process of emotional relearning that good therapy provides. But emotional relearning can also come about in everyday life; the problem is that our defenses keep us from experiences that can help us. This is not new thinking. Alexander and French said this in *Psychoanalytic Therapy* in 1946, when they encouraged patients to seek the "corrective emotional experience." That phrase went down in psychoanalytic infamy because it came to be associated with the idea that the therapist should play a role with the patient—deliberately behave in a manner to induce the desired experience, rather than being authentic. But, as Wachtel (1993) and others have pointed out, we have long recognized the hollowness of mere "intellectual insight" as opposed to true "emotional insight," and nowadays almost no one believes that insight alone leads to recovery. Truly corrective emotional experiences can happen not only in psychotherapy but also in life, if we can learn how to let them happen to us.

Good therapy for depression requires a delicate balance between all of our old principles: Start where the client is; follow the affect; interpret the defenses, etc.—and the need to keep strategic goals in mind. Patients with depression want, and deserve, relief from their pain as quickly as possible. If their self-destructive behavior is contributing to their pain, let's help them stop first, then explore the reasons why (if it's still important when they've already stopped). If they're not able to sleep, let's help them sleep. If they can't concentrate, let's help them make decisions. If they're beset by problematic relationships, let's help them set limits. Choosing where to intervene based on strategic goals may not only provide relief, it may also set in motion a healing process that requires little more than guidance and direction from us.

CHAPTER 3

The Functional Symptoms/ Skills of Depression

I N UNDOING DEPRESSION I referred to certain defense mechanisms and the emotional, cognitive, and behavioral habits that sustain them as "skills of depression." Much like the cigarette smoker who has learned how to light a cigarette in a high wind, how to flick ashes into the ashtray without missing, and who always knows without counting how many cigarettes are left in the pack he's carrying, we become adept at things that aren't good for us. These habits or skills come to seem very natural to us, part of our self.

I know a research scientist who is very precise, logical, and extremely thorough. He never comes to a conclusion without having carefully considered all the possible explanations, no matter how unlikely. I know a bonds trader who is highly focused, energetic, and very competitive. He wins his tennis matches through sheer determination. Both men are highly successful in their fields and extremely unsuccessful in their families. They take the same habits that serve them well at their employment and try to make them work at home. The scientist's wife complains that he's a cold fish who doesn't trust her or love her. The trader's son experiences his father as domineering and selfish.

Like these men, the depressed person has ways of living that serve a purpose in certain circumstances, but that in other circumstances lead to grief. These ways of living, or habits or skills of depression, perpetuate the disease. We become caught in a vicious circle from which there seems to be no escape.

For instance: Joe was raised by a narcissistic, self-involved mother and a strict, demanding, emotionally abusive father; he grew into a meek, compliant individual who has difficulty being assertive. In terms of the skills of depression, he has learned passivity, denial, and intellectualization, but he often feels taken advantage of, neglected, or unnoticed. These experiences are likely to make him feel angry, but his passivity, denial, and intellectualization help him not to be aware of the angry feelings. Instead, he goes on being self-effacing, which leads to more anger, which leads to redoubled defenses. As Paul Wachtel (1993) has noted, this pattern may have its origins in the past, but Joe's anger and inhibition in the present are about real, current experiences of being overlooked or taken for granted, ironically generated by his own efforts not to feel anger.

These patterns are not likely to go away because the patient's serotonin has been balanced, or because he's gained insight into the nature of his problems. They are only going to go away if they are replaced by other skills, and the only way we can learn other skills is by practice, repetition, drill, rote, practice again and again. What used to be called "working through" when psychotherapy was expected to take years was a long period of practicing new ways of living. The patient had the luxury of coming back to the therapist's office and reviewing progress. The therapist had the luxury of not having to prescribe, but of letting the patient learn through experience, through successive approximation. No longer. Now we must prescribe, and prepare our patients for the knowledge that they will have to keep practicing long after our therapeutic contact is ended. Worse yet, under times of stress the skills of depression will reassert themselves, will feel normal again when the newer skills seem uncertain or contrived. This makes the patient more vulnerable to relapse, and we have to plan for that eventuality as well.

Calling these attributes "skills" is appealing to many patients who have some appreciation of the black humor of depression. I think it's important to convey to all patients that depression is hard work, that to a great extent it consists of habits that we have learned, habits that make sense in important aspects of our lives but that have unexpected negative consequences. Use of the word "skills" is also meant to be disarming, to get under the defensiveness of patients who are desperate to hold on to the idea that their depression is caused by their parents, their genes, or their failure to find the right medication yet. By implicitly praising patients for being good at something they do not want to admit they do, we reframe their experience. If we can speak as "experts" on depression, they are more likely still to be willing to entertain our point of view.

COGNITIVE SKILLS

Pessimism

Expecting the worst protects the depressed patient from disappointment. Perhaps because of traumatic disappointment in the past, disappointment may be experienced as a uniquely aversive event by the depressed, to be avoided at all costs. In fact, disappointment is frequently one of the narcissistic injuries that can precipitate a depressive episode.

Complicating matters is the phenomenon of "depressive realism." In many ways, people with depression seem to be more accurate perceivers of reality than people without depression. In repeated laboratory experiments where individuals are given a task over which they actually have no control but are told they do (like rolling dice), depressed people are much quicker to realize that they are not able to influence events. When asked to judge their performance on a simple interpersonal task, like giving an impromptu speech in front of an audience, depressed individuals' ratings of their own performance are much closer to the audience ratings than those of nondepressed individuals, who consistently overestimate their own interpersonal skill. It seems sometimes that nondepressed people have a kind of unrealistic optimism about their abilities and the future in general. "The primary active ingredient in cognitive therapy may be the training of depressed clients to engage in the sort of optimistic biases and illusions that nondepressives typically construct, rather than the enhancement of realistic self-appraisal" (Alloy & Abramson, 1988). In a postmodern world, where we question the objectivity of any reality, perhaps we can be open to question about what exactly defines an illusion. It may be that the nondepressives' biases and illusions are really accurate in the world they construct: that in a self-fulfilling prophecy, people *do* like them, and they *are* accurate predictors of reality because things go their way more often than not; but in a strict laboratory setting, where their biases and illusions are prevented from having an impact on events, their judgment appears inaccurate. Meanwhile, realistic pessimism may have some actual benefit for depressives in terms of making them less likely to take unrealistic risks, more likely to prepare for bad outcomes, etc. Still, it is probable that these benefits are offset by the absence of the self-confidence—even if unrealistic—that permits people to be outgoing, to reach out to new friends, to take on formidable tasks.

Negative Self-Talk

The "automatic negative thoughts" noted by Beck (1967) sometimes seem like a knee-jerk reaction designed to counter any good feeling. Diane noticed how one day when she started to listen to the praise people were giving her about her performance, immediately other thoughts began to intrude: "Oh, no, they don't know the real you, they don't know how pathetic you are, they don't know what a loser you are." It's important that she recognize that voice is a distortion and this way of thinking is a habit that can be broken. Most patients, once they are made aware of this pattern, experience a certain grim joy in recognizing how they "do it" to themselves. Some like the shorthand ANTS for automatic negative thoughts, because like ants they seem to creep in from nowhere to spoil the picnic. Patients can learn to counter such thoughts by simple commands to the self: *Don't go there. Don't listen to that voice. Worry about that later. That's not my problem.* Some patients learn to substitute positive self-affirmations, although I cringe; rather than fatuous global affirmations, challenging negative beliefs with the force of logic seems to be more empowering: *What's the evidence for believing you're a loser? Is there other evidence you're not paying attention to? What do other people seem to think? What if you just act as if you don't believe it?*

Passivity

Depressed people are unlikely to view themselves as "centers of initiative." They see themselves as acted upon, rather than actors; as victims, not aggressors. They are more prone to errors of omission than commission. Passivity, as the absence of something that should be there, compared to negative self-talk which is the presence of something that should not be there, can be much more difficult for patients to notice. They are much more likely to notice the anger and disappointment that come with the realization that one has been overlooked or missed an important opportunity again—too late to take advantage of the situation. When this happens, it's important that the therapist not try to make the pain go away but to acknowledge the legitimacy of the suffering and suggest to the patient that he resolve not to let it happen again. With this as motivation, the patient will be more amenable to a detailed exploration of how he turns a blind eye to opportunities to think more proactively about his experience.

Selective Attention

Selective attention was one of the "security operations" pointed out by Harry Stack Sullivan (Safran, 1984)—not unique to depression, but a powerful element in its maintenance. By selectively paying attention only to what confirms our expectations, we avoid anxiety. For the depressed person, not seeing opportunities, not registering the affection and respect of others, not paying attention to the beauty of the physical world, helps to maintain an even keel. In addition, selective attention reaffirms our sense of the essential correctness of our belief system, because no challenging evidence is ever registered.

Depressed Logic

In a later section we will discuss in more depth what cognitive-behavioral therapy teaches us about depressed thinking. Here I want to mention briefly what I consider to be one of the most common and insidious logical errors made in depression: emotional reasoning. We have the idea that whatever we feel is true, and the stronger we feel it, the more true it is. If I have the belief that I can't live without my girlfriend's love, I'm not likely to challenge that belief, but will humiliate and abase myself to please her. If I have the belief that I'm a failure if I don't have a million in the bank by the time I'm 35, I may sacrifice fulfilling work and time with my family in pursuit of that goal. It's an odd kind of closed-system thinking. Schneidman (1984) talks about counseling a pregnant college student who had made up her mind that the only thing she could do was commit suicide. Instead of arguing with her about the suicide, he simply said *you can always do that later* and got her to list all the other alternatives possible—adoption, abortion, marriage, single motherhood. Even though she said each was impossible, by the end of the discussion she had come around to agreeing that some were less impossible than others, and she was no longer a suicide risk that day. We become so flooded with our feelings that we are unable to question our assumptions.

EMOTIONAL SKILLS

Isolation of Affect

The ability to remain calm in stressful situations is a highly useful skill. The problem with depression is that we haven't learned to let ourselves feel the emotion after the stress is removed. And we use isolation in other ways: The sudden urge to hurt oneself, the morbid thoughts of death, seemingly unconnected to what's going on around us. We play mentally with forbidden impulses, not fully recognizing their horror, but still frightening ourselves. "I thought I was the only one who ever thought about driving into oncoming traffic," said a visitor to my Web site.

The function of affect is to call attention to the stimulus that precipitates it (Tomkins, 1962, 1963). The fear response dramatically calls our attention to the feared object; the interest/excitement response heightens our ability to attend to the novel situation. When we isolate affect, we deprive ourselves of information that may be vital in making decisions. Kristin stayed calm and cool when her boyfriend made violent threats against her in the midst of an argument, then "forgot" about them. Only years later in a session did she feel the terror caused by what he had said. Affective response patterns also communicate our emotions to others, as anyone who has ever watched a baby knows. The baby's ability to communicate affectively triggers emotional mirroring and appropriate caretaking by adults. When depression constricts our experience and expression of affect, others do not understand us, find us distant, cold, or odd. Empathy and intimacy are damaged.

People with depression have learned not to communicate affect because of their experience with an unresponsive or hostile environment. In some families, in some situations, to let others know how you feel is dangerous; it gives people ammunition to be used against you. Isolation of affect is an adaptive skill in such situations, but the depressed become unable to turn it off, to express emotions again when it is safe and appropriate to do so.

Somatization

I use this term to mean the use of the body as a metaphor to express a psychological state. Many people with depression complain of physical symptoms that suggest an interpersonal message—pain that can't be helped by conventional medication, fatigue that isn't relieved by rest, being irritated by multiple stimuli, being easily nauseated or having an irritable bowel. By unconsciously magnifying our physical symptoms, we can avoid difficult situations, punish people we are afraid to confront directly, or reinforce our own self-pity. We get to act on or benefit from our emotions without having to experience them.

Denial

A depressed father with an adult, alcoholic son who has lost his driving privileges drives the son around town absorbing his abuse: "What a lousy driver you are. Can't you drive a little faster? You're always late. You're worthless." Telling me about this, he is embarrassed about his son's bad behavior, not about his own passivity in the face of abuse. When I ask him how this makes him feel, he is completely unaware of feeling angry—but remains depressed. He's not afraid of his son, he just avoids conflict and emotional engagement of any sort.

Denial is the defense that drives a wedge between reality and our internal experience. It's not a psychotic process—we see correctly what's going on, we just don't make the connection. The wife of the alcoholic believes it when he says he's going to reform; the kid in the speeding car knows he's putting himself at risk, he just doesn't feel the risk. Denial supports depression by helping us stay in an awful situation and pretend it doesn't affect us, by protecting us from the realization that our irritability and self-absorption are driving people away, and even by insulating us from the sadness and hopelessness of depressed affect, leaving us just empty, overwhelmed, or preoccupied with physical symptoms.

Intellectualization

A patient has been stuck on a novel for years. He comes to sessions with a relaxed, carefree manner, and wants to talk, as he has done in his previous treatment, about his childhood; this is despite the fact that he is practically homeless and destitute. When I point out that his previous treatment didn't work, and suggest that he sit at his desk and work on his novel for an hour each day, and report back to me on how it feels, he drops out of treatment. Intelligent people can protect themselves from awareness of the damage they do to themselves and others in the present by using their brains to focus on the past or the future; and sometimes psychotherapy can be used to assist in this process. Intellectualization is a sophisticated form of denial.

Projection

In projection, we take our own feelings and attribute them to others. In depression, projection allows us not to feel many things that we experience as uncomfortable or unworthy—sexuality, anger, revenge, envy. It enables a passive attitude, watching life go by amused at how others are making fools of themselves. Projection is often the basis for the self-fulfilling prophecy. We apologize for ourselves so much, eventually people start to believe we *are* to blame.

A husband who is depressed over losing his job won't accept his wife's reassurance, believing firmly that she blames him. When he rejects her reassurances over and over again, she eventually stops trying; he feels rejected but finally has the evidence he sought for his belief.

Externalization and Internalization

A wife gets up during the night to use the bathroom, leaving the light off so as not to disturb her sleeping husband. On her way back to bed, she stumbles against a chair that had been left out of its usual position in the room. "Oh, how clumsy of me," she thinks to herself.

The movement of the bed as she returns awakens her husband, and he gets up to use the bathroom in turn. As he makes his way back to bed, he also stumbles against the same chair. "Who put that goddamn chair there?" he curses silently.

An old joke that plays on common stereotypes. We smile because we recognize the truth. Men are generally more quick to blame others, and women are generally more inclined to blame themselves. Real (1997), reviewing the data on incidence of depression in the National Comorbidity Study (Kessler et al., 1994)—which found twice as many women as men depressed—noted that when the incidence of antisocial personality and drug dependence is added in, psychopathology in the sexes balances out. He makes a convincing case that much of male externalizing—making others suffer—is an expression of hidden male depression.

Internalization of blame clearly perpetuates depression; it can be a *skill* of depression because it can make the world go smoothly, it can help us avoid confrontation. Externalization of blame is a skill because it can make others suffer more than we ourselves do, keep others uncertain and on the defensive while we preserve an image of bravado and confidence. But it also perpetuates depression because it prevents intimacy and moral growth.

Rageaholism There are many people who have learned to get their way through tantrums and intimidation. Contrary to popular belief, this behavior pattern is not confined to groups of low socioeconomic status. I know some quite intelligent and well-to-do people who function exactly the same way, but the pattern is a little more subtle. A wife says to her husband, "You're making me feel bad, you're going to ruin my mood for the whole day, it'll be your fault if I get a migraine." A husband who has never touched his wife in anger has learned that if he just yells loud enough, she will let him have his way. Of course, we end up alienating the people we do this to.

Anger is easier than sadness. The wife in the previous paragraph doesn't have to feel all her conflicts about her career. The husband gets to make his wife depressed instead of recognizing his own depression. Righteous indignation fills us with purpose and its ventilation leads to a sense of mastery. The trouble is, it's addictive, and we don't always know when we really are righteous.

Anhedonia

The inability to experience pleasure of any sort is one of the most devastating symptoms of depression—and one of the most pathognomic. To consider it a "skill" of depression may seem like a stretch. But consider this: The ability to experience pleasure requires the ability to be in the moment. If we want to be in the moment we have to relinquish control, take risks, expose ourselves to the chance of failure or loss. Avoiding joy is like avoiding hope; it preserves a homeostasis we are desperate to hold on to. Not experiencing joy preserves our pride; we never fail because we don't try (Snyder & Frankel, 1989).

Envy and Begrudgery

One of the biggest taboo subjects in depression support groups is envy; but once the ice is broken everyone joins in with evident relief. People are finally able to talk about how jealous they are of people without depression, people who seem to be popular and successful. As the talk goes on it becomes clear that envy is a dominant theme in many patients' lives; they spend a great deal of time wishing they had what they covet in others. Most feel quite guilty about these feelings, aware that they are indulging in a self-destructive habit no matter how legitimate the envy seems to be. Envy protects us from depression by mobilizing rage; although we feel inadequate compared to the envied other, our thoughts tend toward aggression, toward devaluing or destroying the other, rather than our own shortcomings (Morrison, 1999). And of course envy gives us an easy rationalization: "He's just been lucky. I never get the breaks." Contempt, closely allied, is depression projected on another: "It's not I who am loathsome, it's you."

Begrudgery is a recognized social problem in Ireland, and seems to be a common theme among many cultures, including the Congressional Republican leadership. Closely related to *schadenfreude*, it implies an active intent to spoil the good fortune of others.

These are skills of depression in that they reinforce the feeling that one is victimized by malign fate instead of being responsible for one's own happiness. But they maintain depression by dragging us down to levels of behavior and feeling we can take no pride in, and by emphasizing our own powerlessness and passivity. People who are full of envy and begrudgery are not pleasant to spend time with, and so they become more isolated and yet more envious of others.

Hopelessness

The terrible pain that hope can bring to the depressive is addressed in chapter 6. But not permitting ourselves to feel hope qualifies as a "skill" of depression because it both protects us from pain and perpetuates the disease. Intense, unrelieved despair is a hallmark of acute depression that no one would choose; many depressed patients will acknowledge that when something good happens, when they begin to experience a little hope, they consciously banish the feeling. The process protects them from what they feel will be an inevitable disappointment, but it also prevents them from feeling energetic and alive, from seeing the world from a more optimistic frame of mind, and from experiencing themselves as capable of influencing their fate.

Apathy

Apathy protects the depressed from disappointment, like pessimism, but also from close emotional engagement. We don't participate in the game, or even actively cheer the team on, but remain high up in the stands, aloof and remote. Not committing ourselves to goals, ideals, or causes, we coast through life without the bonds of partnership or camaraderie. We may have an active fantasy life, *à la* Walter Mitty, which can give us some internal satisfaction without putting us at risk.

BEHAVIORAL SKILLS

Procrastination

Members of my groups wonder what we get out of procrastination. Many of us know very well that we procrastinate on many tasks, and that we make ourselves miserable by worry and guilt when it would be so easy just to sit down and attend to business. It may be that the anxious, guilty state is so familiar that it is disquieting to feel any other way; or perhaps that procrastinating over little things helps us avoid giving attention to more important subjects, like relationships or goals; or perhaps it is the adrenaline junkie's way of feeling alive only under stress. I suspect that procrastination does serve a protective function, in the sense that other people and life in general seem to leave us alone when we're in a frenzy to keep up with mundane tasks.

Another function of procrastination is that it can provide a kind of perverse joy or pride. By putting things off to the last minute we handicap ourselves, we make the task more challenging; we come closer to the flow experience and away from the tedium of too much time, not enough to do. And of course it gives us a great excuse for mediocre results.

Lethargy

Chris, who was described in *Undoing Depression*, speaks of her depression as a big, soft comforter. It's not really comforting, but it's safe and familiar. Sometimes she feels as if she's entitled to be depressed, to quit struggling, to snuggle down and watch old movies and feel sorry for herself. While you're in a haze of television or solitaire or romance novels, some decisions get resolved on their own.

You can miss an opportunity but not notice it because you've shut down your awareness. Opportunities are uncomfortable challenges when you're depressed.

Work Till You Drop

Most people with depression have no understanding of the concepts of pace, timing, preparation, and relaxation; they only have two modes, on and off. Working to the point of exhaustion, perversely, may feel good to the depressive, because exhaustion is an objective state. He doesn't have to stand back and evaluate whether or not he did a good job, or even whether his work actually accomplished anything; he knows he's exhausted, and that's good enough.

Compulsions

The link between true obsessive-compulsive disorder and depression is very strong, and not well understood. Some antidepressant medications (e.g., Anafranil, Prozac and Luvox) have demonstrated their effectiveness against OCD. So has cognitive-behavioral therapy. But many patients with depression use obsessive-compulsive defenses without meeting the criteria for OCD. These can be behavior patterns that pass the time and distract from the pain of depression, or rituals that we use to propitiate the gods of depression. Cleanliness and messiness are areas of life where many people enact their depression. Some are highly distressed because things are not just perfect, others are distressed because they are completely overwhelmed by clutter and mess. Both can be so preoccupied with the issue that they have little time or energy left for anything else.

Adrenaline Addiction

Some individuals become addicted to risk-taking as a way of counteracting depression. Sometimes the risks are obvious, as with gambling problems or self-destructive adolescent acting out. Sometimes the risks are more subtle and have to do with arranging one's life so that one is perennially snatching victory from the jaws of defeat. People who work on deadlines often report that they feel alive only when the weekly or monthly crisis comes around. The regular jolt of adrenaline gives us the illusion that what we are doing is important, even if it isn't.

Inability to Prioritize

One of our children's therapists pointed this out about a mother she works with: Her two children are remarkably aggressive with each other, with their preschool and kindergarten mates, and with adults. In addition, both are enuretic. Mother doesn't seem appropriately concerned; it's as if she doesn't hear their escalation, doesn't respond to cues that would warn most mothers it's time to intervene before someone gets hurt. Yet, it's very important to her that the children say please and thank you.

People with depression confuse what's urgent with what's important, always putting out fires without ever separating the fuel and the spark. Again, it's a way of sustaining a feeling of busyness and importance without questioning the direction your life is drifting in.

Victimizing, Violence, and Acting Out

The differences in the ways men and women express pain and experience depression are quite complex; a more complete discussion follows in chapter 7. For now, let us accept the stereotypes: Men are much more likely than women to turn to violence or verbal aggression when in distress. Victimizing others through intimidation can become a characterological pattern, often rewarded in that one gets one's own way. Acting out—escaping from conflictual situations through action—can be an effective distraction.

But violence is usually a response to shame, an ineffective response because (a) it doesn't address the individual's vulnerability to shame in the first place, and (b) the consequences of violence frequently are the subject for more shame. Though we don't typically think of violence as a symptom of depression, we should recognize that violent men typically have very unstable self-esteem, and that their violent behavior is another vicious circle which doesn't solve the underlying problem.

Victimization, Acting In, and Self-Mutilation

Women are much more likely than men to harm themselves, through suicide attempts or self-mutilation. Women can get stuck in a victim role, often through marriage to a victimizing man, but also in relationships with parents and siblings, employment, and sometimes with their own children. To be treated sadistically is better than being ignored; to treat the self sadistically can affirm a sense of reality, provide a sense of focus, calm, or pseudointegration during times of great distress.

The Link with ADHD

Hallowell & Ratey (1994, p. 19), describe the consequences of childhood ADHD for self-esteem and social acceptance:

> Due to repeated failures, misunderstandings, mislabelings, and all manner of other emotional mishaps, children with ADD usually develop problems with their self-image and self-esteem. Throughout childhood, at home and at school they are told they are defective. They are called dumb, stupid, lazy, stubborn, willful, or obnoxious. . . . They are blamed for the chaos of family mealtimes or the disaster of

family vacations. They are reprimanded for classroom disturbances of all sorts and they are easily scapegoated at school . . . Time and again, an exasperated teacher meets a frustrated parent in a meeting that later explodes all over the child who isn't there.

To make friends, you have to be able to pay attention. To get along in a group, you have to be able to follow what is being said in the group. Social cues are often subtle: the narrowing of eyes, the raising of eyebrows, a slight change in tone of voice, a tilting of the head. Often the person with ADD doesn't pick up on these cues. This can lead to real social gaffes or a general sense of being out of it. Particularly in childhood, where social transactions happen so rapidly and the transgressor of norms is dealt with so pitilessly, a lapse in social awareness due to the distractibility or impulsivity of ADD can preclude acceptance by a group or deny understanding from a friend.

It's now recognized that children with ADHD are at high risk for depression (Cytryn & McKnew, 1996). In my practice, many adults with depression, especially males, report having had learning problems in school and continue to manifest symptoms of adult ADHD. Whether these conditions develop separately in response to common stressors, whether there is a common neurochemical factor at work, or whether depression is an expectable response to the frustrations of ADHD, are questions that may be decided by future research. Some adult manifestations of ADHD can be considered skills of depression because they come to serve a defensive purpose. Impulsivity and distractibility, for instance, can keep an individual busy for a lifetime while little is accomplished in the long run. The ability to hyperfocus can help us rescue the failed project at the last possible moment, supporting procrastination and adrenaline addiction.

INTERPERSONAL SKILLS

Recruiting Accomplices

Living with depression creates a reality that is objectively depressing. One way this happens is that our friends, relatives, and acquaintances are quite likely to live up to our expectations of them, to be "accomplices" in our self-destructive cycle (Wachtel, 1993). When I am always a nice guy, putting others first, always on the periphery, not trying to be a standout, I'm likely to find myself in groups that like having me in that role. I'm likely to have friends who take advantage of me, in ways that can range from just not taking my needs into consideration to outright manipulation. If I'm the more bearlike depressive, I'm likely to drive people away through my intimidation and explosiveness. I'm not likely to develop relationships characterized by great intimacy, stimulation, or challenge.

Social Isolation

Depressed people tend to become social isolates through a variety of means, from shyness to lack of assertiveness to flattened emotional response to others.

Many people with depression are desperately aware of their loneliness, but for others isolation can come to feel normal, familiar, and safe, and we may not recognize our need for interaction with others. Instead of Kohut's "sea of selfobjects," we swim in sterile water, devoid of life, and eventually we starve for nutrients. But this can be such a gradual starvation that it never comes to our attention.

Many depressed people establish connections second hand. Isolated people have found the Internet as a new vehicle for connecting with others. But early research on the effects of Internet usage is not encouraging. Contrary to expectations, Kraut and colleagues (1998) found that people who spend even a few hours a week in Internet use—including interactive communications such as chat rooms and e-mail—become more depressed and more lonely. Participants who were lonely and depressed to begin with were not any more drawn to the Internet than others, but they tended to spend less time with families and narrow their social circles with increased Internet use. Communication on the Internet, however, seemed to lack the innate rewards of communication with living people.

Dependency

People who fit the *DSM-IV* criteria for dependent personality disorder are highly vulnerable to depression (Millon & Kotik-Harper, 1995). But dependency doesn't have to go that far to create a vulnerability. Anyone who relies on a limited number of relationships with others for a good feeling about the self will be subject to depression when those relationships are lost or threatened. People who are excessively dependent are likely to subordinate their needs to those of others, believing their own needs are signs of weakness. This leads them into forming stable attachments with people who are gratified by a one-up, one-down relationship. Others may get sadistic gratification from threatening abandonment of the dependent person, leading to continual crises and depressive episodes. I view dependency as a skill because it takes a great deal of fortitude and practice to continually put others first, a certain amount of interpersonal adroitness to constantly please difficult people. When dependency, shyness, or unassertiveness are framed as deficits, the depressed person is likely to feel unable to learn the required lessons; when these qualities are reframed as strengths, the patient is more likely to feel he has something to build on.

Counterdependency

Many individuals get through adulthood avoiding close relationships of any kind. They may appear as if they are independent and self-sufficient, but in fact either think of themselves as undesirable or think of the world as cruel and dangerous, or both. Their difficulty seeking support from others makes them vulnerable to depression (Hartlage et al., 1998). Extreme cases like this are unlikely to be diagnosed with depression because they are unlikely to ever tell anyone how they feel. But mental health professionals are very familiar with less extreme cases that come to our attention through marital or family counseling. There is an intense fear of close relationships, of being weak, vulnerable, or dependent, which is masked by coldness, intimidation, or distancing. These defensive maneuvers are likewise skills of depression; the individual avoids what he fears, but what he fears is what he needs.

Perseveration

There is a whole theory of depression predicated on the observation that depressive episodes are set in motion by the individual's inability to accept the finality of a loss. Continued efforts to regain the lost object, long after another person would have given up and moved on, result in continued trauma. Rather than accept the reality principle, the depressed person feels guilty or blameworthy, personally responsible for the death, rejection, or disappointment. The vicious circle of depression ensues. But persisting in the face of long odds requires attributes that really are skills of depression—determination, patience, stamina. These are skills which can be put to better use in other ways to help overcome depression.

Passive Aggression

Passive aggression involves getting others to express our own anger. When I make a mess in the kitchen and leave it for my wife to clean up, sometimes it's just because I'm preoccupied, but sometimes it's because I'm mad at her. But if I get her to yell at me about the mess in the kitchen, I get to feel self-righteous and aggrieved (and I also get her to clean up after me). Some people are so skilled at passive aggression that they raise it to the level of a high art form; they get enmeshed in stable conflictual relationships that are so tangled there is no undoing them, and their partner is usually the one who is left feeling crazy or out of control. Their habits perpetuate depression by inviting rejection and preventing the patient from expressing his needs in an assertive and direct manner. Passive aggressive patients can be very difficult to work with (see chapter 5), and are usually too smart or well-defended to fall for simply reframing their defense. Nevertheless, some of the abilities that support passive-aggressive behavior—to follow instructions to the letter; to have the kind of empathy to know so accurately what will make the other person mad; the extraordinary patience and attention to detail that makes passive aggression work—can be adapted and used for more constructive purposes.

Porous Boundaries

Most people with depression have boundaries that are too permeable, so that it is hard to tell where they end and others begin. We assume that others know how we feel, and that we know accurately how they feel. We take responsibility for things that are not of our making, and we blame circumstances for things we are indeed partially responsible for. We are easily contaminated by the moods and behavior of others. If our partner is grouchy, we feel terrible, anxious, and guilty; if people around us are panicking, we will too. These attributes imply some abilities that in other situations, under greater control, can be real strengths: The ability to feel what others are feeling is an essential ingredient for intimacy, if we can avoid being taken over by the feeling. The conflict over responsibility implies a certain level of awareness of fair play, of right and wrong, that can serve as a useful foundation. Training in empiricism, communications, and assertiveness skills can give the patient a better foundation on which to construct less permeable boundaries.

TREATMENT OF THE SELF

Depression is fundamentally a disorder of the self. There is a lack of fit between who we think we are and who we think we should be. While this is true of almost everyone, not everyone is depressed; it is only when the gap becomes too wide that we feel depressed, hopeless, defeated. Sometimes the disparity between our desired self and our real self is a painful issue that's been with us since childhood; we grow into a narcissistically vulnerable personality, feeling empty when not connected to an external source of good feeling, and we manifest the symptoms of an empty, anxious depression when things are bad. Sometimes the disparity is the result of a more recent change: We've become sick, and we're no longer as strong as we used to be; our spouse has died, and we never realized how much we relied on her for our self-esteem.

"Self" is a term loaded with meaning and ambiguity. In a later chapter I will discuss depression from the viewpoint of self psychology, a term used to describe the new perspective brought to psychoanalysis by Heinz Kohut and his followers. Here I want to focus on the everyday meanings of the term: *He's too hard on himself. Take good care of yourself. Self-defeating behavior.*

Impossible Goals, Low Expectations

People with depression are rarely satisfied with their own performance or achievement. This is partly due to our tendency to overestimate the happiness or power of others. When people are told that their button-pressing will turn on a light, but the light actually goes on at random intervals, depressed people will realize that the button and the light are not connected, but nondepressed people develop the "illusion of control" (Alloy & Abramson, 1979). But when asked to judge *another* person's ability to influence random events, depressed people overestimate the other's control, while nondepressed people are more accurate observers. The same phenomenon has been found in estimating the social acceptance of self and others. Nondepressed people think that others like them, even if they don't; depressed people think that others don't like them, even if they do. The implication is that "depressive realism" and "nondepressive illusions" may be specific to the self (Martin, Abramson, & Alloy, 1984).

Overestimating the abilities of others, we set impossible goals for ourselves. Beck (1976) has described some of these: *In order for me to be happy, I must be liked by everyone. If someone disagrees with me, it means they hate me.* Some have to do with our consumer culture: *How can I be happy when I don't have that (car, house in the suburbs, trip to the Bahamas, etc.)?* Some fuel competition in the workplace: *I'm a failure if I haven't made a million by the time I'm 30, if I lose that case, if I don't get that promotion.* Some goals have to do with others in our lives: *If Johnny doesn't make the soccer team, he won't get into the right prep school, and that means he won't go to Yale. My husband has put on so much weight that it's an embarrassment to be seen with him.* All these aspirations have two things in common: (1) They are largely outside the individual's control; all we can do is do our best, and recognize that the ultimate outcome is highly subject to luck and the influence of others. (2) They are all examples of catastrophizing, assuming that if the desired outcome doesn't come to pass, it will be the end of the world. In fact, it is possible to be quite happy if some people don't like us, if our son doesn't make the soccer team, and if our husband doesn't lose weight.

While we set these impossible goals, we "know" we'll never be able to attain them. There is a preconscious knowledge lurking in the back of our awareness that we're setting ourselves up for disaster. We have our overly pessimistic view of ourselves and all our previous experience with disappointment (screened by selective attention), to tell us we'll never make it. But we try frantically to quiet that voice, redoubling our efforts to achieve. *This time will be different, this time I'll do it, and then I'll be happy.*

People with depression tend to be diligent and hardworking. We don't cheat or take unfair advantage. We want to get ahead by following the rules. We care what others think about us. These characteristics imply some of the true skills of depression—determination, a sense of justice and fairness, a concern for others—that can be put to real use in overcoming the disease.

Inability to Nurture, Sustain, and Soothe

Most people with depression don't take good care of their bodies, don't know how to play or relax, don't know how to calm themselves down when upset. Although these are deficits, not skills, they suggest other attributes that are indeed skills of depression—hard work, intense focus, self-sacrifice. And ironically, many people with depression are quite skilled at taking care of others. Although a mother's overt depression can be damaging to her children and upsetting to her husband, in the prodromal phase of self-sacrifice many mothers become adept at nurturing their families. They will insist that everyone eat well, nurse the sick, cheer up the sad, and manage life so that conflict is minimized. These abilities can be used to help the self, once the patient understands that self-care is necessary and justified. The therapist can serve as a nurturing selfobject, reminding the patient to take care. Often this function is an unintentional by-product of the treatment. A manic-depressive patient recounted how her psychiatrist went through a list with her every month, in a stern voice: *Have you been sleeping? Have you been driving fast? Have you been spending too much? Have you been drinking too much?* He intimidated her into good self-care.

Passive Aggression Against the Self

Much of depression is a kind of passive aggression against the self. When I make a mess in the kitchen and deliberately leave it for myself to clean up later, feeling too oppressed and overwhelmed in the present, I'm going to be angry at myself later. The future me is going to be mad at the past me who left this mess behind. Plus, the future me is going to feel hopeless and helpless, reconfirmed in the belief that I'll never change and never catch up with life.

A more important application of the same process has to do with the depressive's treatment of his body. By neglecting reasonable self-care now, we are only leaving a mess for ourselves to clean up later. Smoking, neglect of diet and exercise, working too hard, not taking time to relax and play, all can be subtle forms of reinforcing the depressed position of being out of control and helpless to change. What I find a remarkable skill of depression is that most patients know very well what they should be doing to take care of themselves; they don't do it, but the awareness and the knowledge are there. It's not ignorance.

Active Aggression Against the Self;
Masochism and Suicide

Humans and animals will seek things that hurt them when they have learned that things that hurt them lead to more powerful positive reinforcers; so a dog will react with pleasure to a mild shock that he knows precedes food. Or, when a self-injurious behavior has served to prevent a greater injury in the past, or when a self-injurious behavior has served to reduce the delay of another predictable positive stimulus, people will persist in the self-injurious behavior even when it doesn't work any more if they believe they have no other alternatives. Rather than being motivated by a death instinct, people hurt themselves because they aren't aware of alternatives, because it leads to greater rewards, or because it forestalls punishment. The complication of being human is that rewards and punishments can come from inside ourselves.

The depressed patient's drug-taking, self-mutilation, and other self-destructive behavior up to and including suicide implies an awareness of rage and shame that other people thankfully lack. Hatred of the self comes about from being treated hatefully by others. Getting in touch with the rage at people who have mistreated you in the past can be an important transitional stage between masochism and a mature acceptance of reality. Although our overall therapeutic strategy may be to disempower the rage through improved reality testing, a sustaining transference relationship, etc., at the same time the patient's sense of righteous indignation can be a part of his identity we can encourage and build on. Revenge may be reprehensible, but a determination to right wrongs is admirable.

Each of these skills of depression is an example of a solution having become a problem. In an effort to adapt to difficult circumstances, to prevent future pain, we develop these patterns of behavior that may have made sense at that time, in that context, but in the larger course of our lives have direct negative consequences and perpetuate the vicious circle of depression. In the next section I want to introduce the principles of active treatment, which has the goal of developing the patient's awareness of how he uses the skills of depression, and helping him learn more effective alternative strategies. In doing so, however, we want to build on the skills he has already. The skills of depression have given the patient a lot of strength; a great deal of our job is simply to redirect that strength.

INTERVENTION PRINCIPLES

The overall approach to practice that I advocate is called "active treatment" because I want to remind the therapist that it's necessary to abandon the passive stance we are generally taught if we want to help depressed patients. The patient also must be "active" in order to recover, but more on that later.

We all have been trained with some vestige of the rule of abstinence in psychotherapy. "The analyst must not offer his patients any transference satisfactions. The fulfillment of what the patient longs for most in the analysis serves as a resistance to further analysis and therefore must be refused him" (Fenichel, 1941). This principle has its roots in the idea that all wishes for gratification from the therapist are inherently transferences from past relationships, by their very nature archaic and inappropriate to adult life. But is this really how we still conceive of the patient-therapist relationship? Many therapists seem to operate from the fear that if we grant the patient one little favor, one little exception, it will merely gratify a need that will turn out to be insatiable, and the patient will end up on the therapist's doorstep at 11:00 some night, bags packed and ready to move in. Is this really the case, or could we assume rather that our patients have the maturity to accept a disappointment when we have a legitimate reason for not gratifying a wish?

Following the tradition of the rule of abstinence, we are generally taught to be, at least at the outset of therapy, emotionally cool and somewhat reserved. Rather than guiding the patient, we want to let the patient's story unfold with minimal prompting. We note, rather than confront, defenses. We don't make pointed inquiries about information the patient doesn't bring up voluntarily. Believing so strongly in self-determination, we don't try to "hook" the patient or sell him on the idea that the individual practitioner, or even psychotherapy in general, is the answer to his problems.

These practices have developed for many good reasons, and serve many patients well. But with depression, we must be willing to adapt these modes of operation in order to engage the patient initially and keep him engaged in the ongoing work. The depressed patient lacks hope of ever feeling better, blames himself for his condition, and is acutely ashamed of asking for help. We must find ways of lending hope, we must help the patient change blaming himself to taking responsibility for himself, and we must be acutely sensitive to the patient's shame. The patient does not see the connections between his actions and his state of mind, so he doesn't tell us about how he gets into trouble, and we must inquire. We must be willing to address issues in the patient's world outside the consulting room, to give advice or share our knowledge when we can, to encourage the patient to take risks, to be available to family members when we can help the patient that way. We have to advocate for the use of medication, and nonmedical practitioners must both educate themselves about antidepressants and develop relationships with MDs that will serve their mutual patients' interests. We have to take an active role in planning the treatment, and we need to engage the patient in that process, because it will give him structure and hope. We have to educate the patient about the subtle discrimination he faces because of his disease, and help him understand how that reinforces his condition. We have to assign homework and follow up on it so that the patient begins to learn that his actions can affect his depression.

This is where activity is needed on the patient's part. Letting the patient believe that the magic of therapy takes place in the consulting room is a mistake. We—people with depression—desperately wish for a transforming experience, for a mother or a lover or a therapist with the magic to make us never hurt again. We—therapists—may easily find ourselves seduced by being given that kind of power; besides, it can be hard sometimes to tell our patients the cruel facts of life. But we—all of us—will inevitably go on being hurt, disappointed, abandoned, treated unfairly by circumstance, and we have to get used to it. The depressed patient has to practice different ways of thinking, behaving, and interacting with others for full recovery to take place. And *practice* is very important. The old, depressed ways have come to feel normal. We have to keep trying new patterns until they can become second nature; and the therapist has to be willing to be a *nudge* sometimes to keep the patient practicing.

The best news that comes from understanding the cyclical nature of depression is the implication that we can *intervene opportunistically*, where the resources are greatest and the resistance is least. If depression is a self-reinforcing cycle it's possible that change anywhere can interrupt the cycle, and changes in multiple points in the cycle may have synergistic effects; we can assign cognitive homework to help the patient stop his depressed thinking habits; our acceptance of the patient may help him overcome his sense of shame; medication may help him regain a sense of emotional control; counseling may help keep him from making some mistakes that will later reinforce the depression. Intervention in any area may open up the opportunity for the kind of corrective emotional experience that can contribute to lasting change, an experience that the patient has been using all the skills of depression to avoid.

But at the same time, it's vital to keep in mind that one of the major reasons why the patient is depressed is that he's trying not to feel his emotions. The patient's defensive pattern of trying not to feel anything will be played out in the relationship with the therapist. The relative safety and lack of contamination in the therapeutic relationship can facilitate deep emotional engagement so that, in fact, there are transforming experiences that do take place in the consulting room. But the blank screen approach doesn't work for depressed patients. We need to be emotionally available, honest, and direct, and we need to use our empathic skills in a highly active way to help the patient learn to name, and experience, real emotions.

The "middle phase" of treatment, which formerly suggested a period of several years during which defenses and resistances were systematically explored, now often means only six to eight therapy sessions. Patients no longer have the luxury of lengthy time spans during which they can integrate the lessons of therapy. The "skills of depression"—those habits that depression teaches us, which paradoxically only perpetuate the disease—can't be unlearned with brief therapy and medication. Instead, we have to teach patients a cognitive model of the disease and its particular impact on their individual functioning. The cognitive lessons are only learned, however, when the patient's emotions are fully engaged in the treatment process. The therapist must find ways of making sure that sparks are flying—either through exploration of a strong relationship between the patient and therapist, or through detailed exploration of the patient's interaction with the world—for lasting change to take place.

I've organized discussion of active treatment for depression around a set of principles, each of which is discussed in detail in the following chapters. Briefly, these principles are:

1. *Conduct a thorough biopsychosocial assessment.* Depression is maintained by many forces in the patient's world, all of which are potential avenues for intervention. Without a systematic assessment, treatment can fail.
2. *Engage the patient's emotions.* People with depression are trying hard to feel nothing; unless they can learn from experience with the therapist that the experience of emotions—even painful feelings—helps to lift depression, they will remain stuck.
3. *Pay attention to feelings of grief, entitlement, rage, and hope.* The essential dilemma of depression is that although the patient feels

unfairly deprived of what he needs most, he also doubts his own worth. The therapist must provide hope for a new way out of this paradox.

4. *Use medications appropriately.* Antidepressant medications can be a highly effective source of relief and need to be a part of any comprehensive treatment plan. The nonmedical practitioner must actively support medication treatment.

5. *Use yourself wisely.* More of the success of treatment than we want to admit depends on the therapist's personal style. We must be ourselves with the patient and yet not ourselves. We have to help the patient learn to play with us, and at the same time we have to take care of ourselves.

6. *Maintain a therapeutic focus.* People with depression are in real pain, and as their disease progresses they often do lasting damage to their lives. We can provide efficient treatment best by focusing on a central issue most meaningful to the patient. An effective way of understanding the central issue is that it will be manifested in the chief complaint, the first episode of depression, and the patient's present relationships, including the relationship with the therapist.

7. *Address the patient's social and interpersonal world.* The longer depression has lasted in the patient's life, the more he is likely to be mired in a network of stable, dysfunctional relationships. These include not only his intimates, but also his relationships with social institutions. The patient will need real help correcting these relationships.

8. *Challenge depressed thinking.* Many of the observations of cognitive-behavior therapy have proven accurate, understandable to patients, and effective in helping patients to change. Any therapist working with depressed patients needs to be familiar with these treatment methods.

9. *Teach self-care.* The patient needs to be helped to see how his own actions and inactions contribute to his situation, and provided with more effective alternative behaviors. I choose learning to treat oneself with respect and care as a theme on which to build an educational approach.

10. *Practice, practice, practice.* The patient doesn't realize that the skills of depression are acquired habits, not an integral part of the self. New, more adaptive behaviors will seem awkward and ego-alien. The therapist has to keep the patient practicing until new skills begin to seem part of the self.

11. *Prepare for termination.* Depression is likely to be a lifelong disease. We need to educate the patient about the disease and about the need for continuing self-care. We need to help him recognize when to get help again and know how to get it.

CHAPTER 4

A Biopsychosocial Assessment

THE PREVAILING VIEW of health and disease in Western science has been biological and reductionistic (see U. S. Department of Health and Human Services, "Mental Health: A Report of the Surgeon General," 1999). Explaining events in terms of biological processes has been seen as the goal of science, and such explanations are commonly accepted as complete. Thus, we think of diabetes as "caused" by the failure of the pancreas to produce insulin, a heart attack as "caused" by the blockage of a coronary artery, despite the fact that we all know that diet, exercise, and stress are also intimately involved in causing these conditions. We tend to think that the proper role of healing is to replace the missing insulin or remove the arterial blockage, without considering that it may be more important to teach the patient about health.

This model has been inadequate in addressing even diseases that are primarily physiological in nature. How much less adequate, then, to be applied to conditions that are complicated by the impact of the patient's mind, his relationships, and the culture that he lives in. General systems theory (von Bertalanffy, 1968; see also Gyarfas, 1980) pointed to the error of inflating the importance of one system—even the biological—at the expense of another; forces from other systems are likely to complicate change in any particular system, and change in any particular system is likely to have unforeseen consequences in others. Engel (1977, 1980) further challenged psychiatry and medicine in proposing a *biopsychosocial* model of mental functioning. The biopsychosocial model recognizes that, in any particular mental disorder or trait, a single factor—biological, psychological, or social—may weigh very heavily or may have little impact, but that all play a role. Posttraumatic stress disorder, for example, is caused primarily by psychological events—but not every victim of trauma develops PTSD. Genetic vulnerabilities may play a part, and social supports most certainly do.

When it comes to depression, the need for a biopsychosocial point of view seems inarguable. People develop depression not only because they (may) have a genetic predisposition, but also because they are under stress. Stress results both from problems and difficulties in the social sphere and what those problems mean to us psychologically. While an adjustment in biology may be enough for some lucky patients to be reenergized sufficiently to remedy their stressful situation without any other treatment, experience with psychopharmacology so far suggests that most patients with depression remain damaged and vulnerable even after successful medication treatment. A biological point of view suggests that the medications have been unable to fix the underlying problem in the brain. A biopsychosocial point of view suggests that these patients remain under stress. Treating symptoms without addressing the person and the social situation is likely to be ineffective treatment for depression.

ASSESSMENT AND ENGAGEMENT

Development of an understanding of the nature of the patient's situation cannot be separated from the process of engaging the patient in participating in the treatment, though for practical purposes I've had to write two separate chapters here. I find it necessary to emphasize the role of assessment because too many psychotherapy texts start with the unacknowledged assumption that the patient can be helped by psychotherapy alone. That assumption frequently leads to a negative outcome—sometimes a disastrous outcome—for the patient. Without a thorough understanding of the patient's interior, social, and physical world, we can go down too many garden paths leading nowhere. A complete and systematic evaluation not only provides the therapist with a roadmap, it also provides the patient with a sense that the practitioner is competent, thorough, and professional. And I find, ironically, that some questions that may seem rude or intrusive later in the therapy can be raised at the outset without making the patient feel defensive. When a patient after ten sessions has never talked about his sex life, or substance use, or anger, for instance, he has more or less made it clear that he doesn't want to talk about those subjects, and the therapist may feel awkward asking directly; but when those topics have been raised in the first two or three sessions, they seem a natural part of a full inquiry and are on the table for future discussion.

At the same time, the cold application of a questionnaire can interfere with the art of psychotherapy—the therapist's ability to listen to the music, not just the words, in the patient's story, to play hunches, to express humanity—and of course with the patient's ability to feel hope, to develop a therapeutic alliance, to want to return for another appointment. I do not advocate for an assessment *interview* following the guidelines presented here by rote, but an assessment *process* that can be expected to take two to four sessions before all these questions are answered. And, as the reader will quickly see, these are all leading questions which suggest direction for intervention.

The Role of Bias in Diagnosis

We all tend to stereotype, even when we are highly trained not to. An interesting study by Loring and Powell (1988) presented a group of 290 psychiatrists with case descriptions of patients who were actually being treated for schizophrenia. Most agreed with the diagnosis. But when informed that the patient was female, male psychiatrists often diagnosed a recurrent depressive disorder instead, and frequently added an Axis II diagnosis as well. Female psychiatrists were more likely to diagnose a brief reactive psychosis when informed that the patient was a white female, but were more accurate in their diagnoses when told that the patient was a black female.

At least part of the observed predominance of depression among women has to do with our difficulty recognizing it in men. Seniors with depression are likely to have it dismissed as a normal part of aging that no one can do anything about. Violent men are likely to be dismissed as having a character disorder until someone takes the time to understand what provokes the violence. Women in unhappy marriages who go to their doctors with vague complaints are likely to get treated symptomatically.

After reading the literature extensively, I've recognized some unspoken assumptions: Whereas psychiatrists tend to think that most mildly depressed patients consult general practice physicians first, other mental health professionals, including myself, assume that mildly depressed patients consult mental health professionals about problems in living. I have never read a case report from a psychologist or social worker where the patient was referred by a physician, and I have never read a case report from a psychiatrist where the patient sought advice. (One conclusion I've reached is that general practice physicians only refer to psychiatrists.) The self-selection bias at work here has probably had enormous impact on the disease model of depression. Psychiatrists largely see people who are complaining of symptoms, other mental health professionals see people who are complaining of problems. But focus on either one to the exclusion of the other is only half the story.

Our frame of reference dictates how we interpret what we see. When Rosenhan's (1973) mock patients had themselves admitted to psychiatric hospitals, their most normal behavior was interpreted by the staff as another symptom. Where a pastoral counselor is likely to see grief, a family counselor to see family conflict, a psychopharmacologist to see an unbalanced neurochemistry, I am likely to see a depression treatable by individual treatment. All of us owe our patients the duty of continually stepping out of our limited frames—to have colleagues who challenge us, to read professional material that puts our experience in a different perspective, to be sufficiently informed about the world, society, culture, race, and gender that we at least know where our biases and blind spots are likely to be. We need to acknowledge our own preferences about how we understand depression and how we prefer to work.

REVIEW OF SYSTEMS

The Presenting Problem and the Therapeutic Focus

Something has happened today to make the patient pick up the phone and make a call, and it's important to understand what it is. In a later chapter I will discuss the topic of the presenting problem as a manifestation of a recurrent theme in the patient's life; here it's important to note that this is a key element in motivation. Something has got the patient to the point where he says, in effect, *I can't handle it alone anymore; I have to have help.* It may be that he is afraid of hurting himself or someone else, either through violence or through inaction; it may be that he is experiencing overwhelming anxiety, the sense that he is falling apart; it may be a more gradual recognition that his mood is worse than circumstances suggest, and his efforts to correct it on his own have failed. Whatever it is, giving proper respect and consideration to the patient's stated concerns is essential to engaging the patient in a relationship that we expect to be characterized by mutual respect and collaboration. When we get to formulating a treatment plan, the presenting problem should be high on the list of goals.

This is not to ignore the fact that many patients will have difficulty stating the precipitant clearly. Some are consciously aware, but don't trust us or themselves well enough to talk about it openly: the man who's afraid he's going to hurt his wife, the adolescent who's been having suicidal thoughts. In such cases, it can be helpful for the therapist to articulate the unspoken thoughts: *I wonder if you've been thinking about . . .* In other cases, the patient may be defended against his own anxieties; he may tell us about troubling symptoms that seem to be disconnected from his social or emotional life. In these circumstances, the therapist should honor the defense, at least in the initial sessions, and take seriously the request for symptom relief.

Physical Systems

For the nonmedical practitioner, and even for the psychiatrist who does not focus on physical symptoms, it is essential to have an understanding of the patient's general health. The patient should have a relationship with a primary care physician that includes regular check-ups and consultations, and especially a recent check-up to determine if there are any underlying health problems contributing to the depression. Endocrine problems, systemic infections, and neurological problems may make their first appearance in the form of depression—and it's simply malpractice to provide psychotherapy for an underactive thyroid. The patient should be asked directly about his overall health, his energy level, whether there are any acute illnesses or chronic conditions, what medications he is currently taking, his use of tobacco*, etc. All of these may be indicators of problems that, unbeknownst to the patient, may be related to his condition. The list of medications should include over-the-counter medications and herbal preparations, and the therapist should also ask whether the patient uses any alternative therapies, including chiropractic and massage. Both prescription medicines (beta blockers, steroids, sedatives, opiates) and nonprescription items (cold and cough medicine, for example) can contribute to depression. Needless to say, the therapist should be sufficiently knowledgeable about health-related issues and depression to understand the possible implications of the patient's responses.

Nervous System Difficulty concentrating is a primary symptom of depression, and the patient may not be aware of that fact—may only blame it on age or losing his mind—until the therapist makes the connection. But difficulty concentrating may also be a lifelong problem suggestive of ADHD, which may be a contributing factor in depression. The therapist should be alert to signs of impulsivity, tangential thinking, or restlessness that accompany ADHD. Depression may also be a manifestation of multiple sclerosis, brain tumor, or stroke, and the therapist should be alert to signs such as numbness or tingling in the limbs, vision problems, slurred speech, or sudden alterations in mental status, and be ready to make a referral to a neurologist if necessary.

Endocrine System The thyroid, hypothalamus, pituitary, adrenals, and reproductive system can be involved with depression in a complex cause-and-effect system. Though again we tend to think of the relationship as one-way, the body affecting the mind, the picture is more complicated than that. For instance, some interesting research has found that successful psychotherapy for depression directly affects thyroid action (Joffe, Segal, & Singer, 1996).

The pituitary is intimately intertwined with the hypothalamus and those parts of the brain that have to do with sleep, libido, appetite, and pleasure. Since the pituitary is the "master gland," which coordinates the functions of the rest of the endocrine system, physicians usually become aware of pituitary disorders only as the result of dysfunction elsewhere. Underactive thyroid, or hypothyroidism, a common contributing factor for depression, may be a result of pituitary disease or other problems. Hypothyroidism, unless caused by a tumor or injury, often develops very slowly. Metabolism slows, energy level drops, and the patient feels lethargic and passive. Overproduction of corticosteroids by the adrenals (Cushing's syndrome) greatly increases risk for depression, and there is literature to support conflicting hypotheses: that both Cushing's syndrome and

---

* Smoking is a risk factor for depression, and the patient should be helped to quit; but smokers are so defensive these days that it's wise to abstain from too much disapproval in the initial session.

depression are responses to long-term stress, or that Cushing's syndrome is a primary pathology with depression as a result (Stevens et al., 1995). Addison's disease, the underproduction of corticosteroids, results in weakness, loss of appetite, muscle aches, nausea, and diarrhea. Often the symptoms are only manifested at times of stress, so the patient may seek only psychological help. Ironically, treatment with lithium for manic depression can contribute to malfunction in the thyroid, pituitary, and adrenals. The therapist should be alert to the gross signs of hypothyroidism (puffy face, droopy eyelids, thickening of the skin), and of Cushing's syndrome (moon face, buffalo hump).

Though there is much controversy about the role of the reproductive system in women's depression (see chapter 6), it seems safe to say that at least some depression in women is linked to the fluctuations in hormone levels associated with the menstrual cycle, menopause, and pregnancy and birth, which make the patient extremely sensitive to perceived criticism and rejection. Hormone therapy or use of oral contraceptives can sometimes be an effective treatment that also relieves the depressive symptoms. Because of the passivity that accompanies depression, some women are likely to accept their physical discomfort and mood swings as simply their lot in life; the therapist needs to help them find a gynecologist who understands the mind-body connection and can help them find symptom relief.

Depression inhibits sexual desire and makes the patient feel ugly and unattractive. Most of the newer antidepressants, which are reputed to have few side effects, do have a significant negative impact on both sexual desire and performance. Between these two factors, it is the rare depressed patient who is able to maintain a satisfactory sex life. Of course this situation just perpetuates the depression. The patient feels guilty for letting his partner down, he feels continued isolation and unlovability, and he feels ashamed on account of the sexual problem. It's essential that the therapist make clear in the early sessions that these are normal complications of depression and that it's okay to talk about them. (Many visitors to my Web site complain that their therapist's silence on sexuality has been unhelpful and express outrage that it's only through their own reading that they've learned that sexual dysfunction is part of depression.) Some patients may prefer not to talk about the subject, and we may respect their wishes; but if we don't open it up, many patients will assume it's not a fit topic for conversation and have their shame only further reinforced.

Nutrition, Appetite, and the Gastrointestinal System An acute depression most often suppresses appetite; the patient doesn't feel hungry, food has lost its taste, he can't keep things down, he doesn't have the energy to prepare a meal and eat. Long-term depression often results in "depressed eating"—filling up an emptiness with comfort foods high in carbohydrates (ice cream, pasta, chips), which actually give a temporary high by boosting blood sugar but also lead to an inevitable crash. Eating like this reinforces depression by making the patient feel ugly, helpless, and out of control. It can also lead to bulimia. At the same time, anorectic and bulimic behavior, which starts apparently from concerns about one's appearance, can be a manifestation of or a contributing factor to depression.

Many patients with depression will also suffer from constipation, diarrhea, nausea, or painful abdominal conditions but never mention these to the therapist out of embarrassment. But all of these conditions can: (a) be indicators of a serious underlying health problem or contribute to development of a long-term health problem; (b) interfere with recovery from depression by inducing fatigue, difficulty concentrating, etc.; (c) continue to contribute to the shame of depression as they are kept secret. The responsible therapist should actively inquire about eating patterns, nutrition, and digestive symptoms in the early sessions, making it clear that these subjects can be important to recovery, and that they should be on the table for discussion. When problems are apparent, the therapist should continue to inquire during the course of treatment until the patient is comfortable talking about the subject voluntarily.

Senses Sensory problems can be both symptomatic of depression and contribute to its development. The anhedonia of depression is frequently experienced by patients in that favorite foods have lost their zest, while they seem to have a heightened sensitivity to bad odors, including their own body odors. More than one patient has mentioned that the world actually seems colorless during depression—it's not just a metaphor, it's an actual experience. The return of colors, taste, and pleasant smells can be an early sign of beginning recovery, sometimes the first indicator that the patient takes seriously because it seems so "biological."

Loss of hearing associated with aging can contribute greatly to depression; the patient finds himself more irritable, yelling at people to speak up, then ashamed of himself rather than appreciating that he has an actual hearing loss. The same is true of loss of visual acuity, particularly night vision, which interferes with the ability to drive and thus threatens independence. These can be realistic problems, which should be addressed in the treatment plan so that the patient can benefit as much as possible from assistive devices and be helped to adjust to the realistic changes associated with age.

Pain The relationship between chronic pain and depression is complex enough to warrant an extended discussion (see chapter 12). In the assessment process, it can be very important for the therapist to actively inquire about the patient's pain status and use of pain medications. Although most patients who have a serious chronic pain condition will fully realize that the pain and disability contribute to their depression, disassociation and denial can be so strong that a few do not make the connection at all. And even patients who are aware of the connection may still minimize the effects of pain and use their condition as another stick to beat themselves up with: *I should be able to get over this. I shouldn't let it get me down.* Depression can be an insurmountable roadblock interfering with one's ability to engage in the kind of self-care necessary to recover from chronic pain conditions. Treatment may need to focus on the mood journal (see the next chapter) in order to uncover the pain-depression cycle that sustains both conditions for many patients. Overuse of analgesic medications may be a real problem for depressed patients, not only because of their addictive properties but also because they mimic some symptoms of depression—lethargy, passivity—while enabling the patient to feel insulated and detached.

Other patients, who may have been referred by a physician because they have a pain condition that is not optimally responsive to conventional treatment, are likely to feel defensive and resentful about a mental health referral, believing their problems are being dismissed as "all in my head." Some may be worried that their dependence on opiate medications is being threatened. These patients need to be reassured that their problems are indeed real. It can be most helpful to them to present depression as a natural result of their condition, a result that carries its own implications for recovery. The therapist takes an educational role at first in describing depression's impact, the role of antidepressant medication, and the actions needed by the patient, therapist, and physician to help promote recovery.

Exercise Patterns of exercise and fitness are a frequent issue accompanying depression. Typically, the patient does not get as much exercise as he needs; sometimes he overexerts in a compulsive, joyless manner. The general guideline of a brisk aerobic workout for 20–30 minutes three times a week, plus additional stretching, walking, and sports, should be taken as a standard that most people should follow.

Substance Use Problematic alcohol use and illicit drug use (including prescription drugs) are very likely for people with depression. Most patients, feeling understandable shame about behavior they suspect is contributing to the problem, will not volunteer information on this subject, and the therapist has to ask. *What's your pattern of alcohol use? What drugs do you take regularly? What's been the pattern in the past week, month? Has it ever gotten you in trouble? Have you attempted to quit?* When people suffer with depression, the temptation to find a quick fix in an intoxicated state is very understandable, but some therapists who have never experienced that desire have trouble communicating tactfully around these issues. These therapists can come to a better understanding as they listen to patients' stories of the seductive effects of drugs, but they will never hear these stories unless they can communicate that they are willing to listen. That starts with asking the questions.

When it's apparent that there is a problem with alcohol or drug abuse, the next step depends on the severity of the problem. When patients are getting intoxicated every day, or more often than not during the week, I agree with those who believe that not much therapy can take place until the patient stops getting high. There are just too many mood-altering chemicals in the patient's system for psychotherapy or medication therapy to have any sustained effect. That means we don't talk about anything other than sobriety in treatment until the patient attains it. That may require joining AA or going into detox or rehab before I can work with the patient. On the other hand, when the patient's pattern is always to use to the point of intoxication but to restrict his use to once or perhaps twice a week, I am usually willing to give therapy a try—but I am also very vigilant about the effects of intoxicants and keep recommending sobriety. This is admittedly a gray area, one where most therapists have to find their own way; but clearly we should never dismiss or ignore any indicators of substance abuse.

A special problem occurs with patients who are abusing prescription drugs, often with their physician's approval; this includes, for example, chronic pain patients on methadone, Vicodin, and other morphine-like drugs, chronically anxious patients on high doses of Xanax or Klonopin, and patients abusing sleeping pills or amphetamines. The nonmedical therapist is at a disadvantage when the patient's drug abuse is supported by his physician. It's sometimes necessary to have other physicians to consult with, particularly those who have an interest or awareness of drug abuse. We need to feel confident enough to tell the patient we suspect there is a problem and we want to confer with the prescribing MD. If that doesn't yield results, I sometimes suggest to the patient that he get another doctor.

The Interpersonal World

Family of Origin Most patients expect to talk about their childhood. Whatever the current problem is, it usually engenders feelings that seem very familiar from childhood experience, much like scurvy makes old wounds weep.

It's most useful in the assessment phase to begin a developmental history with general questions—*tell me about your family; tell me what it was like for you growing up*—and see both what the patient thinks is important and what he omits. He may begin with what he thinks is dynamically related to the presenting problem, which can be an indication of initiative and motivation on his part and also an important clue toward formulating a meaningful central issue. Or he may simply relate unconnected facts, which may be an indicator of passivity or distrust. In any case, when the patient gets to describing his parents (or parent surrogates and, to a greater or lesser extent, siblings) he is describing something about the kinds of interpersonal relationships that he still maintains to the present day. If he was abused, there is a part of him that still expects abuse; if neglected, there is a part that still believes himself unworthy of attention. If he was the star of the family, now fallen on hard times, he's likely to feel shame. If he was the little adult, he's likely to still try to solve all his problems intellectually.

Whatever the objective truth of an individual patient's background or the validity of this theory, I find that when patients are talking to me about what they missed from their parents they are telling me a powerful story about their depression and about how they expect to recover from it. I know I will be expected to supply some of what was missed, and I know I will try but fall short, and we will need to deal with the patient's disappointment in me.

A psychodynamic theory of depression espoused by Miller (1981) holds that the foundation for depression is laid down early in the child's development in a faulty connection between parent and child. When a parent is continually stressed, preoccupied, or depressed, he can't adequately mirror the child's emotional state. Instead, he only sees aspects of himself or his problems when he looks at the child. The child is used by the parent as a container for the parent's problems, and the child adapts to this situation. It is in his own best interests to do what the parent wants; to not be a burden, to reassure, to succeed. The child "learns that feelings like anger, anxiety, jealousy, and despair, and that impulses like playing in the dirt, fighting, or crying are not what the parent wants. In fact, the parent can't accept these things. However the parent may respond on a behavioral level, the child experiences a momentary loss of the connection with the parent that is vital to a positive self-feeling. Gradually, the child begins to feel that such emotions or impulses are alien to the self, so they are not felt anymore. *The ability to feel is lost*" (O'Connor, 1997, pp. 66–67). Depression is the resultant atrophy of parts of the self. Thus, the quality of the parental relationship is vital in determining the adult's personality, defenses, and feelings about the self.

I also find it helpful to ask people to describe themselves as children. *Were you just an average kid? Did you worry a lot? Were you good at sports? The teacher's pet? Were you popular or shy? Did you fight your parents, or did you try to be good?* The answers to these questions inevitably reflect the patient's present self as well. *I didn't have many friends. I tried to do the right thing, but it seemed like I was always in trouble anyway.* Statements like these are often quite direct clues to what the treatment focus should be, a deeply felt wish to be loved, to feel security, pride, or passion that always seems doomed to disappointment. The same issue can be expected to come up later in the therapeutic relationship.

There is no particular family background that is typical of depression. Depressed people come from depressed families, alcoholic families, abusive families, loving and supportive families, families with rigid and demanding standards, and families with no standards at all. If anything is typical, it is that at some point the child learned that certain parts of himself, certain feelings or wishes, were not acceptable to those he depended on for life. The pervasiveness of the depression is roughly correlated to how much of the child's self was made to feel unacceptable, so that children whose parents made it clear that they were simply in the way are likely to be more vulnerable than those whose parents tried only to deny or minimize a particular aspect of the child, like his independence or sexuality. But pathology takes many forms, and children can derive strength from many sources, so we can find improbably resilient adults in our offices who come from backgrounds of appalling deprivation, while others suffer miserably though their childhood seems well within the range of normal.

The therapist must have in his mind a clear set of developmental milestones, and must notice which have not been mentioned in the course of an unfocused discussion. *What was adolescence like for you? When did you first live on your own? Tell me about your first love.* Depressed patients often omit talking about areas of strength or accomplishment, but these can be potentially invaluable resources in recovery.

Of course, with depression we are interested in hearing about what the experience of loss was like for the patient as a child. Sometimes we hear of a loss that was clearly traumatic: the death of a child's mother, the abandonment of the family by the father. Even a generation later, the work of the therapy can be to facilitate a mourning process so that the patient can move on. Sometimes a loss destabilized a parent, resulting in a secondary loss to the child: the death of a grandparent or of a child's sibling, resulting in a parent's depression, alcoholism, or withdrawal. Often in such a recounting we hear the frozen affect of the depressed.

I find that almost inevitably when patients describe a childhood in which one parent appeared depressed or inadequate while the other resented it, the patient's childish perception, while it has the aura of revealed truth within the family, is off the mark. Usually the "stronger" parent was highly defended against his/her own depression and used the "weaker" spouse as a receptacle for blame and self-loathing. Usually the patient wants to identify with the "stronger" parent but feels depressed anyway. Sometimes the patient is aware of deep affection for the "weaker" parent but feels confused and guilty about the bond. When we understand that the strengths the patient is trying to emulate are really rather fragile defenses against depression, we can help the patient understand why he continues to experience himself as a weakling, a failure, despite his own often significant accomplishments. Sometimes we can find with the patient a different perspective on the "weaker" parent—perhaps only as someone who was unfairly blamed, but perhaps as someone with real strengths that were mislabeled by the spouse and the child. For instance, a parent who became depressed when the family moved away from its hometown to seek opportunity may be seen as capable of deep attachment, a quality the supposedly stronger parent lacks, rather than as needy and dependent.

Intimate Partners It is the remarkable depressed patient who does not also suffer from disturbed relationships with the people closest to him. If, as is sometimes the case, the depression has burst seemingly "out of the blue" into a stable marriage or family, it may not be long before relationships begin to suffer as a result of the depression. More often, depression and a history of unhappy, unsatisfying relationships go hand in hand. I hear about four major themes from depressed patients:

- Isolation and estrangement. The patient has withdrawn from most social contact or, if he continues to engage, does so with disastrous results, reinforcing his sense of being different and inadequate.

- Conflict. There is a pattern of overt or covert conflict between the patient and his loved ones, which the patient never seems to resolve. It reinforces his sense of being unloved, misunderstood, and out of control.
- Victimization. The pattern is of being taken advantage of by others. Often patients are unaware of this and don't report it. The therapist sometimes does not catch on in the initial interviews.
- Patterns of idealization/disappointment. The patient has a history of relationships that begin with unrealistic expectations and end in disappointment and mutual recrimination.

Many patients do not come in asking for help with depression; they ask for help dealing with the effects of a disturbed relationship. Sometimes that's all they need and they can go on without repeating the same self-destructive interpersonal patterns. In other cases, though, it can be helpful at the outset to begin to tie together the interpersonal conflict that is the patient's chief complaint with other symptoms of depression, which he may be aware of but believes to be unconnected or simply a result of "stress."

Children The children of the depressed adult are at grave risk. As adults, they are much more likely than average to have psychiatric disorders of their own (Beardslee, Versage, & Gladstone, 1998); as children, they frequently manifest behavior problems that can permanently interfere with their own social and cognitive development (Hammen, 1991; Hammen, Rudolph, Weisz, Rao, & Burge, 1999). We owe it to our own and our patient's consciences to assess the home situation thoroughly and help the patient minimize the "collateral damage" the children are experiencing. In the initial interviews, this is another subject where the therapist has the latitude to ask questions that might seem intrusive later in the treatment: *Do your kids listen to you? How do you get them to behave? What happens when you lose your temper with them? Do you think they're worried about you?* The therapist can convey these questions with the message that these are normative and understandable issues that arise as part of the depression, and the patient may be greatly relieved of some of the guilt and shame he feels by being able to talk openly about behavior he knows is not the best parenting.

Work/School Work for the adult, school for the child, is the primary opportunity we have for creativity and mastery. Being successful at work builds self-esteem. Depression interferes with our ability to work: We can't concentrate or make decisions, we can't keep regular hours, we have more difficulty getting along with people, our energy level is diminished. By the same token, much in the work environment can reinforce depression. Depressed people are targets for discrimination, bringing out the bully in their bosses and coworkers. Depressed people exaggerate the inadequacy of their performance and beat themselves up about it. Going to work every day can seem like a horrible trial; each day becomes a monumental struggle just to get through without breaking down. And of course with depression there is no psychic reward for having survived the day, just the dread that the next day will be worse.

The new world of work has made things worse for the depressed. If your job was to run a machine, no one cared if you were cranky. If you're in a service job, you have to pretend to be cheerful. I've heard many patients complain about going home at night with cramped facial muscles from forced smiles. Putting on a false front like this all day constantly reinforces the feeling that one is a hypocrite.

And, with everyone supposedly getting rich from the booming economy, those who are not making it will inevitably feel it's their own fault. But the boom is really a mirage. In the past 25 years, the average American work week has increased from slightly over 40 hours per week to slightly over 50; and the amount of time we have left over for leisure has declined from over 26 hours per week to under 20 (Goozner, 1998). Alan Greenspan and the Bureau of Labor Statistics don't like to talk about it very much, but the vaunted growth in American productivity is illusory. People are working longer hours and usually not getting paid for it. People have to work much harder nowadays—a 25 percent increase in the work week, and a corresponding 25 percent decrease in leisure time—to maintain the standard of living we expected 25 years ago.

And this statistic applies only to individuals; people who are married know things are worse. The two-career family is now the norm and the stay-at-home wife is the exception. Our social institutions—like schools—may still be stuck in the 1950s (schools still dismiss at 2:30 every day and take summers off, like Mom is going to be there to supervise the kids) but Mom isn't. However, she gets to feel guilty about it. And of course, if she is a stay-at-home mother, she gets to feel guilty about that as well.

Social Role Performance Depression is on the increase in established economies, and it makes sense to hypothesize that the increase has to do with social change. It seems like the brass ring is always a little out of reach. Last year's luxury becomes this year's necessity. Last year you couldn't afford a cell phone, this year you can't get by without it. If you ask Americans what it takes to have a comfortable income, it's always just a little bit more than they have, usually about $2,000 more (Schor, 1998). And when we work harder and start making that much more, it's still not enough because our wants have increased. No wonder we always feel stressed out and inadequate; we never make enough money to afford what we tell ourselves we need.

Our expectations are defined less and less by family and friends, more and more by mass culture, television, and advertising. If we set out deliberately to demoralize people, to make them feel incompetent and inadequate, we couldn't do a better job than we are doing. Why doesn't my life have a laugh track? Why can't all my problems get resolved in half an hour, less time for commercials? Why can't I be as sexy, witty, and rich as the people I see every day? Why do bad things happen to me? There must be something wrong with me, because on television, only the bad get punished. We get the idea that life should be easy. Our grandparents knew that life wasn't supposed to be easy. My grandfathers worked in factories and considered themselves lucky to have jobs that provided for their families. My grandmothers worked in the home from dawn to dusk. They knew how to enjoy themselves, but they didn't expect to be enjoying themselves all the time; they didn't feel like there was something wrong with them if they weren't grabbing for the gusto every second.

This is not to say that depression is illusory, a whiny yuppie disease. On the contrary, at least part of depression comes from falling short of our expectations of ourselves. The less those expectations are grounded in reality, the more likely we are to be disappointed in ourselves and depressed. By helping our patients see the objective truth of their situation, we can help them break free from the cycle of self-blame and inadequacy they keep themselves in.

Gender Gender-based expectations are another potential source of stress in the patient's life. We need to be able to talk with the patient about what his gender means, the extent of his satisfaction/dissatisfaction with his gender role and his fit into that role. Most depressed men will acknowledge that they feel they fall short of a macho ideal; most women will acknowledge that they are unhappy with their looks. Homosexual patients who are secure in their sexual identity have their own pressures to deal with. Almost everyone feels constrained by conventional expectations but guilty about not living up to them.

This is the time to bring up more sensitive questions. We should take a reproductive history with every female patient; miscarriages and abortions especially can play a role in current depression that the patient isn't aware of. Infertility in women and impotence in men may be part of the presenting problem but not discussed unless we bring them up. Male parents who are estranged from children from a previous marriage are likely never to volunteer this information or connect it with their present state. Both men and women need to be asked about experiences of abuse and victimization. Women, at least, are generally savvy enough nowadays to recognize childhood sexual abuse and consider that it might be related to present depression. Men often don't even recognize childhood sexual abuse when it's happened to them—but some of these men still go around struggling with issues of passivity, humiliation, and shame.

Class, Race, and Economic Status There is serious research going on into what makes people happy in life, and one observation is confirmed again and again: Once we're past a certain level of want, where basic necessities are taken care of and we have a little leisure time, increased income has almost no relationship to increased happiness. "Moreover, our incomes don't noticeably influence our satisfactions with marriage, family, friendships, or ourselves—all of which do predict our sense of well-being. If not wracked by hunger or hurt, people at all income levels can enjoy one another and experience comparable joy" (Myers, 1992, p. 39).

Yet it's important to recognize that many of our patients are or have been "wracked by hunger or hurt." It's also very true that, although money doesn't buy happiness, the lack of money contributes significantly to misery. Low socioeconomic status is a predictor for depression (Kaelber et al., 1995). So is victimization and discrimination. Minority group status makes one more vulnerable to both low SES and discrimination. Most studies show no differences in rates of depression for different ethnic groups when the effects of SES are controlled for (Regier et al., 1990), but in real life the effects of SES are not controlled for. Being poor makes recovery from depression more difficult: There will be less marginal income to pay for treatment, time will be in shorter supply, work will be less likely to give time off for treatment. Most important, one's sense of adequacy is constantly undercut by poverty.

Psychological Systems

Psychiatric History In working with patients who are depressed, one of the most important questions is, when did the patient first realize he was depressed? People will often say they have felt "different" since childhood or adolescence, but only in retrospect do they realize those feelings had to do with depression. I find that those early experiences are important data, because they give clues about the patient's central issue (an early loss, feeling misunderstood or deprived, feeling rejected and helpless) and indicate areas where there may be developmental lags. A patient who has felt isolated and different since elementary school has probably not integrated knowledge about how to get along with people that is much more developmentally advanced than childhood. When a serious depression has developed in childhood, not only does the child feel that the depressed state is "normal" but he also suffers a severe developmental arrest because the depression makes it impossible for him to learn, to interact with peers, to feel good about himself. "Depression is no less a developmental trauma than abuse, neglect, separation, or death. In the evolution of self-concept, it may be worse" (Schuchter et al., 1996, p. 74).

The second most important question is, what has this experience of depression meant to the patient? Does it mean a permanently damaged self? Does the patient view himself as fragile, incapable, or unlovable? Perhaps there are circumstances associated with the patient's individual experience that have made the meaning of it worse than it really is—a coerced hospitalization, a disapproving therapist. Is the patient prepared for the idea that there is something he can do about the depression, or is it all supposed to be up to the therapist?

I want to know about all previous forms of treatment the patient has tried, and what was helpful and what was not in those experiences. If the patient has had many previous therapists and been dissatisfied with them all, chances are he's going to be dissatisfied with me too, but I can reduce the odds by trying hard not to repeat their mistakes. The meanings of experiences such as hospitalizations and electroconvulsive treatments are also highly individual. Some patients feel like hospitalization was one of the best things that ever happened to them, because they were treated well, reassured that the problem was not their fault, and perhaps their family started to take them seriously. For others, hospitalization has meant a bitter defeat, a mark of Cain. Patients who are in this state can greatly benefit from participation in a support group to help break the sense of stigma.

I also want to know about the psychiatric and substance abuse history of the patient's family. If there is a family history of manic depression or schizophrenia, those conditions need to be ruled out for the patient. There is a genetic loading for simple depression as well, and the patient may feel a little less blameworthy if a careful history helps him see how depression has affected others in his family. I also want to be alert for undiagnosed mental illness, substance abuse, and learning disabilities in the family. This information rarely comes out in the initial phase but there may be indications that there is something to explore later. Besides the hereditary component of mental illness, I am interested in the impact of the relative's illness on the patient and significant others in his life. We are all aware of the impact an alcoholic father or a depressed mother can have on a child; but often the child, now our patient, has not acknowledged the parent's pathology.

One of the goals of active treatment is the patient's acceptance of the disease concept of depression and, with that acceptance, learning to take care of himself as would anyone who has a chronic disease. An initial step toward this goal is establishing the patient's idiosyncratic patterns of depression. It is helpful for both the patient and therapist to know all there is to know about previous episodes of depression. What were the precipitants and stresses, the external circumstances, the earliest indications? How long did the episode last, what helped, what made it worse? This is not only useful information for its predictive value, but it is also useful in helping the patient see that depression is a real entity with a course of its own. How does this episode compare with others in terms of severity and duration? If the course of previous episodes suggests that this one will be severe, intensive treatment should be begun as early as possible.

The Personality Structure and Developmental Level "Personality disorder" is a term loaded down with too many meanings. In my experience, it's often used as a way of blaming the patient—as in "what can you expect from a borderline personality." Further, too much good psychoanalytic brain power has gone into a metapsychology of personality disorders, as if all borderlines, narcissists, and others had the same etiology, the same kind of difficult parental relationship, that is the "cause" of their present problems. This view neglects the effects of some things that are largely givens—temperament, intelligence, resourcefulness—and ironically minimizes the effects of real, repeated trauma, like physical and sexual abuse. Finally, there is also a tendency to minimize the impact of developmental arrest, "caused" by the trauma or incipient pathology, which can leave the individual with severe deficits in living skills.

But despite my reservations about the concept, there is an important distinction between patients who have symptoms and patients who seem to "live" their problems, as the idea of personality disorder suggests. And I have to acknowledge that there are syndromes of problems that seem to be related to each other and define a "type," which can be useful in conceiving of a case. So if someone is admitted to the ER in an affect storm after a suicide attempt following a rejection by a loved one, you start to explore about other aspects of a borderline personality—substance abuse in the present, child abuse in the past—and you have some preliminary ideas about how to treat the patient (e.g., Linehan, 1987).

In thinking of personality, it's the reification and circular thinking that causes the most trouble. Researchers report that greater personality pathology among depressed patients means that successful treatment will take longer (Bearden, Lavellen, Buysse, Karp, & Frank, 1996) as if it's validation that personality disorders are real entities and have an objective existence that complicates recovery, like a chronic infection making it difficult to recover from an acute infection. In fact, it should be self-evident that the attributes that characterize personality pathology—impulsiveness, risk-taking, narcissism, passivity—are going to interfere with engagement in treatment, cooperation with treatment plans, and with life in general.

The concept of developmental level is usefully related to the question of whether patients live their problems or have symptoms. In depression, patients who come from more traumatic, deprived backgrounds are more likely to be chronically and pervasively depressed. Their lives are likely to be such a mess—conflictual interpersonal relations or none at all, school and employment failure, poverty, poor health, no insurance—that if they sleep poorly or have lost interest or pleasure in ordinary activities or their activity level has slowed down no one is likely to notice it against the background of constant struggle in their lives. They "live" their depression. But when patients have been treated fairly by life, when they have some satisfactory social relationships and have achieved some independence of functioning, if they suddenly become depressed, their symptoms stand out. They no longer feel like themselves.

We don't have a single theory of development, and things are complicated even more by the generally accepted notion of "developmental lines"—that individuals can be further advanced developmentally in some areas than in others. There are parts of ourselves that grow with life: intelligence, ability to tolerate affect, capacity for intimacy, fund of knowledge, for example. An arrest of any line can happen for a number of reasons. The lines are intertwined, so that an arrest of one will have impact on the others. Innately low intelligence will interfere with the capacity to develop a fund of knowledge; ability to tolerate affect will have an impact on capacity for intimacy. A mild depression may not interfere greatly with acquisition of knowledge, but may keep the patient stuck with limited ability to engage in intimate relationships. And the patient may become more out of step as his peers continue to grow around him.

Especially important in deciding how to treat the individual depressed patient is the line of development of defense mechanisms. There are mature and immature defenses (Vaillant, 1993). There is a developmental line for each defensive process, and it is important to recognize the distinction between so-called immature defenses (which prohibit awareness of intrapsychic conflict) and similar processes that arise because the psychic structure to appreciate reality is damaged—a distinction between the defensive denial of an event and the developmental inability to register and affirm its reality. To borrow Fonagy's metaphor (Fonagy, Moran, Edgcumbe, Kennedy, & Target, 1993), we may not hear the tune either because the patient isn't playing it (an active defense against emotional awareness), or because the patient doesn't have a violin (absent or damaged structure). With some patients, confronting or interpreting defenses like intellectualization or denial may be enough to help them reengage in intimate relationships after a depressive episode. But others may use what sounds like intellectualization or denial to mask their incapacity for intimacy, and we may need a long-term supportive relationship to help them develop that capacity.

Differential Diagnosis

This is not the book to explain how to determine if a particular patient is, indeed, suffering from depression or another psychiatric condition. Although I tend to minimize the distinction between dysthymia and major depression, there are very important distinctions between these conditions and other illnesses that can sometimes look the same—manic depression, schizophrenia, PTSD, anxiety disorders, family conflict, adjustment disorders. My lack of attention here should not be taken as an indication that I believe differentiating these conditions is unimportant, but rather as an acknowledgement that I should not try to do what others have done better. The reader is referred to the *DSM-IV* (American Psychiatric Association, 1994) and other references (Frances, First, & Pincus, 1995; Spitzer, Gibbon, Skodol, & First, 1994).

Major Depression and Dysthymia As I've argued in chapter 1, the distinction between major depression and dysthymia seems rather artificial and has contributed to the trivialization of research. But it does seem to me that there are important implications in the course of depression, whether it develops gradually and insidiously or whether it takes the form of a sudden collapse. In rural Connecticut where we see many different kinds of people, from old money to old poverty, it's unusual for someone to call us up and say "I'm very depressed and I need help," "I feel overwhelmed," "I feel sad and I don't know why," "I have low self-esteem," or "I think I could be a better person." People generally don't call us because of subjective feelings; they call us because of an external crisis. Maybe it was different in the '50s and '60s when analysis was popular, maybe it's still different in California, but it seems to me that it takes a lot of distress for people to ask for help.

It's very, very common for us to see people who have called us because their marriage is falling apart, their children are in trouble in school, their drinking has gotten them in difficulty, they are afraid of losing their jobs—what seems to them to be a rather recent development—but when we talk to them we recognize that a depression has been building for some time. They may have gone for much longer than the two years required by the *DSM*, feeling sad, anxious, or irritable most of the time, with poor sleep, digestive problems, difficulty concentrating, and low energy—all the indicia for dysthymia. It's just been so gradual in its development that they think it's normal. In fact, their hopelessness about things ever getting better—their delay in asking for help until a crisis makes them desperate—is itself a symptom of their depression.

When we recognize a depression of slow onset like this, we must take care to engage the patient in a way that takes into account how he expects to be helped. To say, in effect, *You simply have depression, it's a chemical imbalance in the brain, take these pills and come back and see me in two weeks,* may be music to some patients' ears, but others may feel rebuffed by such a detached attitude after they've poured out their soul. Though I think that the disease model of depression is ultimately helpful for most patients, many will need time to acclimate themselves to the idea. And the therapist will need time to build up credibility.

On the other hand, there are many patients who will experience a major depressive episode as a sudden massive change from a previously normal level of functioning. Sometimes there is a clear precipitating crisis, sometimes the patient will later recognize that he had been depressed for a long while before he let himself feel it, but sometimes depression does seem to be a sudden event with no precipitant or warning. These patients generally seem to be much more open to medication as a first intervention. Feeling such a clear demarcation between the old self and how they seem now, they are ready to believe that a chemical imbalance has happened and that they need to be put right. They often resist the idea of psychotherapy, and indeed there is no need to force it on an unwilling patient. But sometimes these people are so unstrung that they need supportive contact, sometimes they are ready to make unfortunate decisions that will have lasting consequences, and sometimes the therapist can see a pattern that will likely lead to further depressive episodes unless the patient can change his behavior.

There is evidence that those who experience a major depressive episode without warning have a better prognosis than those who develop it gradually. One major study (Wells, Burnam, Rogers, Hays, & Camp, 1992), differentiating among patients with dysthymia, major depression, and "double depression" (a major depressive episode in addition to dysthymia), found that, while patients with double depression fared worst, patients with dysthymia alone had more symptoms of depression during each follow-up period than those with major depression. The researchers also found that subclinical symptoms of depression were important indicators of future major depressive episodes; in their sample, 25 percent of patients who had any symptoms at all went on to develop major depression within two years (as opposed to 3 percent of a random sample). In another study (Klein et al., 1998), patients with dysthymia alone were found to be largely unimproved at a 30-month follow-up compared to patients with episodic major depression. The study confirmed the general observation that patients with major depression have more severe symptoms during episodes than patients with dysthymia but that dysthymia is more difficult to treat.

The Resources

Although the focus of the assessment process is on problems and symptoms, it is also vital to ask about (and point out to the patient, at times) his strengths and resources. Treatment should capitalize on the patient's strengths, and a fairly systematic review is very helpful. The therapist should make it clear that the patient who is in the midst of a depressive episode is likely to underestimate or overlook some very real strengths, and for that reason we should look not only at the current situation but at previous attainments and levels of functioning as well. What areas of the patient's life have remained untouched by the depression? In what roles does he still function successfully? In what areas are feelings of pleasure, competence, or agency still possible? What relationships does he have to call on for support, affirmation, and structure?

Suicide

The risk of suicide for any patient with depression should never be underestimated; somewhere between one and two out of ten people with depression eventually take their own lives. Therefore it's vital to make a risk assessment as part of the overall assessment procedure. In fact, it's practically insulting to a depressed patient if we don't ask about suicide. *Do you have thoughts of hurting yourself? Have you ever acted on those thoughts? Are you afraid that you might?* Questions like these never put the idea of suicide into anyone's mind. On the contrary, patients feel understood and comforted if we make it clear that such thoughts and impulses are an expected part of the disease and that we know how to help. It should go without saying that our presentation of these questions should be confident and matter-of-fact; if the patient has a plan or is concerned for his own safety we must know what to do, including how to arrange hospitalization if necessary. For the nonmedical therapist in private practice, this is another very good reason to have an ongoing relationship with a psychiatrist. The ability to arrange an emergency admission to a good inpatient program where the psychiatrist and therapist will both be permitted to follow the case, without having to subject the patient to the emergency room, can greatly reduce the trauma of hospitalization.

On March 25, 1999, *The New York Times* ran a story about the suicide of Sam Hingston (Zielbauer, 1999). Sam was a 17-year-old student at the Wilton, CT, high school, a captain on the school's football team, already accepted at the college of his choice, a front-runner for the "best looking" and "most likely to succeed" awards, who doused himself with gasoline in the locked bathroom of his family home and set himself on fire. No one who knew him could offer any explanation. According to his grandmother, Sam had been complaining of headaches for a few weeks. But on the night of his death, Sam had dinner and watched "Jeopardy" with his family and went to bed around 11:00. Sometime around 3:00 he got up, filled a Gatorade bottle with gasoline from the garage, and locked himself in the bathroom.

This story is only remarkable in that the suicide seems even more incomprehensible than usual; but most suicides are incomprehensible. We don't know, and can't know, what will push a particular individual to find, as the black joke goes, a permanent solution to a temporary problem. Was Sam Hingston suffering from a depression? Apparently not, from all indicators. We can argue that he must have been terribly depressed but hiding it well, but that is hairsplitting. At the same time, we want to hope that if Sam had had some contact with a mental health professional, something could have been done for him.

When we work with depressed patients we must come to terms with the fact that suicide is a possible outcome, and that it is likely that over the course of a career, we will lose patients. We need to be prepared to do everything we can to protect the patient's life, assuming that a failure to intervene appropriately is a countertransference act. At the same time we must accept the fact that we are not omniscient and that a truly determined patient will find a way, even in a good hospital, to end his life. We need to understand that, for some patients, suicidal threats and talk are an expression of despair and a form of release, not an active intention, and that such patients need us to hear the affect, not the content. But deciding when suicidal talk is or isn't an emergent danger is one of the most difficult skills that a therapist can learn.

Fifteen percent of people with a severe major depressive episode of a month or more duration will die of suicide (Guze & Robins, 1970). Approximately two-thirds of suicides have a diagnosed depressive disorder at the time of their deaths (American Association of Suicidology [AAS], 1997). Suicide is approximately 30 times more likely to be the cause of death among those with depression compared to the general population (Guze & Robins, 1970).

In 1996, the year for which most recent data are available, suicide was the ninth leading cause of death in the United States, responsible for nearly 31,000 deaths, 85 suicides a day. Risk of death from suicide in the United States is more than one and a half times greater than risk of death from homicide, but the resources and attention given to homicide are immeasurably higher than to suicide (U. S. Public Health Service, 1999).

Over 5,000 people under 25 in the United States commit suicide every year, 2,000 of them teenagers; and there are somewhere between 300 and 350 serious attempts for every completed suicide (Slaby & Garfinkel, 1994). The Centers for Disease Control and Prevention reported in 1997 that one in 10 American youths have attempted suicide (*The New York Times*, Aug. 14, 1998). The rate for children and youth has increased over 300 percent since the 1950s (AAS, 1997). For young people aged 15–24 years old, suicide is the third most common cause of death, and there have been recent disturbing increases in the rate of suicide among children. Suicide is the fourth leading cause of death among children between the ages of 10 and 14 (U. S. Public Health Service, 1999).

The rate of suicide increases with age, reaching its peak among white males age 65 and over. Recognition of suicide risk among the elderly by health care professionals and the mental health community remains a serious problem. Most older people thinking of suicide see their physician within the month before the act, and 40 percent within the week (Brody, 1998a). But physicians are less likely to provide treatment when a depressed suicidal patient is older, apparently from the belief that depression is a natural consequence of aging (Uncapher & Areán, 2000).

There are large differences in suicide patterns by gender. Men are at least four times more likely to die from suicide than women, but women make two to three more times as many attempts as men (Jamison, 1999).

Suicide is usually the result of overwhelming distress, for which the patient sees no other solution. There is often also a message of reproach to people whom the patient feels injured by or disappointed in, but this is usually only a secondary motive. Leenaars (1988, 1992), who has made a career of studying suicide notes, finds that textual analysis reveals these recurrent themes:

- unbearable psychological pain
- feeling isolated and alone
- anger or ambivalence at a rejecting other
- inability to adjust to a change
- indirect expressions of psychic conflict
- escape from a painful situation
- anger or shame at the self
- thinking constricted to the problem, not permitting alternatives

Suicide is not about death but about relief. We must differentiate between a "wish to be relieved of the tension or pain associated with consciousness from a wish to embrace death, fully comprehended as permanent nonbeing" (Hoffman, 1998, p. 38). Most suicides can be best understood as resulting when an individual's level of pain has exceeded, or is expected to soon exceed, his level of tolerance at that moment (Motto, 1992). This suggests that if we can relieve the pain, raise the level of tolerance, or extend the moment (by preventing impulsive actions), we can hope to prevent suicide (Schneidman, 1984).

Some suicides are not the result of depression or other mental illness. For some people, there comes a point in the fight against disease, disability, and pain when the patient needs to be able to put an end to his own suffering. Freud himself died from an overdose of morphine, which he requested his physician to administer. Many physicians who practice among the elderly have an unspoken understanding with patients who have stockpiled lethal doses of medication. As we see life artificially prolonged, we all become more comfortable with the idea of "do not resuscitate" orders. The question we all will face is defining at what point death makes more sense than life. Indeed, for many of us, the biggest fear is that we will slip into senility without being able to make that decision ourselves.

Acceptance of pain and disability moves in stages, and depression is most frequently evident at the transition between stages. When we first get the diagnosis, when we learn that the chemo didn't work, or when the cancer spreads to a new organ and increases our pain—at those times our anxiety skyrockets. We fear that we will only feel worse from now on, and depression can take hold. But most people are able to adapt to bad news, disability, or pain, and within a few days life has returned to some degree of normality, and we find ourselves experiencing some joy again. It's important that the therapist and physician help people not to act impulsively during those times of adjustment.

Controlling Risk There are volumes written specifically on suicide assessment and prediction (e.g., Maris, Berman, Maltsberger & Yufit, 1992), a journal on the subject (*Suicide and Life-threatening Behavior*), and many published protocols to follow on conducting a suicide assessment (see Rothberg & Geer-Williams [1992] for a review). Table 4.1 presents my own compilation of the most salient risk factors, based on Schuyler (1998) and U. S. Public Health Service (1999).

All of these factors should be considered part of the picture that may get a patient to the point where he is contemplating suicide. Our therapeutic goal is to lift the depression and restore hope (reduce the pain and increase the level of tolerance); but with a potentially suicidal patient our immediate goal is to make sure the patient is safe. To keep the patient safe, in my opinion there are only four primary things to consider: *history of impulsive acts, access to lethal means, drug or alcohol use, and social support.* An important "psychological autopsy" study (Appleby, Cooper, Amos, & Faragher, 1999) compared suicides with controls matched for age and gender. The researchers found a great many differences between the two groups. Suicides were much more likely to be unemployed, isolated, and transient; they were more likely to be in mental health treatment (45 percent of cases); they were much more likely to have a diagnosable mental disorder (90 percent vs. 27 percent), and more likely to abuse alcohol or drugs (57 percent vs. 11 percent). They were much more likely to have a history of self-injury (68 percent vs. 6 percent). Finally, they were also much more likely to have experienced a negative life event within the past week (69 percent vs.

TABLE 4.1
Suicide Risk Factors

Stated plans

Delusions, hallucinations, or paranoid ideation

Mixed or transitory affective states

Family history

Recent (6–12 months) discharge from hospital

Previous attempt

Poor medication response

Noncompliance with treatment

Substance abuse

History of violence or impulsivity

Communication of suicide intent to others

Social isolation or withdrawal

Lethality and accessibility of plans

Recent psychosocial loss

Barriers to treatment

Contagion—identification with friends or public figures
    who have committed suicide

Physical illness

Hopelessness

---

13 percent) and to be experiencing moderate to severe interpersonal problems. The picture was of a socially isolated individual, dependent on relatively few relationships which are themselves unstable, with a drug or alcohol problem, who has been destabilized by a recent disappointment or injury to the self system.

Medication is a major factor in controlling risk. Jamison (1999) makes a strong case that lithium is the most effective suicide preventer, whether for manic depression or simple depression, an argument that too many psychiatrists seem unfamiliar with. The newer antidepressants have the distinct advantage over the tricyclics of being much less lethal in overdose. And medication will generally provide much more rapid relief from some of the most frightening symptoms of depression than psychotherapy alone. Although anxiolytics are generally not prescribed for depression, I find that many patients who are at the highest risk of suicide are in an agitated state, and that responsible use of medication to provide relief from tension and ability to get some rest can be very helpful in getting through the crisis.

The patient must be separated as much as possible from lethal means. If there are guns in the house, they have to go. Guns account for 59 percent of all deaths from suicide. Among children ages 15–19, gun deaths account for 96 percent of the increase in the suicide rate since 1980 (U. S. Public Health Service, 1999). At 3:00 in the morning, in the dark night of the soul, patients may survive an overdose and are unlikely to get into their cars and drive into a bridge abutment, but the gun on the closet shelf can be too tempting. Potentially lethal drugs must go as well. Patients who refuse to go along with these steps should probably go to the hospital.

If the patient is abusing drugs or alcohol, that has to stop. If he has a pattern of sporadic but excessive use, drugs and alcohol should not be in the house. Intoxicants lower inhibitions. More often than not, when there is a completed suicide the patient is in an intoxicated state. If the patient cannot abstain, he should be in a hospital.

The patient's support network must be part of the assessment. If loved ones are not appropriately concerned, the therapist should take steps to raise their concern. If they give any mixed messages about the patient's love and worth, the patient must be protected from them. If they minimize the importance of re-moving lethal means from the house, the patient is not safe in the house.

If the patient has a history of violence or other impulsive behavior, the therapist's concern should be redoubled. Someone who has a history of ar-rests for disturbing the peace or domestic violence and is currently contem-plating suicide should be considered at high risk. Someone who has made previous attempts obviously is at high risk. Someone who has a history of ac-cidents or injuries—even if not clearly self-destructive—is likewise at high risk.

The ability of the patient to contract for his own safety should be respected, within limits. It's often said that such contracts—usually an agreement that the patient will contact the therapist or go to the emergency room before killing himself—are really designed more for the therapist's comfort than the patient's benefit. Sometimes this is clearly the case.

I know a patient whose analyst had her sign a contract, before she started treatment with him, that if she chose to kill herself she must discontinue treat-ment first. She *was* a suicide risk, with a history of attempts and self-mutilation and other self-destructive behavior. She looked horribly depressed, thin as a rail, and very fragile. And, her analyst told her, shortly before she began seeing him, he had a patient complete suicide. So he was scared. But is it any wonder that the patient was tormented by doubts about the analyst's ability to help her? By setting up a contract in which she was free to kill herself if she absolved the analyst of culpability, the analyst was communicating to the patient that his overriding concern was not her safety but his comfort.

On the other hand, many patients will hear the more usual form of the contract—*Promise me that you'll get in touch with me if you feel like hurting yourself*—as a communication of caring from the therapist. The therapist is giv-ing the patient the respect due a rational adult, one who is capable of entering into and living up to a bargain. The message of caring and respect can be a powerful intervention and, coupled with the knowledge that there is a safety plan, can go a long way toward alleviating the patient's distress.

But the therapist is taking a risk in proposing such a contract. If the patient refuses, the therapist really has no choice except to attempt to get the patient into a hospital; to let a patient go when he is not able to vouch for his own safety is abandonment in both the legal and the clinical sense. Still, this is a risk that is inherent in holding oneself out to the community as a mental health professional; it presupposes that the therapist has the knowledge or power to arrange a hospitalization if necessary.

FORMULATION AND TREATMENT PLAN

When we can be relatively certain that the patient is safe and that psychotherapy is indicated for his complaint (hopefully during the initial interview), it behooves the therapist to make an offer to the patient. This can be done in fairly general terms: *It sounds to me like you are struggling with depression, and that there are a number of problems in your life that are connected with it, especially your relationship with your daughter. Would you like to work on this with me?* Then if the patient has questions about what's expected of him or what the therapist will be doing, these should be answered. But as the first few sessions go on, there should be a natural progression to a clearer definition of the problem, a better understanding of the mutual roles of the therapist and patient, and some explicit discussion of what the goals of therapy are to be.

So, toward the end of the assessment process, there should be an emerging picture of the problem that will be the focus of the therapy (see chapter 9). How the therapist communicates that problem can be a vital link to the patient, a message that the therapist deeply understands and that there is reason for hope.

It is useful in treating depression to take as a starting hypothesis the idea that there is an important link between the patient's first experience of depression and the precipitant for the present episode. The first episode may have been to do with the loss of the mother's love through death; the current episode may be connected with the threatened loss of the spouse's love through her preoccupation with a new job. (The connection is, alas, often not nearly so obvious.) James Mann suggests that this be presented to the patient as an empathic statement about the self: *It seems as if you doubt that you're truly worthy of being loved.* Rather than suggesting that the patient had ambivalent feelings about his mother which made him unable to mourn her, or that he is jealous of his wife's new job, we make it unnecessary for the patient to get defensive by phrasing the problem in terms of a preconscious statement about the self: "a chronic feeling about the self that periodically flits into consciousness but is equally quickly suppressed, denied, and warded off from full awareness by bringing into use well-established coping devices" (Mann, 1981, p. 33).

It is then useful to take as a secondary hypothesis the idea that the same "well-established coping devices" that are ordinarily used to keep the problem out of consciousness will also be used in the therapy to impede progress on resolution of the problem. In other words, the same skills of depression that the patient uses to keep himself from feeling are going to be a problem in the therapy. In still other words, the initial hurt, the present problem, and the patient's resistance in the transference are all variations on the same theme, which should be the focus of treatment.

The same issues may also be played out in setting goals. The patient may state *I want my wife to make more time for me.* We may think *You have to accept that she has other interests and become more autonomous*—but the patient would just experience that as confirmation that he is indeed damaged and unworthy. It is more helpful for the patient for us to think and say *Feeling that your wife is growing away from you has shaken you badly. Let's understand why this is so and see what you can do about it.*

The patient has a right to know the approximate length of treatment; however, this is notoriously difficult to predict. The therapist should at least prepare the patient for the idea that treatment is likely to take a few months (although some relief of symptoms should come earlier), and that patients often choose to continue after that because they find the process helpful in addressing other problems in their lives. I think we owe it to our patients to be as respectful of their time and money as possible—the cost of therapy shouldn't add unnecessarily to the patient's problems—and to realize that when we are working in a managed care situation in which it is clear from the outset that only 20 sessions per year will be authorized, there is a clear obligation to do the best work possible within the parameters given. There are many excellent texts on short-term treatment that incorporate the time limit in a therapeutic way (e.g., Davanloo, 1978; Gustafson, 1986; Malan, 1976; Mann, 1973), and of course both cognitive-behavioral and interpersonal psychotherapy for depression are designed to be short-term in nature. Following such a model is much better practice than following one's usual open-ended style and allowing it to be truncated by managed care, which is likely to make the patient feel cheated and depressed again.

We also need to recognize that many depressed patients, even if not suicidal, are in a state of acute distress and desire immediate relief from their suffering. Feeling pressured to come up with quick solutions for very complex situations that we are only beginning to understand, we may miss some opportunities to be of real help because we underestimate their potential value to the patient. Or we may begin to resent the patient who apparently has not heard us just explain that psychotherapy can take some time. For instance, when the patient demands to know if we think he should quit his job immediately, we can relieve the pressure greatly simply by asking *How would it be if you don't make a decision on that until we have had a chance to talk about it more?* The patient may see that there are, in fact, no adverse consequences to delaying a decision. When the patient feels that others in his life are making intolerable demands, we can help by teaching some simple time-out skills: Count to ten, leave the room, go for a walk, spend more time outside the house. When the patient is overwhelmed by an important task, reminders to prepare as thoroughly as possible and take time to relax can be very effective. It only reinforces the patient's depression for us to act as if we are above giving concrete advice.

There is a great deal to be done in the assessment phase with a depressed individual. We need to begin to determine the interplay between biological, psychological, and social factors in the current illness. We need to make sure the patient is safe. We need to take steps to alleviate acute distress. We need to begin to develop a therapeutic focus. We need to begin to strategize about what points in the vicious circle of depression may be the best targets for intervention. We need to begin to educate the patient about how we work, and we need to begin to learn about how the patient's mind works. And although we have to do a lot, we also have to begin to get the patient actively invested in the process of helping himself—the subject of the next chapter.

CHAPTER 5

Engage the Patient's Emotions

The therapeutic alliance is more critical than the techniques a therapist employs or the drugs that may be prescribed. This is currently not a popular view among many researchers, and it isn't what health care insurers want to hear either. (Strupp, 1997, p. 21)

THE MAJOR TASK OF the beginning phase of treatment is to engage the patient in a relationship marked by common purpose and an expectation of direct communication. Both the purpose and the communication are immediate obstacles for the depressed patient. Engaging in a relationship with clear-cut goals is a new experience for most people with depression. Lacking hope, we do not set goals. Not accustomed to seeing ourselves as centers of initiative, we function as reactors, not actors, in our lives. Not appreciating that sustained effort pays off, we give up too easily.

The communications side of the relationship also presents new challenges. We do not know how to talk in the language of emotions that engages people in a close relationship. We especially do not understand anger and how we express it, so we act out passive-aggressively when we are disappointed. We often seem to be stuck in grief, but exactly what we lost is not clear. We present a mask to most of the world, convinced that people will be repulsed by the "true self" we keep hidden; yet at the same time, we have the fantasy that someday someone will appreciate, respect, and love that hidden self. So we keep the therapist at arms' length—through a variety of characterological styles—all the while wishing for a transforming experience. No wonder so many depressed patients drop out in the initial stages of treatment. Therapists must be ready to bend the rules, must be very alert to subtle forms of communication, must understand the patient's shame and desire for hope, at the same time as beginning carefully to challenge the patient's assumptions and encourage/expect changes in behavior, in order to successfully begin treatment.

It can be useful to assume that, at the outset of treatment, the patient is likely to see the therapist both as a powerful, omniscient authority and as a dangerous threat to his stability and self-esteem. When we attribute to someone the power to heal us, we also give him the power to hurt us. The extent to which the individual patient experiences these infantile transferences will vary a great deal, depending on factors like the patient's overall maturity and the extent of his destabilization at the time, but nevertheless they play a role with all patients. In active treatment, our goal is to help the patient move to a point where the therapist is experienced as a mentor or coach, a collaborator with the patient in the shared task of overcoming depression, eventually a trusted friend. The patient is not expected to be a passive participant but an active agent in changing his own life.

REACHING OUT WITHOUT FALLING IN

Several studies of therapeutic process in the NIMH Treatment of Depression Collaborative Research Program yielded results that are highly pertinent to the subject of affective engagement. The larger project (Elkin et al., 1989) had studied 250 participants with major depression, who were randomly assigned to one of four conditions: interpersonal therapy (IPT; Klerman, Weissman, Rounsaville, & Chevron, 1984), cognitive-behavioral therapy (CBT; Beck, Rush, Shaw, & Emery, 1979), imipramine plus clinical management, and clinical management only. The three treatment groups were all more effective than clinical management, but the differences between the groups were small; instead, differences between patients and therapists were much more powerful predictors of effectiveness. For instance, the degree to which the patients experienced their therapists as empathic, caring, open, and sincere *at the end of the second session* significantly predicted outcome at termination (Blatt, Zuroff, Quinlan, & Pilkonis, 1996). The most effective therapists—including two who were providing only medication and clinical management—reported that they tended to treat most of their patients with psychotherapy alone and rarely used medication, and that they tended to view the etiology of depression as psychological and environmental rather than biological. They also expected that their patients would take a longer time to begin to benefit from treatment than did the less effective therapists (Blatt, Sanislow, Zuroff, & Pilkonis, 1996).

Ablon and Jones (1999) conducted detailed analyses of the taped interviews, and demonstrated that the therapists had indeed been following their prescribed models. IPT therapists, for example, were very likely to focus on issues in the patient's interpersonal life, and were judged to be sensitive and attuned to the patient's feelings. CBT treatment, on the other hand, centered on the patient's beliefs and constructs, and the therapists were often teacherlike and gave explicit advice. The interesting finding is that none of these variables were correlated with outcome. The only process items that predicted outcome were found in both therapies, and they reflected the patient's motivation or capacity, or the therapeutic relationship itself. For example, "patient conveys positive expectations about therapy," "patient is clear and organized in self-expression," "patient readily explores inner thoughts and feelings," "humor is used"—all were positively related to outcome. Negatively associated with outcome, on the other hand, were variables like "patient rejects therapist's comments or observations," "patient does not feel understood," "patient experiences ambivalent or conflicted feelings about the therapist." Furthermore, these patterns of relatedness were already stable by the fourth session of treatment. In other words, it's hard to rescue a therapy that's going wrong.

Yet, therapists too often persist in doing what seems safe and comfortable, even in the face of the patient's signals that it isn't working. Sometimes we have unshakeable belief in impeccable authority to substantiate doing just what we want to do. Stephen Mitchell (1993) has a trenchant observation about the need for flexibility:

> The problem with the principle of standing firm is the assumption that it must mean to the patient what the analyst wants it to mean. Sometimes it does, and that patient feels encouraged by the analyst's ability to set limits, stand by his faith in the analytic process, resist allowing himself to be seduced into dangerous departures.
>
> However, while the analyst thinks she is standing firm, the patient may feel he is being brutalized in a very familiar fashion. Many patients are lost because they feel utterly abandoned or betrayed by analysts who think they are maintaining the purity of the analytic frame. The frame is preserved; the operation is a success; but the patient leaves, climbing off the operating table in the middle of the procedure. (p. 194)

From the first phone call, we must work at establishing conditions for treatment of depression that are likely to lead to a successful outcome. This may not come naturally. As professionals, we vary from extremes: from the analyst who may permit a brief handshake at the end of a five-year analysis to the "new age" therapist who opens and closes every session with a bear hug; from the academician who wears a lab coat and sits behind his desk to the therapist who greets his patients in a sweater and fills his office with overstuffed furniture that makes it clear this is egalitarian seating. We can share jokes with the patient or we can be all business. And these all are respectable extremes, perhaps too austere or too loose for individual taste, but clearly not malpractice. These ways we have of indulging our personal preferences have tremendous impact on how the patient experiences us.

Extremes are not right for most depressed patients; they can become more depressed by our coldness or frightened and overwhelmed by our intrusiveness. We can say baldly "here is what you must do" or we can implicitly reassure the patient that our positive regard will be enough to solve the problem. Expressing our personal preferences in these ways can be an effective tool for screening out the patients we can't work with. Or we can take a middle course, listen carefully, practice flexibility, and accept the danger that we may get difficult cases who will challenge us and make us uncomfortable.

We want to be able to engage the patient emotionally but not be overcome by our own emotional reactions to the patient's depression—whether those emotions make us feel depressed and hopeless ourselves, panicky and overwhelmed, angry and sadistic, a messiah-like rescuer. We want to respond to the patient's distress like a sympathetic human being, but a special kind of human being— someone who not only has the expertise to help but who also respects this other person's unique situation.

Telling a new patient in the first session that depression is a chronic disease and that he's going to have to learn to live with it is probably not a wise thing to do. But telling that patient that all the things that are bothering him, all the things he worries about, like self-destructive thoughts, crying for no reason, trouble concentrating and remembering, yelling at the kids, are all tied together and have a name can be very helpful. Aside from the depression, the patient is suffering from confusion and anxiety, and feels overwhelmed by new and unfamiliar symptoms and behavior that seemingly make no sense. We can alleviate some of this confusion at the outset with a simple message: *You are suffering from depression. We can help you.*

GOALS OF ENGAGEMENT

Hope

William Styron told me a story (personal communication, 1998): When he was at the very bottom, when every morning was torture and he didn't believe he could last another day, he asked his doctor how long it generally takes to recover. And the doctor told him "with a little smile" that it would take six months to a year. Perhaps this was true, depending on how the doctor defines recovery, but the truth can be used sadistically. It would have been so much more helpful to the patient's current state of mind and willingness to engage to tell him something true but not cruel: *Most people start to feel better within a few weeks.*

Depressives are very afraid to ask for hope directly. We always have the dread that no matter how horrible things seem right now, we haven't seen the worst yet. The therapist must offer hope, and remind the patient sometimes when things are bleakest that they do get better; but at the same time people with depression have exquisitely sensitive bullshit detectors, and you must be honest. So it's honest and tactful to say *I think you can expect some relief soon.* It's not honest to say *You will feel better soon.* It's not tactful to say *Everyone is different, time will tell.* It's not helpful to say *Don't worry, we'll take good care of you, everything will be fine.* We depressives know the sound of false reassurance, because we hear it all the time, and we know that it means we're not being taken seriously anymore. The listener has turned from sympathetic and helpful to patronizing and dismissive.

The ability to lend hope comes from confidence that depression can be reversed, from the experience of having seen other patients, perhaps ourselves, through the same process. Perhaps even more important than the content of what's said are the therapist's tone and conviction—the music, not the words.

> The aspect of active hope that affirms a commitment to life is probably not generally communicated in the content of what is said but, rather, in the fervor of the tone, in the strength of conviction that may be signaled by directness and forcefulness of speech. (Buechler, 1995, p. 72)

Hope means desire, and many depressed people avoid experiencing desire. If you come from a background of abuse, chronic disappointment, exploitation, or traumatic loss, you may experience desire as a frightening vulnerability, a weakness which others will only exploit or which will only open old wounds. If you have experiences where your own difficulty controlling impulses has brought you to grief, you may experience desire as an overwhelming force to be avoided at all costs. In extreme situations, experiencing desire can feel dangerous to the core of the self, as if you will blow up, fall apart, or go crazy unless you are careful to feel nothing. For prison inmates, the time just prior to release is that of the greatest stress, when suicide or homicide attempts are most likely (Gilligan, 1996).

The fear of hope and desire is a powerful obstacle to the depressed patient's engagement in treatment, and one reason why medication seems like an attractive solution for many patients. There is comfort in conceiving of the self as a helpless victim. For one thing, it interferes with the experience of desire, which can be a terrifying vulnerability or an overwhelming impulse. The medical model provides absolution from responsibility. Further, medication comes without a relationship, and has the mystique of solving the depression without requiring the patient to change himself. But psychotherapy awakens desire for love, intimacy, protection, affirmation, emotional resonance—desires that depressed patients avoid. So the patient is acutely sensitive to narcissistic injury from the first moment—to the therapist's vanity, exploitation, rejection.

I find it most helpful to most patients to mobilize hope as much as possible at the outset by using my authority as an "expert" and to keep my personality in the background. I do not want to be especially charismatic or clever, but to let the patient know I understand his condition, I have a great deal of experience with it, and I know how to help him. Our relationship will be built on conjoint work and mutual respect, and affection may develop as an added benefit.

Absolution

Being in a state of depression usually means you blame yourself for your own condition. Depressed patients generally agree with the conventional wisdom that if they really wanted to get better they could pull themselves up by their own bootstraps. They tend to feel that depression is not a "real" illness. Though more sophisticated patients will attribute these attitudes to society or to family members and deny them in themselves, this is often mere projection. The negative self-evaluations of depression, of feeling as if one is "weak" or "lacks character," don't disappear just because the patient recognizes intellectually that they are unfair. So most patients come to treatment in hopes that the therapist can absolve them of the self-blame they feel so bitterly.

Ironically, the best antidote for self-blame, since it is an artifactual distortion of self-image caused by the disease, is recovery from the disease itself. At the same time, work to resolve the distortion aids in recovery from the disease. Over the course of treatment, the therapist's continued acceptance of the patient despite revelation of guilty or shameful secrets contributes immeasurably to adoption of a more forgiving attitude toward the self. But at the outset of treatment, the therapist must be very sensitive to the patient's need for forgiveness; and as with hope, the patient is also very attuned to false reassurance.

The Catholic Church has a fine model for forgiveness of sins; it requires both sincere repentance and a firm intention to sin no more. The depressed patient is usually filled with regret over a host of (generally imagined or exaggerated) sins, weaknesses, and defects, but he can't hold the intention to reform because he feels powerless. The therapist provides a model for absolution with responsibility via the message that there are tools to help the patient reform. This does not mean that the therapist accepts the validity of the patient's self-blame; on the contrary, we need to be explicit that it is a manifestation of the disease. But we recognize that the patient's suffering is real, even if the cause for it is not.

Affective Connection

Depressed self-absorption keeps the patient from engaging in intimacy, including the intimacy of therapy. Therapists need to recognize at the outset that there are powerful forces at work to keep the patient from connecting with us, and that it is part of our job to address those forces in a planful way. Depressed patients are prone to flat affect, understatement, emotional muting, slow reactions, and unassertive behavior. They are acutely sensitive to any form of rejection. Everyone ignores their feelings, takes them for granted, or treats them like a china doll. We have to listen very carefully, with all our senses. We have to key in to subtle cues of feelings. We may have to teach the patient what's normal: *Most people would feel _____ when something like that happens.* We have to let them know we have confidence we can help, and that we are sincerely interested in them as individuals.

At the end of the nineteenth century in Vienna, women wore galoshes when the streets were muddy. Traditionally, it fell to the host to help them on and off with their galoshes when they visited. Sigmund Freud helped his female patients get their galoshes on and off at every session. Jung had a romantic relationship with a patient; Klein analyzed her own family. Yet we have inherited this analytic ideal of a remote, reserved, brittle therapist. When Kohut allowed a patient to hold on to two fingers (not three), he was aware that he was transgressing a major taboo (Hedges, 1992). Because as soon as you say, all right, holding on to two fingers is okay, someone else is going to say that holding hands is okay, hugs are okay, holding on to something else entirely is okay. And this is more difficult for inexperienced therapists, because with experience we really do get a sixth sense for our own and our client's needs so that these tricky and seductive situations don't come up so often—but we don't want to admit that because we're desperate to prove we're a science and not an art, and to be a science you have to be able to write down how it works and teach it to people. It all leads to a lot of trouble.

Let us recognize that fragile patients can be frightened away by effusiveness, that many people resent being hugged or patted or treated with false affection; but also let's recognize that not to behave normally is a rebuff—to be friendly, to smile, to give encouragement, to help put on a coat, to offer a cup of coffee. At the same time, we must keep in mind that the patient is trusting us not to exploit him for our own purposes, much as he seems to ask for it at times. We do not want to gratify the patient's wishes to be taken care of by us, to be loved by us, or to have a sexual relationship with us, but we do want to respond to the patient's *growth needs* (Casement, 1990)—needs for active concern, empathy, even direction and encouragement when attempting new developmental tasks.

> [It is too easy for us to deny] both the extent of our authority and the extent of our intimate involvement with our patients as they risk doing or not doing one thing or another, both inside and outside the analytic situation. In trying so hard to stay out of it, we can really be "out of it." Opportune moments for action come and go. They do not necessarily recur, and they certainly do not last forever. The analyst is right there in the patient's life as those moments pass by. There is no risk-free position to which he or she can retreat. (Hoffman, 1998, p. 73)

There is evidence that much of the discussion about the "frame" and the importance of maintaining rigid professional boundaries in the relationship is of more theoretical than real importance. Johnston and Farber (1996) surveyed 500 randomly selected members of the American Psychological Association's Division 29 (psychotherapy) concerning their actual behavior with patients. The 213 respondents had an average age of 50 years, with an average of 19 years of experience, most in full-time private practice. Most reported that they generally accommodated patients' requests to rearrange an appointment or renegotiate a fee. Most reported that they made themselves available between sessions, made personal disclosures and expressed personal feelings about their patients (within narrow limits), and practiced the usual social amenities or discussed current events. Most drew the line, however, at having a social (nonsexual) relationship with the patient.

Renik (1995) advocates for self-disclosure for purposes of self-explanation. In other words, that it's useful for the therapist to try to make sure that the patient understands why he's doing what he's doing (to the extent that the therapist understands it). One advantage is that it keeps the patient from being distracted by always trying to figure out what we really want, what's really on our minds. "A stance of non-self-disclosure tends to place the analyst center stage. It makes the analyst into a mystery, and paves the way for regarding the analyst as an omniscient sphinx whose ways cannot be known and whose authority, therefore, cannot be questioned" (p. 483). It's not only analysts who take advantage of this mystifying omniscience, of course, but also many practitioners in the family therapy tradition who use Ericksonian techniques, some psychopharmacologists, and even some cognitive therapists who like the mantle of authority. Another, more compelling, advantage of self-disclosure about the therapist's intentions is that it establishes an atmosphere of candor and authenticity in the relationship. It is too easy for therapy to degenerate into an intellectualized game with an "as-if" quality, the patient feeling license to explore all kinds of recesses in the brain without direct consequence. When the therapist talks directly about what's going on in the relationship, including his own doubts or convictions about what he's doing, the patient is challenged to respond on the same level, to take what we're doing as serious business. A third advantage is that it helps keep the therapist honest; if we have established an atmosphere where we are expected to report why we did something that the patient may have experienced as rejecting, we may be less likely to do it in the first place.

The therapist must monitor his own emotional experience of the patient at all times. The old psychoanalytic ideal that the therapist must provide an uncontaminated field in which only the patient's subjectivity is to be explored— like the cognitive behavioral ideal that the therapist is a detached expert who has only special knowledge to offer and whose personality is immaterial—has to be abandoned. We must accept that our subjective experience of the patient is one of the tools we have to use, and that it is by definition imperfect. We can never be fully analyzed and we can never be fully objective. But when we make a diligent effort to correct for our own pathology and the special role we play in the patient's life, we can be sure that how we feel when we are with the patient is vital data, and we can assume that it is something like how most people feel when they are with the patient.

Maintaining the Emotional Connection Silvan Tomkins (1962, 1963) developed the most widely accepted theory of affects and emotions. Affects are defined as hard-wired innate responses to stimulation. Tomkins lists eight primary affects: surprise, interest/excitement, enjoyment/joy, distress/anguish, contempt/disgust, anger/rage, fear/terror, and shame/humiliation. Affects have the function of amplifying or calling attention to the situations that engender them. They make good things better and bad things worse. When an affect is stimulated, it makes things happen all over our body. Infants are taken over by affects. Adults learn to control the outward manifestations of affect, but the same things are happening inside; we can become full of adrenaline, ready to fight or flee, or shamed and ready to retreat. Damasio (1994) points out that affects are a manifestation of drives and instincts: "In general, drives and instincts operate either by generating a particular behavior directly or by inducing physiological states that lead individuals to behave in a particular way" (p. 115). Affects also have a social function; when we have the facial expression of sadness, we elicit sympathy from those around us; when we swell up with anger, we can scare people.

In the language of emotions developed by Basch (1988) and Nathanson (1992), an *affect* is the innate biological response to a stimulus, a *feeling* is our conscious perception of an affect, and an *emotion* is our individual learned response to an affect, including all the memories and associations that go with it. Affects are pretty much the same in all of us; anger does the same thing inside you that it does inside me. But emotions are unique: How I experience anger depends on all my previous experiences of anger. Emotions also are self-reinforcing; they engender memories and thoughts that perpetuate the affect. "An affect lasts but a few seconds, a feeling long enough for us to make the flash of recognition, and an emotion as long as we keep finding memories that continue to trigger that affect" (Nathanson, p. 51). A *mood* is a persistent state of emotion, one that we cannot shake easily by changing our thoughts or our environment.

In other words, feelings are like toenails, things that have a life of their own, that happen to us whether we want them to or not. But the depressed patient has learned to fear his own emotions; he believes it is better not to feel. Depression is seen by some (e.g., Basch, 1988; Bowlby, 1980; Gut, 1989; Haynal, 1976/1985; Nesse, 2000) as an adaptive state, a regrouping of the self when we've done everything we know how to do and it hasn't solved the problem—a systemwide brownout of emotional intensity. Others, like Miller (1981), see depression as an effort to deny one's own feelings, an effort that requires a continual supply of psychic energy. Both formulations tie the patient's flattened affect and diminished responsiveness to the lethargy, lack of agency, and hopelessness of depression. Regardless of the theoretical explanation, however, recovery from depression implies recapturing the ability to experience emotions, an ability that will enliven the patient's apathetic, anhedonic state.

> An emotion is usually transient and responsive to the thoughts, activities, and social situations of the day. Moods, in contrast, may last for hours, days, or even months in the case of some depressions. Moods also have their own halo effect: They recruit memory and any ongoing experience and color these with the prevailing mood state. . . . [E]xpressed emotion is evidence of the homeostatic regulator at work, while mood is the set point around which it oscillates—a set point that for most people is fairly neutral and stable, much as an active thermostat maintains the steady temperature of a room. Thus it is our mood, the state of our emotional balance, that powerfully influences the way we interact and perceive the world. (Whybrow, 1997, p. 19)

By definition, the depressed patient is stuck in a depressed mood, a state where the only emotions likely to be experienced are negative ones. Naturally, the patient tries to control his experience of these emotions, but this does not lift the depressed mood. Paradoxically, he needs to exert less control, to allow himself to feel a full range of emotions in their moment-to-moment fluctuation as life happens.

A place to start is to help the patient differentiate between mood and emotion. Much of the focus of treatment must be on getting the patient to realize that mood changes don't come "out of the blue" but are connected to external reality. One of the greatest skills of depression is the ability not to see those connections. The mood journal (see p. 107) is my suggestion for helping to regain that lost ability. I ask the patient to keep track of times when he experiences a mood change (which does not have to be in a negative direction; it's very useful to find out what makes the patient feel good), and to note the external circumstances going on at the time, as well as the internal circumstances (thoughts, dreams, associations). Review of this material in session inevitably demonstrates that the patient's change in mood had a precipitant. Something happened that would have made a nondepressed person feel an emotion—usually anger, frustration, or rejection but sometimes joy, pride, or excitement—but the depressed person, instead of experiencing the emotion, experiences a mood change.

This need not be onerous homework. I find that two or three examples are all we can successfully review in a session. Some patients quickly catch on, however, and get a lot out of using the mood journal on their own.

There are several important lessons that come from the mood journal. One is the obvious one, that the patient's reactions to events are seen by the therapist as legitimate and understandable given the circumstances. This helps the patient become more tolerant of himself and begin to feel that he's not particularly loathsome for feeling angry when someone hurts him. A second lesson is that moods change. In the midst of feeling absolutely horrible, the patient's subjective belief is that he will always feel this way. But, except for the severely depressed, most patients do have fluctuations in mood, times when they feel better than their worst.

Another message is more subtle: By demonstrating that there are reasons why the patient's moods go up and down, we are showing the patient that he is not crazy. As we have discussed, the fear of loss of emotional control is one of the greatest secret worries of depression. The patient experiences his mood changes as forces that overwhelm him, apparently for no reason whatsoever, and he fears that he is losing his mind. When we show the patient that there is a *reason* for his mood change, we give him hope. That the extent of the mood change may be vastly out of proportion to the event that causes it is a secondary problem. If mood changes have to do with events, there are things we can do with events; we can avoid some, control others, and learn to accept what we have no other choice about. The patient can begin to adopt a wait-and-see attitude toward mood changes, a little detachment. Moods are like buses, another will come along soon enough.

MOOD JOURNAL*

DATE, TIME	MOOD CHANGE	EXTERNALS (WHO, WHAT, WHERE, OTHER UNUSUAL CIRCUMSTANCES)	INTERNALS (THOUGHTS, FANTASIES MEMORIES)

Instructions: When you detect a shift in mood, write down the change (e.g., from neutral to sad), the external circumstances (what you were doing, where, with whom), and the internal circumstances (what you were thinking about, daydreaming, or remembering).

*From *Undoing Depression* by Richard O'Connor. Copyright © 1997 by Richard O'Connor. By permission of Little, Brown and Company (Inc.).

Some patients will report not feeling anything. Something important happens in their lives, and they are not aware of feeling any particular way about it. Or they come to treatment and don't know what to say. This can be frustrating for the therapist, but hammering away at times like these can be terribly destructive for the patient. Wachtel (1993) proposes two strategies. One is to suggest that the patient may be feeling something, just not what he thinks he's supposed to feel. The patient who has suffered a loss, for instance, may report just feeling numb, believing he ought to be feeling overwhelming grief. But sometimes with a loss we don't feel sad, we may feel relieved or angry or hurt. Suggesting that feelings other than the conventional expectation are possible may open a door to fruitful exploration. Wachtel's other suggestion is to point out to the patient that he *is* feeling something—that feeling numb, bored, or indifferent is not feeling nothing. *In fact, you seem to be feeling a great deal of indifference. What's that about?* Both these approaches get around the accusatory power struggle of trying to convince the patient that he must be feeling something, which often ends up with him feeling angry at the therapist or feeling deeply defective, less than human.

Another technique described by Wachtel and used, sometimes unwittingly, by many different therapists, is what he calls "strategic attribution." This is the process of telling the patient that he is feeling something before he's fully aware of it himself. *Your anger at your husband is beginning to get to you. It sounds like you're getting ready to make a decision about your job.* Put forth baldly here on the page, comments like these can sound disingenuous, but I do think this is common practice, and it's better for us to be fully conscious of our methods than not. Sometimes therapists who view themselves as merely empathic are actually actively prompting the patient on how to feel. Whatever the rationale, when we do this right—when we are indeed not too far ahead of the patient, when we are speaking of something that is preconscious or even conscious sometimes, just not right now—it can be a way of giving permission to feel, of conveying the idea that a warded-off emotion is natural and acceptable under the circumstances. Such comments—which if accurate are really nothing more than deep empathy—can be an important step toward beginning identification with or internalization of the therapist as a more benign, less dangerous object.

Grief and Therapeutic Focus Most patients can tell you what happened the first time they got depressed, and it usually has something to do with loss. If in subsequent episodes it's taken a less perceptible cause to precipitate the depression, grief still seems to be the first cause for most people.

Freud's hypothesis was that grief leads to depression when we can't mourn the person we've lost because of our intensely ambivalent feelings. Our unconscious feelings of hate or rage toward the person whom we loved make it impossible for us to complete the mourning process. A more acceptable formulation today is that many things can interfere with grief: ambivalent feelings, certainly, but also a high degree of dependency, a sense that the lost person was the only source of vital resources, external circumstances that interfere with the grieving process.

In many cases of depression the therapist's goal is simply to facilitate normal grief. When the current episode has been precipitated by a recent loss, or when a recent loss has stirred up old feelings of depression associated with previous losses, it should be fairly clear to the therapist that this is the way to proceed. Often, however, the connection between the immediate stress and the old loss is so subjective to the patient, and outside his awareness, that we can find ourselves helping a patient do the work of mourning for a relationship lost years ago, a loss whose impact he did not feel at the time. Sometimes we find an anniversary reaction, a new experience of grief at a date of significance in the relationship; sometimes we find a depression coinciding with a phase of life in the old relationship. A mother whose own mother died while she was in college developed a depression when her daughter left for college. A man whose father became severely depressed when he retired feared the same reaction in himself.

The goals of treating patients who have a delayed grief reaction are to facilitate normal grief and to help the patient establish new relationships to take the place of what has been lost. The initial goal is simply to get the patient to think about and talk about the loss: the qualities of the individual, what the relationship meant, the circumstances of the loss. In doing this, the patient should be able to experience feelings of sadness, fear, and anger that have been suppressed. Many patients will need reassurance that their emotions will not overwhelm them or that they are not going crazy. Klerman and colleagues (1984) suggest that many patients will be fixated on the death itself, and will be uncomfortable talking realistically about the relationship. Feelings of anger, hurt, abandonment, and betrayal are very common, but the depressed person believes them to be unacceptable and fears expressing them. The therapist has to normalize and universalize such feelings, and assure the patient that with time he will find a realistic balance of feelings about the relationship, the ability to see its good points and bad points. Eventually the patient should be able to reengage in substitute activities and relationships.

In many patients with recurrent depression, however, the patient's efforts to find substitute relationships have been sabotaged by his own self-destructive behavior, and it is less the loss than the subsequent effects of incomplete mourning that are the therapeutic focus. For example, the patient may have integrated a deeply shameful self-image—*You hated your own father; what kind of a cold-hearted bastard are you?*—that lies at the heart of symptoms like violence and substance abuse that seem to be unrelated to the loss. Or a parent's cruelty to the child may have been introjected and then projected, so that a mother finds herself behaving sadistically to her children despite her fervent desire not to repeat her own mother's mistakes. Nevertheless, if good therapeutic work can help the patient gain control over his acting out or projection, some of the most powerful work of treatment can take place in finally completing the mourning process. The therapist's positive regard comes to feel something like the lost object's love. Though it is never enough to compensate for the loss, the therapist's continued acceptance in the face of the patient's sabotage helps the patient finally accept the loss and go on.

Guilt, Shame, and Blame

Excessive, pervasive feelings of guilt are among the most familiar hallmarks of depression. The patient is tortured by guilt feelings which he may know logically are out of proportion to the offense, or he may have a sense of guilt that colors every thing he does. Most patients receive the news of the psychodynamic doctrine of unconscious guilt with surprise, despite the ubiquity of knowledge about Freud and the Oedipal theory. It comes as unpleasant news to hear that you may feel guilty over feelings of desire and rage that you are not even conscious of. But it doesn't take much psychoanalytic training to begin to appreciate the universality of the phenomenon; we might think of Lady Macbeth or *Sophie's Choice*. I find that once the subject is explored and the patient is helped to make the connection that there is a real reason for his excessive guilt, he usually becomes interested in other manifestations of the idea.

Deirdre's mother had died five years ago, but each year on the anniversary of the death Deirdre experienced weeks of anxiety, depression, and guilt. At these times Deirdre talked about how she had faithfully tended to mother during her last years, but she was tormented by feelings of guilt that she had let her mother down. She made a big ritual out of visiting her mother's grave and arranging flowers, and was enraged at other members of her family who did not feel these rituals were so important. In contrast, at other times during the year Deirdre talked about her

experiences of physical and sexual abuse as a child, and her mother's severe alco-
holism and unavailability to Deirdre when she needed her. There seemed to be no
connection between the idealized mother when Deirdre was mourning and the
more objective mother she saw at other times.

Deirdre's rage at her abandoning mother was completely split off, but she still
got to feel guilty about it, the guilt that continued to torment her as she did every-
thing she could to be a dutiful daughter.

There are many factors that can help patients with excessive guilt. The therapist's acceptance of the patient as he is, warts and all, goes a long way. As
the patient becomes more trusting that he won't be condemned or rejected for
what he reveals, he reveals more to himself as well; secrets that he keeps in the
preconscious can get examined in the light of day. The resolution of cognitive distortions also relieves guilt. When we understand that we systematically blame ourselves for bad things and give others the credit for good things, we can begin to
challenge the validity of our assumptions. When we learn that we consistently
forget compliments and remember criticisms, we can force ourselves to pay more
attention to compliments and to have a better perspective on others' criticism.

Other forces we can utilize against excessive guilt include medication, which
seems to help reduce the frequency and intensity of obsessive guilt-ridden
thoughts, as well as mobilizing energy for changes in personal habits (neglect
of self-care) that have been reinforcing the guilt. Friends and family also
frequently make the patient feel guilty. "Guilt tripping" can be a very effective
manipulation to get one's own way, but many children of depressed mothers
know how to play mother like a violin without any deliberate intention to induce guilt; it's just a habit they've acquired in the family system. Helping the
patient learn his rights and responsibilities in relationships, as well as assertive
behavior principles, can teach others in the patient's life that inducing guilt is
no longer rewarded, eventually destabilizing the perpetual cycle of guilt in which
the patient is caught.

In psychodynamic terms, we may understand that the excessively guilty
patient has an overly punitive superego. The patient may talk about a mother
who never approved, a father who was always cold and critical. Helping the
patient understand that such experiences do indeed contribute to depression
by instilling impossible standards or withholding self-soothing can be effective
in getting the patient to lighten up on himself. Sometimes we can joke—*There's*
Mom's voice again, telling you you're not pretty enough; that's Dad, telling you
you're weak and whiny. By encouraging and accepting the anger and sadness
that accompany these childhood experiences, we help the patient a great deal
in learning to forgive himself. Eventually we may move beyond this to a mature
perspective on parents as people with problems of their own that interfered with
their ability to provide our patient with what he needed.

Times have changed, though, and it is the rare patient who will be shocked
by the news that his repressed rage at his parents has something to do with

depression. More patients come in now already angry, feeling cheated and deprived of something they had a perfect right to expect. Therapy with such patients that doesn't go beyond these themes is generally a fruitless exercise in intellectualization. I find that the mood journal can be helpful with these patients, because it helps us focus on what's going on in the present to push the patient's buttons. Excessive guilt may be an old wound, but it gets reopened by current experience. The patient's problems are in his interaction with his boss or his wife now, not how his father or mother treated him long ago.

Shame is so inherently painful that when we see someone in an embarrass-ing situation, we naturally cringe and look away. Lewis (1987) argues that is exactly what therapists have been doing about their patients' shame ever since psychotherapy began. The patient feels ashamed of himself for the mere fact of needing therapy. We ignore that or dismiss it and then later when the patient becomes enraged at our condescending treatment over a minor incident, we think we have a borderline patient on our hands, not realizing that our com-placent assumption of omnipotence is in fact enraging (cf. Brandchaft & Stolorow, 1984). Depressed patients, however, are sometimes only too eager to stifle the rage and keep the shame to themselves.

Guilt is about what we do, shame is about who we are (cf. Karen, 1992; Morrison, 1989, 1999; Nathanson, 1992). The Freudian structural theory, with its emphasis on conflict between libidinal drives and the superego, has tended to focus attention on guilt as the primary problem in depression and in other pathological states. Until very recently, shame has been all but overlooked. And yet it seems to be shame that is the primary motive force behind much of depression, as well as racial and religious conflict, international diplomacy, and angry males with automatic weapons.

Though we tend to think of shame as inherently pathological or damaging, and we are taught to avoid making our children feel ashamed of themselves, that was not always the case. In the past, to be capable of shame meant to be modest, to have character, to be respectful of boundaries and one's own limita-tions (Karen, 1992). And even now, to be shameless still means to merit disap-proval in most situations; even on the Jerry Springer show, the attraction is that the participants are the sideshow geeks, the modern-day freak show. So to be capable of shame is not a bad thing; to experience a painful feeling when we have done something to be ashamed of teaches us a lesson. For the infant who experiences the precursors of shame when the mother's desired response is not forthcoming, the retreat into the self keeps a bad situation from becoming worse by protecting the mother from further importuning and the child from destabilization. For the adult who is doing something foolish, the early warnings of shame can prevent outright mortification. It is a hidden, repressed shame that we strive to keep out of consciousness that often leads to depression; we force ourselves to behave in ways that keep these self-doubts out of consciousness, which reinforces the idea that we are fooling everyone. Women's doubts about their appearance, men's doubts about their masculinity, all Americans' doubts about dependency—these get stuffed away and overcompensated for. In Karen's words, we run from the belief:

> that one is at core a deformed being, fundamentally unlovable and unworthy of membership in the human community. It is the self regarding the self with the withering and unforgiving eye of contempt. And most people are unable to face it. It is too annihilating. (1992, p. 43)

I find that much of adult shame seems to have its origin in a parent's tin ear to the child's experience. When a child feels that his most basic feelings are consistently misunderstood or ignored, feelings of defectiveness seem inevitable. Ruth, an attractive young woman who was destabilized after being rejected by her boyfriend, remained insecure about her looks. She remembered always feeling this way, but was always accused of being vain. When she was 13, hopelessly anxious about her appearance, she would compulsively brush her hair in the mirror, feeling that it was her only attractive feature. Her mother, however, missed the point completely: "You're too conceited." Ruth felt that her very insecurity was shameful.

The overtly narcissistic patient is a different kind of example. To all appearances controlling, self-centered, and manipulative, always needing to be in the spotlight, their way of interacting drives others away. But let's call them narcissistically vulnerable* instead of merely narcissistic; and when we understand that the appearance masks a deep sense of shame, of being different, helpless, and scared, we can see how the patient's attempts to compensate only perpetuate the fear.

Morrison (1989, p. 73) states the clinical problem of shame very definitively: "For guilt, the antidote is forgiveness; for shame, it is the healing power of acceptance of the self, despite its weakness, defects, and failures. The self-object/therapist must strive to facilitate self acceptance through his own protracted immersion in the patient's psychological depths. Modification of grandiose ambitions and the ideal of perfection may then eventuate through understanding, and through identification with the accepting, empathic therapist." But the patient faces an apparently insoluble dilemma: You can earn forgiveness, through good deeds, acts of contrition, making amends. You can't earn acceptance, it's a gift; and the patient who feels unworthy, who doesn't trust, who fears intimacy, is not likely to accept gifts. The mere act of accepting a gift—though never refused by the unassertive depressed patient—can be experienced as shameful. That is why active treatment is framed as hard work, shared mutually. The patient begins to accept himself as a diligent partner with the therapist, able to experience and master fear and rage, able to experience joy and sorrow without crumbling, able to accept help without feeling shamed.

---

*Wachtel (1993) makes a suggestion which I heartily endorse, that we dispense with the whole diagnosis of narcissistic personality disorder (with its roots in the idea that libido is a fixed quantity) and begin to refer instead to self-esteem disorder.

Annie (mentioned in chapter 2) and I have a minor misunderstanding at the end of our first session, largely because I'm not tuned into what's on her mind. She came in to the office acutely sensitive to who might see her seeking help, although my office is 30 miles away from her home. But she does a good job during the session of letting her guard down and telling me her story. At the end of the session, believing that it's a rare experience for her to cry and feel deeply, I ask "How are you feeling now?"—meaning, in effect, are you in shape to drive home? But she has her coat and hat on, and has already put on the mask that she wears for the world, and her answer is "It would be worse if there were people in the other offices," referring again to her acute self-consciousness. She was reminding me of how embarrassed she felt about asking for help.

The fact that being a patient is inherently shame-inducing has been overlooked by theorists for far too long (cf. Lewis, 1987). The mere act of acknowledging that life is too much and laying bare one's deepest secrets to a relative stranger is fraught with shame. We must always keep in mind that depressed patients feel deeply defective and that asking for help is just one more manifestation of that defect. In fact, although they desperately desire our help, they feel unworthy of it. The worst of psychoanalytic methodology was very shame-inducing: the analyst as a remote, idealized presence who never showed warmth or interest, and selectively reinforced with his attention the patient's most humiliating revelations. The worst of medication treatment today remains shame-inducing: The busy physician ignores the content of what the patient says to focus on how his verbal productions manifest his level of pathology, rushes the patient out after 15 minutes, and somehow makes him feel to blame if the medications don't help. We need to acknowledge the patient's difficulty asking for help, the discomfort he feels at being in a supplicant's position. We can say directly that although it's natural to be embarrassed at not being fully in control of oneself, the depth of the patient's mortification is unjustified and in fact part of the disease. Many of the patients who contact me make it clear that my openness about depression has helped them feel that I won't look down on them.

We must remain acutely sensitive to our patient's experiences of shame in the treatment. Not only are such experiences almost inevitable, how we handle them is also critical. If we try to pretend that nothing happened, looking away, the natural reaction to shame, we only reinforce the patient's idea that he is inherently shameful. If, on the other hand, we can quickly respond, we bring real feelings into the consulting room.

Sally had been widowed approximately five years before, leaving her with two young children. She became depressed and sought treatment after breaking off with a man whom she felt was taking advantage of her. She felt that she had let herself be treated like a doormat, and feared that she would never be able to be appropriately assertive. She had a difficult family history, with a highly narcissistic mother and a distant father.

In an early session Sally mentioned that she was getting a large payment from her husband's insurance company, and that she was going to use it to buy property. She then went on to talk about early life experiences with her mother and father. I thought this material was an intellectualized digression from more pressing matters; I also thought about the coming week between sessions and Sally's seemingly quick decision to buy a house, and my own admonitions about preventing the patient from making hasty decisions in the midst of a depression. I said, "Wait, something is troubling me. Are you certain you want to buy property? You may be able to invest that money and have an income that you can rely on. Have you talked to any financial advisors?"

This enraged Sally. She talked about how she had felt belittled and pitied by bankers and attorneys—all men—at the time of her husband's death; moreover, the advice she had taken was uniformly bad and her finances had worsened. She reminded me that she had been a bank officer before her marriage. I quickly apologized, and pointed out how I had fallen into the trap of pitying her and treating her as an incompetent, just as so many other men in her life had done. She said, "Thank you for acknowledging that," with a huge smile of relief. This subject— what she called the "pity trap"—became a focus for treatment: the pull she felt between her own real accomplishments and her deep belief that she was indeed good for nothing except to reflect glory on her mother; and that since her widowhood, the "pity trap" was an attractive, though ultimately destructive, adaptation, for by engaging people's pity she got to have some aspects of a real relationship without engaging her real self.

Just as lecturing the patient can be a defense against our own embarrassment, sometimes we do it out of embarrassment for the patient's shame. Sometimes we can see that something has come up that is acutely shameful for the patient, and we feel we can cover it over by distracting both of us with words, typically a long disquisition to the effect of "you needn't feel ashamed, everyone does that." Although very often the information we feel such a need to impart *can* be helpful to the patient, it's important not to let the shame go unacknowledged and unexplored. Colluding with the patient to intellectualize away his feelings of shame is not nearly as helpful as letting him know you're aware of his embarrassment, you care about him, and you want to help him with it.

Psychosomatic Depression

There is a special population of patients who express their depression somatically— through stress-related conditions and other "new diseases" which are resistant to conventional medicine. These conditions (explored in more depth in chapter 12) include fibromyalgia, chronic fatigue syndrome, intractable pain, and certain other conditions like multiple chemical sensitivity and irritable bowel syndrome. They all share one thing that shows the link with depression: the element of reproach.

The sufferer is in pain or distress, and no one is able to help. The implication is that no one is trying hard enough. When the cause of pain is obvious—cancer, surgery, injury—we provide analgesics and make the patient as comfortable as possible and no one feels guilty. But when the cause is obscure, there is a burden on others not to rest until we nail it down, so that we can be sure we are doing all we can for the patient.

I find that many of these patients are also by nature rather reproachful. They feel they are working harder and sacrificing more than anyone else, and they find little ways of reminding others in their life about that. But the tone is always long-suffering, never directly angry. If the therapist makes a small mistake—forgetting to make a phone call on behalf of the patient—he's put into a position of feeling embarrassed and ashamed. This is an important clue, because shame is what these patients feel. Their veneer of moral superiority is really quite thin; underneath there is always a history of being made to feel unwanted, unloved, and unlovable. Controlling others is a way of staying safe.

When people continually make us feel guilty and inadequate, eventually we get mad at them. In television comedies, an irritating stock character is the person who controls others through multiple chemical sensitivities; Molière wrote a scathing comedy about a hypochondriac. In the workplace, we roll our eyes behind the back of the complainer.

A similar dynamic goes on with the patient who acts out self-destructively, through smoking, drug or alcohol abuse, risky sex, or excessive risk taking, and blithely declares that he can't help himself. The therapist and people who love the patient are made to feel powerless.

The task for the therapist is to help these patients feel cared about. We have to challenge the patient's destructive beliefs—that he is permanently damaged and any exercise will make things worse; that he has an allergy to the world and must control it rather than strengthen his resistances—and at the same time let him know that we take his symptoms seriously. The pain or sensitivity is a vast metaphor, another statement of the focal problem, of feeling unfairly injured by life; but like any other skill of depression, the symptom makes it impossible to solve the problem. In fact, the symptom guarantees that the patient will continue to feel victimized.

We need to look at the triangle: first episode, presenting complaint, transference problem. The transference problem is that the therapist is likely to want to reject the patient just like everyone else does. We must get the patient back to talking about the first episode, the primary loss, the events that gave him the belief he was permanently disabled. We may be able to engage the patient's sadness, sense of loss, and vulnerability around these issues more effectively than we can about how he's discriminated against in the present. Having thus convinced the patient that we understand his pain, we may be able then to engage him in the kind of habits that will ease his pain: more exercise; physical therapy and massage; graduated exposure to the feared stimuli; less hyperfocus on somatic sensations and more attention to emotions and pleasures.

We may be able to help the patient complete his unfinished grief work without ever mentioning the word "depression." Since so many of these patients are acutely sensitive about being told the disease is all their minds, we may never want to confront the problem. Instead, psychotherapy and medication can be presented as supportive mechanisms to help the patient cope more effectively with his condition. The word "stress" seems to have an almost magical ability to smooth over much of the resistance that patients may feel about having to consult a psychotherapist for what they insist is a physical condition. "Stress" seems to be an intuitive concept that we use to bridge mind-body problems. *You have the stress of your disease, and you have the stress of your alcoholic husband and a very difficult boss. No wonder you can't sleep and worry all the time. Let's see if there are some things you can do to help yourself feel a little better.*

Anger, Irritability, and Bearishness

Among the many faces that depression wears, one of the least recognized is irritability. People who continually strike out against those close to them, who blow up over little things, whose looks quite literally could kill, who project contempt and disdain for those around them, who are intolerant of mistakes—among other things may be depressed. The individual is likely to feel overburdened, struggling alone against Herculean tasks, unable to rely on others because they're such fools. Depressed men frequently become like a bear who can't get to sleep— retreating into the den, desperate to be left alone but never feeling refreshed, growling and swatting at anything that comes within reach. Depressed women in a similar state remind me more of cranky cats, but the interpersonal effect is the same: People who are able to keep a wide berth avoid the individual, while loved ones suffer and the depression continues. Projection is the principal defense: it is not I, but everyone else, who is overwhelmed by life.

When people like this come to therapy they are predictably reluctant and skeptical. They are likely to be unimpressed by a therapist who merely makes sympathetic noises, as they feel that the last thing they want is sympathy (of course, they want it very much, but it must be on certain terms). They often come in because of an external crisis. Their spouse has served notice of divorce, their teenager has run away from home; and of course they feel betrayed by the rejection, because they've only been doing their best.

It's important that the therapist actively give direction at this point, because the efforts that the patient is likely to try to rectify the crisis will only make it worse: to dismiss the wife's complaints as silliness, to order the teenager to return home. I find that an explanation of cyclical psychodynamics can be very helpful at this point; it respects the patient's defenses but clarifies the self-destructive pattern of his behavior: *You have a great deal on your plate and I recognize that you have only been doing the best you know how with your family (job, boss, health). But when things are getting to you, you only try to control them more. You're doing what you think is helpful but the people around you resent it because they don't feel you're respecting them. You're going to have to learn how to back off, disengage, not be provoked, and try to figure out what they want from you — not what you think they need but what they want.*

If we're successful in stopping the patient's destructive behavior at this point and he can learn better listening skills and self-control, the crisis may resolve itself and that may be the extent of our involvement. But many people like this have been too damaged by their underlying depression to be able to stop the pattern of control and anger. The therapeutic task then becomes to focus on the present and chronically endured pain (see chapter 9) — the old loss, the recent injury, and the defense against change. I find that patients like this appreciate direct questions. *You love your wife, but you drive her away. In fact, you've made yourself very isolated from almost everyone. Why are you so afraid of depending on others? Were you abused, neglected, abandoned?*

A straightforward interpretation of the defensive function of anger is also necessary: *It's easier to be angry than sad. Anger makes us feel powerful, and sadness makes us feel weak. But when we're hurt we feel both, and we have to recognize both. And if we're only angry, we only drive others away.*

Anxiety

Most patients with depression experience a significant amount of anxiety as well. Research estimates of anxiety disorder co-occurring with major depression range from 50 to 70 percent, and comorbidity is a negative prognostic indicator for both conditions. In depression, anxiety is usually experienced as the fear of loss of emotional control. The patient fears he is losing his mind, that he will collapse or have a fit in public, will hurt himself or someone else, will be dragged away by the men in white coats.[*]

Anxiety is an intimately visceral experience, the flight component of the flight or fight adrenaline rush. Our stomachs knot, hearts pound, hands sweat, intestines churn. We feel dizzy, can't catch our breath, develop tunnel vision, become acutely sensitive to sound. Primitive states like this easily become conditioned responses to any stimulus that is associated with the feeling. Diane went back to her hometown dentist two years after her last appointment, which was in the middle of a course of ECT. On walking into the office, she was immediately overwhelmed with the sense of muddle and confusion she had experienced then, even the burnt-sugar taste in her mouth that had been part of her experience. She had to sit down and catch her breath. I, having eaten lunch at my desk for 12 years, one block from the volunteer firehouse where they test the siren each

---

[*] I find it remarkable how the fear of the mental hospital as the snake pit from which there is no escape has endured despite the revolution of managed care, which has meant in effect that no patient is detained one second longer than necessary. It is a powerful myth, which speaks of the fragility of our sense of control.

day at noon, now salivate like one of Pavlov's dogs whenever I hear the fire siren. This kind of conditioning, especially that of the anxiety response, doesn't go away because we understand that our fear is illogical. It goes away when we reexperience the stimulus without the response, and that takes practice.

It's naïve for the practitioner to focus on the depression, the past loss, and expect that anxiety symptoms will fall away once the depression is healed. Anxiety symptoms develop just as strong a functional autonomy as depression. The therapist must be prepared to practice proven cognitive-behavioral techniques for managing anxiety, and should be open to considering medication as part of the intervention. Although anxiolytic medication may increase feelings of depression in some patients, this effect is likely to be more than offset in other circumstances. For the acutely distressed patient, to go on a tranquilizer for a month while the therapist and patient work to alleviate the stress is just common sense. For the phobic patient, to be encouraged to confront the phobic situation with the assistance of a mild tranquilizer or a beta blocker may be an enormously helpful intervention.

The patient should be encouraged to view anxiety, like depression, as something that is happening to him, a familiar "disease" that has a predictable course, rather than as a sign that he is falling apart. And, as with depression, there are things the patient can do to help himself: relaxation exercises, meditation, cognitive restructuring, fitness training, stimulus control. The therapist should be active in prescribing any intervention that will lower the patient's experience of distress.

Anxiety, of course, is also a defense against feeling. The patient is so focused on his inner subjective state that he doesn't attend to moment-to-moment feelings of sadness, anger, hurt, or pleasure. While the therapist must engage the patient's emotions for treatment to work, interpreting the defensive function of anxiety doesn't do any good while the patient is caught up in it. Better to provide relief.

"Stuck Listening to Whining"—
Passive Aggression in the Consulting Room

Many depressed patients feel a kind of self-righteous anger that overshadows all other emotions. It can seem like anger, bitterness, and self-pity are all that's left in the patient's pantry, and the therapist can come to dread the patient's visits. It's important to keep in mind that this kind of anger is a defense against other feelings that are even worse. The patient's rejection of the therapist's help, the angry attitude that "no one can help me," can be understood as defiance and revenge against previous abandonments, much as children sometimes increase their acting out when a depressed parent is recovering: *You're ready to be a parent now but where were you when I needed you? You have to pay for abandoning me!*

For many patients, especially but not necessarily men, it is difficult to let the therapist's empathic expressions penetrate beyond the barrier of denial and anger that they live behind. Insofar as this is an effect of the shame the patient feels at being in a dependent relationship, the collegial atmosphere between patient and therapist, the notion of therapy as a difficult task we share, can help lower this barrier somewhat. But often this pattern is a manifestation of a lifelong habit of rejecting support because accepting even a little bit threatens to open the floodgates, to overwhelm the patient with the need and rage he has kept bottled up for so long. It is vital that the patient understand that his pattern of rejecting support contributes to the trouble he is in. The therapist can easily fall into the trap of accusatory, condescending statements: *Have you noticed how when I try to get you to talk about this painful area, you change the subject?* It is more useful just to comment on the patient's discomfort — *Talking about this is difficult for you* — and to explore what the patient understands of the discomfort.

When we get to thinking that a patient is "playing games" with us, deliberately not moving, not listening, rejecting everything we have to say, we need to remember that passive aggression is a reasonably normal response when an individual with little authority is feeling picked on by someone with more authority. Perhaps the patient is seeing the therapist as an authority figure, and perhaps the therapist is acting like one? Perhaps we are not in agreement about the goals or methods of treatment, and the patient feels we are trying to stuff our own agenda down his throat? If so, we can hardly blame the patient for telling us where we can stuff our agenda.

Often, depressed patients who are making us feel stuck and ineffectual are treating us the way they were treated as children. We can feel dehumanized, much as they might have experienced little or no emotional engagement in childhood; we can feel helpless, as they were made to feel that their initiative was irrelevant to the course of events in their lives. We can feel scorned and emotionally abused, as they themselves were made to feel growing up with narcissistic or erratic parents. We can feel not trusted. In all these situations, getting underneath our anger and sharing with the patient our understanding that the process in the consulting room is much like his experience as a child can be a first step in breaking the pattern. *You know, it seems to be a pattern between us that when I make a suggestion for you, you never really find it helpful. And when I note my own reactions to the pattern, I find myself feeling a little helpless and ineffectual. I wonder if you are trying to show me just a little bit of how you felt as a child when so often your parents just brushed you off or dismissed you and left you feeling that your concerns were of no importance.*

It's not always necessary to know where to direct the treatment. It can be enough to say that the way it's going is not helpful, to say to the patient *I want to help, but this is not going anywhere,* to put some of the burden back on the patient. The patient may be hurt or angry, and is likely to be confused, because after all he's only been acting the only way he knows how. So it's important to convey interest and concern, at the same time as refusing to be a masochistic receptacle for the patient. Allowing the patient to continue "acting out" the depression in this way just reinforces the patient's view of himself as hopeless.

The archetypal passive-aggressive technique, of course, is to follow orders so thoroughly and by the book that the intent of the order is sabotaged and the authority is made to feel stupid for having given the order in the first place. The patient can act out this pattern with the therapist, particularly around therapeutic homework. This is a problem that doesn't seem to happen often with me, although people at my conferences complain about it a lot, and I think that part of the reason is that there is always a spirit of play at work when I'm assigning homework. I rarely, if ever, think that the homework is going to solve a major problem for the patient; instead, I tend to think that whatever the results are, they are going to be interesting. If the patient forgets about the assignment totally, of course that's going to be very interesting; if the results are good, that's great; if the results are mixed or bad (and I try never to suggest anything as homework where the actual outcome will have a significant impact on the client's life), that is also very useful data. Very often the patient and I have differing memories about just what the assignment was—but I usually keep silent about that, because I assume that the patient had good reasons for distorting the assignment.

A little playfulness also goes a long way toward disarming passive aggression. The comedian David Steinberg had among his characters a psychiatrist who would tell his patients with great glee "Everything counts!"—the normal rules of polite conversation don't apply in the consulting room—*If you look away, perspire, change the subject, or mumble, I get to talk about it.* Sometimes I use Steinberg's caricature as a way of explaining the rules of psychotherapy to patients who seem stubbornly unwilling to examine their own experience.

It seems to me that much of what passes for the patient's passive aggression with the therapist is an iatrogenic effect of the therapist's way of conducting business. If we start with the assumption that our role is to discover the patient's secrets, to catch every little bit of acting out and nip it in the bud—or if we assume that everything the patient does that doesn't conform to our idea of how therapy should work is automatically resistance—we are infantilizing the patient, and we only have ourselves to blame if he lives up to our self-fulfilling prophecies and behaves childishly. On the other hand, if we assume that our role is to help someone in conflict with himself, that defensiveness or acting out only get manifested when we are making the patient insecure, that part of our job is to teach the patient what's expected of him, I generally find that people rise to the level of our expectations. They are less likely to miss sessions or payments, get stuck in treatment and expect me to do the work, or drop out and make us both feel like failures. It's easy for us to get angry, critical, cynical about the patient who doesn't move; the point to remember is that depression, not the patient, is the enemy.

Michael Yapko (1997b) has a harsh but effective lesson for therapists who attend his conferences: He asks them to think about a problem they have struggled with for a long time, something that is painful and deeply personal; to think about all the time, effort, and money they've put into trying to fix the problem, all the times when hopes were raised only to be disappointed; to reflect on the shame and guilt they've felt over the years about their problem, their feelings of inadequacy and hopelessness that it never gets resolved. Then he tells them: "If you *really* wanted to get over it, you would have by now." Of course, we would never say that to a patient, but many of us believe it at one time or another. Imagine the patient's mortification if he knew our thoughts. But I suggest that on some unconscious level he does know; he knows that we are blaming him just as he is blaming himself. We should try very hard not to do that.

In the end I find it helpful, when my patience and empathy are being severely taxed, to focus on the patient's "inner bereaved child," in Raphael's (1983) poignant phrase, to remind myself that this adult before me feels at the moment like the frightened or abandoned child he once was.

It was difficult at times to maintain my empathic connection with Cynthia, an elderly woman who tended to perseverate on regrets. Sometimes all she could talk about was how much she missed the little house she had left behind to move in with her son. She obsessively worried about whether she had made the right decision.

Cynthia's son had contacted me hoping I could pull a rabbit out of a hat for him. Cynthia had already been to the best psychopharmacologists in New York, and medication helped some, but not enough. Her continued worry, sad affect, and anhedonia was driving everyone in the house crazy. He didn't give me much history, though he did make an arch comment about mental illness "back in the family somewhere." But Cynthia herself had had no previous treatment.

After Cynthia and I had talked for a few sessions I could feel myself having some of the same feelings as her family, tired of the repetition and the automatic rejection of any help. I switched gears and asked her to tell me about herself, and as we sat in her wealthy son's sunny garden I heard stories of horror and tragedy I'd never suspected. When Cynthia was 6, her mother killed herself and Cynthia's little brother while Cynthia banged on the door trying to get in. After a time, her father took in an immigrant housekeeper who became Cynthia's surrogate mother, but she became mentally ill when Cynthia was a teen and died in a state hospital years later—Cynthia faithfully visited her every month. Father remarried, and Cynthia and the stepmother hated each other. When the war came along, Cynthia jumped at the chance to work in a defense plant and leave home—she met her husband, got married, had children, and never complained.

I never lost patience with her again.

In attempting to engage people with depression in psychotherapy, it's vital to keep in mind that the depression itself is a resistance to engagement. Depression is an effort not to feel. Having integrated the message that certain aspects of ourselves are unacceptable, we try hard to keep those thoughts, feelings, wishes, and experiences out of awareness. Therapy feels unnatural and frightening to the patient, so we must create an atmosphere of safety. But if we play it too safe, nothing happens, and the therapist becomes another part of the patient's stable dysfunctional interpersonal world. We need to help the patient begin to reexperience his emotional life in this safe setting. By helping the patient begin to name his feelings and understand his experience, we provide both hope and absolution, a promise of a way out of depression.

CHAPTER 6

Grief, Entitlement, Rage, and Hope

ALTHOUGH THE INDIVIDUAL with depression tries not to feel normal emotions, he often feels in the grip of powerful emotional forces over which he has no control. He finds himself sometimes exactly like someone who has just lost a loved one—crying for no apparent reason, unable to be comforted, unable *not* to think about the pain, loneliness, or deprivation. At the same time that he recognizes that this state is self-destructive and perhaps out of proportion to the real situation he's in, he will often fiercely deny that recognition, pretending that no one is more entitled to be depressed than he is. Feeling himself diminished and dependent on others for a good feeling about the self, he becomes acutely sensitive to slights and rebuffs. In general, the sexes respond differently to these injuries: Men retaliate on the injuring party, raising the stakes and sometimes turning to violence, while women more often internalize the injury, making it part of themselves. For men, there is a separate vicious circle of shame that is put in motion when depression lasts for any length of time. They feel vulnerable, then ashamed of being vulnerable, then ashamed of their shame, so eventually they turn to rage to feel whole again.

Some methods of treatment of depression have had the unfortunate effect of inducing shame, then blaming the patient for acting out or not getting better. Psychoanalysis has been such a dominant force in how we understand ourselves that it pervades our thinking in ways we have a hard time being aware of—not only as professionals, but also as members of a society whose basic assumptions about the human mind have been dramatically altered by Freud and his followers. The effects come sometimes not so much from what Freud said but what we think he said. In the case of depression, some real damage was done, I feel, by a psychoanalytic view of the disease that has the effect of reinforcing the patient's shame about being depressed. Progress in understanding the condition has been delayed by an effort to shoehorn observations to fit a theory that has become outdated and rickety. At the same time, the highly developed observational skills of the analytic method and the middle-level theoretical abstractions of defense, resistance, adaptation, and ego development have made essential contributions to understanding both depression and how individual psychotherapy works. A deeper understanding of the nature of shame, in particular, has greatly increased both our ability to appreciate the nature of depression and the patient's inherent difficulty accepting help and our difficulty offering the patient what he needs.

EARLY PSYCHODYNAMICS:
DEPRESSION *IS* SHAMEFUL

Karl Abraham (1911/1979), an early member of Freud's inner circle, wrote the first paper in the psychoanalytic movement that dealt directly with depression. At that time all neurosis was thought to be caused by repressed libido. Abraham counterpoised depression with anxiety: Anxiety was thought to be the result of repression, which prevented the attainment of desired gratification when gratification was still possible; depression resulted when the individual had given up hope of attaining gratification. Abraham found among his depressed patients a deep ambivalence toward others, in which a wish for love is blocked by strong feelings of hate, which in turn are repressed because the individual cannot acknowledge them. The repressed hatred is then projected and turned on the self: "I do not hate others; they hate *me*." Thus the individual cannot progress in relationships, and thus the depressive's overinvolvement with the self, sometimes to the extent of taking pleasure in suffering. The theme of hatred for a lost or renounced object, turned and projected onto the self, continues to reverberate in analytic thinking to the present day.

Freud's short paper "Mourning and Melancholia" (1917) not only set the stage for how we still think about depression, it was also the beginning of his mature work, the first time he branched out from his assumption that all psychological distress was simply caused by blocked libido. He noted the similarities between mourning and depression—sadness, anhedonia, lethargy, preoccupation with the self—and some critical differences. Only in melancholia is there loss of self-esteem and guilt or expectation of punishment. Also, because people in depression are unable to state clearly the nature of what they have lost, Freud concluded that the loss is internal and unconscious: "In grief, the world has become poor and empty; in melancholia it is the ego itself" (p. 249).

In this pre–structural theory paper, Freud speculates that the ego has split, with one part (which he refers to as the conscience here) setting itself up to judge the other as an external object. The remainder of the ego, he feels, has identified with the lost object; the castigation of the self in depression is actually castigation of the ambivalently experienced and lost object.

Freud (1917) postulated that the propensity for melancholia is laid down in childhood, in a traumatic disappointment with a loved person which resulted in a withdrawal of libido from others into the self; but this libido remained attached to a representation of the other which was incorporated into the ego. "Thus the shadow of the object fell upon the ego, so that the latter could henceforth be criticized by a special mental faculty like an object, like the forsaken object" (p. 251). Later losses reactivate the primary loss and cause the patient's rage and disappointment to be directed at the incorporated object within the self—through self-defeating or self-destructive behavior and, in extreme cases, through suicide. But for most melancholics an episode of self-reproach is sufficient to vent the rage, and the patient returns to previous functioning until another loss precipitates another episode.

Although beautiful poetry, this formulation has been difficult to apply clinically. Getting the patient to express his rage directly rather than against the self hasn't been particularly effective in relieving depression. The idea of the ego introject has been pursued by the Kleinians, with more orthodox Freudians tending to see depression as the result of the actual self falling short of the ego ideal. Nevertheless, the essential idea of the perception of oneself as inferior or deflated, and the object being overly idealized, with the groundwork for this situation laid in a traumatic experience of loss or threat of loss in childhood, and a resultant dependency in adult relationships, still has much appeal.

Sandor Rado was instrumental in further developing the psychoanalytic understanding of depression. In his influential paper "The Problem of Melancholia" (1928/1994), Rado described what he observed of depressives' interpersonal relations: "As soon as they are sure of the affection or devotion of another person . . . their behavior undergoes a complete change. They accept the devoted love of the beloved person with a sublime nonchalance, as a matter of course, and become more and more domineering and autocratic, displaying an increasingly unbridled egoism, until their attitude becomes one of full-blown tyranny" (p. 74). This pattern would go on until the other person finally would reject the patient, precipitating a depressive episode. Rado felt that, although he bullies and tests the love object, the depressive desperately needs the other's constant nurturance. He needs to be showered with love and admiration and will not tolerate frustration of this need. "[The depressive] will push the test of love to the limits of tolerance in any relationship during periods of security and relative health. During periods of depression which occur after the object have (sic) been driven away, the individual resorts to a different method of coercion. He becomes remorseful and contrite, begging for forgiveness, and hopes to regain the lost object through inducing pity and guilt" (Arieti & Bemporad, 1978, p. 25). Rado traces this pattern back to infancy, when the child learned that he could regain the connection to his mother by atonement and remorse. Rado explicates the notion of the "bad object," the individual's internalized representation of the hated and frustrating side of the parent (and hence the individual himself), while the "good object" becomes introjected into the superego. The bad object becomes the "whipping boy" of the superego.

Rado had the reputation of a compassionate and caring therapist—despite his emphasis on the depressive's supposed narcissism it was he who recognized depression as "a great despairing cry for love"—and it is unfortunate that some of his more extreme positions became incorporated into psychoanalytic orthodoxy without the tempering effect of his personality. Thus Fenichel (1945) spoke of depressives as love addicts who care little about the actual person who is the source of love, and the stereotype of the depressive as narcissist gained acceptance. Klein (1940) and Jacobson (1971) took theoretical refinement and elaboration to extremes in ways that in the end turned into rather Procrustean beds for treatment of depression.

In all these analytic formulations except that of Freud and to a lesser extent of Rado, one gets a sense that the authors find depression slightly distasteful and their depressed patients rather unlikable. There is a strong element of condescension; depressives are willful children who have to grow up and accept the reality principle. In refreshing contrast, Bibring (1953) humanized his patients, whom he understood to have developed depression after difficult life events. He defined depression much more empirically, as the emotional indication of a state of helplessness and powerlessness of the ego, irrespective of what may have caused the breakdown of the mechanisms that established self-esteem. Central to Bibring's formulation is the perception of helplessness in the face of superior force, and the tension between what the self aspires to and what it seems can actually be attained. Putting depression in the ego, as Bibring did, immediately obviated a lot of psychoanalytic hairsplitting that had been going on between "normal," "neurotic," and "psychotic" depression. Most important, it shifted the focus from the patient's intrapsychic world to his interaction with the real world. Aggression from the superego to the ego was relegated to the role of a complicating factor. The problem became the ego's inability to maintain a positive self-representation (self-esteem) in the light of negative experience.

Still more tolerant understanding of depression came from Bowlby (1980) and Winnicott (1965). By substituting the word "attachment" for "dependence" Bowlby removed much of the disdain from the field of object relations. Attachment implies a mature, volitional relationship, one that (anticipating Kohut) provides a secure base (the "holding environment") necessary for confidence and action. Attachment relationships are reciprocal; dependent relationships, one-way. Winnicott viewed the self not as a mechanism for channeling drives but as a being with unique innate qualities that develop only through relationships with others; there is a push for development of the self, not for expression of drives (Rubin, 1997). Depression came about through lost potential; there was a lack, a deficit, which therapy could repair, not a conflict to be resolved. The basic technique was to hold, not to interpret.

But Bowlby and Winnicott, lionized now, were voices in the wilderness in the 1960s and '70s. A few respected writers such as Arieti and Bemporad (1978) advocated much of what we would find appealing today: a strong emphasis on the therapeutic alliance, no regression, the patient as agent to solve his own problems with the therapist as guide and support, an understanding that much of depression's pain comes from the patient's falling short of his own realistic expectation of himself, an openness to medication as part of the treatment. On the other hand there were many writers who were reduced to investigating the phenomenon of the "negative therapeutic reaction"—the worsening of symptoms in response to the "correct" interpretation—which was clearly assumed to be the patient's, not the therapist's, fault. Even Basch (1975), a warm and compassionate therapist, was writing about the depressive's "immature level of narcissistic development that is dominated by some form of an infantile sense of entitlement" (p. 529). As Luhrmann (2000) points out, the problem with psychoanalytic theory was that, since it could never be disproved, when the patient didn't get better it couldn't be that the theory was wrong. Either the therapist or the patient was to blame. When a depressed patient didn't improve through analytic treatment, it was easy to blame him.

Self Psychology

Heinz Kohut's writings, and the development of self psychology as a "school" within classical analysis, constituted a revolution within the psychoanalytic movement (Kohut, 1971, 1977, 1984; see also Deitz, 1991; Goldberg, 1998). Kohut started with the problem of the narcissistic patient, who was thought to be unanalyzable because he would fly into a rage when the analyst did not support his grandiosity or idealization of the therapist. Instead of viewing the patient's expression of anger or rage toward the therapist as an inevitable, desirable result of the collapse of a childish transference which the patient simply had to get over, Kohut proposed to work with the transference and to view the patient's rage or disappointment as a result of an empathic failure. In fact, Kohut in his later work more or less dismissed the whole drive theory of psychoanalysis and came to believe that rage, far from being the inevitable manifestation of a drive to kill or win, was instead a byproduct of intense disappointment. Kohut argued that our relationships—with other people, with roles such as work or school, with institutions like the church or the nation—constitute selfobjects that are necessary to sustain a positive self-regard; that primitive selfobject relationships can be dependent or narcissistic but that there is a line of development between these relationships and the self that leads to mature, reciprocal, relationships; and that most disorders of the self are the result of a failure in this line of development due to traumatic disappointment or absence of necessary selfobjects in childhood.

Disappointment or rage at the therapist, then, was seen as a reenactment of trauma; recovery came from a sustained selfobject relationship that would inevitably lead to growth through a gradual, guided confrontation with the reality principle. The goal of analysis was not the attainment of autonomy but the acceptance of interdependence.

One of the great technical problems with the classical analytic stance toward treatment of depression had its origins in the idea that depression is the result of rage, originally directed at the lost and ambivalently loved object, now redirected from the superego to the ego itself. From this point of view, the patient's development of an idealizing transference, with its manifestations typical of depressed relationships—dependency, passivity, rejection sensitivity, passive aggression—was seen as a defensive strategy to avoid expressing and experiencing rage. Dynamic therapy was designed to mobilize the patient's rage and encourage its expression. Depressed patients sometimes did not understand what was being expected of them and experienced the therapist/analyst as provocative or sadistic. When they expressed anger or frustration over lack of progress in treatment or over their analyst's behavior, this would be seen by the analyst as an indication that treatment was going well and be interpreted to the patient as a manifestation of a transference reaction based on rage at the lost love object (Deitz, 1989). To the objective observer, this might seem to be a rage-inducing response; but the patient's anger was seen as a further sign of progress by the analyst, and led to long, bitter, humiliating treatment for some analytic patients.

In contrast, the self psychologist was expected to use empathic communication to convey acceptance of the patient's sense of deprivation and entitlement, establishing a sustained selfobject transference.* The patient feels held and supported, and experiences a nondepressed state of energy, confidence, and optimism. The goal of treatment is for the patient to internalize those positive states of the selfobject transference gradually. This comes about through a process of "optimal frustration"—when the patient gradually realizes that the therapist is not perfect or all-powerful—and "optimal responsiveness." Inevitable empathic disruptions are worked through in the context of a trusting relationship. Through a process of "transmuting internalization" the patient is enabled to "draw more successfully on internal functions that previously could only be provided externally. More cohesive, flexible, vital, and enduringly self-regulating structures emerge from the process" (Donner, 1985, p. 53).

In self psychology, depression is understood as a manifestation of a "depleted self," a defensive adaptation to a failure to achieve a healthy idealized relationship with a parent which would enable the child to feel safe and powerful. The child who is disappointed or frustrated in these age-appropriate needs grows up lacking internal standards and means of self-soothing:

> In general, the depleted self represents a response to the absence of the sought after, omnipotent, idealized selfobject and accompanying internalized ideals, with consequent empty depression.
> Kohut connected the primary structural defect in the nuclear self to genetic failure of the mother as a selfobject to mirror the child's healthy, age-appropriate ex-

---

* Empathy is much more than just a technique of communication, and much has been written about just what empathy is and what it can do (cf. Berger, 1987; Kohut, 1984). Regardless of one's point of view, it should be emphasized that conveying empathy for a patient who seems relentlessly self-pitying and help-rejecting does not come naturally to most people, and requires a real immersion in the patient's world.

hibitionism. Defects in the self's compensatory structures, on the other hand, frequently reflect failure of the father as selfobject to respond to the child's needs for idealizations. . . . Depletion, I suggest, reflects most prominently failures in compensatory structures of a self in the process of attaining tenuous cohesion, seeking to make up for its enfeeblement through merger with an idealized selfobject. . . . The absence of ideals and goals as a result of failure of compensatory structures is, then, a major source of self-depletion.

From the perspective of self psychology, the process of psychoanalytic treatment involves either repair of the self's nuclear defect through repeated transmuting internalizations (utilizing connection with the mostly empathic analyst as a responsive selfobject) or through modification of compensatory structures by establishing more flexible and realistic ambitions, goals, and ideals. Modification of grandiose ambitions and/or the ideal of perfection may eventuate through identification with the accepting empathic selfobject/analyst, with important consequences for the palliation of shame. (Morrison, 1989, pp. 73–74)

Treatment for an enfeebled self, from the standpoint of self psychology, is a sustained selfobject relationship with an empathic therapist. But from the standpoint of treatment of depression, while it may be true that a sustained selfobject transference is an effective treatment, it is time-consuming, expensive, and neither necessary nor feasible for most people. And, in my experience, most depressed patients mobilize an active defense against the process by rejecting or avoiding or having contempt for the empathic therapist/selfobject. That's what makes depressed people so difficult to love. At the same time, *when* the patient needs an empathic selfobject, the therapist needs to be ready to meet his needs, or else more traumatic disappointment may be the result.

Constructivism and Intersubjectivity

Psychoanalysis has endured not one but two paradigm shifts in recent years (Rubin, 1997). Kohut and the self psychologists moved human motivation from a drive-reduction to a relational basis. The other shift, more difficult to summarize, has been away from a positivistic outlook that defined the analyst's role as the uncovering of objective truth, to a constructivist position that emphasizes the analytic relationship as co-creating a new reality for the patient, with both the therapist and the analyst contributing elements that are helpful and elements that are detrimental to healing (Gill, 1994; Hoffman, 1998; Mitchell, 1993). Even more broadly, there has been a postmodern reassessment which takes into account the fact that concepts like health and recovery are socially constructed.

Constructivism, in Gill's words, is "the proposition that all human perception and thinking is a construction rather than a direct reflection of current reality as such" (1994, p. 1). An "objectivist" view of the therapeutic situation assumes that it is possible for the therapist to know exactly what it is about the patient that needs to be changed. A "constructivist" view suggests that it is difficult to separate neurotic anxiety from real anxiety, that the patient often has to make choices that combine elements of both, and that the therapist is expected to help the patient make a choice without the ability to clearly differentiate between the neurotic and the healthy (Hoffman, 1998). Indeed, the therapist must acknowledge that his definition of "neurotic" and "healthy" is colored by his personal biases as well as his professional knowledge. For instance, when a patient is considering a decision to stay in or leave a relationship that is less than perfect—one of many common human dilemmas for which there is no clear right answer—the therapist's own experience with and biases about divorce are intimately involved in his thinking.

The constructivist therapist is not neutral or detached but very involved with the patient in the analysis of their communications, wishes, and expectations, which creates a relationship of a certain transparency and high emotional intensity. He assumes a much more respectful, less shame-inducing stance than the old analyst who saw his job as uncovering the patient's secrets. His position is even more respectful than the self psychologist, who still viewed himself as the expert, empathy as an objective tool. Instead, therapist and patient are in it together, trying to figure out how to go about living. Gratifying appropriate developmental needs is acceptable, but the therapist and patient struggle together to determine what is appropriate and possible given the constraints of the relationship. It is the combination of all three factors—gratification, mutual struggle, and loss (acceptance of limits)—that leads to growth. The basic problem for the therapist becomes how to use his personality, clinical biases, and moment-to-moment experiencing to co-create this changing, charged relationship, and to keep it moving in a way that leads to health (the definition of which is subject to change depending on perspective).

Reality depends on punctuation. If a depressed patient recovers with medications alone during a three-month study period, he is deemed to be a successful case. If he relapses a year later, he's still a success. But if the study period is two years, he's not a success anymore. If my elderly patient recovers from a depression resulting from his retirement, but has a heart attack and dies three years later, he's a successful case. But if he survives his heart attack only to have his wife die shortly afterwards, and he develops depression again because of that loss, perhaps he cannot be considered a success anymore. To the constructivist, health and disease are relative states, recovery is a social construct, and diagnosis is out of the question. While this removes a lot of the shame from depression and humanizes the therapist, it leaves a certain ambiguity about how to best help patients.

Contemporary analysts recognize that "throwing away the book" can lead to the most powerful interchanges in treatment (Ehrenberg, 1992; Hoffman, 1998; Mitchell, 1993). Exchanges which take place in "liminal space," which "bend the frame," which push the boundaries of the therapeutic relationship, are understood to have particular meaning to the patient—to be, in other words, potentially corrective emotional experiences. Analysts thus come around to considering interventions like giving advice, inquiring about the patient's health, expressing sympathy, assigning homework, advocating for medication, revealing aspects of their own experience—interventions which have been supported in other frames of reference but not in analytic orthodoxy. The particular power of these interventions in analysis derives from the context of abstinence which over-shadows everything, the old idea that, whatever happens, the patient's wishes are *not* to be gratified. When gratification is such a taboo, the willingness of the an-alyst to transgress is a magical gift to the patient.

Ehrenberg (1992) describes an interaction that can serve as an example of "throwing away the book." She was working with a difficult, withdrawn, distrustful patient who had had many previous negative therapeutic experiences. After much work on trust, the patient had agreed to come in three days a week. Then Ehrenberg had to cancel a session unexpectedly. The patient became enraged and refused to be comforted:

> I stated that I understood how painful this was to her, but I also emphasized how inconsiderate and punitive she was being toward me. I insisted that on the basis of our work so far, though she seemed to feel she had the "right" to now wipe the floor with me, I had at least earned the right for her to consider that my cancel-ing the session might not have been frivolous or uncaring or irresponsible. Furthermore, if she felt she couldn't give me the benefit of the doubt, and even forgive me, then I felt I had as much right to be angry at her as she had to be an-gry at me. At this point I told her that I had actually canceled to go to the funeral of a friend. (p. 71)

What a contrast from the remote, aloof analyst who can't be touched by any-thing the patient says! Yet Ehrenberg's willingness to express her anger at her pa-tient only served to strengthen and deepen the relationship, and to break through the kind of therapeutic impasse that had likely made treatment impossible in the past. In fact, one could make a case that, in this situation, it is the breaking of the therapeutic rules in itself that makes the interchange so powerful. After all, everyone, including the patient, knows that the therapist is not supposed to get angry and above all not to be guilt-inducing. But I think the little dig at the patient's expense shows that the patient has gotten under the therapist's skin — has had a real impact, not just a bought-and-paid-for professional impact, on the therapist. And that is what this patient needs, to be reassured that she is real and that this therapist will be honest with her. The patient responds, with a hint of a smile, "If you are poor and starving you can't afford to be generous."

DESPERATELY CLINGING TO DEPRESSION

> In childhood, one should have the opportunity to experience oneself as more at the center of another person's concern than is possible later, and it behooves the caregivers to indulge this need, to foster this "illusion" through an optimal de-gree of self-subordination. The individual who has been cheated out of this op-portunity, who has been, instead, more exploited than recognized as a child, of-ten cannot readily tolerate the factor of self-interest that he or she must encounter in every other person in adult life. That factor may become toxic while a sense of entitlement to an impossible, selfless love generates depressive rage at the world for offering so little of what the person feels he or she needs. (Hoffman, 1998, p. 17)

Perhaps the most difficult resistance to recovery in depression is the patient's belief that he's entitled to be depressed. Depression, which started as an adaptation to an irreparable loss, has become a mechanism of cohesion, a defense against growth. The price of accepting that depressed moods don't just come out of the blue is that the patient must accept some responsibility for his own depression. But this is a horrible admission for the depressed, who feel that depression is so unfair to begin with that to be expected to work on your own recovery is simply cruel.

Diane is a young woman in her mid-20s; she first contacted me when she was a graduate student in business. She has been hospitalized twice for depression, once in her freshman year in college and again in her senior year. Despite this, she managed to graduate cum laude from her prestigious university. Before entering graduate school, she had another major depressive episode and received a course of ECT. Before she contacted me she told the administration at school about her history and in fact registered as a "special needs" student, which gave her access to special counseling services. Diane's opportunity to vent to the counselor was very important in giving her the feeling of a sympathetic ear at school. With the counselor's support, Diane established a tutoring program for other students that was highly praised by both the students and the administration. As we worked together during the final year of her program, Diane's school performance was stellar; she received straight As, strong encouragement to continue in an academic career, and offers of graduate assistantships. But she would come to my office and cry desperately; despite all the good things happening to her, she remained depressed and desperately lonely. It was as if no amount of success was enough to reach the "dead child" inside. Indeed, she wished to be dead, for God to say, "Okay, this is enough, this is a good enough ending, you can die now."

The pattern was repeated after graduation. She took a job full of hope and promise, only to be bitterly disappointed and treated sadistically by her supervisor. This led to another major depressive episode and brief hospitalization. She bounced back from this episode more quickly than in the past, and within a few months had found a new job that she liked and where she felt appreciated. Again, however, she was back to the situation of doing well on the outside but feeling lonely, unloved, and hopeless about the prospects of change.

There is plenty of history to explain this. Diane was made to feel resented through most of her childhood and adolescence; she was often verbally abused by both parents, sometimes physically abused. Shortly after Diane's birth, her mother's mother died, and mother was hospitalized for depression. Though Diane's mother made a substantial recovery and indeed embarked on a career in which she has been very successful, she remained subject to fits of overpowering rage which were usually directed at Diane. Diane's father seemed oddly distant and almost amused at times by Diane's distress. In her teens, a school counselor reported the family to protective services because Diane had visible bruises on her body; her mother's response was to ask Diane if she thought any foster parents were going to pay for college. *Diane's older brother joined with the parents in scapegoating Diane while her younger sister was pampered and spoiled. Throughout secondary school, Diane was desperate to be liked by her peers, but usually ostracized. Her consistently outstanding grades didn't gain her popularity.*

Diane has been helped substantially by previous treatment and her own self-discipline. The self-destructive behaviors have largely stopped, and she has entered a new phase of her relationship with her parents, who seem much more accepting and patient with her; indeed, she feels at times that her mother is her closest friend. Diane is also quite sophisticated clinically. She has been told, and believes, that in addition to major depression she has a borderline personality organization. She's been in treatment since she was a teenager, and though she's had two very good relationships with therapists, she's had some disasters. She frustrates psychiatrists because she does not respond to medication. She feels that therapists abandon her and blame her for her own condition.

The circumstances of her referral are remarkable. Diane called me after having read some of Undoing Depression, *and reported a dream to me in the initial phone call: We took an X-ray of her brain, and we could see a black spot there, which was the cause of all her suffering. I told her we could take it out, but that she might die; Diane wanted the operation anyway. Her mother was there, but detached, not looking at her. Diane felt that this was a very hopeful dream, despite the evident warning.*

Now the problem we inevitably run into in the therapy is that I don't have an X-ray machine or an operating room to take out the black spot, and Diane continues to suffer. I can pat myself on the back that she is doing so well on the outside, and even give myself a little credit for helping her avoid destructive choices, but I can't reach the "dead child." I begin to wonder about the secondary gain she gets through her depression, but at the same time I feel guilty and don't want to be another therapist blaming her or dismissing her as borderline.

I ask myself what she needs from me. When I attempt to use principles of cognitive behavioral therapy with her, she is always ahead of me; she's been there and done that. She tries very hard to counter depressed thinking habits, but still she wants to die. When I suggest practical strategies to prevent and cope with loneliness, she's scornful. She clearly doesn't want to have "mere" loneliness; for all her angst and pain to be cured by making friends or falling in love would be a supreme anticlimax.

Her frustrating me, making me feel powerless to help her, could be seen as passive-aggressive acting out. But it's more useful to Diane for me to acknowledge her fear, the horrible emptiness she feels when she feels alone, which she has reified as "the depression."

There is plenty of support from the psychodynamic school that what she really needs is a holding relationship, optimal disappointment, that will allow her eventually to take in the caring and respectful side of the therapist so that eventually she will feel better. After all, she has already made substantial progress, and there is no reason to expect that she won't continue unless I fumble badly or life deals her a bad hand. And from an existential point of view, all I really have to give her is my support as she copes with her terror which, after all, has much basis in reality. I feel a strong sense of identification with the idea that she suffers from "depressive realism"—a better than normal sense that life is fragile and that meaning is hard to find. But at the same time there is a resistance here that we need to work through. In Diane's mind, her depression is her self, and if we remove it, she will no longer exist.

We often think of depression as an adaptation to bad news, an attempt to compromise with the reality principle. Having lost the ambivalently loved object, we introject both the good and bad feelings and end up unable to love ourselves without hating ourselves at the same time. In other words, depressed. But the depression, painful as it is, is an adaptation to loss, one that presumably protects us from the full consciousness of our abandonment, guilt, and rage.

But for some patients, the depression itself takes on selfobject functions. It is an identity that holds the self together, a familiar and safe role. Reluctance to give it up is not about secondary gain, but about an attempt to prevent another loss, this time a loss of the depressed self, the old friend, Churchill's pet black dog. Such patients can be restored to functioning with the help of a sustaining therapeutic relationship, but leaving the depression behind will take patience and energy from both the therapist and patient. We have to find a way to wrestle with the patient without reinjuring him, help him build strength by using our strength. We have to recognize that among the patient's skills of depression will be efforts to make us blame him, reject him, reenact the trauma that set depression in motion in the first place. And though we want an intense affective engagement with the patient, we don't want treatment to become solely focused on our interchange—so we talk about medication, support, self-care, relationships with others, because these can be equally effective ways of helping the patient.

RESISTANCE AND THE
THERAPEUTIC FOCUS

Let us assume that the patient's particular pattern of skills of depression will be manifested in the central issue and in the transference. The patient's self-defeating habits are already interfering with recovery; they will continue to interfere as the therapy challenges defenses and suggests new patterns of functioning. In short, whatever "resistance" the patient shows is a repetition of his characteristic means of functioning; and having it occur in the treatment room gives the therapist a great opportunity to help the patient do something about it. But with depression, we address resistance in a particularly careful way.

If the patient comes to treatment armed with his defenses, our goal is to disarm him, not defeat him. Psychotherapy is not an adversarial process. The notion of "resistance" never was intended to suggest that every time a patient disagrees with us, changes the subject, or fails to appreciate the glorious wisdom of our interpretation, the patient is resisting. Resistance means use of intrapsychic defense mechanisms or acting out to avoid the conscious experience of a difficult feeling engendered by the therapy that is necessary for further growth to take place. If we are overly adversarial with our patients, we can engender all kinds of difficult feelings that are merely artifacts of bad technique. If we see the patient's need for support as a manifestation of a power struggle in which his role is to seek gratification and our role is to deny it, we frame the therapeutic experience as a kind of zero-sum game. We need to keep in mind the patient's conflict: the need for affirmation of his present state and the push to better himself; the desire to feel better and the fear of change. We have a way of looking down on resistance—*This patient simply wants to feel better; he doesn't want to change*—that dismisses all too cavalierly the patient's predicament. The patient didn't want to be depressed and doesn't understand how he got that way. He may buy the idea that some of his own habits contribute to his situation, and believe he is ready to change those habits, but he cannot know how difficult and frightening this task is going to be. *Of course he wants to feel better but doesn't want to change. Who wouldn't?* As therapists, we must respect the patient's dilemma. Often, this means focusing on both sides of the conflict: *You want to change, but you're frightened of what the future will be. It's a hard position; that's part of what keeps you depressed.*

The model for therapy is hard, shared work, and we need to cultivate a tone of "you do your part and I'll do mine." Blaming, self-pity, helplessness, and manipulation are tolerated as part of the disease but not accepted as part of the person. Well-timed confrontations of these defenses early in the therapy set a tone of mutual expectation and respect in an emotionally charged atmosphere that will be a different relationship from any most depressives have experienced. And it precludes the power struggle in which the patient frustrates the therapist's attempts to make him better; the battle instead is within the patient, between the parts of himself that want to recover and those that don't.

Part of avoiding resistance involves treating the patient with respect. When we have a suggestion to make, let's make it as a suggestion, not a leading question. We have the stereotype that it's somehow taboo for the therapist to give advice, yet we often have a viewpoint or information that we wish to share with the patient. Sometimes we have good reason to believe that the patient is set on a course of action that will have severe negative consequences. A common way out of this dilemma is to avoid giving direct guidance by asking leading questions. *You must be worried that if you quit your job, your family will starve. Do you feel like you've fully considered all the consequences of quitting medical school to take up the dulcimer?* I think that experiencing these kinds of comments is shaming for the patient and leads to distrust of the therapist. The patient is likely to conclude that the therapist really believes he's a fool, but is humoring him because he can't handle the truth. Far better to be direct. *What will you do for money if you quit your job? I think you're making a hasty decision about quitting school.* We cannot *not* influence our patients, and to pretend we're not trying to when we really are demeans us both. A patient once told me he could tell I liked his old girlfriend better than the new one, because whenever he started talking about the new one I changed the subject back to the old girlfriend.

Of course, there is a great deal of danger from our exerting too much influence over our patients' lives, and I don't want to advocate that we take control just because we can. But the process of making ourselves honest about exerting control may actually reduce the amount of influence we exert without acknowledging it. Also, it must be stressed that this kind of direct influence should only take place in the context of a relationship where the patient is empowered to disagree. That means there must be a tone of mutual respect and directness on both sides, and that the therapist must have earned the patient's trust, not by being right all the time, but by being genuinely concerned all the time.

One of the most difficult problems is that of the patient who just doesn't keep appointments, because without the patient in the room no work can occur. When I sense that this is likely to be a problem, I sometimes try to make an overt alliance with the patient's healthy side: *There is a part of you that strongly wants to get better, and I want to help you. At the same time, there seems to be a part that sabotages your efforts, and I don't want to help that part. So let's be clear that we're going to work on this consistently together, and that if something comes up that means you're too busy, or too sick, or just forget our appointments, that's the sabotaging part of you. For the first few weeks I'm going to call you if you're just a few minutes late for an appointment and I'm going to speak to the side of you that wants to get well, and we'll see what we can do to use your time better.*

People can get angry at the implication that their depression can be resolved by changing their behavior. They feel invested in finding a dramatic solution, a big discovery: a career change, a spouse change, the right medication, a treatment epiphany. Anything less seems like a betrayal of all the suffering they've been through. I find that I can confront the defense directly because I have the authority of experience; I acknowledge my own struggle with depression and express both sympathy and reality: *I know your suffering is way out of proportion, that you never wished it on yourself, that it doesn't seem fair to have to change. But your only choice is to change or to continue to be depressed.* I'm afraid that therapists sometimes underestimate the power of this resistance, and can end up making the patient feel blamed or shamed again. It is an issue that must be attacked with great tact and delicacy.

The single greatest obstacle to the treatment of depression, however, is the patient's ability to sever the connections between experience and affect:

Rachel came back to our self-help group, reporting that she had had a bad time. She had been overcome with the impulse to cut herself—an impulse she'd had under control for some months. "But this time, I don't know what it was, just out of the blue, I was in the kitchen and I saw the knife, and I got the idea in my head, and nothing would do till I cut myself. And then I felt better. But now I feel ashamed and depressed again, like I'll never get well."

The group spent half an hour with Rachel, trying to help her figure out what had triggered this impulse. It was fruitless. To every inquiry, Rachel just repeated her litany: "I don't know what it was about. It was just an impulse, out of the blue." Finally the group gave up and moved on to other things.

At the end of the meeting, as we were putting the chairs away, someone asked Rachel if she'd had a good visit with her grandchildren over the holidays. "Oh, no," said Rachel. "That was a big disappointment. My son-in-law picked a fight with me, and they stayed away." It was as if you could see a series of little light bulbs going off over the heads of all the other group members. We all knew how important the grandchildren were to Rachel, and how much she'd been looking forward to this visit. We knew the history of her conflict with her son-in-law, who used Rachel's one suicide attempt and hospitalization as evidence that she was somehow a menace to her grandchildren. It was plain as day to us—though not to Rachel—that there was a connection between her disappointment, anger, and shame at the cancelled visit and her impulse to cut herself.

All over the country, at any given time, depressed patients are sitting in their therapists' offices, repeating words like Rachel's—"out of the blue," "all of a sudden," "for no reason," "out of nowhere"—to describe how they experience the sudden reappearance of a depressed mood. In other cases, they may have learned how to avoid altogether the mood change and go directly to the consequent self-destructive symptom: to drink, to cut, to binge, to pick a fight. Sometimes it is neither a mood change nor an impulse, but a physiological event: a seized back, an attack of colitis. It is remarkable how people with depression have learned to sever the connection between events that have an emotional impact and the consequent subjective change in feeling. We can call this denial, isolation, intellectualization, repression, acting out, somatization—but whatever we call it, it remains a very powerful mechanism in depression.

The mechanism has been empirically demonstrated in college students (Stader & Hokanson, 1998). Nondepressed students filled out a daily experiences questionnaire every day for 45 days. The questionnaire measured their subjective experience of depression as well as three variables that were hypothesized to be linked temporally to depressive experiences: dependency (questionnaire items like "You needed acceptance or affection from someone"); interpersonal stress ("Your feelings were hurt by someone"); and negative cognitions ("Your attention was focused on problems or negative things"). Time-series analysis showed that feelings of dependency and interpersonal stress reliably preceded experiences of depression, while negative cognitions tended to coincide with depressed experiences. These normal college students tended to recover from their dysphoric moods within a day; for individuals already suffering from depression, experiences of dependency and stress will likely precipitate episodes that are not so quickly recovered from.

The basic psychodynamic paradigm holds that pathology results from conflict between a wish and a fear. *I want to get my own way but I fear retaliation.*
I want love but I fear rejection. When the process is conscious, we can make a
deliberate decision not to act on the wish, and we may feel sad or angry but we
don't develop pathology. Trouble comes when the wish, fear, and conflict are
unconscious. Under those circumstances, the conflict causes anxiety. Defense
mechanisms help us avoid the experience of anxiety. The interplay between our
wishes, fears, defenses, and reality leads to pathology which, classically, could
be expressed as either symptom or character. Symptoms are relatively clearly defined behavior patterns that are experienced by the individual as alien, as not a
part of himself; problematic character patterns are more generalized behavior
patterns that are either not experienced as undesirable or are seen as part of one's
nature.

Thus, for example, a person who wishes to soil but fears punishment and has
learned undoing as a defense mechanism may develop obsessive-compulsive
symptoms such as stylized cleaning rituals which help keep the impulse out of
consciousness, or compulsive character traits like neatness and control which
serve the same purpose. In reality, the distinction between symptom and character for any particular individual is likely to be quite blurred. Most people with
OCD symptoms have compulsive character traits, many people with compulsive character traits may become symptomatic under stress, and even the question of whether a behavioral pattern is a "symptom" is largely determined by
context.

The premise of psychoanalysis was that by enabling the patient to become
conscious of the underlying wish and fear, anxiety could be confronted, defenses
would fall away, and symptoms and pathological behavior patterns would remit.
As experience has shown that the premise rarely leads to the dramatic change
implied, there has been a gradual evolution in analytic thinking about the meaning and role of defense mechanisms (Morrison, 1999; Vaillant, 1993). "An examination of the history of the concept of defense indicates that while ideas
about *what* a defense wards off have evolved, the concept of defense itself has
remained static" (Stolorow & Lachmann, 1980, p. 89). Instead of being seen as
obstacles to the work of therapy, defenses are treated more respectfully, as an integral part of the person, not to be done away with but to be understood. Kohut
(1984) viewed defenses as attempts to protect the integrity of the self from
experiences of fragmentation. More adaptive defenses are to be strengthened,

and as the self becomes less vulnerable to fragmentation, less adaptive defenses fall away. At the same time, the psychoanalytic model of depression has been changing as well: Depression has come to be viewed neither as a symptom nor a character pattern resulting from conflict, but as a general system slowdown, a brownout resulting from too much stress, too little supply (Basch, 1988).

In the common sense model of depression, the factors that mediate depression—neurochemical changes, depressed thinking, behavioral problems, etc.—function as defenses against recovery, resistances against therapy. The viciousness of the vicious circle is the automatic, reflexive negative response of other mediating variables when one begins to change. When we try a new behavior, our automatic thoughts tell us we won't succeed. When we express ourselves emotionally, we feel embarrassed and ashamed. When we begin to feel close to the therapist, we also feel a need to put up obstacles to this intimacy.

The communicative aspect of depression is to express the wish and the fear simultaneously: *Please love me, even though I'm so loathsome. I want to hurt you, but I'm afraid you'll hurt me. I want to be in control because I fear chaos so intensely. Please take care of me, even though I don't deserve it.* Expressing contradictory messages is of course a self-defeating strategy. We confuse people, who eventually will distance themselves from us. The job of the therapist is to tolerate the confusion and help the patient express both sides of the conflict appropriately.

In the end, defenses protect us from acceptance of the reality principle. Life is not fair. You can't get everything you want. Goodness is not always rewarded. You're bound to feel lonely sometimes. You will die. Everyone knows that these statements are true, but most of us, most of the time, act as if we don't believe them. Why else do we feel angry, bitter, jealous, sorry for ourselves, cheated? Getting along in life means finding ways to keep these feelings at bay, not to be constantly preoccupied with death. That's what good defenses can do: control reality but not distort it excessively. People generally come to therapy because they still struggle with the reality principle, they still want magic. All psychotherapy is about mourning, about giving up the wish for omnipotence, immortality, perfection, return to the mother, and accepting that life is short and joy is fleeting (cf. Haynal, 1976/1985). Psychotherapy means taking apart the defenses that seek to protect us from reality but interfere with our growth and creativity.

GENDER DIFFERENCES

The traditional socialization of boys and girls hurts them both, each in particular, complementary ways. Girls, and later women, tend to internalize pain. They blame themselves and draw distress into themselves. Boys, and later men, tend to externalize pain; they are more likely to feel victimized by others and to discharge distress through action. Hospitalized male psychiatric patients far outnumber female patients in their rate of violent incidents; women outnumber men in self-mutilation. . . . A depressed woman's internalization of pain weakens her and hampers her capacity for direct communication. A depressed man's tendency to extrude pain often does more than simply impede his capacity for intimacy. It may render him psychologically dangerous. Too often, the wounded boy grows up to become a wounding man, inflicting upon those closest to him the very distress he refuses to acknowledge within himself. (Real, 1997, p. 24)

Though women are much more likely than men to be diagnosed with depression, men are three times as likely to take their own lives. The proportion of women diagnosed with affective, anxious, or psychosomatic disorders is the same as the proportion of men diagnosed with affective, substance use, or personality disorders (see Table 6.1), suggesting that men express the same conflicts in different ways than women, ways that are less likely to be understood as a mental illness and more likely to be seen as a social problem. There is strong support for the idea that men are just as likely to be depressed as women, but they externalize the pain, seeing themselves as victims of injustice or unfairness, and making others suffer in consequence.

It has long been known that rates of mental illness are higher among poor and disadvantaged groups than in the general population. Conflicting explana-

TABLE 6.1
Lifetime Incidence of Mental Disorders as Percentage of the Population

	MEN	WOMEN	BOTH
Affective Disorders			
Major depressive episode	12.7	21.3	17.1
Manic episode	1.6	1.7	6.4
Dysthymia	4.8	8.0	6.4
Anxiety Disorders			
Panic disorder	2.0	5.0	3.5
Agoraphobia	3.5	7.0	5.3
Social phobia	11.1	15.5	13.3
Simple phobia	6.7	15.7	11.3
Generalized anxiety disorder	3.6	6.6	5.1
Substance Absuse Disorders			
Alcohol abuse	12.5	6.4	9.4
Alcohol dependence	20.2	8.2	14.1
Drug abuse	5.4	3.5	4.4
Drug dependence	9.2	5.9	7.5
Other Disorders			
Antisocial personality	5.8	1.2	3.5
Nonaffective psychosis	0.6	0.6	0.7
Totals	48.7	47.3	48.0

From Kessler et al., 1994. Copyright © 1994 American Medical Association. Used with permission.

tions for this observation favor either *causation* (the lives of the poor are more difficult, resulting in greater mental illness) or *selection* (those with mental illness inevitably find themselves in the lower socioeconomic strata because of their poor functioning). In an elegant experiment designed to investigate this question, Dohrenwend and his colleagues (1992) compared incidence of schizophrenia, major depression, antisocial personality, and substance abuse between matched samples of European and North African young adult Jews in Israel. African Jews in Israel face discrimination and poverty unlike European Jews, hence are more vulnerable to factors associated with social causation. On the research question, the investigators concluded that the selection hypothesis was supported for schizophrenia, but that life stress was the major factor influencing development of depression, antisocial personality, and drug use. Of interest here, however, were the gender differences. While differences between the sexes among European Jews were moderate, African Jews responded differently to stress. Females were much more likely to develop depression, and males more likely to develop antisocial personalities or substance abuse problems. All in all, the findings are strong support for the observation that men and women respond to stress in different ways: men act out, and women internalize.

Women

Women are generally found to suffer from depression about twice as frequently as men (Nolen-Hoeksema, 1990; Weissman & Klerman, 1977). The reasons for this differential are subject to much debate. Pajer (1995) identifies three general lines of explanation:

- The artifact hypothesis suggests that the differential is due to errors in how we count—that women are more likely to seek treatment than men, that the definitions of depression are influenced by stereotypes of the feminine role.
- The biological hypothesis is that because women are apparently more subject to changes in hormonal levels than are men, these changes trigger depression in vulnerable women or directly cause depression themselves.
- The psychosocial hypothesis is really two explanations. One is that women are inherently more dependent, hence more vulnerable to rejection, and that they tend to internalize stress more than men. The other is that since women's social role and power are less than men in most societies, women are less able to take effective action when they experience stress. The combination of internalizing stress at the same time as being less able to relieve it leads to greater incidence of depression in women.

In all likelihood, all three explanations have some impact on how we observe the incidence of depression among the genders. For women, there are several implications for assessment and treatment. Because of regular hormonal changes, and because of increased comorbidity with somatic symptoms among women, pharmacotherapy for women may be more complex than for men. Factors that affect hormone production should be stabilized in addition to treating depressive symptoms. There may be variations in mood and in medication response that coincide with the menstrual cycle; psychotherapy may help the individual patient anticipate and control these variations, but new medications and greater experience in their administration may lead to more finely tuned pharmacotherapy. An assessment of the patient's feelings about her gender role and identity may help the patient identify negative assumptions about the self that she does not connect with her depression; likewise a reproductive history may establish links between sexual experiences, abortions, postpartum episodes, etc. and the onset of depressive symptoms. A sensitive knowledge of a woman's role expectations—for instance, a need to provide child care that interferes with her ability to comply with treatment recommendations—may prevent unfair labeling by the practitioner. There is evidence that group therapy combined with individual treatment may be particularly effective with women (Pajer, 1995).

The roles of abuse and poverty in depression for women are far too often overlooked. In the general population of women, the incidence of childhood sexual abuse has been found to range from 22 to 37 percent. The incidence of battering by an intimate partner may range from 25 to 50 percent of women. Between 10 and 15 percent of women are estimated to have an experience of date or spousal rape (McGrath & Keita, 1990). At this point, little is known for certain about the long-term effects of victimization, but depression occurs at a much higher rate among abuse victims than among other people. The incidence of depression among lower income groups is greater than that for more affluent populations. Most of the poor are women and children; poverty decreases choices of all types for women and puts them in conflict about their children. Much of what looks like depression or borderline personality disorder in women may actually be the delayed manifestations of posttraumatic stress disorder; much of what seems like hopelessness may be a well-founded belief that it is impossible to escape the cycle of poverty. The clinician treating a depressed woman should inquire specifically about issues like a history of abuse; symptoms like nightmares, blackouts, seizures, or depersonalization experiences; and possible head or internal injuries (which often contribute to endocrine malfunction). We should also inquire directly about current abuse, and be knowledgeable about the reality of life for low-income women. Mothers of young children are especially vulnerable to depression, and the more children there are in the home, the greater the likelihood of depression.

Sadowski and colleagues (1999) found that childhood stress was significantly linked with adult depression, but that boys and girls were vulnerable to different stresses. Both groups were vulnerable to social dependence, overcrowding, and family/marital instability. Girls appeared to be more highly affected than boys by poor physical care and poor mothering. The researchers hypothesize that girls exposed to poor mothering "may be particularly liable to develop in-secure attachments giving rise to low self-esteem and poor relational skills" (p. 117)—in other words, more likely to develop dependent relationships which in turn can be upset by stress—than boys whose emotional stability is less likely to be threatened by insecure attachments.

Women's depression is also related to personality and cognitive differences. Behavior patterns that are avoidant, passive, or dependent are directly associated with depression and contribute to a vicious circle of negative life events that re-inforces the depression. Pessimistic cognitive style contributes to depression, and may be more prevalent among women than men because of higher likelihood of learned helplessness experiences associated with being a woman (McGrath & Keita, 1990). Nolen-Hoeksema (1990) suggested that, while men may respond to a feeling of dysphoria by "instrumental" behavior—active attempts at mastery or distraction—women are more likely to ruminate over their feelings. Ruminative styles interfere with problem-solving behavior, reinforce self-blaming explanations for events, and lead to further negative associations, all of which may amplify and prolong a depressive episode.

The incidence of depression among children of both sexes, which is ap-proximately equal before puberty, dramatically increases among girls during ado-lescence. Hankin and his colleagues (1998) reported on findings from a ten-year study of development of depression in a birth cohort of a thousand children in New Zealand. At age 11, slightly more boys than girls were depressed (1.79 per-cent to 0.31 percent). At age 13, an additional 2 percent of each sex had devel-oped depression. At 15, the accelerated rate among girls had begun; 4.39 per-cent more girls had become depressed, compared to 0.56 percent more boys ($p < .01$). At 18, depression had increased dramatically among both sexes, but the increase for girls was markedly higher; almost 10 percent of the boys had become depressed, but almost 21 percent of the girls ($p < .001$). At age 21, the rate of increase among boys had slowed, to 6.58 percent, and though the rate slowed among girls as well it was only to 15.05 percent ($p < .001$). Cumulatively, by age 21, 11 percent of the boys and 25 percent of the girls were depressed, as determined by careful structured clinical interviews. Clearly, the years between 15 and 18 are a critical time for development of depression in both sexes, but even more so for women. Two explanations for this trend seem possible: One is that as girls age, they become more aware of the limitations of the traditional fe-male role and less optimistic about their own future. The other is that, while boys' bodies in adolescence become more like the masculine ideal (big and strong), girls' bodies become less like our society's distorted feminine ideal (model-thin and heroin-chic). Either way, girls in adolescence are at extremely high risk for depression.

One more reason why women are so much more likely to be diagnosed with depression is that the criteria are weighted toward somatic complaints. Silverstein (1999; Silverstein, Caceres, Perdue, & Cimarolli, 1995) has reanalyzed data from many of the large epidemiological studies on incidence of mental illness, differentiating between "somatic depression" (patients who complain of fatigue, appetite, or sleep disturbance, along with other symptoms) and "pure depression" (patients who do not report any of those somatic symptoms). He finds that somatic depression is typically twice as common among women as men but that pure depression is close to the same rate in both sexes. I think that if the diagnostic criteria for depression were more balanced, the gender differences might be minimized. For instance, if we were to include as symptoms of depression problems like irritability or self-destructive behavior that are more typical manifestations among men, and if "masculine" traits like assertiveness and "feminine" traits like interdependence were not defined as healthy and pathological respectively, we might understand that men can be depressed without meeting the current *DSM* criteria.

Men

> We tend not to recognize depression in men because the disorder itself is seen as unmanly. Depression carries, to many people, a double stain—the stigma of mental illness and also the stigma of "feminine" emotionality. Those in a relationship with a depressed man are themselves often faced with a painful dilemma. They can either confront his condition—which may further shame him—or else collude with him in minimizing it, a course that offers no hope for relief. (Real, 1997, p. 22)

It remains true that substantially more women than men request psychiatric help. Men are supposed to be tough and self-reliant. We don't even ask for directions when we're lost; how can we be expected to ask for help with intimate problems or feelings of inadequacy? And men know that the land of therapy is dangerous territory. People are expected to cry and hug.

But it's not all men's fault. At least one of the problems associated with getting male patients into the office is their suspicion that they are going to be blamed for whatever is going wrong, a suspicion that can seem well-founded. It's no longer socially acceptable to make sexist generalizations, unless the sex is male:

> In a survey of 1000 random advertisements, one hundred percent of the jerks singled out in male-female relationships were male. . . . One hundred percent of the ignorant ones were male. One hundred percent of the incompetent ones were male. . . . 3M sells a variety of Post-it notes such as "The more I know about men, the more I like my dog," and "There are only two things wrong with men . . . everything they say and everything they do." A 3M spokesperson added that they have no intention of selling similarly anti-female products. (Thompson, 1991, p. 74)

Men manifest their suffering in different ways. Self-respect is very important to men. To be weak, to need help, is bad enough; to allow oneself to be taken advantage of, used, or disrespected, is unacceptable. If the male doesn't know how to remedy the situation constructively, violence is the result. Violence can be an attempt to ward off depression.

All violence is an attempt to achieve justice, or what the violent person per-
ceives as justice. The violent person feels he has been wronged; more strongly,
he feels he has been shamed. But we try to ignore the role of shame in violence.
We prefer to call batterers "senseless," the Littleton boys "crazy." We should be
clued in to the importance of shame by the very triviality of the incidents that
lead to violence—a dirty look from the spouse, flirting in a bar, too much complaining about not enough money. It is precisely because these incidents are so
trivial and yet rankle that the violent individual becomes ashamed of being
ashamed; ashamed of the awareness of his dependency on the spouse for self-
esteem, ashamed of being vulnerable. These are men who need to feel in control at all times, because that sustains the all-important illusion that the dependency in the relationship flows one way only. These are boys who prefer to
feel rage than the daily humiliation of their peers.

The act of beating one's wife needs to be understood as an act of depression.
To take the one person in life who loves you and attempt to destroy that person
in rage is ultimately an act of self-destruction. Battering men are dependent on
their spouses for a stable sense of self; the smallest sign of disruption in the "holding environment," or a blow to the self-esteem that the wife can't soothe, is
enough to precipitate a crisis—a mini-depression, which is quickly covered over
with violence.

Often overlooked in the shootings at Columbine and in most of the recent
episodes of mass murder is that these events are suicides as well as murder. In
fact, the suicide rate among men who have committed homicide is several hundred times higher than among other men. But this is not usually a phenomenon of remorse; both the homicide and the suicide are manifestations of a pre-
existing condition, a feeling that the self has already died. There is a peculiar
type of psychotic depression, often described by men who have killed, that they
are not living tissue—that they are made up of ropes or wires, that they are controlled by other beings, that they stink of putrefaction even though they go
through the motions of living. If imprisoned and unable to kill themselves, these
men often turn to horrible and bizarre forms of self-mutilation; though typically
numb during the act, they know that the pain of healing will help them feel
real again.

Gilligan (1996) believes that because of the experience of torture, incest, beat-
ings, and violence inflicted on violent offenders by their parents, their selves
have died. I think perhaps that the self has become permeated by violence and
shame; the positive cathexis between the two poles of Kohut's self has become
a negative cathexis, and it is shame and rage, not love and respect, that holds
the self together. Violence is usually about shame; a man, a movement, or a nation, feels it has been dissed—humiliated, mortified; and given a lack of self-
control or the absence of other alternatives or a culture that promotes violence,
violence is the result. It was true of post–World War I Germany, true of the
Columbine boys, true of African-American street kids. I fear it's true of Russia
today, and we are just waiting for the inevitable violent response to national

shame. The first murder was about shame—God respected Abel's sacrifice, but disrespected Cain's. We don't usually focus on the excessively vulnerable self-esteem of the violent offender, but if we could help men develop skills they can be proud of, if we could change culture in the high school and on the street and in international politics so that the way to get ahead is not by humiliating others—we might get somewhere.

Intuitively, it makes sense that men and women use different defenses against shame and painful affect. In general, men externalize and women internalize. Both genders may try to defend against loss and grief, but in our culture only men experience those feelings as shameful and unmanly. Depression can serve as an adaptation, an organizing principle, for either gender, but men are more likely to reject it and organize themselves around rage instead.

When depression has become part of the self like this, the patient experiences his suffering but is blind to how he participates in its creation and maintenance. His desire for Hoffman's (1998) "impossible, selfless love" generates rage, shame, and rejection. The challenge for the therapist is to help the patient understand these processes without adding to his shame and self-blame.

CHAPTER 7

Use Medications Appropriately

Although there is still no definitive lab test for depression, it makes sense to assume that some neurochemical change has taken place in the brains of people with depression, a change that is not easily reversible. Treatment with antidepressant medication seems to be effective in helping to stabilize this process, though at this point no one can say definitively how medications work (Berman & Charney, 1999). Medications can help patients feel better more quickly than psychotherapy alone. They seem to "raise the bottom" so that the patient's depressed moods are not quite so intense and overwhelming. They also can help restore a natural sleep cycle, improve concentration, and raise energy level. For most patients, side effects are tolerable, and there is no research yet suggesting negative effects of long-term use. Antidepressant medication should definitely be considered as part of treatment for all patients with depression. Exceptions should be those who have a history of negative effects, a history of failure of medication, and those patients who are relatively stable and have made a decision not to use medication for strong personal reasons which the therapist can be sure are not self-sabotaging.

MEDICATION AND THERAPY COMBINED

It doesn't stretch a point too far to view pharmacology vs. psychotherapy as an Oedipal battle; certainly that's the way I've seen it get played out in clinics. The (typically) male psychiatrist, cold, controlling, and self-certain, wants us to insert things into our bodies. The (typically) female therapist, warm, supportive, and vague, wants us to linger in her cozy den. The psychiatrist becomes angry and rejecting when we don't respond to his prescriptions, often blaming us for being bad patients. The therapist becomes helpless and overwhelmed when we don't respond, sending us back to the psychiatrist in hopes of something more potent from his arsenal. The patient is caught in the middle, often feeling that to obey one is to betray the other, like a child caught between feuding parents. Of course the child needs parents who can put aside their differences and work together in his best interests, and the patient needs for his therapist and psychopharmacologist also to act like adults. Despite any doubts therapists may have about the exaggerated claims of the pharmaceutical marketplace, medications usually offer quicker relief than psychotherapy and can have important lasting benefits; and we do our depressed patients a disservice if we don't actively encourage them to pursue medication.

It remains to be conclusively demonstrated that treatment combining medication and psychotherapy is more effective than either treatment alone, although several studies point in that direction (Eells, 1999; Hollon et al., 1992; Keller et al., 2000; Klerman et al., 1994; Manning, Markowitz, & Frances, 1992). Some observers have reported that medication alone leads to a higher number of treatment failures and a higher dropout rate (Wexler & Chicchetti, 1992), but clearly there are enough dropouts from psychotherapy that therapists shouldn't brag. A serious drawback with almost all of these studies is that treatment is usually of short (twelve weeks) duration and that results are measured only during and at the end of treatment, with posttreatment follow-up extremely rare (Eells, 1999). There is good reason to believe that combined treatment will lead to more lasting recovery, but it will take further investigation to demonstrate it.

Lack of good research should not hold back common-sense practice, however. Schuchter and colleagues (1996) present a model for Biologically Informed Psychotherapy for Depression (BIPD) that is comprehensive and eclectic. It should be reviewed by any nonmedical practitioner dealing with depressed patients.

Therapists' Resistance to Medication

Schuchter and colleagues (1996) discuss a number of objections that psychotherapists raise concerning pharmacological treatment of depression:

1. *Drug treatment introduces a placebo effect that increases the patient's dependency and magical expectations.* These are legitimate concerns, especially for a profession that has tried so hard to practice egalitarian values. In reality, however, though we don't like to acknowledge it, much of the success of psychotherapy comes about through exactly these same forces. When a veteran police officer walks into my office to ask for help and tells me it's the hardest thing he's ever done, more difficult than highway fatalities and bomb disposal, I'm going to respect and make use of the power he's ascribing to me. On the one hand, there are certainly many patients who are simply waiting for the pill to work, angry and resentful that their doctor hasn't found the right pill yet. On the other hand, there are many patients who *have* been helped significantly by the right pill. Should we deny them that help because we fear creating a problem in other patients? Perhaps the patients who are just waiting for the pill to work would

have been somewhat passive in psychotherapy anyway; perhaps it is the promise of the pill that got them in our door in the first place.

2. *By reducing symptomatic distress, drug treatment reduces the patient's motivation for psychotherapy.* This idea bases its legitimacy on the belief that everyone has unresolved conflicts, that psychotherapy is good for everyone, and that the current distress is just a manifestation of a deep-seated issue that will take psychotherapy to resolve. Schuchter and others (1996) argue that despite a hundred years of experience, no one has been able to demonstrate that these assumptions are true (though the *Consumer Reports* (1995) study might be introduced as evidence). I would argue that the value of reducing symptomatic distress not be dismissed so lightly, that we have to be absolutely certain we have something more valuable to offer before we deny the patient access to quick relief. The trend in the research seems to be that medication treatment is not sufficient by itself to provide long-term recovery; as this knowledge becomes more accepted by the professions and by the public, it will reinforce the understanding that many patients have already, that they need to change their lives before they can truly feel better.

3. *By undermining the patient's defenses, medication may simply result in symptom substitution.* No research has ever been able to demonstrate that this belief has any validity. The premise of symptom substitution was based on old linear thinking, the idea that depression has a single cause deep in the patient's unconscious which, if not identified, is capable of manifesting itself in a variety of symptoms. Understanding that depression is a circular process suggests that multiple interventions, including medication, can be most helpful.

4. *Patients who are treated with medication may have the "sick role" unduly reinforced.* Again, this is a legitimate concern. Patients may feel additionally stigmatized by needing medication, and in fact this is a major source of patients' resistance to medication. Other patients may feel that having a disease absolves them from responsibility. This is something to be addressed in psychotherapy, and part of the reason why medication and psychotherapy should be provided together.

Despite these resistances, the trend has been toward greater acceptance of the use of medication by psychotherapists. Their successful application with a particular patient will be affected by the therapist's respect for the treatment method. We can collude with patients who skip doses or want to change medications impulsively, or we can become unduly alarmed about side effects if we are not properly informed. We can subtly reinforce the perception that medications are a crutch that a truly strong person should be able to do without. Or, we can recognize that depression is at least partly biochemical in nature, and that our first duty is to reduce suffering.

If nonmedical practitioners have resistance to medication, it's fair to point out that many psychiatrists are resistant to psychotherapy (e.g., Bennett, 1996). It's not unusual at all for me to hear from a patient that he has been fired by his psychiatrist. Usually this happens when the patient has tried five or six medications, and nothing has worked. The most difficult situation seems to be when the patient has an initial honeymoon with a new medication, only to find that after a few weeks the effects wear off. The doctor throws his metaphorical hands in the air, saying, in effect: *You're beyond help. Try psychotherapy as a last resort.* Of course, this all has the effect of reinforcing—in a highly punitive and demoralizing way—the patient's depressed view of himself as worthless and hopeless, and it sets up the therapist for failure as well.

Patient's Resistance to Medication

We should feel no shame about trying to "sell" the patient on pharmaceutical intervention. This should be based on the therapist's belief in and understanding of the efficacy of medication and the desire to help the patient get relief from unnecessary suffering. Many patients are understandably reluctant to take any medication that affects brain functioning. The brain is what we depend on to make all of our decisions, after all, and though we may feel we know the effects of alcohol well enough to allow it to impair our judgment temporarily, fears about something that is less familiar, has less history, and is more subtle in its effects seem quite rational. These fears should be countered by rational argument, not dismissed as unreasonable. In fact, this discussion with the patient can be the subject of much of the therapeutic work, a part of educating the patient about the disease model, a part of accepting that depression affects the brain in ways that we may be completely unaware of.

Once a patient has accepted the initial prescription for medication, his continued use will depend on its efficacy and his tolerance for it. There are unpleasant side effects associated with most antidepressants, and the nonmedical therapist should have a general knowledge of these effects—what phenomena are expectable, what are likely to be unrelated, which effects are likely to be transitory, which require medical advice. Another of the ironies of depression is that for the first few weeks on medication the patient is likely only to feel the side effects and not to feel any improvement. The therapist will need to feel safe knowing when to encourage patients to hang in there. There are other patients who will want to stop their medication as soon as they have experienced some relief from an episode. The impulse to give up in the face of side effects and the impulse to quit as soon as relief is achieved have to be countered by education. Education need not come exclusively from the therapist or the prescribing MD. The patient should be encouraged to learn as much as he can about his disease and its treatment.

Most episodes of major depression will improve substantially after four months' medication treatment. After this, the odds of success decline steadily with the passage of time (Coryell et al., 1994). There is a strong indication that patients are also more susceptible to the suggestion and hope of placebo effects early on in the course of an episode. For these reasons, it makes sense to get patients medicated as quickly as possible; if there is a six-week delay between the onset of an episode and seeking treatment, then another delay for an assessment or referral, then another while the medication builds up to a therapeutic level in the body, the golden moment when recovery has its best chance may be lost.

I continue to be surprised at the high proportion of patients who, successfully stabilized on antidepressants, experiencing few side effects, still wish to get off their medication as soon as possible. They feel weak or ashamed, "dependent" on drugs. I don't know patients who need insulin, antihypertensives, allergy medication, or many other drugs that will require lifetime use, who feel personally diminished because they can't get along without the medication. Certainly, many resent the expense, the nuisance, and the side effects, but that is not the same as feeling blameworthy for needing drugs. This sense of guilt for dependence on medication should be interpreted as yet another manifestation of depression.

If this sense of guilt continues to be the case for patients who are well stabilized on antidepressants, think of how complex the feelings must be for new patients who are considering taking something for the first time. The drugs, after all, affect our brain, which is where we live, where our mind is, who we are. We invest the drugs with all the power and fear we give a witch doctor, who can make us well but also put a curse on us.

Lauren had friends who had had negative experiences with Prozac but were happy with Zoloft. When the doctor first tried to prescribe Prozac, Lauren mentioned her friends' experiences, and the doctor cooperatively changed the medication. When she saw me the next day, Lauren was irate, and didn't want any medication at all. "Is that science? It's more like give me the red lollipop instead of the green one. Do I have to be a guinea pig? Isn't there some way to predict which one is better for me?" It didn't help matters any when the doctor and I both explained that individual reactions to the medications are highly idiosyncratic. She felt like she'd been to see the great and powerful Oz, but instead glimpsed the man behind the curtain.

It is ironically predictable that those patients who are most sensitive in general are most sensitive to the side effects of medication. People who are hypervigilant about their bodies will be especially attuned to every headache, upset stomach, and dizzy spell. Often this seems to get in the way of getting up to a therapeutic dose, and can seem like another piece of unconscious self-destructiveness on the patient's part. It's very important to clarify that the side effects come first, and generally wear off, before there is a therapeutic effect.

Unfortunately, there are a great many patients—no one knows how many, but I suspect it ranges from 25 to 50 percent—who do not respond to medication. Many psychiatrists will be careful and patient, replacing a failed medication with a new one or adding more. We all know of many patients who are taking an SSRI, a mood stabilizer, Trazodone to help with sleep, and a major or a minor tranquilizer. Some are taking more than one SSRI or a tricyclic and an SSRI. Psychiatrists who prescribe so many medications are often using only anecdotal information and their own clinical experience. As Fawcett (1998) points out, no one—drug companies, NIMH, foundations—is interested in studying the effects of more than one drug at a time. It's not clean research; the results are bound to be complicated and confusing. And no one—except patients—will benefit. MDs who really want to help their nonresponsive patients are left to their own devices.

SENSIBLE MEDICATION POLICY

Despite the fact that some patients do not respond, the possibility of success makes it incumbent on us to suggest to any new patient who is experiencing depression sufficient to meet the criteria for dysthymia or major depression that he consider medication as part of treatment. This should be an absolute requirement if the patient is suicidal, and a firm recommendation if the patient is in great subjective distress or if he has primarily vegetative symptoms. We need to make it clear that medication can provide relief from some of the worst symptoms before psychotherapy can be expected to, and that there is no reason to wait. If the patient is reluctant, I may use the common-sense model of depression to explain how neurochemical changes are part of the process of depression, changes that cannot be expected to reverse quickly through psychotherapy or positive life experience. We should talk openly about shame and stigma, and explain that sometimes reluctance to take help is another example of depressed self-defeating behavior. At the same time, we need to listen to and respect the patient's legitimate concerns about medication. We want to understand what information he has and how accurate it is, and point him to more reliable information if it's needed. In the end, if the patient is not at great risk, I feel I have to honor his wishes and provide psychotherapy alone if he is adamant, reserving the right to introduce the subject again if he continues in distress.

This policy presupposes that the therapist has a relationship of mutual respect with a psychiatrist who can provide medication for his patients. For the non-medical therapist in private practice this can be a real obstacle. I am fortunate to have several such relationships, though I understand that in some parts of the country psychiatrists are in such short supply that they can refuse to collaborate in this way. In order to develop and sustain these connections, it behooves the therapist in private practice to call the psychiatrist and share his observations, concerns, and initial treatment plan before the patient's first psychiatric consultation. After a few weeks of medication, the therapist should make a second call to report his observations. The psychiatrist will never call the therapist; that's the pecking order and we just have to live with it. I leave prescribing up to the doctor, unless I feel that I have information that the psychiatrist just doesn't have—for instance, if the patient reveals symptoms to me that he hasn't discussed with the MD. This is unfortunately too frequent a problem, as psychiatric appointments are rushed and the patient sometimes feels pressured to present a rosy picture or not waste the doctor's time.

Assuming that the patient is stabilized on medication, the therapist and psychiatrist should maintain contact to discuss changes in the patient's status and any major changes in treatment plan, especially any steps toward termination.

The foregoing discussion applies to patients who are new to antidepressant medication, a dwindling minority as medication is marketed so aggressively and supplied to many patients by general practitioners, obstetricians, and other specialists. These patients are likely to seek the therapist out when medication hasn't lived up to its promise. For such patients, it's essential to determine if a therapeutic dose has been prescribed in the first place and if the patient has been taking it as prescribed. The therapist needs access to information about usual dosage ranges for antidepressants, and should actively ask the patient how he has been taking the pills. If there is an inadequate dose or the patient has not been compliant, either the patient or the therapist—preferably the patient—needs to inform the prescribing MD. I find it helpful to follow up the patient's call with a call of my own to the doctor, to report my observations and to inquire about the physician's comfort level in prescribing antidepressants. If there is any suicidal potential, or if there is a diagnostic question or an unusual medication response, I want the patient to see a psychiatrist for an evaluation. Most MDs are happy to hear from the therapist, relieved that their patient is getting help, aware that the pills they've been prescribing are not a panacea, and pleased to share the responsibility.

A more difficult situation for the therapist comes with the patient who appears to be overmedicated. I had a patient who, when he arrived, was being prescribed Lithium, Depakote, Prozac, Ritalin, Topomax, Lomictol, Trazodone, and Klonopin. His affect was inappropriate, his thoughts trailed off into nowhere, his skin was broken out, and his chief complaint was that he couldn't get out of bed. Naturally it was very hard for me to tell which of his symptoms were due to illness and which were side effects of medication. Also naturally, he had taken to medicating himself: If he had to do something that required energy, he would take a Ritalin, then take a Klonopin to slow down again as soon as his chore was accomplished. After my repeated calls to the psychiatrist went unreturned (the patient had warned me he was difficult to get ahold of) I finally suggested that the patient see someone else.

Another problem frequently overlooked is the patient who abuses alcohol or other drugs while taking antidepressants. Since alcohol will counter the effects of the medications, this is clearly a self-defeating strategy. Anxiolytics and analgesics can have the same effect. But patients who are in denial about their alcohol or drug problem will blithely take the medication and expect it to work. The therapist who wants to work with depressed patients must be comfortable with asking direct questions about substance use, and focusing attention on the subject when there is a problem.

I find that I am frequently walking a fine line with patients who are reasonably stable and taking an adequate dose of their medication. On the one hand, the patient is mourning the myth of the magic pill. He is disappointed that the medication has not been a transforming experience that insulates him from all unhappiness and makes him the person he always thought he should be. The fact that there are still days when he doesn't want to get out of bed, when he dreads going to work, when he still feels inadequate, when he knows that he's still somewhat anhedonic, not participating fully in life's pleasures—this is a true disappointment, one we must help him grieve. At the same time, we must help him appreciate that very often the medication *is* having a significant beneficial effect—he is sleeping better, has some more energy, recovers more quickly from transient depressed moods, is better able to distance himself from automatic negative thoughts, is less irritable. We do not want him to go off medication in order to appreciate those benefits. The same kind of de-idealization process that used to be expected in termination of analysis—seeing the analyst as human, imperfect, capable of error—now has to be worked through in terms of medication. And like the analyst, the pill doesn't have to be perfect to be helpful.

CHAPTER 8

Use Yourself Wisely

THE THERAPIST MAY BELIEVE himself to be armed with authority, technique, theory, and intervention plans, but these weapons are useless unless the therapist is a whole person. If the patient is under a microscope, so equally is the therapist. In addition to wanting relief from suffering, the patient will want desperately to like, trust, and respect us. But most depressed patients, with their history of traumatic disappointments, will be very vigilant for any sign that we are not capable of living up to their hopes. While it is possible to fool some of the people some of the time, the therapist who is putting on an act is likely to be found out eventually; besides, the psychic cost of pretending to be someone other than who we are is higher than most of us want to pay. In the end, honesty is the best policy.

Buechler (1995) has a wonderful observation on the patient's need for the therapist's authenticity:

> I don't believe it is, specifically, the analyst's hope that engenders hope in the patient, but the analyst's whole relationship to life. The patient observes the analyst's struggle to make sense of things, keep going in the face of seemingly insurmountable obstacles, retain humor and courage in situations that seem to inspire neither. The analyst stumbles, reacts without self-hate, works to recover. The analyst is willing to work hard. She is honest without being crippled by shame. She wants to live even in the most difficult moments. She doesn't shrink from what is ugly in herself or the other. She is more interested in growth than in being right, more curious than self-protective. She can be wounded but refuses to be made dead. While in part this attitude may provide a model, and it may be contagious, I think that what mainly creates hope is the patient's experience of finding a way to relate to such a person. For many, this task requires substantive changes, alterations in all components of the emotional system. The deepened curiosity and joy, the lightened envy and hate that results engenders hope. (p. 72)

HOW THE PATIENT MAKES US FEEL

The special danger of working with depressed patients, of course, is that we are vulnerable to catching the disease ourselves. The disease can take many forms; there are many types of depressed patients, who affect different therapists differently. Many of us might be drawn to a young, attractive, verbal, intelligent, successful patient with a reactive depression, but a patient who is schizoid and experiences a long-term sense of futility and hopelessness is a different story. Some depressed patients are angry, some are passive aggressive, some are dependent, some are psychophysiological. All of these can, in Kleinian terms, put their depression into us. We become a container. Within ourselves, we need to develop a professional container, with firm boundaries between our work and our core self. Without functioning internal boundaries, and without good external supports, the patient's depression can get beyond our professional "container" and into our selves.

For instance, in what seems like a simple reactive depression, where the patient is reacting to the loss of an ambivalently loved object and cannot experience the anger side of the ambivalence, and thus moves from simple grief into depression, our goal may be to help the patient experience both sides of the ambivalence. When the patient can't do this, and gets into another ambivalent relationship and gets rejected again, and especially if this happens again and again, we might feel frustrated with the patient and with our own failure as therapists, and we might begin to experience contempt for the patient. But contempt is only another defense against depression. Our feelings of contempt are only going to get in the way of good practice, not only for the obvious reasons but also because they are a way of avoiding the patient's projections.

We may find ourselves feeling especially challenged by patients whose issues push our own buttons. We all have been victimized to some degree. We all face some issues with a certain amount of anxiety or hopelessness. How do we treat a patient who is struggling with the issues we ourselves have trouble with?

Jane's son shot himself without warning one night while she slept in the next room. *She had had a difficult, unhappy life and was chronically depressed, but after this event her depression became severe. She had headaches, backaches, cried constantly, couldn't get to work, and of course tortured herself with blame for her son's death.*

Given my own family history of suicide, this was a very difficult case for me. I was angry; I saw Jane as the victim in this case, her son as the aggressor. But I controlled my anger, recognizing that it could do Jane no good. I have vivid memories of long silences in our sessions while she cried and mourned, and I felt powerless, like Yossarian with the dying gunner, only able to say "there, there."

As difficult and painful as it was, I was able to keep from getting depressed by this case and be helpful to Jane because of two experiences: One was having worked

---

*This case was discussed in more depth in *Undoing Depression*.

in a group home early in my career and learned the discipline of leaving work at work. The other was having been through analysis and having experienced the healing power of silent understanding. I felt like I had a strong empathic connection and that I knew when she needed me to say something and when she needed me to be silent. I had faith in the process and the idea that she would eventually recover if she was helped to explore and express her feelings. I felt good about my work with her because I felt like I was in control of my aggressive/ rescuing impulses, and that I wasn't going to act on them.

The content of the session can be depressing but the experience of mastery is not—a very important distinction to maintain while working with the depressed. At the same time I must acknowledge that at other points in my life, before and after, this case would have gotten to me. We need to feel that we can say no to cases that push our buttons. This is a sign of strength, not weakness.

If we want to become an effective container for the patient's depression we must build within ourselves a professional self, which becomes the container for our patient's projections. We must use our ego to maintain this container, to be aware of when it's getting too full, and then to find healthy ways to detoxify ourselves—a balloon that inflates and deflates in response to stress, that we must deflate intentionally before it bursts.

One way our ego can monitor our container is through watching our mistakes. So many of our interventions are really efforts to control our own anxiety, not to advance the therapy. To give advice, to give a prescription, to give a premature interpretation, to shift the modality of treatment, all may be done in reaction to our needs to ward off depression or anxiety rather than to listen to the patient. These patients do make us very anxious. We want to be good at our jobs. We worry about suicide, about the patient's interactions with others—children, job, spouse. Our mistakes are valuable material for us, nothing to be ashamed of; they are normal reactions to the patient's projections which we should never expect to avoid. The supervisor, and our desire to please or impress him or her, the staff group, and our fears of criticism must also be brought into the paradigm. The supervisor and/or staff group can pick up the patient's projections, perhaps in a purer form than the therapist, because less of their narcissism is on the line.

We have a tendency to be kinder to our patients than to ourselves. We certainly do not expect them not to make mistakes. We shouldn't expect ourselves to be in a human relationship without making mistakes. As we get more experienced, we might expect our mistakes to get more interesting, or for us to have a deeper understanding of mistakes, but not to not make them.

TALKING ABOUT THE RELATIONSHIP

But it's always a mistake not to listen to the patient. If he experiences us in a particular way, and has the courage to point it out—if he sees us as angry, cold, depressed, or rejecting—let's give him the courtesy of assuming that the experience has some basis in reality. Above all, let's not assume that it's merely transference, let's never deny or patronize: *Isn't it interesting that you think I'm angry. Perhaps you see me as your father, always full of rage.* Instead, let's assume that there is some good reason for the patient to feel as he does, and that we have contributed to the situation in some way, perhaps some way we're not aware of, most likely in some way that finding out about it will make us uncomfortable. We are only naïve if we expect that the patient will accept what we choose to share about ourselves at face value, to believe that we have no unconscious motivations. We must be ready to model for the patient a deliberate and open self-exploration.

Having signaled that we are interested in hearing about how the patient experiences us, we open the door to sharing our own experience. To shut it prematurely becomes sadistic, "tantalizing" (Aron, 1991). We have to be ready to share what we understand of our experience and consider that the patient's alternative experience might also be valid; we are just as capable of fooling ourselves to maintain our self-image as the next person is.

I made a mistake with Diane (see p. 132) when she brought in correspondence with an old friend. Diane had felt taken for granted by the friend's infrequent correspondence and phone calls. I thought I could see in the friend's letter that she was irritated with Diane for taking things too personally—she wanted to blame her carelessness on being too busy. I wanted to convey to Diane that her friend was sending her a clear signal to lighten up and return to the status quo, and that Diane had to accept that if she wanted to maintain any kind of a relationship with this particular person. But in doing so, I stepped out of my empathic connection with Diane, making her feel like I was just another in a long line of people who told her she was "too needy."

I didn't figure this out right away, though I was certainly conscious of feeling disturbed by the outcome of the session. Next week Diane came in with a story about having been sexually harassed. She felt she was helpless to do anything about it herself, but had to enlist allies. I couldn't understand where her own anger about this incident had gone, and wasn't understanding that in a way I was the harasser. We continued to talk about these two issues for another session, until Diane said something that my unconscious paid attention to. Lamenting her friend and others who she felt dismissed by, she said with great feeling, "No one ever apologizes, no one ever says they're sorry." I realized she was talking about me, and at that point did offer an apology for taking her friend's side. We then could open up the subject of how Diane could feel safe in letting me know more directly when she felt injured or threatened. At the same time, this gave us the opportunity to explore a major resistance, which was her perception that any suggestion she do things differently meant that she was being told her problems were all her own fault.

MIRRORING AND IDEALIZATION

The therapist's attention shapes behavior, selectively rewarding desirable alternatives. We have to be aware of and comfortable with the patient's need for mirroring, for a positive response from us. We have to provide the "unconditional positive regard" of the Rogerian therapists for the patient as a whole, and at the same time acknowledge that there are aspects of the patient that we will like more than others. The patient's need for mirroring can lead to uncomfortable moments; the patient is likely to continuously scan the therapist's face, tone, affect, and posture for indications of rejection or disapproval. This can be experienced as an intrusive demand. Freud is said to have started using the couch partly because he didn't like being stared at, and Sullivan suggested placing the therapist's and patient's chairs at right angles so that it wasn't awkward to look away from each other. I prefer an arrangement like Sullivan's, but recommend that the therapist try to match the patient in alertness. If we are working hard and fully tuned in, we should be aware when we are upsetting or discomforting the patient, and we can explore what happened together in our relationship of mutual respect.

Because of the enormous differences in power (one asks for help, the other gives it) and self-revelation (one is completely open, the other hardly at all), the therapist is set up to be an idealized object. The therapist's interest and warmth can become a kind of magical gift that provides sustenance for the patient and eventually can be integrated into a new view of the self. This is why the therapist's active emotional engagement with the patient has such power. The cold, objective, detached therapist promotes regression; the emotionally connected therapist promotes hope and adaptation.

The therapist also needs to be comfortable being used as an idealized object. And although I advocate for self-disclosure in some circumstances, many patients need to see us as stable and solid, if not perfect, and careless self-disclosure can interfere with that needed relationship.

John had been a patient for some time. He came from an odd family where both parents seemed helpless and inadequate. Highly ambitious, John put himself through school and embarked on a successful career. But when he married and had children, he was clueless about what to do. The intimacy and conflict were intensely destabilizing to him. We developed as a metaphor for therapy the fact that he didn't have "the manual" for family life, and that therapy was designed to help him write the manual. Although he knew that I didn't have all the answers, it was very important for John to believe that I was a wise guide who would help him find the way.

There came a point in the therapy when John talked about his sexual interest in other women. When I indicated that such interest was a normal part of being male, John was undone. The idea suggested to him that I might be unhappy in my marriage. He made it very clear that he didn't want to hear any more on the subject from me, and I went along with it. At a later point in the therapy, we were able to discuss the same issues without his feeling threatened.

COAXING THE PATIENT
TO COME OUT AND PLAY

Winnicott (1971) taught that play is essential to growth: "It is in playing and only in playing that the individual child or adult is able to be creative and to use the whole personality, and it is only in being creative that the individual discovers the self" (p. 54). Play gives us the opportunity to learn, practice, and master feelings that are in fact dangerous—aggression, sexual desire, competition—in a safe setting (see Ehrenberg, 1992, for a thoughtful discussion of therapist-patient play).

But people with depression have generally lost the ability to play. Though we want to encourage them to recapture this ability in the real world, it's also helpful to engage in an element of play in the consulting room. The depressed patient is often like a whipped dog, anxious, needing to be coaxed and reassured. Sometimes the message of playful teasing is *No matter how bad things are, it's not the end of the world. You may have the resources to handle this.*

I find that many depressed patients are masters of black humor. They fully appreciate the irony of life. This is a healthy adaptation. When I began to discuss with Diane the fact that I would like to use parts of her story in my book, her immediate comeback was "Do I get cured?" When another, very depressed patient told me he was planning for a manic episode next so he could have a little fun, I didn't at first get that this was a joke, and he was crestfallen, because it was the first feeble attempt at humor he had made in a long time. The patient's use of irony or self-deprecation in this way is an attempt to play with the therapist, something we must make ourselves receptive to. I find many patients telling me about how their jokes with previous therapists or current psychopharmacologists have fallen flat; they are telling me that they value our connection through humor.

Ruvelson (1988) discusses her use of sarcasm in working with patients who are narcissistically vulnerable. She feels that empathic, well-timed sarcasm, in the context of a safe, trusting relationship, directed at people in the patient's life who have proved disappointing—including the therapist—helps such patients maintain a reliable therapeutic alliance. It can validate their feelings—including the most painful and disorganizing abandonment fears and narcissistic rage—and help contain them at the same time. I would argue that it can do more; that playfulness like this in the session can teach the patient the value of humor as a defense. Humor in the face of disappointment implies a certain acceptance that reality is disappointing and you might as well make the best of it. Wit, by its very nature, is disarming. It subverts, rather than attacks, defenses. We are all better off when we can laugh at ourselves, when we don't take ourselves too seriously. Humor is one of the most mature defenses, a way of taking the grimmest news and standing it on its head, seeing things in a whole new light.

At the same time, wit is all about timing—and unempathic humor can be experienced by the patient as a devastating rupture. Ruvelson (1988) suggests that when a joke is experienced as unempathic, it can represent an attempt to ward off the patient's pain or a retaliation for a narcissistic injury suffered by the therapist. Wolf (1979) suggests that sometimes in such cases the therapist is using the patient as a mirror for his own narcissistic needs, showing off his own wit or erudition at the patient's expense. But even though wit can be dangerous, we should bear in mind that sometimes silence is an empathic rupture; even a joke that falls flat can change the context of the relationship. The fact that the therapist wants the patient to enjoy something he has to offer is a powerful gift in itself. By exploring why the joke failed and openly acknowledging that the problem may be as much, if not more, the therapist's than the patient's, we may able to build a deeper relationship.

An element of playfulness about the boundaries of psychotherapy can be a strong affective connection. Our patients are full of fantasies about who we really are and how we really feel. Engaging the patient in play about those fantasies is a way of enlivening a relationship and teaching the value of play and the patient's capacity to play. For example, I have on the wall in my office a collection of "couch" cartoons clipped from *The New Yorker* and other magazines. Many of these are very witty comments about life in general and the ironies of our profession in particular. Patients add to my collection from time to time, and it is a harmless pleasure we can share together.

SPONTANEITY AND SELF-DISCLOSURE

We have less choice than we want to believe about using our own countertransference reactions. The patient tunes in to what we feel, whether we're open about our feelings or not, and thus is immediately aware of inauthenticity (Ehrenberg, 1992). How we feel in this session today with this particular patient is some of the most important data we have—our affective response to the patient's affect. Do we feel bored, threatened, playful, protective, angry, depressed? Although we should never act blindly on the basis of our own emotional response, an effort to deny our responsiveness, to overcontrol it by remaining detached and professional, can result in a stale, dry therapy. In fact, sometimes our detachment can be an enactment of our own need to withhold. While some patients may take comfort in an unflappable therapist who enforces the boundaries of the professional relationship consistently, others might experience the same therapist as cold and uncaring. And some therapists might stay detached and aloof to facilitate a therapeutic goal, while others do it to control their own anxiety (cf. Mitchell, 1993).

> Patients seek to connect to their analysts, to know them, to probe beneath their professional façade, and to reach their psychic centers much in the same way that children seek to connect to and penetrate their parents' inner worlds. This aggressive probing may be mistaken for hostile attempts at destruction. (Aron, 1991)

Self-revelation, especially about what is going on in the therapeutic relationship, is often a useful tool for mobilizing an affective connection. Staying in the here and now, focusing on what's happening in the patient's immediate experience—sometimes using the therapist's own experience as a telltale—brings an intimacy that many depressed patients have never experienced before. The willingness to examine microscopically the nuances of communication between therapist and patient demonstrates an interest in the patient's experience but also teaches by example that emotions have reasons.

Sometimes the patient, when he is talking about aspects of himself or about other people in his life, is also talking about how he experiences the therapist. "Patients tune in, consciously and unconsciously, to the analyst's attitudes and feelings toward them, but inasmuch as they believe that these observations touch on sensitive aspects of the analyst's character, patients are likely to communicate these observations only indirectly through allusions to others, as displacements, or through descriptions of these characteristics as aspects of themselves" (Aron, 1991, p. 36). This mechanism operates in everyday life; every important person in our life has a taboo territory that we are (or should be) endlessly curious about, which we populate with fantasies. And we communicate only indirectly to the other about the nature of those fantasies. The process of developing intimacy can be said to be one of opening up realistic communication, exploring the taboo, demystifying fantasies, owning projections, replacing the fantasy with the real. But depressed patients have had the curiosity beaten out of them, and we should expect that it is part of our job to nurture it back to health by being able to talk about it, and sometimes to gratify it.

There is an implicit bargain in all therapy. You give me money, and that's all you have to give me. You don't have to give me respect, affection, sex, sympathy, loyalty, kindness, friendship, or any of the other things that are part of the exchange in all other human relationships. (We say we expect honesty, but we don't really expect it, because we expect our patients to have defenses, shame, and guilt, which get in the way of full disclosure.) Money is all you owe me. In return, you get my implicit promise to act in your best interests at all times, putting aside all my own needs in our relationship. So I don't exploit you, I don't use you, I don't get you to worship me, I don't try to make you love me or like me or be like me.

This axiom leads to two corollaries we generally assume about revealing details about our personal lives to patients: (a) patients don't want to and don't need to know, and keeping ourselves relatively anonymous at the same time as being warm and concerned is simply respectful of the patient's needs; and

(b) patients who want to know about our personal lives are trouble, because they don't understand the implicit bargain, and if they don't understand that, therapy isn't going to work. In general, those assumptions are very true. And, of course, they are supported by the Freudian theoretical position that the therapist should be a blank screen, that the therapy should provide a sterile medium so that we can be sure that whatever develops within it is a contribution from the patient, not the therapist.

And in depression, we don't want patients worrying about or taking care of us. So when my patient is talking about his conflictual relationship with his father, to tell him I understand because of my conflictual relationship with my father is disrespectful. He's paying for the hour; he doesn't want to hear about my problems. Even if it sounds like a normal, human, nice piece of commiseration, most of the time it will come back to haunt us. The concern raised by Gill (1983) seems very valid: that the patient is less likely to talk about his feelings about his father after my self-disclosure just because he fears that hearing anything more about me will make him uncomfortable.

But can't telling the patient something about myself *ever* be in his best interests? Can't we argue that sometimes the best thing I can do on the patient's behalf involves letting him know something about me? As we've discussed, some analytic theorists are now arguing that some of the most curative moments occur when the frame is bent a little, when boundaries are violated a little, because that's when emotions are most fully engaged. Thus Hoffman (1998) suggests that limited direct self-disclosure can enliven the process. Answering a direct personal question before engaging in a discussion about why the patient asks will likely lead to a much different outcome than not answering but having the same discussion. The answer is a small gratification, just as not answering is a rebuff. Many depressed patients will benefit from small gratifications. Therapist self-disclosure can be understood as a form of empathic attunement. As Goldstein (1997) comments, "Correct attunement is the key to the successful use of self-disclosure, whether it is deliberate or spontaneous."

Just as it's neater and cleaner to prohibit all physical contact between therapist and patient, rather than open up a discussion of what kind of contact might be permissible under what circumstances, we can have the same trouble drawing the line about self-revelation. It's easier to say never. It's harder to say sometimes, because then you have to thoroughly understand the principles involved. Gabbard and Lester (1995) suggest as a guideline that helpful self-disclosure generally relates to an aspect of the therapist's experience in the here-and-now of the interaction, and that disclosure of the therapist's current personal problems or childhood history is a sign of trouble. Nevertheless, I think that sometimes it can be in the patient's best interest to know something about our personal history. Having published *Undoing Depression* and told my story, I am more or less forced to defend this position, but I believe it anyway.

Depressed patients desperately need hope, and they suffer from terrible shame, and self-disclosure can help us engage across those barriers. Sometimes we have expert knowledge from our own experience, and to withhold that knowledge is not in the patient's best interest. We don't always have to say that it comes from our own experience, but sometimes it helps to say it. When I'm trying to get someone to understand that mood changes are caused by life events, but we depressives practice isolation, intellectualization, and repression so we don't see the connections, the first thing is to show the patient the connection. *You woke up depressed this morning, and you have no idea why. But when you review the events of the previous day with me, you tell me you had a fight with your wife last night at bedtime. You had a fight with your wife, and you woke up feeling depressed, but it doesn't seem to you that these are connected.* Humor and self-revelation can soften the confrontation of his defensive system. *Well, it certainly seems to me that they are connected, and I'll bet most of the rest of the world would say they are, so it's interesting that you don't see it. I would say you're fooling yourself, except that I do the same thing. Last week I had a horrible backache, and I was so upset that my back was acting up, because it had been good for a while and now I thought it was just going out of control again. But then I remembered that we were being accredited, and that meant a lot of tension for me, which I was feeling in my back, and a little while after I realized there was a reason, my backache went away.* This is not a model interchange; I don't hold this out as the best or the only way to get the patient to see the connection, but it is a way that works sometimes, and the value of it is that it disarms his shame. People with depression think that they are more dysfunctional than anyone else, because they never hear about how anyone else's mind works, and it can help sometimes to let them know that we are human too.

And sometimes in extreme situations, we can use ourselves to give hope. Styron (1990) is especially eloquent on this point. Sometimes all anyone can do for the depressed patient is just keep reminding him that the most intense pain never lasts. And if we can use ourselves as a model for that, so much the better. It can be very hard to say anything that doesn't sound like false reassurance, yet horrible to say nothing at all. So if we can speak from experience, if we can remind the patient that we know this will pass, we should.

At the same time I must say directly that self-revelation, especially of there-and-then material, should always be for a clear, strategic purpose. Most impulses therapists feel to talk about their own story are manifestations of their own anxiety rather than purposeful. Patients are likely to experience such revelations as an empathic disruption: *Why are you thinking about yourself—you're supposed to be concentrating on me!* My experience with patients who have read *Undoing Depression* is instructive. Most never ask anything more about me, except sometimes to seek hope or reassurance. I have the impression that many patients have repressed some details of my history; it is as if they are comforted by the fact that I am a survivor or authority, but they want to maintain me as a somewhat impersonal figure. That is exactly as it should be. For me to break this tacit understanding by gratuitous sharing of my own experience would be intrusive, exploitative, a violation of the implicit bargain of therapy.

THE THERAPIST'S DEPRESSION

We are just as vulnerable to depression as anyone else, if not more so. Failures in our work or in our personal lives can increase vulnerability. We can catch depression not only through our patients' projections, but also just because of life. By strengthening our internal boundaries we can remain receptive to but not overwhelmed by patients' projections, but we can still become depressed.

However, the therapist should not only expect to be in control of his own depression, but also to have a generally optimistic outlook and to have a positive view of other people. Therapists who are overly cynical, critical, bitter, and who enjoy finding pathology and are threatened by the patient's strengths are not what a depressed patient needs. Such attitudes will only reinforce the depression. But a great deal of flexibility is expected from the therapist—to be able to move from genuine empathy with the patient's real pain to confrontation of self-destructive behavior to sincere appreciation of progress. Shallow, self-satisfied cheerleaders aren't needed either.

Schuchter and colleagues (1996) sound a strong warning about the potential impact of depression on the therapist's effectiveness:

> [Therapists who are experiencing depression themselves] resonate more profoundly with themes of depression and have more difficulty extricating themselves from this state. They are also less likely to mobilize those intellectual skills that are necessary for both making clinical decisions and maintaining appropriate distance. Some therapists' boundaries become more fluid when they are depressed, forcing them to withdraw emotionally just to protect themselves. . . . They may see themselves as people who want to control and manipulate others rather than help them; as voyeuristic in contrast to curious and interested; as nurturing their own dependency and narcissism; and, in response to their protective detachment, as uncaring, unfeeling persons just doing a job.
>
> If all of these forces are operating without perspective—without the recognition that this is "depression talking," and that this state is time-limited and state-dependent, depressed therapists may perceive their state as a career-related existential crisis whose solution is change. (p. 66)

In other words, the therapist turns the distorting lens of depression on himself and ascribes to himself the worst possible motives and least possible competence. The solution clearly is for the therapist to have a therapist, a mentor, or consultant to turn to when times are hard. In fact, it seems to me that our work is so demanding that the therapist who cuts himself off from colleagues, teachers, or a former therapist is plainly acting out in a self-destructive manner.

We also have to be aware of the insidiousness of depression within ourselves. Schuchter and colleagues (1996) are appropriately concerned about the effects of a clear-cut depressive episode upon the therapist. I see many more therapists who just seem to lack depth, a quality I attribute to a depressed adaptation. Patients tell me about their former therapists, or about their pharmacologists: "It's like talking to a wall." They complain of a lack of resonance, a feeling that they keep dropping pebbles down the well but hear no splash. The therapist who's not enjoying life, who doesn't have relationships and interests outside his work that bring fulfillment and challenge, probably should not be working with the depressed.

In terms of the therapist's impact on the patient, Goldstein (1997) talks about the damage to the patient when changes in the therapist that he can observe are never acknowledged or validated. Like so many patients' childhood experience, the evidence of the senses is denied; there is a family secret. When the therapist has a serious physical health problem, it can be visible—the therapist loses weight, appears frail. When there is an emotional strain on the therapist—a death in the family, a divorce—it may be equally visible. The therapist may be preoccupied, have difficulty concentrating, be less empathically available. Goldstein has the grace to acknowledge what all of us have felt during times of great stress: When the patient is demanding or his concerns seem trivial, he ought to be glad we're present at all. When we're feeling this beleaguered, it's very difficult to be our usual self, and we have to be ready to acknowledge it to our patient.

Morrison (1997), writing of her experience dealing with life-threatening cancer, observes:

> To me, the main positive effect of occasional, ordinary self-disclosure, is in its humanizing of the relationship. In an extraordinary situation, such as the serious illness of the therapist, which has ultimate ramifications for the patient, the main effect, I think, is in the therapist's offering of authenticity and honesty, in what I consider a real relationship, beyond the transference. . . . Conversely, nondisclosure risks that the patient will feel excluded, unimportant, and perhaps even betrayed, when she or he later learns that the therapist was undergoing such a major experience. (pp. 236–237)

The ideal therapist should never get so depressed that it significantly affects his work; but ideals are in their very nature impossible to achieve. We have the idealized parental imago of Freud, his mouth eaten away by cancer, suffering from painful, ill-fitting prostheses, continuing to attend his patients without a seeming trace of self-pity. But of course his condition did affect Freud's work unconsciously, and of course it is too much to expect of any of us that we never get depressed, and that it never affects our work. Our course should be to practice what we preach: Depression is not a cancer against which we are helpless, but a complex condition which our own determination can—usually—keep under control.

So in some circumstances, when the depression intrudes upon the therapy, the therapist may need to talk about his own depression with his patient. Many therapists are much more comfortable with the idea of self-disclosure about the therapist's reactions to the patient in the here-and-now as opposed to disclosing information about the therapist outside the context of the relationship, especially when it comes to vulnerabilities. But more and more writers are recognizing that the transference is never a sterile medium, that the therapist or analyst inevitably gives himself away in countless ways he's not even aware of, and that the patient's reactions to such "self-disclosure" are just more grist for the mill of therapy. This should not be seen as constituting a blanket endorsement of reck-less self-disclosure but a recognition that much of the rationale for avoiding it is based on a flawed assumption. As Aron (1991) comments, "Self-revelation is not an option; it is an inevitability."

Good timing and attentive sensitivity to the patient's needs are essential. Some may need to idealize us more in the early sessions. I am certainly less likely to acknowledge any current difficulties I may be having to such a patient than to one I have known for some time where we have developed a rueful mutual re-spect for life's ups and downs. However, I am more likely to trade on my hav-ing overcome depression in the past with a new patient, if it will help establish credibility and trust.* But I hope it goes without saying that any self-disclosure on the therapist's part, especially on such a sensitive topic as his own troubles, should always be for a strategic purpose, most likely clarifying the patient's per-ception. Like Johnston and Farber (1996), who found that most patients were highly respectful of the boundaries therapists established around their private lives, I find that while patients may be curious, their need for information about me is extremely limited; limited, in fact, to only that which affects our work.

We have to feel free not to talk about ourselves as well. We cannot be good therapists if we feel the pressure we normally feel in social settings to share some-thing of ourselves in response to hearing our friend's secrets. This is where the implicit bargain of therapy comes back into consideration, and we should be prepared to explain it to our patients: *Sometimes I won't answer questions you may have about me. I can't be a good therapist for you if I get caught up in think-ing about myself. If I can't raise issues with you without being certain that I won't be expected to explore those same issues within myself, I'm going to be limited in what I can do for you.*

TAKING CARE OF THE THERAPIST'S SELF

Just as we encourage our patients to do, we ourselves must learn to practice good self-care. This means learning to relax, to play, to take care of our bodies, and to adapt to stress. But in particular for therapists treating depression, we must accept that we are vulnerable. Like a depressed patient, we must learn to iden-tify our own individual warning signs. Sometimes we experience depression di-rectly, but at other times we may find ourselves not working optimally, acting out, withdrawing, or becoming apathetic. We need to have strategies in place that we can use when we notice these warning signs. These strategies can range from a vacation to a refocusing of one's work habits, from a tennis date to a con-sultation with a trusted colleague.

---

*Renik (1995) argues persuasively that the chief function of analytic anonymity was to protect the analyst's comfortable idealized position; I acknowledge that here I am sug-gesting we substitute one form of idealization for another, with a strategic purpose in mind. As any therapeutic relationship endures, we should expect a gradual shift away from idealization to mutuality.

An important element of good self-care is to permit ourselves to appreciate the very real pleasures of our work. Among the primary pleasures, in my opinion, is the opportunity it gives us to engage emotionally with others. Every session is an emotional workout, and we continually build our stamina and stretch our selves. Humans need to feel affectively connected in order to feel human, and our lives are enriched by our opportunity to connect with our patients; we even get to do it in a relatively safe way, where we set most of the rules and do most of the deciding about when to go deeper, when to back off.

Our work also gives us the opportunity to experience mastery of difficult material. We have learned, or are learning, not to be overwhelmed by emotions. Like a surgeon who is not distracted by the gore of the patient's injuries, we also focus on the task before us. We are able to put up a temporary barrier between ourselves and the panic and the horror in the room, something that does not come naturally to most people. By demonstrating to ourselves that we have what people call courage, we enhance our self-esteem and maintain our confidence that we can do a very demanding job. And by being trusted and living up to the responsibility that others give us, we reaffirm our sense of ourselves as capable and worthwhile.

Psychotherapy is also a highly creative task. No two patients, no two hours are ever alike, and if we begin to experience our work as boring, that's probably a reflection of what's going on inside ourselves rather than our work. We get to help patients find new understanding and new solutions. We get to help them practice creative thinking. "During treatment psychotherapists can also have the creative feeling of providing a responsive environment in which the patient, perhaps for the first time, can know joy . . . the joy of participating in effective psychotherapy (doing or receiving) is ultimately the unique fulfillment of discovering and fostering a nuclear self, either in another person or even in ourselves. It is being present on the day of creation" (White & Weiner, 1986, p. 185).

We also are given the opportunity to practice altruism, in my opinion a highly underrated virtue. Anna Freud (1937/1966) referred to altruism as a higher order defense, the vicarious satisfaction of our own needs through another. In Vaillant's (1993) terms it means doing for others as one would be done by. But it is not masochistic renunciation; we take joy in the happiness of those we give to. And by giving them happiness, we feel more capable of dealing with our own needs.

And that is the last and greatest pleasure of our work. We get help with our own pathology. We can see ourselves in our patients, we can hear the mistakes that they made that we would make too, and hopefully we will be less likely to make such mistakes. When I hear a patient making some of the familiar cognitive errors of depression, I recognize myself. My antennae become more finely tuned and I become more conscious of my own errors. When I hear how a patient can't get out of bed, I'm reminded that it's important for me to exercise. When I hear someone behaving selfishly, I become a little more sensitive to my own selfishness. Our work, properly done, continually makes us a little wiser and better.

Occupational Hazards

Just as much as there are joys inherent in our work, there are also pitfalls. Not everyone can do it. Not everyone understands the lessons our patients are trying to teach us. We can resist these lessons, burn ourselves out, or merely reinforce our own damaged perception of ourselves.

Perhaps many of us are born caretakers. Reiser (1986), himself the son of a psychoanalyst, writes of his experience treating the adult children of psychiatrists during the final years of his own analysis. These people were in the process of psychiatric training themselves. He describes their depression, their hunger for attention, the tendency toward idealization and disappointment, and the relentless drive toward perfectionism—but notes that these are people who function well, who are lively, sensitive, gifted, capable of love, capable of great empathy; in fact, perhaps, too empathic. The problem, indeed, seemed to come from "the inability of these children, as adults, to turn their own exquisite empathy inward. Though they were highly attuned to the authenticity and significance of emotions in others, they seem strangely oblivious, even ridiculing, of emotions in themselves." Despite the absence of overt pathology in their upbringing, they seemed to be able to function only as selfobjects for others. The problem is, of course, that unless we have a healthy respect for our own feelings, we can get so drained and confused by others' conflicting needs that eventually we can become an empty vessel, the life sucked out of us.

Relying on our patients to provide us with a sense of connectedness is also dangerous. Aron (1991) suggests that one of the reasons why we are drawn to this kind of work is because of our own conflicts about knowing and being known, about being in control of what we reveal about ourselves. We can transmute our own grandiose wishes into becoming the world's foremost authority on the patient, denying our own wish to be seen. These notions suggest that self-revelation is a highly seductive subject for the therapist, that the act of "revealing" oneself is fraught with narcissistic, competitive, and libidinal baggage—which it is. Therapists are fascinated with this subject, just as patients are often fascinated with trying to analyze the therapist. This can become a problem in the therapy when "playing with the boundaries" becomes a precious, seductive, or merely distracting game. The therapist who finds himself in such relationships with his patients is well advised to get a life. We need attachments outside the consulting room to keep us humble and real.

And as refreshing as altruism can be, we must be watchful that it doesn't cross the line into overidentification. When we see ourselves too perfectly in the patient, we are not seeing the patient at all. We may influence him to take certain courses of action in order to give ourselves vicarious fulfillment. *Go ahead, walk out on that abusive husband! Stand up to your boss! What's wrong with a little affair?* Or we may be so overcome with the patient's helplessness that we become helpless ourselves. We need to be able to stand back, get our bearings, regain control of our emotions, and remember to act in the patient's best interests.

We must also keep in mind that this is very difficult work, and the odds are not with us. We will have failures. There are many patients we won't be able to help. Sometimes this will even be our fault; we will make an error that the patient won't be able to forgive, but we must learn to forgive ourselves. More often our helplessness will simply be due to circumstances, and we must have other sources of optimism. Sometimes our failures will have tragic consequences. Gitlin (1999), discussing his reaction to a patient's suicide when he was beginning his practice, describes all the features of PTSD in himself, including a course that ran for longer than a year and a permanent effect on his practice. We need to keep in mind that depression is a grave disease and that suicide is a common outcome; a patient's suicide is not by definition the therapist's responsibility.

Therapeutic Sadism

A special problem in our work is what I call sadistic authoritarianism. Speaking for myself but also, I suspect, for many others, part of the attraction of the profession for me was the idea of becoming, in Sullivan's terms, an "expert in interpersonal relations." What a seductive idea! We were to become proficient at "seeing through" people and by implication able to get what we want. Although my professional training and experience has helped me get through life in many profound ways, I have not found that it's given me any special advantage in getting what I want from people—except, sometimes, with my patients, and that's very dangerous.

I have been asking visitors to my Web site and people who attend my lectures to share with me their stories about memorable events in therapy—especially wonderful events or especially difficult events. Most people who reply seem to want to strike a balance, and if they have a complaint about a therapist they also have something good to say, sometimes about the same therapist. One response that seemed to me to be thoughtfully reflective about the situation told me of the following incident:

The therapist and patient were both young women, the therapist having just completed her professional licensing and begun her own private practice. One day the patient saw the therapist in the locker room at the health club that they both, apparently, had joined. The patient said something like, "Now I understand why you always seem so fit." The therapist turned on her and in front of other women in the locker room lectured her about how it was inappropriate for her to address the therapist outside of the office. In the next session the therapist insisted that the patient change health clubs.

Now, we obviously don't know the whole story. Perhaps the patient's memory has been distorted over time, so that what she said was actually more intrusive, the therapist's response less rude. Probably the therapist was young and insecure, and with more experience would have handled the situation more tactfully. There are many mitigating factors we could think of that would change the story or help us understand the therapist's response, but the point is that almost every patient I meet can tell stories like that. Almost everyone has a story about what drove them out of therapy, and too often it seems to be an act that they interpret as one of cruelty or disrespect.

Depressed people sometimes bring out the worst in others, and depressed patients can bring out the worst in therapists. Diane, mentioned above, seems to bring out the sadist in most authority figures. I think of the schoolyard bully, someone who actually enjoys humiliating others, and I think that is the exact experience many patients have had with some therapists. Another patient told me that her therapist had forgotten a session yet billed her for it, and whenever she brought up the subject he met her with silence—for six months, until she finally dropped him.

There are theoretical positions that encourage, if not prescribe, such a sadistic outlook on our patients. Think of Fenichel's (1945) depiction of the depressive as someone who treats others as only a source of narcissistic supply, and how that stance can affect the treatment of a patient who is really grieving a loss. Think of Langs (1973) and the assumption that all the patient's verbalizations are about the transference, or a defense against the transference, and how destructive that attitude can be for a patient who is having problems in real life and just wants help with them. The depressive thinks of himself, and often presents himself, as a lowly worm; we don't need to be encouraged to treat him the same way. We need to do the opposite, to treat him with dignity.

We all have an unconscious. I have "forgotten" appointments with patients; or, just as bad and much more common, forgotten in today's session the continuity with previous sessions. I have known very gentle and caring therapists who have been driven to distraction by certain clients. Rather than acting out our sadistic anger, and rather than merely analyzing and trying to understand it— for that can be too easy, we get the idea that we can keep doing it if we keep analyzing it—let us try to transmute it into energy for the therapy. We could start by acknowledging it when we've done someone an injury—but this seems to be such a difficult thing for most therapists to do, a vestige of the fear that if we allow one small gratification the patient will want to move in with us.

BEING OPEN TO HELP

Too many therapists I know have turned their backs on therapy. They've had a course of treatment early in their career, decided that they're fixed, and not felt it necessary to get any further help or have a sustaining relationship. They maintain a rather brittle façade of competence. If they have a continuing consulting relationship, it usually involves mutual idealization; there is no challenge or growth going on.

We can be a highly judgmental profession. There is a lot of blaming of patients that goes on between therapists. In case staffings, jokes at the patient's expense are common, and loaded words pass moral judgment—needy, passive-aggressive, borderline, poor protoplasm. Diagnostic labels, especially of personality disorders, are used to rationalize our inability to help. In such an atmosphere, no wonder we feel diffident about talking about our uncertainties or vulnerabilities.

Most of the therapists I know are taking antidepressants, but few discuss it openly. In agencies, therapists get together behind closed doors to compare the effects of antidepressants, but never acknowledge publicly that they are taking meds. We perpetuate stigma among ourselves. When I conduct professional workshops, I always ask the audience three questions: (1) How many of you know a colleague who suffers from depression or takes antidepressants?—60 to 80 percent raise their hands. (2) How many of you feel that colleague's work has been impaired by his or her depression?—less than 10 percent raise their hands. (3) How many of you, if you were depressed, would feel safe talking about it among your professional colleagues?—again, only a very small number of positive responses. We cannot practice what we preach.

I know that some of the best therapists—and psychopharmacologists—are especially interested and connected with their patients because of their own experience with mental illness. I'd like to see us more willing to talk about it.

Group processes among professionals in reaction to depression are interesting too. What's the basic task of a case conference or a consultation? Is it to help the patient, the therapist, or the agency? Is the therapist there to complete a ritual, to get help with a case, to validate his or her assumptions about the self? When we hear a presentation by a therapist who seems very confident about his assessment and treatment but we feel something is missing, how do we respond? If we share our concerns, are we acting out sadistic, competitive feelings, or are we acting in the best interests of the patient? Should we consider that the therapist may need to protect himself from aspects of the client's situation that are threatening? When we feel a need to protect a therapist who seems uncertain about a case but appears somewhat defensive about it, what is our best response? The best antidote for depression is to be allowed/enabled/encouraged/expected to express the true self, to explore one's own unconscious, to express all feelings openly and honestly. The real task of all these meetings is to help the patient. The more we can own that as a shared task, the better off we are. Warm fuzzies and unquestioning support don't help depression; creating the conditions where people are stimulated to explore and share does.

Perhaps we should all be more open to the possibility of failure. We can fail with patients because of any number of reasons, absolutely none of which are to be ashamed of. In my experience, it is very unusual for a therapist to transfer a difficult patient. Usually our patients have to drop out, then come back later for a different therapist. What's so bad about acknowledging we're not getting anywhere with a particular patient?

And also maybe we should be more open to the possibility of failure as a profession. Maybe at this point we don't have anything to help a particular individual. For all our theories about and interest in borderline personality disorder, I can't name many cases who have been demonstrably improved by therapy more than by the aging process. Maybe we have swallowed the myth that we sold the public, that we can analyze and understand everything, that our failures are always because the patient dropped out, moved away, or died. Maybe we just don't know enough to really help some people. Maybe we should consider that it might be wise to focus on helping those we know about.

CHAPTER 9
Maintain a
Therapeutic Focus

IN JAMES MANN'S MEMORABLE PHRASE (1973), the precipitant that finally drives the patient to pick up the phone and ask for help can be understood as an example of the "present and chronically endured pain." In psychodynamic terms, there is a fundamental conflict or neurosis, a perseverative attempt to work out the same issue over and over again in life, to reach a different ending. It is Balint's "basic fault" (1979), the issue that can be expected to be brought into the transference as a resistance to change. It is Frank's "focal symptom" (1966), an oblique attempt to gain reassurance from the environment while denying the need for reassurance. It is Luborsky's "core conflictual relationship" (1984), a wish and a defense against the wish. In my terms, it is the patient's failed attempt to use the skills of depression to overcome a problem. The skills of depression all but guarantee failure, the tragic irony of depression that the more one does to avoid a particular outcome, the more one guarantees that outcome. Feelings of frustration and failure stir up bad memories of similar past failures, with their concomitant negative affect and depressed thinking. The failure to solve a life problem not only has intrinsic negative effects, it also precipitates another round of depression.

RECURRENT THEMES

It is clinically useful to start with the hypothesis that there is a meaningful link between the current precipitant and the patient's first episode of depression, and that this link will also represent a problem that the therapy will have to solve.

Almost all initial episodes of depression start with a loss that the patient doesn't totally recover from. Grief is overpowering, the experience of losing emotional control is too terrifying, there is no replacement available for the lost person, the loss precipitates other major losses that have a cumulative impact on the patient's life—whatever the reason, the patient experiences the loss as a trauma. A loss, in my terms, can be very gradual and subtle; the repeated failure of a parent to perform necessary selfobject functions for a child has similar (though more complex) effects on the child's development as a sudden loss through death or divorce. A sudden loss can result in a dramatic change, the first episode of major depression; the cumulative effect of a subtle abandonment results in a gradual change, the development of a depressed self.

In either case, much of the patient's psychic development gets stuck at this point. He begins to learn the skills of depression, which he uses both to find a new solution to the old problem and at the same time to protect himself against future disappointments. By trying to accomplish both purposes at once, he ensures that neither will be entirely successful.

Part of the experience of the unacceptable loss is that—on some level—the patient will blame himself. *Dad rejected me because I'm unlovable. I didn't take good enough care of Mom. If I'd been a better kid, they wouldn't have gotten divorced. I hate them so much, I must be an awful person.* It's quite common for thoughts like these to coexist with much more mature and objective evaluations of the situation. But these thoughts continue, usually at a preconscious level, forgotten for the most part but ready to be dragged out again whenever a new experience rekindles feelings of the old loss. And each of these new experiences reinforces the depression, because the patient can never find a new ending, can never escape that self-blame. If he feels unworthy, he generates rejection by his need for reassurance. If he feels out of control and dangerous, he will keep hurting those who try to love him.

So the patient calls the therapist because something has happened recently to upset his adjustment enough that he feels he can't go on without help, and we take it as a working hypothesis that the current incident is a variation on this old theme. If, in the initial sessions, we can convey to the patient that we understand this connection, we make it clear to the patient that we understand his troubles in a deep and powerful way. If we put this in terms of an empathic statement about the self (see chapter 5), we avoid making him feel defensive—*It seems as if in all your relationships there is something you can't forgive yourself for. It seems that you really doubt that anyone could ever love you. I wonder if you don't fear that your needs are just too overwhelming, that you're doomed to drive everyone away.* We help him feel hope, and we help him feel an intimate connection with us. But developing a treatment focus this way is more than a tool of engagement, it is a way of organizing the therapy. Our task is to help the patient write a new ending for his recurrent problem. The job will be difficult because we can expect that the patient's skills of depression will interfere with engagement in the treatment and with emotional relearning. But by not being what the patient expects—by not rejecting him, not giving up on him, not blaming him, not allowing him to isolate himself—we provide a corrective emotional experience.

In the end, it's not that our love makes up for the trauma of the original loss. Nothing can do that, and we do not have the resources anyway. The new ending is that we help the patient experience the needs he tries to pretend he doesn't feel, giving up on those that are impossible to meet and accepting what life has to offer. But we stay with the patient while he suffers with his needs, acknowledging that there are limits to what we can do and yet not abandoning or blaming him. We are willing to face our limitations and the realities of life and to help the patient bear the disappointment.

When Leon first called me I thought he had swallowed a dictionary. His manner of speech was highly idiosyncratic, not only a preference for big words but a predilection for long complex sentences with many subordinate clauses. He had a hard time getting to the point, but the basic story was that he was back living with his mother in New York after a two-year sojourn in Southern California. His job had ended six months ago and he was having a hard time getting started again. He thought he might be depressed and he had heard of my book.

At our first meeting, Leon's affect was anything but depressed. He seemed "perky," hyperalert; his mind was active, his body restless (the psychiatrist I referred him to at first wondered about manic depression). As he chattered on in his unique way I found that if I paid close attention I could follow the trail of his associations, which turned out not only to make sense but also to reflect an active and insightful mind; but if I tuned out even briefly it was very easy to lose the thread and to feel overwhelmed and put off by his manner of speech, as if under verbal assault.

Leon had received a master's in comparative literature a few years before. His original plan had been to pursue a doctorate and an academic career, but he'd been turned off by what he learned of the politics of academia. He turned to his second love, computers, and began freelance consulting, which eventually led to his job in California. He'd loved the climate and the friends he made, but eventually he ran into trouble with his boss, who, Leon felt, did not adequately market or advocate for the needs of their department with the company as a whole. Leon's insistence that his boss shape up led to a lot of friction and the eventual loss of his job. He had then come back to New York and had thought he could quickly find another position, but he realized he was procrastinating. Now six months had passed, he was running out of money, and he had to do something. Could I help?

I thought I was hearing in Leon's story a theme of idealization/disappointment with authority figures and institutions, so I asked him about his father. His parents had separated shortly before Leon left for California, after a long and unhappy marriage. Leon was clearly on his mother's side in the conflict. His father had been a scapegrace all his life, full of potential in his field but never able to put the deal together that would lead to success. Instead, he drifted from job to job, and spent much of Leon's childhood and adolescence trying to work out of the home, but drinking too much for anyone's good. Leon's mother did not like

*the situation but tolerated it—for the sake of the children, as she later told him—
herself working long hours as a teacher. The family lived in the poorest section of
an affluent Long Island suburb, and Leon felt like an outsider at school: not the
right clothes, no car, a nerd. In the present, Leon talked about the current state
of alienation with his father, who rarely communicated with Leon or his sister,
and was trying to get out of a reasonable financial settlement with Leon's mother
by pleading poverty.*

*As we worked together it became clear that Leon's need for a father and rage
at his father's abandonment was the core of a central issue that got played out
throughout Leon's life. Leon had been a hyperactive and gifted child, in the "geek"
track in his large high school, where he felt isolated and unpopular. But he had
the ability to hyperfocus, and he comforted himself in his isolation by reading
everything he could get his hands on. He knew something about everything—his
degree in comparative literature was merely icing on the cake—but like every au-
todidact he didn't know what he didn't know, and that made him anxious. He was
openly bitter about the lack of guidance in school and career; his high school gifted
program had been a major disappointment, and he had ended up at what he considered a second-rate college and graduate school because he was making all the
decisions on his own.*

*I found it easy to provide Leon with the structure that he needed, and he re-
sponded as though he'd been waiting for it all his life, as indeed he had. I insisted
that he find meaningful work, and he contacted some peers in California and immediately got connected with a freelance project. He was surprised that people
were happy to hear from him. I insisted that he save his money and get out of
debt. We talked about his long-term aspirations, and he was clearly happy to be
"held"—taken seriously and understood.*

*The focus for Leon was both his need for guidance and his fear that he was un-
worthy of it. He was very aware of the need for and his consequent resentment of
authority figures in the past and present who let him down, but more defended
against his doubts about himself. These doubts were manifested in his highly idiosyncratic manner of thinking and speaking, which both preserved a precarious self-
esteem and kept others at arm's length. As I got better at tracking his train of
thought, it was hard for me to know sometimes if he was being more direct or if
he was just training me. I had to make an effort to train him to pay attention to
his emotional state and to speak in the language of feelings, where simple words
convey the greatest impact.*

CLUES IN THE PRESENTATION
OF THE SELF

I make it a habit to note exactly what the patient says to me in the first phone
call and in the first session. If it's not volunteered, I will ask directly, *What was
it that finally made you decide it was time to get help? What was going on when*

you picked up the phone? I find that the patient's words often have an uncanny accuracy, foreshadowing much of what we will have to deal with in the therapy, often in a deeply ironic way which I can only understand fully in retrospect. Sometimes I hear a metaphor that will be packed with meaning, allowing the development of a private language between myself and the patient, a verbal short-hand that establishes an atmosphere of intimacy very quickly.

Diane's dream after reading my book—that we could remove the black spot in her brain but she might die in the process—is one vivid example, which had multiple layers of meaning. The black spot could represent her depression, which was so much a part of her identity, or her grandmother's "schizophrenia," which was the secret fear of her family. Later, when Diane's depression had recurred full force and the idealized transference had worn off, we could talk about her frustration that I did not have an X-ray machine or operating room, the magical instruments that could heal her forever.

Sandra, who had been sexually abused by her father and suffered from manic de-pression, only said she needed counseling to help her quit smoking because she might have throat cancer. True enough, and that issue was a priority, but it was also true that she wasn't going to tell me anything more about herself until she got to know me.

Elizabeth, who didn't seem to be able to separate from the lover whose callous treatment made her miserable day after day, whose recent serious auto accident had left her in great pain and with a long road to recovery, mentioned almost in a sarcastic aside in the first few minutes that her father had died six weeks ago ("Oh yeah, and then the cat died, my father died, and the tractor broke down"). She continued to "forget" about this loss throughout the early part of the treatment.

GLORIOUS DETAIL

Some patients paint a vivid picture for us. They bring their lives to life in the consulting room, and the therapist gets a crisp, clear understanding of the nuts and bolts of their interaction with the world. (Some, of course, carry this too far and the therapy becomes overwhelmed with detail.) But most depressed patients aren't good at painting a picture. Their flattened affect dampens color, their im-paired concentration omits detail, and their helplessness vitiates against paying attention. I often find to my chagrin that when I assume I know what is going on in fact I'm going down the primrose path.

There is no such thing as a stupid question in psychotherapy. We need to un-derstand the patient's life in glorious, elaborate, intimate detail. If we don't un-derstand what's going on, we must ask about it. It's only by knowing who said what to whom when and what they were feeling like or looked like at the time, what their manner had to say about the content of their speech, what led up to it, what happened after it, that we can hope to understand the patient's experience. In doing so, we teach the patient important observational skills and give him the opportunity to challenge his assumptions about the world. We are also conveying that his life is important and interesting. To sit back and let the patient go on in a desultory monologue, though it may seem polite to a beginner, is actually disrespectful. Only when we fully understand the intricacies of the patient's world can we be fully engaged in the process.

Jane brought in a story she had written. Though it expressed her anger, loss, and longing, there was no theme and she presented it without commentary. She went on to complain about how her 15-year-old daughter Janice had started acting "babyish" at bedtime, a description I had never heard before.

In the previous session I had found myself in the position of giving Jane permission to let Janice move out and live with Jane's mother. She seemed to be running wild, and Jane was unable to control her. Between Jane's low-income job, her care for her other children, her hostile-dependent relationship with her mother, and the physiological problems that drained her of energy, she seemed to have nothing left over. She felt that she provided a good home, but Janice kept demanding more. I felt that Jane was setting up a situation where her daughter would continue to escalate until there was a catastrophe at home, and asked if she had considered letting Janice have what she wanted. This mild suggestion was all that was necessary for Jane to decide it was a good idea.

But all Jane had to say today was that she was acting "babyish." As I frequently felt with Jane, things seemed to be happening for no clear reason. Janice was "out of control," her mother was "sadistic and sick"—but those were generalities. I asked her to describe what happened the previous day, when Janice ended by acting "babyish."

She and the other children were cleaning the house. Janice came home from an overnight visit at a friend's house, and immediately got on the phone with another friend. Jane asked her to help with the housecleaning, and Janice called her a motherfucker. She told Janice to go to her room, which she did "sort of," but stayed on the phone with her friend. She spent the rest of the evening playing loud music and fixing herself elaborate snacks, pointedly having a good time while the others worked. At bedtime, Janice repeated old bedtime rituals from her childhood in a tone that was much more taunting and condescending than babyish.

I was mortified that it had taken me so long to understand what was going on. I told Jane: "Here's the rule with teenagers. Never give any directive unless you're willing to back it up all the way. If you tell her to go to her room, she goes to her room. Everything else stops until that happens. Until you can do that, she won't respect you." She looked embarrassed but agreed that she let Janice get away with murder. "But I can't do that; I never was the kind of person who could be so firm." As she left the session, she asked ruefully, "Know where I can buy a backbone?"

CHAPTER 10

Address the Interpersonal
and Social World

The communicative aspect of depression implies an entire infraverbal communication, a call for help, for consolation, but at the same time a refusal of help, an insistence on showing oneself inconsolable. . . . Hope—the confident cathexis of an image of self and its future potentialities—is the opposite of depression; it is the feeling that the hurt is not definitive, that reparation is possible. (Haynal, 1976/1985, p. 28)

DEPRESSED PEOPLE CRAVE connection with other people while the nature of the disease makes it impossible for us to connect. In fact, we can be very difficult to live with. We need a great deal from others, but we are embarrassed and confused by our needs, so we don't articulate them well. We need to practice letting down our masks, letting other people get to know us as we see ourselves. But this is a very difficult thing to do, not only because it goes against all the interpersonal skills of depression we have learned, but also because it is likely to be met with opposition in the stable dysfunctional interpersonal world our relationships have become.

The interpersonal world is the stage on which depression plays. Desperate for love, approval, and respect in order to heal the wound within the self, the depressive seeks those qualities from the people who play important roles in his life. But his very desperation frightens people, engages their defenses so that they keep him at arm's length. If they should give him what he says he wants, he remains dissatisfied; if they withhold, he will become enraged or withdraw. Whatever happens, no one gets what they need. The therapist working with the depressed patient must develop a thorough knowledge not only of the patterns of his interpersonal relationships but also of the realities of the people in his life. While depressed patients are good at projection and misinterpretation, the therapist cannot take for granted that every interaction they report is a distortion. Sometimes in relationships the patient's nightmares really do come true.

RELATIONSHIPS AND LOSS

Most first episodes of depression are linked to loss of an important relationship. The experience of grief and that of depression are almost indistinguishable. Freud argued that depression was always about an unfinished mourning process, our inability or unwillingness to accept the finality of a loss. The depression-prone individual, destabilized by both the experience and expression of intense emotions, is likely to try not to grieve, but to end up feeling powerless and over-whelmed, stuck in grief. This leaves the individual vulnerable in new relation-ships to a state of permanent vacillation between the poles of fusion and with-drawal, dependency and counterdependency, with an unstable sense of his own boundaries. We want to believe that others have the power to heal us, and so we desperately pursue them, seeking fusion; and if they disappoint us, we may withdraw into bitter, hurtful isolation. Many people with depression remain in unsatisfactory relationships marked by dependency and aggression, always hop-ing and always disappointed.

A goal of therapy in such cases must be to help the patient learn the value of healthy boundaries. The ideal is to have boundaries that are semipermeable, to be able to merge with others at times of great intimacy, but to be capable of functioning autonomously when needed. We all want to have a degree of conscious control over this process, so that we can *choose* not to fall in love with the pretty lady at the next table who is flirting with us, choose not to lose our head completely in a heated argument, but at the same time allow our-selves to merge and bond with people we can trust in situations of safety. A boundary is simply a demarcation of what's inside the self and what's outside: what's my responsibility and what's yours, what's my emotional state and what's yours.

Alcoholics Anonymous, Al-Anon, and the recovery movement have a great deal to teach professional therapists about boundaries. Alcoholic marriages and families are characterized by identity diffusion; everyone blames everything ex-cept alcohol for the problems in the family, and true responsibility is never ac-knowledged. Much of the work of AA and Al-Anon and addictions counseling in general is about who said what to whom when, trying to pin down evasions and manipulations while encouraging the individual to trust his own observa-tions. This is how healthy boundaries get built. The same fine-grain analysis of interaction likewise needs to take place in psychotherapy with the depressed. In the depressed person's interpersonal world the reason for diffuse boundaries is not collusion to deny the effects of alcohol, but rather to perpetuate the de-pression—to keep the patient confused, stuck, powerless, and overwhelmed.

I firmly believe that people can practice boundary setting and help them-selves recover from depression in the process. Therapists can encourage people to practice simple skills: to insist on privacy; to establish routines; to count to ten before responding; to identify and resist manipulation; to differentiate be-tween what we can control and what we can't, and not feel responsible for what we can't. But many therapists forego opportunities to be of significant help to patients because they believe that education is not part of therapy, or that true change comes only through the therapeutic relationship.

COMMUNICATION SKILLS

Research by Libet and Lewinsohn (1973) investigated the hypothesis that people with depression were less skillful socially than others. The absence of social skill, it was thought, led to fewer successful social interactions and thence to feelings of exclusion, anger, and low self-esteem. Although it's going too far to argue that the absence of social skill is a stable trait of depressives, the investigators found evidence that it is certainly a frequent state. In student analogue experiments, those who were assessed as more depressed emitted substantially less behavior when in small-group situations than normals. When they did interact interpersonally, their behavior was met with fewer rewarding comments (of approval or inclusion) and more punishing comments (ignoring, changing the subject). To the extent that we can arm the depressed patient with more adaptive social skills, and teach him about the consequences of social withdrawal, we can help break the vicious circle he finds himself in socially.

Emotional Expression

People in a depressed state tend to blunt their affective expression. They stand rigidly, speak in a monotone, and omit the facial expressions and other nonverbal forms of emphasis that typically accompany speech. They tend to engage in communication of any kind less than other people; they tend to react slowly in social situations and thus miss opportunities for engagement. In studies of small-group behavior, it is clear that those who engage in communication become the focus of attention, while those who communicate less are left on the fringes.

The therapist-patient interaction with depressed patients can degenerate into a dull monotony. The therapist must take the responsibility for energizing the therapy. This may mean, at times, specifically commenting on the patient's muted expression and its impact on the listener; at other times, deliberately mirroring and reinforcing more intense expressions of affect.

"Spilling"

While we want to encourage emotional expression, we must recognize that many people with depression are seemingly unaware of the discomfort they cause others by their open shame about themselves. This phenomenon can range from inappropriate remarks at cocktail parties *(No, I didn't see that movie, I must have been in the psych ward when that came out)* to badgering a lover for reassurance *(You're just saying that you love me, I know you don't mean it)*. Generally, the social impulse is to comfort people who are hurting, but such blatant disregard for convention makes others want to run away. This may be a part of depressives' technique of instigating rejection before a relationship can develop. We sometimes have to point out that such topics of conversation betray a self-absorption that others find off-putting.

Assertiveness

People with depression seem to have a wish that others understand and respect their needs automatically. We tend to be rather naïve about the idea that our motives and desires are constantly in conflict with those of others. Asserting one's rights feels like an unfair burden. And fearing intense emotions, depending on others' approval, the depressive tends to back away from confrontation.

Assertiveness training is simple and effective treatment for these habits. Do-it-yourself manuals are available (Bourne, 1990, Smith, 1985); the patient can do the reading, implement the principles, and review the results with the therapist. One source (Bower, 1975) describes a simple four-step process for assertiveness:

1. *Describe.* Describe exactly what is upsetting you. Be calm and cool. State the problem in objective, noninflammatory terms. Stick to the immediate issue.
2. *Express.* Express exactly how the situation makes you feel. Describe your emotional reaction in terms of I statements. Don't accuse the other of making you feel this way, just state it as part of the problem.
3. *Specify.* Specify exactly what you want the other person to do, what behavior on his part will address the situation.
4. *Consequence.* Describe exactly what you will do if the other person doesn't comply. Again, be calm and cool, not threatening; just state the facts.

Taking responsibility for one's behavior, and expecting the same from others, may be the only way there is to develop self-respect. Generally, people with depression are thought to be, if anything, overresponsible. We accept blame for things that are not our fault, and we can feel horribly guilty about trivial events. But in reality this phenomenon is a result of porous boundaries and cognitive distortion. We're not good at differentiating ourselves from others, and we tend to believe that, when things go wrong, it's our fault. The therapist may have to help the patient learn how to track interpersonal causes and effects, to objectively observe the impact on others of his behavior and of other forces that are outside the patient's control.

Therapists can remind their patients that they are responsible only for their own actions and failures to act. They are not responsible for how they feel, how they look (within limits), their intelligence, connections, or other attributes that come down through inheritance or luck. They are not responsible for the way others feel, except insofar as their actions engendered those feelings. They cannot make themselves responsible for making others happy; instead, they have to be responsible for making themselves happy. They're allowed to be selfish, to put themselves first at times. Continual self-sacrifice is masochistic and irresponsible.

Patients must also be encouraged to expect responsibility from others. As in any human interaction, if we are hurt by another person's behavior, we need to let him know how he has hurt us; to do less diminishes our self-respect. We can, and should, be forgiving; but there is a line between forgiveness and being taken advantage of. When others in the patient's interpersonal world repeatedly manipulate, abuse, or otherwise take advantage, the therapist should be prepared to help the patient develop a heightened sensitivity to the impact of such experiences on his depression, and to review the options open to him in protecting himself from these experiences.

Engaging and Disengaging

In the same sense that depression can manifest itself in the extremes of frozen affect and inappropriate spilling, patients can vacillate between depressed self-absorption and oversensitivity to any feeling anyone in the room is having. "Emotional contagion" is the term for how, for instance, panic runs through a room, communicated more by body language, facial expression, and tone of voice than by the direct experience of a threat. The patient who is overly vulnerable to this process needs to be taught to observe its manifestations in himself and what he can do to defend himself against it. The idea that he has some choice in whether or not to get caught up in how others feel is likely to come as news to many patients, who view themselves as passive responders. Best to simply state it as a matter of scientific fact: *There are simple ways to protect yourself from emotional contagion: Take three deep breaths, count to ten, walk away, notice that your feelings are happening to you and are not, in fact, you.*

The opposite problem is presented by the patient who does not respond appropriately to others' affective communication because of his own depressed self-absorption. These patients are likely to lead rather isolated lives and unlikely to have any insight into the nature of the problem. The only evidence the therapist is likely to hear—other than the patient's isolation from the therapist—is the apparently inexplicable reactions of others in the patient's life. These appear to the patient to be unprovoked attacks, when in fact the other person has been provoked by the patient's failure to respond to their emotional expression in a socially expectable way. When we become aware that this is a pattern with the patient, we need to start teaching the patient how to get along socially. Active listening skills—making a focused effort to understand the other's point of view; echoing and mirroring; asking lots of questions; sitting down and maintaining eye contact rather than allowing oneself to be distracted—are skills that the patient can practice and learn.

Rejection Sensitivity

While it's true that people with depression seem to be more easily destabilized than others by experiences of rejection, it's also true that people with depression are in fact rejected more often than other people. In studies of small-group interaction, Libet and Lewinsohn (1973) found that depressed people were less likely than normals to elicit positive reactions (expressions of affection, approval, interest, etc.) from others, and more likely to elicit negative reactions (criticism, disapproval, interruptions, etc.). It's another of the great ironies of depression: Hurt more than most by rejection, the behavior we adopt to try to avoid it merely guarantees more of it.

Cognitive therapists would have the patient closely question his own perspective: *Is it really rejection or do I just think it is?* I sometimes suggest to patients that they inoculate themselves against the experience by inviting rejection and noticing that they survive it. Newer antidepressant medications are thought by some to raise the threshold of rejection sensitivity, so that the patient doesn't notice or isn't derailed by small slights.

The dynamic of rejection sensitivity is that the patient is excessively dependent on positive feedback from those around him to maintain a feeling of goodness about the self. Experiences of rejection are shaming, flooding the self with negative affect and all the cognitive distortions and problematic behaviors that accompany shame. This process is part of the therapeutic relationship as well; the patient feels acutely shamed just by asking for help, and any sign of disinterest or disapproval on the therapist's part will be experienced as a hurt. When the patient's defense is to withdraw, we can lose the patient without ever knowing why; when the defense is to attack, we may also lose the patient but at least we have a chance to address the issue. But when the patient's pattern is to internalize, to assume that the therapist is indeed rejecting but that it's the patient's own fault, we can reinforce depression without being aware we are doing so. And it's very difficult to get patients who internalize to be aware of what they're doing in the first place and then to trust that it's safe to talk about how they experience the therapist. It becomes incumbent on the therapist to pay close attention to the patient's moment-to-moment experience in the hour: Does he grow more engaged, his affect brighter, his communication more direct? Or does he become more vague, withdrawn, passive? These changes, while of course partially determined by the content of the session, are also manifestations of the patient's feeling of being held and accepted by the therapist. Eventually, with time and skill, even the internalizing patient may come to feel that it's safe to mention it when he doesn't experience the therapist as being in tune; and thence to understand that his moods are not just an out-of-control internal process but a response to how he feels people treat him.

INTERPERSONAL PSYCHOTHERAPY

Interpersonal psychotherapy (IPT) is a well-known treatment method for depression which has been empirically validated as approximately as effective as cognitive-behavioral therapy and medication. As the name implies, IPT focuses on the patient's interpersonal world. It was developed as a pluralistic approach to treatment of depression, drawing from differing theoretical points of view, but emphasizing always the current interpersonal relations of the patient. From the beginning, there was an emphasis on empirical validation of the method and the techniques (Klerman et al., 1984). Also from the beginning, the approach was conceptualized as a focused, time-limited, treatment method. Klerman and his colleagues trace their roots to Meyer and Sullivan, Fromm-Reichmann, Becker, Frank, and Arieti and Bemporad.

A depressed state will disrupt an individual's interpersonal relations, and troubles in relationships will affect an individual's mood. IPT challenges the therapist and patient to reverse the usual psychodynamic and psychopharmacological bias, and consider the idea that disturbed relationships are the primary problem, depressed mood the result. Or at least, since the method is empirical, to entertain the idea that repairing disturbances in social relations can repair depression, regardless of which is the cause and which is the effect.

IPT assumes that the need for attachment bonds is universal and innate, and that when those bonds are threatened the experience of depressed affect and the display of depressed demeanor are probably universal and innate as well. The display, if not the affect, has survival value for the mammalian infant, eliciting care. The experience of mourning, also innate, is a close cousin to the experience of depression, but the presence of other attachments prevents a full depressive cycle from initiating. IPT hypothesizes that experiences of loss in childhood, especially the loss of parental figures where there has been a problematic attachment or when the quality of replacement relationships is inadequate, contribute to vulnerability to depression in adulthood. Depression in parents, parental rejection or hostility, and family discord are also thought to contribute to vulnerability to depression in adulthood.

Likewise, certain common difficulties in adulthood are associated with development of depression. Marital discord, loss or threat of loss of other meaningful relations, physical illness, job stress, financial difficulties, transitioning from one role to another—all are recognized as often preceding episodes of depression. And depression leads to further difficulties in interpersonal relations. Studies in social psychology have shown that people seek to avoid or escape from communication with depressed individuals. While the normal response to sadness or distress is sympathy and comfort, after a certain amount of time we expect the individual to respond; when the depressive doesn't respond, we feel frustrated, perhaps angry or depressed ourselves. Mates of depressed patients are themselves at high risk for depression or other mental illness, a phenomenon that increases with the duration of the relationship; and the researchers feel they have strong indication that this is not a phenomenon of assortative mating (depressed people only marry other depressed people) but of interpersonal toxicity (depressed people can make their mates depressed).

Finally, IPT argues that there is empirical evidence that there are enduring personality traits that both predispose to depression and prevent complete recovery. These traits include being introverted, dependent, lacking self-confidence, unassertive, pessimistic, and a damaged or inadequate self-image.

But in essence, IPT relies little on theory, and the connections between its methods and theoretical underpinnings are not clearly spelled out (Joiner, Coyne, & Blalock, 1999). IPT is essentially a treatment method, emphasizing empirical investigation and validation, based on the assumption that changing the patient's interpersonal relations will help assuage the depression, but not going much further in efforts to explain or predict, and largely avoiding the chicken-or-egg question of which comes first.

IPT for depression is conducted with two goals in mind: to reduce depressive symptoms and to address the interpersonal problems associated with the symptoms. Though there is a hope that accomplishing these goals will lead to at least partial resolution of the personality issues just named, or contribute to prevention of future episodes, the stated goals have only to do with resolution of the current episode.

PROJECTION AND PROJECTIVE
IDENTIFICATION, SPLITTING
AND REPETITION COMPULSION

These are some of the skills of depression which make relationships with the depressed person so difficult and problematic. Projection is understood to be a process whereby painful feelings or ideas originating in the self are experienced as emanating in someone or something else (an "object," in psychoanalytic terms, can be a person, a group, a movement, an idea; political battles are the source of much projection). Incorporation is the reverse, when aspects of another are attributed to the self. Incorporation is usually thought of as a comforting process in grief whereby we take into ourselves aspects of the lost object. However, we may also incorporate aspects of another that we dislike, as Freud argued in "Mourning and Melancholia."

Trying to resolve a conflict with someone who is projecting is fruitless, and to say "you're projecting" only raises the stakes and makes matters worse. When the therapist hears about repetitive disputes in the patient's life, he should consider whether a projection process is occurring, and whether it might also be getting played out in the transference. The therapist should then focus on the patient's felt experience: *It seems like you feel that I'm attacking you. I'm trying not to, but maybe I'm not aware of something that's going on here. Can we talk about this?* It is, of course, usually hate, rage, rejection, disapproval that is split off and attributed to the therapist or object. These are feelings the patient may have initially experienced from the parent or other lost object, which have now become internalized, perpetuating the vicious circle of depression.

Projective identification is a major element in recruiting accomplices into the patient's stable, dysfunctional interpersonal world. It involves others correctly understanding the subtext of the patient's messages, the unconscious expectations he has that people will reject him, ignore him, treat him with contempt or sadism. When the therapist finds himself experiencing some of these feelings about the patient, we may understand it to be part of a process of projective identification, but to interpret it to the patient as such is merely acting out sadistically. *It's your fault that I'm rejecting you.* This is a major stumbling block for many patients with depression, who will hear any suggestion that they change their behavior as an accusation that their problems are all their own fault. Tact, timing, and patience, a willingness to look openly at the therapist's contribution to all misunderstandings, and a determination to solve the problem in the face of doubt and uncertainty are required elements in the therapist.

It is easy for the therapist to come to participate in the irony of depression. If, for instance, we consistently point out how the patient puts himself down, we are putting him down; if we keep emphasizing how he minimizes progress, we also are minimizing progress. The patient can come to believe that he is not a good-enough patient, just as he believes he is not good enough in other aspects of his life. Instead of always pointing out the defense against feeling good, it may be better to ignore it sometimes and get back to what caused the good feeling in the first place. If there is a healthy give-and-take in our relationship, the patient will come to the time when he can explore what is so anxiety-provoking about feeling good; but if he expects that we too are never satisfied with him, he will just acknowledge that it is difficult and blame himself. Especially if the general thrust of the patient's efforts has been in a positive direction, for us to keep pointing out the negatives verges on therapeutic sadism.

The patient comes to the therapeutic relationship with a kind of fatalism, expecting that this once again will be a relationship that will fail to satisfy him, to cure the "basic fault." At the same time, he wishes and hopes that this will be a different relationship. The therapist's task is to prevent the patient's self-fulfilling prophecy from repeating itself. The therapist is only human, and will be influenced by the patient's projective identification and by his own unconscious motivations, but he must work hard at clarifying ambiguity and moving the process in a direction that addresses the patient's expressed wishes. The depressed patient can resist engagement in many ways—by rejection, by dependency—but the hallmark of depressive resistance is withdrawal, tuning out, refusing to come out and play with the therapist. This attitude leads, pari passu, to the therapist's frustration or giving up on the patient; the patient sees this even when the therapist is unaware of it, and (not aware of his own contribution to the dance) concludes that the therapist is but one more in a long line of people who have disappointed and rejected him. But when the opposite happens, when the therapist jumps on the patient's withdrawal, persistently points it out, brings it to the patient's awareness and the two of them collaborate on figuring out what it means, the opportunity is there for a new "mental representation" (Fonagy et al., 1993) to develop. A new nexus of affect, relationship, behavior, and hope can be laid down.

What is experienced as rejection depends greatly on the uniqueness of the patient. Ehrenberg (1992) reports her embarrassment at becoming drowsy during a patient's sessions and her surprise when he reported experiencing it as comforting. To the patient, it meant that she felt safe with him, a man who did not feel safe with his own impulses, and it reminded him of comforting, intimate nap times with his mother who was otherwise anxious, unstable, and threatening.

But therapists are prone to some forms of acting out that clearly betray a rejecting component: forgetting appointments, starting the appointment late or ending it early, not giving notice of vacations and interruptions. On a micro level, finding ourselves distracted or bored, losing the thread, sighing, yawning, changing the subject—depressed patients are infinitely sensitive to these insults, always looking to the therapist for signs of loss of love and approval. We may in fact be feeling bored by the patient, or angry at him for a reason we might not be able to identify; we might simply be feeling overwhelmed, sorry for ourselves, needing a nondepressed patient who can perk us up a little; or we might not know why we are rejecting the patient. Regardless, if ever we are confronted by the patient, the worst thing we can do is deny what we are doing, try to disconfirm the evidence of his own senses. It is far better to acknowledge what's happened, explore the patient's reactions, explain the meaning from our perspective insofar as we know it, and mutually explore the implications for the relationship.

> There is no way for the analyst to know, with certainty, what course to pursue with respect to the balance between spontaneous, personal responsiveness and adherence to psychoanalytic rituals at any given moment, nor can the balance that is struck be one that the analyst can completely control. The basis for the patient's trust is often best established through evidence of the analyst's struggle with the issue and through his or her openness to reflect critically on whatever paths he or she has taken, prompted more or less by the patient's reactions and direct and indirect communications. (Hoffman, 1998, p. 225)

Many depressed patients will never complain, no matter how much we abuse them. Some will drop out, and some will settle into a masochistic "therapeutic" relationship that can become the most important relationship in the patient's life and last for many years. Just as the patient continually scans us for signs of disapproval, we must be alert for subtle indications that the patient isn't happy with the way things are going. Dreams of rejecting parents, lovers, or bosses, complaints of careless treatment at the hands of others, usually have plenty of basis in reality but also may be a communication from the patient's unconscious about the therapist. A simple comment like *There are so many experiences in your life when you are made to feel inadequate, I wonder how often it happens in here but you don't feel comfortable mentioning it* may open a door.

DAMAGE CONTROL

Most people with depression are only too aware that their illness is hurting their loved ones. In a telephone survey, more than 90 percent of respondents said their families had been an important influence on their decision to seek treatment (Brody, 1998b). Depressed parents often worry that their depression has a negative impact on their children, and unfortunately their fears are justified. When parents have major depression, approximately 60 percent of their children will develop a psychiatric disorder during childhood or adolescence, and are four times more likely to develop an affective disorder than children of nondepressed parents. By the age of 20, a child with an affectively ill parent has a 40 percent chance of experiencing an episode of depression; by 25, the odds rise to 60 percent (Beardslee et al., 1998; see also Weissman, Warner, Wickramaratne, Moreau, & Olfson, 1997). Children of depressed mothers are often objectively more difficult to raise, suggesting that there is a reciprocal relationship between parental depression and childhood difficulties that maintains dysfunction and depression for generations (Hammen, 1991; Warner, Weissman, Mufson, & Wickramaratne, 1999). The frequent observation of family therapists is that a child acts out in order to help a parent snap out of a depression, to get back a functional parent who can set limits and provide nurturing in the family.

As therapists, we need to recognize that depression affects the whole family and that we have a positive obligation to help mitigate its effects. Our patients want to be good parents. They are not going to be injured by our direct advice about how to handle difficult parenting situations. Let us be sure that we know what we are talking about, that our view of the problem is complete and objective, not distorted by our feelings about the patient or by stereotypes; but when we can be sure we have something helpful to say, let's say it. *Your battles with your child are making you feel ashamed and ineffectual, and they're not doing him any good either. How can you learn how to handle the situation differently?*

ENGAGEMENT OF OTHERS

A study of family members found that relatives of depressed patients reported just as much distress as relatives of schizophrenic patients. "It was striking to find that, independent of psychiatric disorder or ethnicity, relatives agreed that the most frequent and most distressing symptom is the patient's misery," which was statistically the same for both groups (Jenkins & Schumacher, 1999). Family members, loved ones, and associates of the depressed patient are inevitably involved in the problem, because of the nature of depression. Their involvement can be seen as a destructive element contributing to the patient's suffering or an understandable reaction to the patient's self-defeating interpersonal patterns. In most cases, neither end of the spectrum contains the whole truth. Most people have mixed motives most of the time, and we are best advised to help the patient understand that and use the knowledge.

Depressed patients are ashamed of themselves, ashamed of being a burden to family or friends. It's important for the therapist to listen carefully to reports about the behavior of significant others and help the patient understand what's helpful and what's destructive. *It's okay to lean on reliable others some now, while you're sick, and it's okay to distance yourself from destructive others now.* The therapist should feel comfortable offering to meet with family members or other people in the patient's life and advise them on how they can be helpful to the patient. (All communication between the therapist and others in the patient's life should take place in front of the patient.) Sometimes a social intervention can give much more immediate relief than continuing to be stuck with the patient's helplessness. It's always dangerous to assume that people won't be helpful without giving them a chance. That kind of assumption suggests that the therapist is supporting a paranoid view of the world and encouraging dependency.

Harry and his wife are a devoted, passionate couple. She hates his depression, he hates her weight. Their fights are truly dangerous, involving threatening each other with knives and guns. They need to stop focusing on the other's behavior and be more responsible for themselves. I can help her understand that Harry and I are working on his problems and that there's little she can do now beyond offering encouragement and refraining from provocation. She is responsive to the suggestion; their fights de-escalate into a truce while he and I work on his depression.

In keeping with the philosophy that depression is a chronic illness that the patient will battle throughout his life, it only makes sense to involve significant others in the battle. The patient may be unaware of how his depression is affecting others close to him, and though it may be hard to hear at first, for instance, how a spouse or child is hurt by his irritability or self-preoccupation, it can provide greater motivation for change. The other person may be able for the first time to express some of that anger and hurt in a neutral setting, in a nondestructive way, which can lead to reduced resentment and greater openness of communication in general. Teaching the others about depression—that it is a disease with a predictable course, that many of the patient's irritating habits are not willful selfishness or weakness but instead manifestations of the disease— can help them feel less injured and defuse many of the power struggles they can get into with the depressed patient. Especially with patients who are suicidal or who are slow to pick up on the warning signs that they are heading into another episode, significant others in the patient's life can be used as monitors to help get help before the situation becomes too acute.

A very simple social intervention is similar to the family therapy technique of reframing: *It's the depression talking. He isn't treating me badly because he thinks I've done something wrong, he's treating me badly because he's depressed. I can comfort him instead of feeling like I have to defend myself. She isn't withdrawing and sleeping because she doesn't love me anymore, she's doing it because she's depressed. I have to not take it personally and control my anxiety.* But attributing everything to the illness can be carried too far. In marital and parent-child relations, the depressed partner may have legitimate grievances that can be robbed of their legitimacy by dismissing them as "the depression talking." The therapist needs to maintain a balance, and maintain his alliance with the undepressed self of the patient. When the patient has tried to resolve a conflict, and the therapist can see that he's using the best coping skills he has available, but the other is intransigent or, worse yet, uses the depression to dismiss the patient's argument, the therapist needs to support the assertive, healthy behavior of the patient. Having gotten to know the significant other through early or intermittent contact can put the therapist in a better situation to make such difficult distinctions.

An excellent resource for family members who want to know more about how to help their depressed loved one is *When Someone You Love is Depressed* (Rosen & Amador, 1996). They suggest the following guidelines for parents, siblings, children, spouses, and lovers of the depressed:

1. Learn all you can.
2. Have realistic expectations.
3. Give unqualified support.
4. Keep your routine.
5. Express your feelings.
6. Don't take it personally.
7. Ask for help.
8. Work as a team.

I find that when family members are intimately involved with a patient's depression, periodic meetings with them can best be structured around these principles. Of particular importance is the distinction between giving unqualified support and expressing your own feelings. Families ask rightly enough how they can express their feelings if they are expected to be only supportive. This presents an opportunity to talk about how to express feelings in a constructive rather than critical way. Structure is an absolute requirement for meetings like this, because they can quickly escalate into unproductive blaming. Reiteration of these basic principles and exploration of how they can be put into action can give family members a chance to communicate with each other in a new, more constructive way.

DEPRESSION TESTING
THE LIMITS OF LOVE

As a result of both experiences in childhood and patterns of cognitive bias and sensitivity, depressed individuals anticipate, and as a consequence provoke, responses from others that are hostile, rejecting, alienated, or in other ways aversive or

uncomforting. Such experiences further maintain the depressed person's expectation of and selective sensitivity to rejection from others, making likely once more
behavior that is dysphoric, anxiety provoking, accusatory, and otherwise unpleasant for interactional partners and thus likely to evoke once again from the partner
the responses that will perpetuate the depressive pattern. (Wachtel, 1994)

As Rado (1928/1994) had suggested, some depressed patients seem to want to
punish those who love them. Anticipating rejection, they try to provoke it. They
set up impossible situations for their loved ones, who ultimately do reject them:
*No one can understand how bad I have it. If you try to get me to feel better, it
just proves you don't understand.*

Some patients will take the disease model of depression too far, using it as a
resistance to change or a manipulation of others.

*A patient was going through a very rough time with symptoms of depression and
anxiety, feeling that he was completely overwhelmed at work and getting no support or sympathy at home. The longer the situation lasted, the more irritable and
self-centered he became, to the point where his wife drastically limited communication with him out of her own need for self protection. Of course, this just made
him feel further betrayed. In his mind, the conviction that his depression was a biological process over which he had no control meant that he was entitled to be as
petulant as he wanted, and that his wife's responsibility was simply to take care
of him. Finally, one morning he left her a note alluding to the high death rate
among people with depression and suggesting that his death would be on her
hands.*

*This was one of the relatively few occasions when I think it has clearly helped
me to have been through depression myself. I said, in effect,* Look, you have to be
a mensch. Depression doesn't entitle you to any special treatment. You're having a rough time but that doesn't make it right for you to expect your wife to
treat you like a baby. She really can't help you feel better anyway, and you know
that. All you're doing is alienating her and losing your own self-respect.

*This resulted in one of the most dramatic reversals I've ever seen. The patient
went home that night and apologized to his wife. She was smart enough to accept it. Within a week he had largely stopped his provocative behavior at home
and was starting to feel that there might be some hope for him. Within a month
he had taken a much more active role at work and his mood had greatly improved.*

Other depressed people have defensively adopted a pattern of aloof withdrawal
when they perceive a slight. By acting tough and independent, they make others
think of them as cold, distant, perhaps selfish. After years of this vicious circle,
the patient has learned never to let a need be shown, and no one around him
makes any attempt to get close. Reframing the process can be an effective means
of addressing the problem; we instruct the patient to grant others the privilege
of taking care of him. We predict for the patient how difficult this will be, because

he has plenty of reason not to trust, and how he's taking a chance by letting his needs be known. Practicing this new skill in limited situations with people who are relatively trustworthy can result in experiences of greater intimacy than the patient has felt in years.

THE WITHDRAWING PATIENT

There are occasions when it's responsible to pursue the withdrawing patient. If we take the position that we have an alliance with the patient against his depression which causes him to act out self-destructively, clearly there are occasions when withdrawing from treatment can be just such acting out. For instance, I try never to let a patient terminate in a phone call, but insist on a session to talk about it. In this session I try to get the patient to come to grips with two questions: (1) Is this desire to quit treatment a kind of acting out? (2) Would a different therapist or a different style of treatment help the situation? The answer to the first question is never easy to come by, because the patient's motives are always mixed; but when it's clear that the patient is acting impulsively in the midst of a depressed mood or as an expression of anger or hurt, it's incumbent on me to help reach behind the anger and hurt and rectify the situation.

The question of what to do about the patient who just leaves a phone message discontinuing treatment or who just stops showing up for appointments is an interesting one. In my experience, the therapist's willingness to reach out to the patient is much more a reflection of the therapist's affection for the patient than anything to do with a professional assessment of the patient's needs. Knowing this to be as true about myself as anyone else, I try to follow the same rules for everyone: *Try to reconnect.* And if the patient does come back in, *Am I rejecting him?* Too many depressed patients drop out of treatment because they interpret the therapist's unconscious communication correctly: *You are a burden I can't handle right now. You are boring and unlovable.*

Even when the patient is highly engaged with us there will be times when his rage will make him want to drop out. We have to be able to accept the patient's rage without being destabilized about it. Langs (1973) argues grandly that every illness of the patient is a way of acting out and that therefore it is appropriate to charge for each missed appointment regardless of excuse. From today's point of view, it seems more appropriate to argue that there can be a secondary gain to illness and that missing an appointment is often a message to the therapist that we should pay attention to. Often, the message is that the patient is angry at us. Sometimes, it might take charging the patient for the appointment regardless of the ostensible legitimacy of the excuse in order to get the patient to express the anger directly. Many patients need to see that we are not destroyed by their anger. At the same time, we must acknowledge that the patient's rage is not merely a transference manifestation but has its origin in something in the treatment relationship, which we have a responsibility for. The message to the patient is neither *You're not really angry at me, it's your father,* nor *It's very interesting that you feel angry at me (let's figure out why you're so weird)*, but *Your anger is a subject of real concern, because it feels dangerous to you. I accept that you're very angry at me and that makes it hard for us to work together right now, but let's try very hard to get to the bottom of this.*

In the end, we need to be open to the idea that sometimes when the patient doesn't like us or want to work with us it's not just a transference manifestation but bad chemistry. Sometimes we have gotten off on the wrong foot. Sometimes we are the wrong gender or the wrong age and the patient doesn't feel safe enough with us. We can be naturally too tentative, too self-assured, or too warm or too cold, and the patient won't be able to connect. When this happens, let's help the patient find a new therapist. Let's have the courage to put the issue on the table, rather than forcing the patient to drop out of treatment with another failure to chalk up against himself.

CHAPTER 11

Challenge Depressed Thinking

W E ARE ALL CONSTANTLY ENGAGED in trying to make sense of our experience. On a deeply unconscious level, even the most unreflective individual tries to establish lawful, predictable relationships between events; if *this* happens, *that* is likely to follow. In social events, we tend to be "dispositionists" (Slusher & Anderson, 1989), believing that others behave as they do because of internal motives: *That's just the way he is. Women are like that. He's always been against me.* But dispositionist or not, the payoff for predictability is clear; we are not continually caught off guard by everything that happens; we can integrate our experience into a more or less coherent whole, which provides us with security, mastery, and a reduction of anxiety. We build, in Jerome Frank's (1974) term, an "assumptive world," which we use as the basis for our actions.

But clearly, our belief systems are not always congruent with reality. People with depression, for instance, believe that they are socially awkward even when objective observers can't distinguish them from people who believe they have high social skills. However, incorrect or distorted beliefs can be incredibly tenacious; reality keeps trying to teach us that we're wrong, but we just don't get the message. The causes of this self-defeating pattern can be argued from now till doomsday. Cognitive therapy helps us teach our clients to become aware of these patterns, to challenge their beliefs, and to integrate new ways of thinking and behaving.

COGNITIVE THERAPY

Cognitive therapy for depression is such a well-regarded and effective method of treatment that it's reasonable to say most therapists should not attempt to treat depression without being familiar with the model.

Cognitive therapy is based on the premise that our emotions and behavior are largely determined by the attitudes and assumptions that we use to structure reality. Distortions in thinking—attitudes and assumptions that do not work, that do not predict reality correctly or have unanticipated adverse consequences—arise during development. Some of these distortions in thinking are seen as causing depression. The goals of therapy are to identify, test, and correct cognitive distortions and the dysfunctional beliefs that underlie (or summarize) these distortions.

Beck and colleagues (1979, p. 3 ff) stress three underlying concepts:

1. *The cognitive triad.* The depressed patient views himself, his current experience, and his future in characteristically distorted ways. He sees himself as defective, different from others, unlovable because of these differences, and to blame for his own unhappiness. He tends to have a negative view of his current experience, interpreting ambiguous events as failures or defeats, and assuming that life is too difficult for him to master. His view of the future is pessimistic and bleak. He expects his current problems to continue without relief, and he expects to fail at most tasks.

2. *Schemas.* "Schema" is the term Beck uses to describe an individual cognitive pattern that we use to help us make sense of reality. It is a characteristic way of thinking, one of the assumptions of our "assumptive world," a theory we apply to help us make sense of ambiguous stimuli. When I pass two colleagues in the hall and they giggle together behind my back, I can choose to interpret that event many ways. I can assume their laughter has nothing to do with me. I can assume that it is related to me and that it has to do with what a good-looking fellow I am. I can assume that it is related to me and has to do with what a loser people perceive me to be. While my interpretation on any given day is going to be affected by my general mood and by current events, I have characteristic ways of interpreting reality—schemas—that are relatively fixed over time.

3. *Faulty information processing/cognitive errors.* Beck and others have identified a number of errors in logic which they feel often contribute to depression. In my experience, some of these errors are committed every day by many patients, as well as friends, family, myself, and colleagues—not just the depressed—so it's difficult to argue that they are idiosyncratic of depression. Evans and Hollon (1988) review the evidence that all of us, not just the depressive, can be systematically biased in how we receive information and draw inferences from it. Still, the application of such biases obviously can perpetuate depression.

ATTRIBUTIONAL STYLE

The work of Martin Seligman (1990, 1994) and others on how we interpret reality is highly complementary to Beck's work. If we characteristically believe that we are helpless to control events, we are likely to *act as if* we are helpless.

If we believe that, for instance, it won't matter how much we study for an exam because we just "can't get" the material, we won't study—a self-fulfilling prophecy if there ever was one. And so we add attributional style as a fourth dimension to the subject of how thinking affects depression.

There is extensive research (summarized in Alloy & Abramson, 1988) to show that people with depression make common assumptions, which can be summed up as:

Good things are transitory, limited in scope, and sheer luck.
Bad things are permanent, pervasive in impact, and my fault.

There are three dimensions of attributional style: We can tend to believe that explanations and events are *stable* (if it happened once, it'll happen again) or *unstable* (today was a bad day, but tomorrow may be better), *global* (if it applies here, it'll apply everywhere) or *specific* (if it applies here, it may or may not apply everywhere), and *internal* (I was the cause of that event) or *external* (there were many causes of that event). Generally, a tilt toward either of the extremes of these dimensions may be problematic, making it difficult to interpret reality objectively. For instance, if we consistently lean toward an unstable interpretation of phenomena, we may fail to predict future events accurately, leading to disaster (*It's rained for three days straight, and the water is at the door; but don't worry, it's bound to be dry tomorrow*). If we are overly specific, we may fail to note important probabilities or trends (*So what if Johnny and all his friends were busted for selling dope? My son is a good boy. He is the innocent victim of evil companions*). If we tend to apply external explanations injudiciously, we can avoid taking responsibility when we need to (*I know I'm not supposed to hit her, but she should know better than to get in my face when I'm drinking*). These are all examples of what Beck refers to as emotional reasoning, also known as "if I want to believe it hard enough, it must be so."

But even though choosing unstable, specific, and external explanations consistently can lead to trouble, that is exactly what we want to encourage our depressed patients to try, because they tend to go in the opposite direction, toward the stable (*things are always going to be bad*), global (*everything is bad*), and internal (*it's my fault that everything is always bad*).

Yapko (1997b, p. 165) has a useful exercise. He presents three ambiguous situations:

- There is a meeting held at work to which everyone is invited but you. Why?
- You apply for a job you want. You think the interview goes well, and the interviewer promises to get back to you within a week. Two weeks go by and you don't hear anything. Why?
- You have a date with a close friend, but he seems cold and distant. Why?

What are the consequences of acting as if these things are your fault? What are the consequences of acting as if they are not? It's a good exercise in learning the effects of negative expectations, because if we withdraw or get angry or feel guilty because of our negative expectations, the consequences will be negative. If we remain pleasant, cooperative, curious, assertive, the consequences are unlikely to be any more negative than reality would dictate, but are likely to be better than those suggested by negative assumptions.

DISTORTED PERCEPTION

There is a kind of negative narcissism that perpetuates depression. The patient exaggerates his own role in events, especially his responsibility for negative outcomes. At the same time he assumes that everyone is always paying attention to him, especially when he commits errors. So he assumes he's more responsible for negative outcomes than he is, and he believes that others are always aware of his failures.

It's hard for the therapist to argue the patient out of these beliefs. Though we may be successful in helping the patient see the distortions involved in specific episodes, in my experience this awareness does not lead to a reduction in the tendency to make the same mistakes again. I believe it's more productive to help the patient learn to appreciate the role of other factors in causation, and to learn about how other people interpret reality. Social psychology refers to the *fundamental attribution error* (Slusher & Anderson, 1989), meaning that people in general are much more likely to overestimate the influence of personality and other dispositional factors, and to underestimate the importance of situational factors, in determining their own and others' behavior. Sometimes with clients I will challenge what I call the "truntz" theory of human behavior (in honor of my wife's Jewish grandmother): *He behaves that way because he's got a truntz (a little demon) in him. Let's get the truntz out, then he'll be okay.* By putting a trait-centered explanation of behavior into this humorous and distancing frame, patients can sometimes see (and remember) how silly such explanations are, and open themselves up to considering that, for instance, they feel they have fallen short because their expectations were too high or because the goal was too vaguely defined. Sometimes just taking the time to brainstorm all the possible explanations for a particular event may help the client see how his self-centered frame of reference is distorting his judgment. Sometimes getting the patient distracted—by getting him out to a high-stimulus event—removes the painful self-focus for a while; this experience can be noted for future reference in the therapy.

The depressive continuously undervalues himself in comparison to others. Research has shown that depressed people forget about positive feedback, while nondepressed people forget about negative feedback. Depressed people underestimate their own competence, while nondepressed overestimate theirs. People with depression are also more pessimistic about their future than nondepressed people. Nondepressed people have a positive bias about themselves, predicting their own future success and the likelihood of happy events to be better than average, whereas people with depression expect more sad events to occur to them (Alloy & Abramson, 1988). As people recover from depression, they begin to overestimate themselves again (Lewinsohn, Mischel, Chaplin, & Barton, 1980). To the depressive, others are always more competent, more successful, more attractive, more happy. Some of this seems to be selective perception, as if the only other people who count in the depressive's world are those who are doing better, while those who are obviously doing worse are ignored. Some of it seems to be due to the maximization/minimization error.

Depression thus has an insidious effect on self-concept. Everyone has experiences of failures, setbacks, and rejections. For most of us, these are balanced by positive experiences; people do not actively seek out opportunities to re-experience the negative events. But depression seems to do exactly that: It "actively recruits negative states" (Schuchter et al., 1996, p. 69). All the cognitive errors of depression—selective perception, cognitive distortion—are applied to the self. We examine ourselves through a distorting lens.

It is remarkable how people with depression can get so good at not seeing certain things. It is as if they only see half the spectrum, the blue-indigo-violet shades, and the red-orange-yellow are invisible. This makes the depressed view of the world remarkably resistant to change. We all pay more attention to, and learn more easily, information that fits our preconceptions. Information that challenges our belief system, though it may get our attention momentarily (the Aha! experience of psychotherapy), tends to be quickly forgotten unless it is systematically reinforced.

The therapist must be very sensitive to this phenomenon, because we are all naturally better at noticing the presence of something that shouldn't be there (a symptom like excessive guilt) than the absence of something that should be there (like pleasure). It's easy to get overwhelmed trying to help the patient solve what seem to be emergent problems—making decisions, finding energy, repairing relationships—and not pay attention to what's not in the patient's reporting (things that are going well). We need to maintain Freud's "evenly hovering attention," staying immersed in the patient's immediate affect, yet maintaining a perspective that there are other things going on in the patient's world. We need to comment explicitly at times that there are good things going on in the patient's life, because the patient needs to learn this skill, to raise his head up from the muck and see that there are things to appreciate.

A patient reported a dream about a job situation he had left six months before. The job had been quite stressful and the ending process was ugly, but he was consciously relieved to be out of it and objectively better off. His thought on awakening was "Oh, no, I'm still dreaming about that place; when will I put it behind me?" The therapist pointed out that he could have awakened thinking, "Thank God that was only a dream."

Most depressed patients immediately grasp the irony of depressive realism—the fact that while people with depression often make things seem much more difficult than they really are, the nondepressed seem to be consistently overoptimistic. It becomes a useful source of black humor in sessions. We can joke about others in the patient's life who seem to succeed through naïve optimism, and play with the idea of the patient "faking" the same kind of optimism.

When patients are excessively self-critical, when their expectations for themselves are too high, it can be helpful to ask *What would you think of someone else if he got as far as you? Is it only you who has to be so good?* Often the element of self-criticism becomes a dilemma for the therapist as well. When the patient flagellates himself for not being a good enough patient, for not making enough progress in therapy, what's the therapist to do? To point out that the patient is punishing or underestimating himself is merely to agree that he is not a good patient. To disagree, however, will usually be experienced by the patient as a disingenuous act of "shining on." It can be helpful in such instances to call such self-flagellation a manifestation of an old pattern which, implicitly, the patient is moving beyond. *It's natural that there will be times of stress, like today, when you will feel like beating yourself up again. We can't expect the depression to go away overnight.*

FALSE BELIEFS AND DISTORTED LOGIC

Beck and others have elaborated the theme of cognitive errors of depression far beyond the scope of this book, and the reader who is interested is referred to some of the current literature: Alloy, 1988; Beck et al., 1979; Burns, 1999; Copeland, 1992; Joiner & Coyne, 1999; Yapko, 1997b). At this point I want to focus briefly on how the therapist practicing from a broader perspective can help the patient address some of the most salient issues.

Much of depressed thinking lends itself to caricature; furthermore, the use of a little humor in the session helps the lesson be both heard and remembered. I like to use exaggeration as a tool to highlight the cognitive errors of depression, and sometimes will bring out Table 11.1, A Satire of Depressed Thinking, as part of the discussion. The patient can easily grasp how my hapless young man who keeps having flat tires is distorting reality and making himself more miserable; it's most helpful if the patient can think of a similar kind of situation more relevant to his own life and reflect on his own characteristic patterns of distortion.

The depressed patient's insistence on perfection is the cause of a great deal of his misery. In the NIMH Treatment of Depression Collaborative Research Program (Elkin et al., 1989), those patients who were assessed as most perfectionistic prior to treatment had the worst outcomes in all treatment modalities (Blatt, 1998). The therapist must help the patient learn to accept the imperfect in life. Things will never be exactly as we want, but we can make ourselves miserable by not accepting the value and beauty of the way things are. We cannot

TABLE 11.1
A Satire of Depressed Thinking

Cognitive Error	Underlying Assumption	Example/syllogism
Overgeneralization	If it's true once, it's always true. If it's true in these circumstances, it's true in all similar circumstances.	Jill hates me. Jill is a girl. All girls hate me. I had a flat on the way to the theater. All the tires must be going bad. I can't do anything right.
Selective abstraction/ Disqualifying the positive	Bad events count more than good events.	Everyone said they liked my speech but there was someone in the fifth row who looked bored. It must have been a boring speech. The others are just covering up to make me feel better. I had a flat on the way to the theater, and we missed the opening credits. It ruined the whole evening.
Excessive responsibility	When things go wrong, it's my fault. When things go right, I got lucky.	I had a flat on the way to the theater, and we were late. I should have checked the tires more often.
Assuming temporal causality	If it's been true in the past, it's always going to be true. *Post hoc, ergo propter hoc.*	I had a flat on the way to the theater, and we were late. My date acted like it didn't matter, but she was cold to me later. It's all my fault. I woke up this morning feeling depressed. I'm always going to feel depressed.
Excessive self-reference	Everyone is watching me all the time, especially when I slip up. When things go wrong, it's because of something I did wrong.	No one is going to listen to what I say because I'll be so anxious they'll only pay attention to my nervousness. I had a flat on the way to the theater. Did I act flustered? Did I get too angry? Did I fix it fast enough? She must think I'm a fool.

(Continued)

TABLE 11.1
(*Continued*)

Catastrophizing	Things have to be perfect all the time. The minute any little thing goes wrong, everything will start to fall apart.	I had a flat on the way to the theater. I must need a new set of tires, but I can't afford it. What if they all go bad and I can't drive to work? I'll have to quit my job. I'll never find another job. I'll starve.
Dichotomous thinking	Everything is always good or bad, black or white, with no shades of gray.	I got a B on my paper. The teacher must hate me. I had a flat on the way to the theater. What a lousy car! I should never have bought it.
Emotional reasoning	Whatever I feel is true.	I had a flat on the way to the theater. It put me in a lousy mood. My date said she had a good time, but she was only trying to make me feel better.
Should statements (perfectionism)	Things always have to be a certain way, and if they're not, that's awful.	I had a flat on the way to the theater. I should have known that would happen. I should take better care of the car. I should have a better job so I could have a better car. I should have gone to medical school instead of being an English major.
Magnification/ minimization	Exaggerating the importance and impact of bad events, not paying attention to (not being aware of) good events.	I had a flat on the way to the theater. After the movie my date said she really had a good time. Too bad about the flat, it ruined the whole evening.

always be waiting till the weekend, or summer, or the holidays, to feel good, we have to feel good now. We have to live in present moment, and at the same time we have to cultivate patience. Life is not a dress rehearsal. Happiness is not an end state, it's a process.

My own personal barometer is what happens when I walk out into the garden: Do I see a mess of weeds demanding my immediate attention, with a few poor flowers being crowded out? Or do I see an overall expanse of beauty, color, and texture with an occasional weed intruding on the scene? I admit that I am not a perfect gardener and that the objective reality of the garden is sometimes unfortunately more like the former than the latter description—but so much of how I see it depends on my mood. When I see the weeds and not the flowers I know it's time to pay attention to my mood, to challenge my assumptions. This is a relatively benign piece of self-revelation that I feel comfortable sharing with most patients; we can then work on finding a metaphor that fits their own experience and values more closely.

I try to stay alert to faulty generalizations, to respond reflexively when patients make statements containing the words "always" or "never" (*I'll never be able to manage on my own. She always does that to me*). There are usually exceptions to such generalities, but if we assume there are not, we will not be able to see them. Not only do such beliefs perpetuate depression, they also perpetuate interpersonal conflict. To be told that you are always doing what you shouldn't or never doing what you should is inherently unfair and puts us immediately on the defensive. I try to teach patients to drop these words from their own vocabulary and to educate their loved ones about their negative effects in solving disagreements.

Another aspect of this perfectionistic drive has to do with the depressed patient's obsessive wish to control things, usually either things he can't control at all or things that aren't worth a tenth of the energy he puts into the struggle. All of us have trouble realizing that the more we try to control an aspect of ourselves, the more we are defined by it. If we think our anger is bad, we try to bottle it up, then feel guilty every time we explode or even have an angry thought; we come to think of ourselves as an angry, explosive person. If we are deeply ashamed of our lustful, slothful, gluttonous, etc. thoughts and behavior, we try to deny them, cover them up, but still feel ashamed of ourselves. Reinforcing this problem is the depressive habit of thinking in terms of black and white. Things are moral absolutes, good or bad with no shades of gray. This kind of thinking makes one prejudiced and judgmental. Decisions and actions are taken based on feelings (negative attributions) rather than evidence. The therapist serves an important function by humanizing and minimizing some of these little imperfections that cause so much misery, and by teaching a practical empiricism as an approach to making decisions.

A characteristic piece of depressed thinking is the patient's idea that everyone should like him, and that if someone doesn't like him, it's a catastrophe. The patient with these beliefs is in for a great deal of trouble, because he will constantly find himself compromising his own values and interests in order to maintain superficially friendly relations with others. In fact, this "liking" is by definition shallow; it doesn't mean intimate communication, it means, at best, a pleasant, distant cordiality. Patients can sometimes be helped to address this issue by developing a tolerance for disapproval. I sometimes suggest "disapproval inoculation" exercises—that the patient identify relatively minor issues where there is a disagreement that he has been stifling because of his need to be liked.

If he always drives his teenage daughter around and feels taken advantage of, I suggest he just refuse one night. He could go to a restaurant and send the food back. I suggest that the patient watch himself carefully to see the effects of the inevitable disapproval. Chances are it's not going to be nearly as bad as he imagined. The opportunity to experience disapproval and not be derailed by it can be an important step toward independence.

Another common assumption of depression is that no matter how bad things are now, they are likely only to get worse. Affectively, this way of thinking can cause genuine despair among patients who are already in great misery and yet assume there will be no relief ever. I had an AA veteran attend a few depression groups, who shared with us his own philosophy for dealing with dark times: *I had a really lousy day today. But I'm going to go home, fix myself a nice dinner, watch a little TV and go to bed, and there's a very good chance that tomorrow will be a much better day.* He didn't belong in the group; depressed people don't think that way. But with practice, they can learn.

Depressed thinking leads to anxiety, which leads to more depressed thinking. The depressed patient's anxiety runs away with him, and he turns trivial events into catastrophes. One goal of therapy is to bring this process into awareness; to objectify it, reify it, give it a name. When the patient recognizes that he is catastrophizing, he has taken the first step toward controlling it. The therapist can help the patient recognize that he must stop this process early, because if it is not arrested in time it will go out of control and follow inevitably to its conclusion, a genuine catastrophe. The solution for the patient is to learn to break tasks down into small steps, to prioritize and address the emergent problems first, to organize his thinking and problem-solving to make the best use of his resources.

THE GOOD COGNITIVE THERAPIST

In the end, cognitive therapy for depression seems to me like a marvelous set of mechanic's tools; but the depressed patient, trying to find why his engine won't go, isn't helped by the tools alone. It's the knowledge of how the engine works and the experience that gives you a hunch about where to look for the trouble — without these, the tools aren't useful except as paperweights. This is where the therapist can be of immense help: to focus the patient on what exactly is wrong with him, which of the cognitive errors he makes consistently, which false assumptions distort how he experiences reality—and then to coach and encourage the patient as he tries out new ways of thinking, to help problem-solve as things don't quite work out at first.

But there's something else missing from cognitive therapy. All the cognitive errors, mental distortions, false assumptions have developed as "skills of depression" in the service of helping the patient avoid emotional experience. Take away those defenses and the patient's world will be rocked, and it's the rare patient who can move without difficulty into a more intense and engaged level of emotional experience—or who wants to. People with depression fear feelings.

There is a false promise in cognitive therapy, that depression can be treated without attention to emotions, without accepting hard truths.[*]

Sometimes the engine doesn't *want to start.* Sometimes the patient has the tools, the therapist supplies the knowledge and experience to guide the overhaul, and the engine just won't go. There is a fear of starting, a risk of disappointment, a stubborn self-destructiveness that wants to resist all logical help. We can say such patients are too traumatized, too pathological, or too character-disordered to be helped by cognitive therapy, but this is just a judgmental way of saying they need a different kind of therapy. I think the therapist has to reach way down and engage with both parts of the patient, the part that wants to start and the part that doesn't, and let the patient know that both parts are equally worthy of love. Because that's what the patient fears, that this dark side, the resistant force, the frightened child within, will hide itself away by letting the patient be a good patient, a compliant patient, but one who doesn't get better, and come back out again when it's safe, when the therapist isn't paying attention or when the therapy is over. We want the good child and the bad child to become integrated.

---

[*]I know that there are many accomplished therapists who use cognitive techniques as part of an integrated approach to treatment that is highly engaged with the patient's emotional life. I speak now in reference to some texts which focus on cognitive techniques exclusively without consideration of other aspects of the patient's make-up.

CHAPTER 12

Self-care

S ELF-DEFEATING OR SELF-DESTRUCTIVE behavior is a key element in maintaining the
vicious circle of depression. It seems as if what depressed people do often in-
vites rejection, disappointment, or defeat. Many depressed patients with physical
problems seem to have their own bodies punishing themselves. Yet it is obviously
very difficult for them to change destructive behavior patterns or gain control of
their bodies; there are millions of patients who know what they *should* do, they
just feel they can't do it. But aside from overt self-defeating behavior, a common
but subtler problem with depression is the absence of what should be there—the
absence of normal behavior we generally take for granted. The ability to focus
on a work assignment, to listen carefully to another person's point of view, to relax and unwind—when capacities like these are missing or damaged, the patient
usually isn't aware of the absence, and the therapist can get frustrated and blame
the patient if he assumes the capacities are present and the patient is just being
resistant. Active treatment assumes that by helping the patient do less of what is
bad for him and more of what is good for him, we help to break the vicious circle; we enhance self-esteem, we change moods, we interrupt depressed thinking
patterns, we promote corrective emotional experiences, we improve the patient's
relationship with his body, and we change brain chemistry.

The little aphorisms of Alcoholics Anonymous express great wisdom in one-
syllable words. One standard is "fake it till you make it"—the neophyte trying to
maintain sobriety is encouraged to literally just go through the motions. Just keep
coming to meetings, repeat what you hear, mouth the AA philosophy as if you
understand it, do the steps even if you don't feel particularly honest or sincere.
The wisdom I hear is the recognition that all new behavior feels artificial at first.
When we are trying to learn anything new, from downhill skiing to typing to intimate conversation, we feel clumsy, awkward, self-conscious, even phony. Yet we
often assume that if something doesn't feel natural right away, there's something
seriously wrong. We don't recognize that the skills of depression are in fact

sequences of behavior, thought, and feeling that we have learned, just as we can learn new skills. I hear the disbelief in the voice of my patients: *You mean I should just act like I'm listening to her? You mean I should just pretend I know what I'm doing?* Yes, that is exactly what I mean. Fake it till you make it. Walk the walk, talk the talk. Practice makes perfect. Eventually, what felt awkward and forced becomes part of us.

MANAGING THE DEPRESSION

Since most patients have a somewhat idiosyncratic course of development of symptoms that is stable from one episode of depression to the next, learning to identify the sequence and intensity of symptoms can help provide mastery and hope. Patients can step up their medication, arrange for additional treatment, or simply remedy the stressors that are kicking off an episode. But the experience of depression is so immediately debilitating that most patients will not be able to respond appropriately to early warning signs unless regular and systematic review of symptoms is made a part of treatment, so that the practice becomes a familiar habit to the patient. Schuchter and colleagues (1996) suggest regular use of a self-rating scale like the Beck Depression Inventory (Beck, Ward, Mendelson, Mock, & Erbaugh, 1961) or the Zung Self-Rating Depression Scale (Zung, 1965), or that the patient and therapist collaborate on development of an idiosyncratic scale for the individual patient. The development of a unique "profile"—the patient's idiosyncratic warning signs of the depth of depression—can be especially useful for those who act out rather than feel.

Another method useful for objectifying and gaining some emotional distance from depression is the development of a "lifeline" (Post, Roy-Byrne, & Uhde, 1988) charting previous episodes of depression. A graphical format can display the patient's age, the duration and intensity of each episode, as well as life circumstances and stressors. Treatment should also be charted. Such a technique can help the patient remember that there are periods of recovery between episodes, and can give important clues about precipitating events and effective treatment.

When patients can learn how depression affects judgment, perspective, and impulse control, they can exercise more control over, or at least counterbalance, the destructive behavior. Patients are expected to learn that they have a disease that is talking to them, making them feel they have to do certain things or act in certain ways; they are encouraged to recognize when "it's the depression talking" and make adjustments as necessary.

This stance places the clinician in a position of authority, which sometimes may not feel comfortable. For instance, a depressed patient feeling impelled to take action—to break off a relationship or to quit a job—may be encouraged to delay action until the depression is under control. The reason for this is that depression is understood to be a subtle and pervasive enemy that affects the patient's conception of himself in ways that are likely not to be fully understood until the treatment is well along. The therapist wants to build an alliance with the patient's "undepressed self," which may be largely unknown to the patient, against the common enemy—depression. Especially in the beginning stages of treatment, the therapist has a better idea than the patient does about how depression can pervade the personality. As treatment progresses, the patient will find the depressed self more ego-dystonic, while the undepressed self and the therapist's perspective are in synchrony.

The patient can be helped to understand that damage to self-esteem accompanies any chronic illness, and that the fact that depression can be hidden—unlike a physical defect—only enhances that damage. Keeping a shameful secret only gives it more power. Accepting the reality that the patient has a chronic illness can, ironically, deprive the illness of much of its power.

Schuchter and colleagues (1996) identified certain "moral imperatives" as special problems for management of depression. The patient, because of his distorted world view and because of his intense desire for relief from suffering, develops an irrational belief that if and only if he takes a particular kind of action his problems will be solved and his suffering will end. The three moral imperatives that seem to be most common among depressives are to quit work, to end relationships, or to kill themselves. Leaving aside the question of suicide, the authors note the investment most people have in their work and their relationships, and the difficulty of establishing replacements. The patient must learn to recognize that the urgency of the decision is fueled by the depression, and the seeming wisdom of the decision is a result of cognitive distortion. To tolerate unpleasant affect and to question one's own perception are coping skills that must be learned.

REDUCING DESTRUCTIVE BEHAVIOR

Violence and Rage

James Gilligan (1996), who spent his professional life as a prison psychiatrist in the Massachusetts penal system, has this to say about violence: "I have yet to see a serious act of violence that was not provoked by the experience of feeling shamed and humiliated, disrespected and ridiculed, and that did not represent the attempt to prevent or undo this 'loss of face'—no matter how severe the punishment, even if it includes death. For we misunderstand these men, at our peril, if we do not realize they mean it literally when they say they would rather kill or mutilate others, be killed or mutilated themselves, than live without pride, dignity, and self-respect" (p. 110).

Violence, in other words, is always purposeful. Perhaps a lasting contribution of self psychology has been to clarify that aggression is not an innate drive but a reaction to events (Goldberg, 1998). People become aggressive when they are injured in some way. Rather than seeing destructiveness as an inborn part of human nature that must be tamed or civilized—with the implication that aggression is innately shameful, not fully evolved—we can be more empathic with rage, more open to understanding the injustices, real or perceived, that underlie it. Often, rage is a defense against shame, against conscious awareness of feeling insulted, slighted, chastised. Rage reverses the passivity that we experience with shame, flooding us temporarily with power and self-righteousness. Of course, we often feel ashamed after the outburst; but for many people, feeling embarrassed about losing control is much more acceptable, because it conveys being powerful and scary, than feeling embarrassed about being weak.

Our first task with a depressed patient who is violent must be to stop the violence, because violence can make it impossible for the therapy to work—perhaps by getting the patient incarcerated, by injuring someone in such a way that the patient won't be able to forgive himself, by intimidating the therapist, or by forcing the therapist into collusion. (Suicide is the ultimate act of violence, and of course these observations apply to suicide as well.) It's much like treatment of the drinking patient; you can't accomplish anything as long as the drinking is going on. Our efforts to get the patient to stop can range from persuasion to medication to social intervention (advising loved ones to protect themselves) to hospitalization, if necessary. Once again, we are trying to build an alliance with the patient against his depression, of which the violence is one manifestation.

Clara was stuck in an enmeshed, conflictual relationship with her husband. He avoided her emotional needs in a passive-aggressive way, making her feel weak and ashamed. When she injured her back in a freak accident, the pain, disability, and dependency were too much for her to bear. Confined to a hospital bed in their living room, Clara would beg her husband to approach her, to just hold her, sit with her and hold her hand. When he didn't, her rage took over; she would curse him, verbally abuse him, throw things at him, endanger her own recovery by getting up and storming around the room. He would leave her, and she would then spend hours sobbing, exhausted, abandoned, and in pain.

Later she showed me her diary from this period. She consistently referred to herself as a "big fucking baby" and other contemptuous epithets. Letting herself get out of control and be violent and verbally cruel to her husband not only drove him away but also reinforced her own view of herself as pathetic and loathsome.

It helped Clara that, although I made it clear that she had to stop the violence, it did not indicate to me that she was an unstable or dangerous person. On the contrary, her rage was perfectly understandable given the circumstances; it was her manner of expressing it that reinforced the depression.

Self-Destructive Behavior

Curtis (1989a), in an interesting article attempting to bridge the gap between social psychology and psychoanalytic views of masochism, summarizes observations neatly: The general belief is that people have learned, usually in their interaction with a parent, that behavior that seems self-destructive—such as not performing at one's best, not being assertive, not expressing feelings—functions as a way of maintaining the parent's love or caretaking. A dog will passively accept a shock if it knows the shock will be followed by food. A patient is inhibited in his work performance because being autonomous was a betrayal of his depressed, Holocaust-survivor mother; he says his role was to stay home and watch television with her. Behavior that is assertive or leads to autonomy will provoke anxiety in some parents, who will punish the child, often by withdrawal of attention or approval. Rather than accept this fate, the child will learn behaviors that reduce the parent's anxiety and maintain the flow of narcissistic supplies—but not without rage. Balancing taking care of others and taking care of the self is difficult enough for everyone. When taking care of others means punishing the self, it's a no-win situation. A difficulty is that, in a dysfunctional relationship, the cues that tip us off that our assertiveness makes others anxious are so subtle that our responses are automatic, and our self-sacrificing behavior so habitual, that everyone comes to take advantage of us—a self-fulfilling prophecy, or a projective identification. If the therapist can remain aware of the projection, the fine-grain analysis of communication possible in the therapeutic relationship can be a powerful method of building the patient's awareness. The problem is that autonomous behavior has become a source of anxiety for the patient, who is likely to sabotage the treatment. Stepping down off the therapeutic pedestal and being a real person can help reduce the patient's anxiety (Menaker, 1981).

Alcohol and drug abuse is a special arena for self-destruction. The relationship between alcohol and drug abuse and depression can easily fill another book. When working with depressed patients, we need to make a careful assessment of whether alcohol or other drugs are contributing to or creating problems for the patient; when they are, we need to intervene. This means we have to be comfortable asking nosy questions (see chapter 4 on assessment) in order to get a clear picture, and we have to be alert to behavioral cues for patients who are in denial.

The connection between depression and substance abuse, especially alcohol, is very clear. People with primary depression can become alcoholics because alcohol provides temporary relief from the depression. Many recovered alcoholics find that they are quite depressed, more depressed than the damage they have done to their lives alone would warrant. Professionals need to remember that alcohol is a very effective and reliable drug. Its immediate effects are to give a sense of well-being and confidence and to lower inhibitions, which are very seductive feelings for people with depression. But when the initial euphoria wears off, the depressant effects of alcohol sink in. The person feels weak, guilty, and ashamed, and often has engaged in behavior he will be sorry for.

Alcohol, like Valium and Xanax, is a "sedative-hypnotic." These drugs have a depressant effect on the central nervous system. They make us think more slowly and they interfere with coordination and muscle control. In larger doses they produce unconsciousness and interfere with breathing. But alcohol is popular as a recreational drug because its depressant effect comes in stages. At first it depresses only the inhibitory functions of the brain, reducing inhibitions and anxieties; it makes us feel more smart, interesting, and capable, and it permits us to take risks that we wouldn't otherwise.

But the initial pleasurable effects of alcohol use are only temporary; within a few hours of ingestion, alcohol also depresses the excitatory functions of the brain. We feel sleepy, confused, lethargic, and irritable; we lose motor control, coordination, and balance. With regular use we develop a tolerance for alcohol—it requires larger doses to produce the desired effects—and we develop a dependence on it. At first, the dependence may be only psychological, but eventually the body adapts to alcohol use and will complain—through withdrawal symptoms like anxiety, insomnia, tremors, and hallucinations—when alcohol is stopped.

When drinking or drug use is out of control, it has to stop. If the patient is drinking every day, he has to stop entirely. If he's drinking several times a week to excess, he has to stop entirely. If he's drinking in moderation while depressed (no more than two ounces of alcohol a day for no more than three times a week), he's flirting with disaster, and he'd better stop or monitor himself very carefully. The same is true for recreational use of marijuana. These drugs are seductive for the depressed. They make us forget our troubles and feel too good. We feel too much pleasure when we indulge, and then we feel guilty for indulging, and we reinforce the vicious circle of depression. Then there is the fact that long-term alcohol use is by nature depressing.

In my experience, which is the best thing I have to go on since the research is so politicized, we do patients a great disservice by trying to help the depression and ignoring a substance-abuse problem. With rare exceptions, it's a false hope to believe that relieving the depression will alleviate the need for alcohol or drugs. We need to be educated about the effects of alcohol and drugs on depression. We need to know who to refer to when we can't help. We need to insist sometimes that the patient get sober before we continue treatment.

Self-mutilation is another form of overt self-destructiveness. Though self-mutilation is primarily thought of as a women's symptom, Gilligan (1996) notes how common it is among men in prison. In that setting, men's violence has no other outlet. For both men and women, the experience of acute pain has become a tension reliever for the patient, a way to distract the self from overwhelming feelings of anxiety and depersonalization. "In an individual with a diffuse or dissolving self representation, the masochistic search for acute experiences of pain can be understood as a means of acquiring a feeling of being real and alive and thereby reestablishing a sense of existing as a bounded entity, a cohesive self" (Stolorow & Lachmann, 1980, p. 32).

Again, this is one of those things we'd better ask about in the initial sessions, because the patient may never volunteer it. Once we know that self-mutilation is a pattern for the patient, we need to keep asking about it. Frequently the patient will act out hostile feelings toward the therapist by cutting and not telling us. When we're aware of an empathic disruption, we should be alert to the possibility that self-mutilation may be a response.

Covert Self-Destructiveness

Depressed people have developed many habits that keep them in trouble, functioning far below their optimal level. These are "bad habits" in the classic sense of the term, ways of functioning that I reframe as skills of depression. Some, like shopping and smoking, are guilty pleasures, things that the individual knows very well make things worse for himself but feels unable or unwilling to give up. Others, like procrastination, tend to be accepted as a part of the self that can't be controlled, while still others, like taking unnecessary chances, seem to be denied or split off. These are all things that, in my view, the patient ambivalently wants us to know about, and will drop hints to help us find out. He will feel attended to and more confident about our skills if we do find out, though he fears it will mean giving up the activity. On the other hand, if we don't pick up on the clues, he will feel a little guilty pleasure about having outsmarted us.

There is certainly a risk that if we see our jobs as finding out the patient's bad habits and checking up on them, we will come across as a nag and a scold. We have to make sure we give the patient credit for honest reporting, acknowledging that it's not easy to reveal oneself. We can also use a little humor to soften the nagging tone.

Most depressed patients have no trouble buying in to this idea in the initial phase. You can show them a list of cognitive errors, and they will have an Aha! reaction at four out of five. Talk about procrastination or lack of assertiveness, and they nod their heads in recognition. For some, however, there is an odd kind of split in consciousness; they may say they understand that there must be something about them that contributes to their horrible bad luck, but they may be tremendously defended against confronting any problematic behavior directly. With such patients, it is very important to avoid framing questions in an accusatory manner. Wachtel (1993) suggests what he calls an exculpatory question. *You must have had a good reason for doing that* is a lot easier to explore than *Why did you do that?*

Procrastination is a form of passive aggression against the self. By keeping ourselves disorganized, by jumping from one project to the next without ever finishing, by constantly finding reasons for taking no action, we rebel against the little voice of authority inside our heads that tells us what we should be doing.

Saul was divorced from his wife ten years ago. His son, now 17, is floundering in school. Saul has not really been able to communicate with him since the divorce, despite faithful weekly overnight visits, and he feels terribly guilty about the growing distance in their relationship. They have never talked about the divorce, and Saul has never talked openly about himself with his son. When I suggest that he take the boy out to dinner and begin to open up these areas for discussion, Saul's immediate reaction is to feel that he'll never find the time, because he will also have to make the same kind of time available to his younger daughter, even though neither child has ever shown any jealousy or favoritism. And this is what Saul does: He always sees the obstacles ahead, and seeing only the obstacles, he never takes the first step. In avoiding action, he manages to preserve some self-esteem; he can believe himself to be a kind and good father, whose distant relationship with his son is caused by circumstances outside his control.

In helping a procrastinating patient, it's important to keep in mind that most depressed people don't think they are capable of working effectively unless they are motivated. They don't realize that motivation often follows action, that when we force ourselves to dive into the dreaded task we start feeling better about it. Teaching the patient simple techniques for staying with a task can help over-come this initial resistance. *When you want to stop, work for ten more minutes, then stop if you still want to. Reward yourself with a five-minute break after a half hour of work.*

There are many other simple strategies that help improve work habits: prioritizing work, and getting the most important done first; learning to self-monitor productive and unproductive activity, so that the stimuli for each situation can be controlled; and *chaining*, which means making a desired event contingent on performance of a less-desired event. The patient can learn to reward himself for attending to the mundane chores of everyday life that are so difficult for many depressives with a snack, a television show, a walk in the garden, a hot bath—whatever the patient finds intrinsically rewarding. At first these contingencies need to be very simple and gratification almost instantaneous: "Twenty minutes of fast walking before I let myself watch Rosie." "I'll spend half an hour cleaning before I can have lunch." Gradually, longer duration or greater difficulty, or a chain of several aversive behaviors, can come to be contingent on rewards. This ability to delay gratification is simply how most of us learn to stay at work every day for two weeks before we get paid. Though it sounds simplistic—indeed the depressed patient may have learned these lessons many times before—in the midst of depression the patient can't remember these things, and a reminder from the therapist can be very helpful.

Patients who are overwhelmed with work to the point where they don't know where to begin and keep making false starts can benefit from establishing stimulus control over their working environment: *Work only at your desk and only work at your desk. When you find yourself distracted or anxious or unable to decide what to do next, get up from your desk and give yourself a short break. Don't try to work when you're not at your desk.* Eventually the desk (computer terminal, kitchen, etc.) becomes a less dreaded stimulus because it is only associated with productive activity.

Establishing stimulus control over the problematic behavior can be a powerful method for helping the depressive gain a different perspective on the problem. It means, essentially, confining the behavior to a specific time, place, or circumstance. The patient who worries a lot can learn to save up his worries for his worry time, a specific hour in the evening. The same goes for the patient who can't seem to shake loose from self-criticism. During the rest of the time, he is not to try to stop the problem behavior, but notice it and set it aside for later. As Wachtel (1993) points out, the patient often begins to see the absurdity of the situation—when it gets to be the time period set aside for self-criticism, he can't remember half the things that happened during the day, which seemed at the time to be catastrophic events, that made him feel so awful. He begins to get an idea that depression is something he does to himself and that, to some extent, he can have some control over. If confronted directly with this idea, many depressives will either deny it absolutely or agree but feel worse because they believe that if they were strong enough they could do something about it. Sometimes we can supply the "corrective emotional experience" without needing to interpret the defense or the wish.

It's also vital to keep in mind that the patient may not know how to work. Simple time-management strategies can be very helpful for people with depression. Many of the techniques advocated by Hallowell and Ratey (1994) for coping with adult ADD are quite helpful for people with depression (and there is often a great deal of diagnostic overlap): OHIO (only handle it once); break down large tasks into small ones; work in your own best working environment; establish external structure through lists, notes to yourself, color coding, rituals, reminders, files. One I especially like is to put your life into habits and patterns, and follow them without having to think about them; it greatly reduces the amount of time that goes into decision-making about trivial issues. I've had patients in severe depression report that, when mornings are especially difficult, they get up, shower, brush their teeth and so on without incident until they have to decide what to wear. Confronted with the first real decision of the day, they become overwhelmed with indecision; nothing seems right. One woman regularly burst into tears standing in front of her closet in the morning. She was greatly helped by the advice to pick out her clothes the night before. By the time she got to work, her depression had usually lifted somewhat, and she was able to get through the day without incident.

Sometimes we need to help the patient keep in mind the difference between procrastinating and letting the creative process chew on a problem. Sometimes patients need time to see things from different perspectives, to understand feelings, to collect more data. We can encourage the patient to deliberately decide to put a problem aside for a while and let it simmer until it's done. This is not the same thing as trying to forget about it until it's a crisis. Depressed patients, always thinking the worst of themselves, are not likely to give themselves permission to make use of this kind of reflective time.

Another common phenomenon of depression is that the patient either gives up too easily or doesn't know when to quit. The individual seems to lack persistence, to give up too soon on many tasks; in other situations, it seems as if the depressed person is blind to cues that would make a reasonable person cut his losses. And of course the irony of depression is that patients quit too soon on things that are good for them, like diet and exercise, and keep hanging on to destructive habits, like bad relationships and exploitative jobs. Much of this can be attributed to the depressed person's low estimation of his own abilities and high estimation of task difficulty.

The depressed are more likely to give up sooner on a task they have been told is moderately difficult than they are on one they believe to be very difficult (Snyder & Frankel, 1989). The explanation seems to be that their self-esteem is not at stake on a difficult task; they have nothing to lose by persisting. But on a moderate task they are more likely to feel they are just "not getting it." On the other hand, Snyder and Frankel argue, if the depressed really believed in their inadequacy, it doesn't make sense for them to try harder on difficult tasks. "It is as if the depressed are clinging to the belief that they are competent and seizing an opportunity to demonstrate it" (p. 136) when they have nothing to lose by trying hard. But if they do withhold effort in order to protect self-esteem, they shoot themselves in the foot because they are less likely to achieve their goals. The therapist must be ready to help the patient decide when to hang in there and when to fold his hand and walk away. The cognitive process of emotional reasoning is often at work here—*I want this so badly it has to happen*—and the therapist must help the patient learn a more analytical and empirical method of making decisions.

Money management is another major problem for most people with depression. I hear a lot of what I call "depressed shopping"—going out to buy something because of boredom, because it's a quick thrill, because it might fill up the emptiness or loneliness inside. Inevitably (unless the patient has more money than he needs), this process just makes matters worse because the coveted article doesn't accomplish what he was hoping for, the thrill is fleeting, the boredom returns, and now he's spent money that he shouldn't have. I try to make it clear to patients that financial stability and independence is not impossible and that it will improve their state of mind tremendously, but that it starts with self-discipline. I go over budgets with patients or refer them to financial counselors. I encourage them to save, and help them control depressed spending by identifying activities other than shopping that will give them longer-lasting happiness.

Taking unnecessary chances is another common phenomenon with depression. I don't mean thrill-seeking—that might actually provide some fun—but neglecting to pay attention to cues that most people would do something about. Not following a doctor's advice is very frequent; not getting the car serviced; not having that mole looked at.

Roger is a boyish-looking man approaching middle age who initially sought help because he was concerned about his procrastination and other self-destructive work habits. He was employed as an accountant at a major corporation.

In the very first interview Roger revealed that his wife had threatened to kill him. In the past, she had flown into rages and had attacked him with knives. Now, however, she appeared to have a well-thought-out plan and, from Roger's description, felt nothing for him but extreme anger and contempt. Her training put her in a position to accomplish his death in a way that might avoid detection. Events over the past few weeks made it seem as if the danger to Roger was escalating.

Roger seemed much less concerned about this than I was. He seemed to pooh-pooh me when I asked if he had contacted the police or had another place to stay. If anything, I thought he might have been embarrassed by my concern. When he left the office after the first visit, I thought I had scared him off and did not expect to see him again. When he did come back, he carefully avoided the subject of his wife. As time went on I realized that Roger felt empty and uninteresting inside, and he needed this drama to make him feel really alive. The trouble is, I don't believe he was making it up.

There are many other ways that depressed patients express subtle self-destructive behavior. Smoking is one. Ehrenreich (1999, p. 46) captured perfectly the victim mentality of the depressed, defiant smoker:

> Work is what you do for others; smoking is what you do for yourself. I don't know why the antismoking crusaders have never grasped the element of defiant self-nurturance that makes the habit so endearing to its victims—as if, in the American workplace, the only thing people have to call their own is the tumors they are nourishing and the spare moments they devote to feeding them.

Unprotected sex is another depressed flirtation with disaster. It's as if, when the AIDS, or the cancer, or the murder happens, the individual will somehow feel vindicated. The therapist must be rather cold-blooded in exploring such subjects, conveying to the patient that these are serious issues that need to get talked about. The therapist's mantle of authority as an expert on depression, a disease which is frequently manifested in these kinds of self-destructive behavior, can help the patient overcome his embarrassment.

INCREASING ADAPTIVE BEHAVIOR

As we've said, besides decreasing the frequency of behavior that has aversive consequences, we also want to increase the frequency of behavior that has positive consequences. However, it's often easier for both the therapist and the patient to see how action leads to trouble than how inaction also creates problems. Yet, we've known for a long time that inaction is part of the problem with depression. Libet and Lewinsohn (1973), studying the functioning of depressed individuals in groups, found that they "emitted" less behavior of any kind: They tended to be passive, shy, and withdrawn, to only speak when spoken to, and then to speak in fewer syllables.

In general, it's polite for the therapist to first assume that if the patient is not doing something he should, it's because he doesn't know how, rather than that he doesn't want to, is afraid to, etc. Assertiveness skills is a clear-cut example; Occam's razor suggests that if the patient doesn't emit assertive behavior when it's appropriate, it's because he doesn't know how. To assume that he's unassertive because he's afraid or masochistic or dependent is to invoke a more complicated explanation. One of them may be true, but we owe it to our patient to give him the benefit of the doubt. When we do that, however, we then have to be ready to teach the patient what he needs to know, or at least be prepared to help him find out. This is something not all therapists are comfortable with.

> Whether we like it or not, we are inevitably involved in some measure as *mentors* to our patients. To accept fully that aspect of our role is to appreciate that it is not enough to say that our actions should always be subjected to analytic scrutiny. We also have to try to *act wisely* even while recognizing that whatever wisdom we have is always highly personal and subjective. In fact, because of that recognition, we do not *like* to think that we influence patients in regard to life-shaping questions. (Hoffman, 1998, p. 74)

It therefore behooves us to be broadly conversant with a range of human problems and resources, enough so that we can help the patient identify the skills he needs to learn and how to learn them. At the same time, it's vital that we not feel we have to know all the answers. Being willing to be uncertain with the patient, to work together to find the best information and the most sensible solution but acknowledging that all decisions are gambles and that in these circumstances it is the patient who has to take the brunt of a risk—this enlivens a therapeutic relationship and makes it honest and affectively charged.

But often the absence of a capacity we should take for granted is because of the presence of something else, one of those skills of depression that takes the place of more adaptive behavior. The depressed person's lack of a sense of "agency" is often not just the absence of something, but the presence of something else. Being passive, confused, or helpless and repeatedly engaging in behavior that has unintended negative consequences for self or others can be an expression of disavowed anger, dependency, or other needs or emotions. But it is very difficult for the therapist to confront or interpret this kind of pattern successfully; the patient will usually just experience the same passivity or confusion in response, setting up a vicious circle which leaves the therapist feeling frustrated and the patient feeling accused. The therapist must maintain a relationship with the patient on both sides of the conflict. Comments that speak directly to both sides are the most helpful: *You want to get your husband to listen to you, but when you get his attention you find yourself tongue-tied and confused. Maybe the confusion is a way of expressing your feelings toward him, the anger that you're aware of and the fear about what your anger might do.*

The patient comes to therapy already practicing a number of coping skills: Some help minimize psychic pain, some help prevent or inhibit dysfunction.

Part of the trouble with depression is that often the habits that are chosen to minimize pain—social withdrawal, for example—have negative effects on functioning. The therapist and patient should examine systematically together what works and what doesn't work among the patient's existing coping skills. There may need to be a special inquiry into what has worked in the past, because the patient, in the throes of depression, may have forgotten. The therapist can teach directly or help the patient find and learn about new coping skills. Relaxation techniques, distraction techniques, cultivating small pleasures or rewarding relationships all can be learned and practiced.

One explanation for the absence of activity on the patient's part is provided by the learned helplessness model, which suggests that people with depression fatally underestimate their power to influence events, and thus often never even try. A problem with a simple learned helplessness model is that it doesn't really explain who will get depressed; Seligman (1975) noted that even among dogs in the laboratory, some never gave up trying to escape, and science is at a loss to explain what made them different from other dogs. And we are all familiar with people who are able to maintain a reasonably positive mood even in a state of complete powerlessness—in prison, on welfare, suffering from cancer. Abramson, Seligman, and Teasdale (1978); Alloy and Abramson (1988); and Seligman (1990) added to the theory by stressing the importance of attributional style—that people prone to depression think badly about themselves when faced with adverse events because they tend to think in internal, stable, and global terms. In other words, the lack of agency of depression is reinforced by a tendency to blame the self and to unconsciously assume relative helplessness. I think depressed people also underestimate how much their passivity perpetuates the depression; they don't see that positive action can help and that inaction hurts. A patient who borrowed a light therapy lamp to treat her winter depression but didn't take it out of her car all winter is the perfect example.

A behavioral model for depression suggests that the most prominent feature is "insufficient response-contingent positive reinforcement" (Lewinsohn, 1974; Moss & Boren, 1972). In other words, there are not enough rewards in the depressed person's life, and those that do come are unpredictable and apparently not linked to what the individual does. This in itself is a depressing state of affairs. Complicating it, Lewinsohn (1974) noted the interaction with perception:

- The number of potential reinforcers is seen as diminished.
- The reinforcers are less available to the individual.
- The individual's skill at gaining access to the reinforcers is low.

This is another formulation of the vicious circle of depression. The individual, perhaps because of the loss of a relationship or an opportunity, begins to receive fewer social rewards than he is used to, resulting in a feeling of dysphoria. Dysphoria brings with it feelings of pessimism (fewer rewards, less available) and self-doubt (I can't get what I want), which in turn become self-fulfilling prophecies. People tend to avoid the individual, and his dysphoria and self-doubt interfere with development of social skill. Increased anger or irritability may be a side effect. The result is reduced goal-directed activity. Fewer rewards lead to less effort.

If the problem is that the patient's adaptive efforts are no longer being positively reinforced, then one obvious alternative source of reinforcement that we have near at hand is the therapist himself. The depressed patient acutely desires the therapist's approval, and it is an effective therapist who gives it warmly and genuinely. I alluded in the introduction to the therapist's need to serve as cheerleader, a phrase which I am sure made many wince. But let's be honest. We know that we shape the patient's behavior by showing interest and approval or showing boredom or condemnation. And we know that we can do this very subtly. In Wachtel's (1997, p. 256) phrase, "a half-conscious glance at the clock or an intermittent brushing of lint from one's trousers can serve the very same function as a 'very good' or a 'that's wrong.' " While there is nothing worse than insincere praise, or praise over something that doesn't fit the patient's particular value system, a smile, a nod, an indication that you recognize the patient has accomplished something difficult, an indication that you share the patient's valuation of what he has accomplished, an emotional mirroring of the patient's pride—these can have powerful impact on the depressed patient. I think particularly in working with patients who are competent, hard-working people whom we like as individuals, it is ironically easy for us to be insensitive to the effect a few kind words can have. What we do in the consulting room can lift a depressed mood, give the patient renewed energy and motivation, inspire confidence, reduce shame, open doors to new solutions—it is a great responsibility, and we should use it with skill and deliberation.

We also must keep in mind that focusing on the patient's strengths can be a powerful intervention. By actively inquiring about what made the difference on the occasions when the patient has been successful, we put ourselves in a much stronger position to be helpful to the patient. It may not be hard to identify the pattern behind events when the patient fails, but that knowledge may not be particularly useful to the patient. If we can understand jointly what contributes to success, we identify some factors which are already within the realm of the possible and some behaviors which are already in the patient's repertoire that he may be able to use in the future in achieving his goals. And by establishing this beachhead, as it were, of mutual understanding, we can make it less shaming for the patient to explore the patterns that do lead to failure, and to begin to understand his part in such patterns. In so doing, we open up the possibility of exploring the patient's conflict, the wish and the fear that underlie the problem behavior.

Paradoxical instructions can be problematic in work with depressed patients, but I find them sometimes useful in situations where the patient's own attempts to control the problem behavior are only making things worse. When the patient is engaged in a furious struggle with himself to stop being so self-critical (a paradoxical situation in itself), or so anxious, or so sensitive, it can be help-ful for the therapist to "take control" of the symptom by saying, in effect, *I don't want you to try to stop this now.* This does not have to go so far as the disin-genuous suggestions advocated by some theorists along the lines of *You're not ready to try this yet* or *It would be dangerous to give up worrying at this stage,* but it does not have to be the total honesty of *Stop trying so hard, you're only making things worse for yourself.* The patient is likely to feel powerless to stop trying so hard. But if we say, for instance, *Don't try so hard; let's take the time to understand better why you do this,* we take the burden of fighting the symp-tom off the patient's shoulders for a while. The break from the driven effort to control can give him the opportunity he needs to back off from the problem, look at it from different perspectives, and perhaps come up with different solu-tions. Or we may also try just measuring the problem, as with the mood jour-nal (see p. 107), counting its frequency or paying attention to its precedents and antecedents. Whenever the patient is stuck in a cycle where the only thing he can do is *more of the same* behavior that already is known not to solve the prob-lem, we can often help him best by defusing the power struggle going on within himself.

THE PHYSICAL PATIENT

A special population of depressives exists among patients who manifest their dis-tress through physical symptoms. I see a great number of patients (largely but not exclusively women) who act, look, and feel depressed but don't get diag-nosed that way because they go to their physicians complaining of intractable pain or other symptoms. A close examination of their situation suggests that what is actually going on is a somatized depression; the body, not the psyche, expresses pain, guilt, and recrimination.

There is a such a remarkably high degree of co-occurrence of depression and certain conditions that are thought of as primarily physiological that we have to consider whether some common mechanism is involved. I am referring to con-ditions that are relatively "new," that are not well understood but often seem linked to "stress," that cause subjective distress without any definitive diagnostic test—fibromyalgia, chronic fatigue syndrome, and some others that attract less attention but are still highly linked with depression. It may be that depression, in some people, is manifested in primarily physiological symptoms; or that there is something about the physiological symptoms that makes people highly vul-nerable to depression; or that there is some underlying mechanism at work that results in both depression and physiological symptoms.

Hyams (1998), an epidemiologist, reviewed the diagnostic criteria for many "symptom-based conditions"—chronic fatigue syndrome, fibromyalgia, multiple chemical sensitivity (now known as idiopathic environmental intolerance), silicone-associated rheumatic disease, sick building syndrome, multiple food al-lergies, chronic candidiasis, and Gulf War syndrome. He noted that all are manifested by similar symptoms, principally fatigue but including headache, muscle and joint pain, memory and concentration problems, and sleep problems, and that these symptoms are the only way of diagnosing the disease. There are no laboratory tests or findings on physical exam that don't require subjective interpretation by the patient. Nor has anyone demonstrated a unique causative agent at work in any of these conditions. Hyams notes the overlap with psychiatric conditions, principally depression, and the similarity of these states to the "neurasthenia" of the nineteenth century, including the observation that with the exception of Gulf War syndrome these are all principally diseases of middle-class women. Hyams concludes that at this point we really can't be sure that these conditions represent distinct diagnostic entities. Much of what makes them appear to be distinct comes from our hypotheses about causative factors—exposure to virus, silicone, or Gulf War conditions—which is post hoc reasoning when we really can't be sure we're talking about different conditions to begin with. Much of what makes the differential diagnosis seems to be determined by what medical specialty sufferers seek help from; patients who see a rheumatologist are likely to get a diagnosis involving joint or muscle pain, while those who see a neurologist are likely to be treated for something involving the nerves.

People who are vaguely distressed and in pain respond to prototypes. They try to find an explanation for their suffering. Modern society—through the media, the glamorization of medicine, the sensationalism and fear-mongering of disease—gives them new prototypes. Sometimes the prototype—as in fibromyalgia—is not really an explanation at all, but carries with it the weight of scientific authority. Sometimes the prototype comes from a widely shared and ambiguously frightening experience—as in Gulf War syndrome or silicone rheumatic disease—that suggests a cause even though none can be pinpointed. Sometimes a highly improbable explanation emerges only when the patient becomes thoroughly conditioned by charismatic healers and the media—as in satanic ritual abuse and multiple personality disorder. Too often, these prototypes become the patient's identity, and a life becomes organized around a disease and its treatment.

Still, these are real illnesses, just as depression is a real illness. Wessely (Brody, 1999) noted that trying to categorize them as either simply physiological or simply psychological is a disservice to the patient. "If a patient is told the problem is due to a permanent deficit in the immune system or a persistent virus or chronic disability of the nerves or brain, this just generates helplessness and the patient becomes a victim. And if you say the problem is psychological, this generates anger on the part of patients who don't regard psychological ills as legitimate" (p. C1). These patients live in a world that looks down on psychogenic illness, that regards it as less than real. Much of the patient's self-esteem depends on verification of the physical nature of the illness. Wessely's approach to treatment is cognitive-behavioral: to challenge the patients' destructive beliefs (that they are permanently damaged and any strain will make things worse) and, at the same time, implement a graduated regimen of exercise.

But the treatment of these diseases with antidepressants and analgesics by the rheumatologist or neurologist—a common strategy—is subject to the same objections as treatment of depression by medication alone. It can relieve some distress but it doesn't correct the habits that led to the condition in the first place.

Chronic Fatigue Syndrome

Judith Curren, 42 years old, 5' 1", 260 lbs., a registered nurse who had been unable to work for ten years, wrote to the doctor on whom she had pinned all her hopes for relief: "[After we talked] I finally felt a brief feeling of serenity for the first time in the nineteen years since I became so horribly ill . . . I have very severe auto-immune disease which is now affecting every organ in my body, severe adrenal corticol [sic] insufficiency, severe fibromyalgia, . . . systemic opportunistic fungal infections which are constant and also cause . . . persistent candida vaginally and cause deep fissures in the corners of my mouth and painful lesions on my tongue and oral cavity . . . which also cause terrible abdominal distention, horrendously foul-smelling gas if I attempt to eat anything. . . . I am in constant agonizing pain in all of my joints, constant shooting pains in my legs and arms. . . . I am so weak I cannot brush my own teeth, bathe myself and am incontinent but have no sense of when this happens . . . I cannot read, watch movies or television because while trying to read the words just swim before me making [me] dizzy. I am acutely sensitive to sound which causes seizures. The same is true of odors . . . my memory which was once photographic—is now very poor. . . . I am no longer able to bathe myself and must lie in my own disgusting stench . . . " (Curren, undated).

On August 15, 1996, Ms. Curren got the help she so much desired. She died of a lethal injection in the presence of Dr. Jack Kevorkian. Her husband, a psychiatrist, reported that for the last five years of her life she had been unable to function at all without amphetamines. He said that in 1992, one of her doctors had enraged her by describing chronic fatigue syndrome as a "diagnosis for neurotic women." Soon after that, she contacted Dr. Kevorkian. Dr. Curren blamed "the medical establishment in part for not committing more money to research and understanding of chronic fatigue syndrome" (Anstett, 1997).

Chronic fatigue syndrome (CFS) is characterized by disabling fatigue or exhaustion and a significant reduction in activity level, with a duration of at least six months and no other clearly defined etiology. Incidence is estimated at 0.3 percent of the population, more frequently found among women than men (Schuyler, 1998). Though it's frequently thought of as a sequela to a viral infection—influenza, Epstein-Barr, mononucleosis, Lyme disease, herpes—no confirmed link has ever been found (Bell, 1994). Sufferers of chronic fatigue syndrome tend to see themselves as an oppressed minority. A full page ad in *The New York Times Book Review* for one popular book trumpeted: "This book reveals that a devastating infectious disease is reaching epidemic proportions while government researchers ignore the evidence and the shocking statistics" (Showalter, 1997). The theme that CFS sufferers are the victims of the medical establishment runs throughout their literature, Web sites, and chat rooms. There is an assumption that there is a cure waiting to be found but that no one appreciates the depths of the patient's suffering. Attempts to explain the disease as in part psychological are met with open scorn, another example of the discrimination patients feel they suffer.

There is great overlap between the symptoms of chronic fatigue syndrome and those of major depression. The Centers for Disease Control's definition of chronic fatigue syndrome is as follows (Holmes et al., 1988):

- new onset of debilitating fatigue, present for at least six months
- no identifiable etiology
- objective signs: fever, sore throat, inflamed lymph nodes
- minor symptoms: headache, muscle pain, joint pain, muscle weakness, prolonged fatigue after exercise, "neuropsychiatric symptoms," sleep disturbance, abrupt onset of fatigue

To meet the criteria for diagnosis, the patient must meet the first two standards and have either eight of the minor symptoms or six of the minor symptoms and two of the objective signs.

Many patients, but not all, diagnosed with chronic fatigue syndrome also meet the criteria for major depression. Patients typically do not present complaining of anhedonia or depressed mood, but will acknowledge when asked; and many reject the diagnosis of depression (Lane, Nance, & Matthews, 1994). Jorge and Goodnick (1997) suggest that the only reliable way to distinguish between depression and CFS is a thorough physical exam. But that raises the question of self-selection. Psychiatrists rarely perform a physical, because their patients are complaining primarily of psychological distress; neurologists and rheumatologists, on the other hand, will always perform a physical exam but not a mental status, because patients who seek them out are complaining of physical symptoms. Therefore it is highly unlikely that psychiatrists will find CFS and highly unlikely other MDs will find depression.

Many antidepressant drugs have been tried with chronic fatigue syndrome. No wide-ranging controlled studies are available, but evidence suggests that antidepressant medication is helpful about as often for CFS as it is for depression (Jorge & Goodnick, 1997). Remission of all symptoms is rare, but that is true for depression as well. Cognitive-behavioral treatment specifically adapted to address patients' beliefs about illness and coping behavior has been tested in one sample of 60, and found to be much more effective than medical treatment alone (Sharpe et al., 1996). Interestingly, the treated group continued to improve during the 12-month follow-up period.

The problem with mere palliative treatment is that it falsely reinforces the patient's conception of himself as disabled and contributes to the spread of the "disease." If the recommended treatment for chronic fatigue syndrome is complete bed rest, chances are that the patients who take the advice are likely to continue to be fatigued. And we feed the rumor mill if we permit the myth of a hidden physiological cause to continue; more and more patients who are tired or depressed will believe they have a mysterious disease. Meanwhile people who could be helped by psychotherapy and/or medication are encouraged to get on the merry-go-round of fruitless medical treatment.

Fibromyalgia

The chief symptom of fibromyalgia is generalized somatic pain of no clear etiology. It is diagnosed by the presence of "tender points" where pain is felt when digital pressure is applied. Points are inside the elbows, inside the knees, and in the neck and shoulders. It seems to be a disease discovered most by rheumatologists, whose old specialty, rheumatism, has fallen out of favor. There are no objective physical changes observable by X-ray, laboratory analysis, examination, or autopsy. The prevalence is estimated at about two percent of the population, most over fifty, with a 6:1 female/male ratio (Schuyler, 1998). Depression and sleep disturbance are commonly observed.

An interesting study assessed psychiatric symptomatology among 31 patients with fibromyalgia and 14 with rheumatoid arthritis from the same clinic (Hudson, Hudson, Pliner, Goldenberg, & Pope, 1985). Rheumatoid arthritis was taken as a comparison because it is also a chronic, painful rheumatic disease and patients generally come from the same social class and background as those with fibromyalgia. The investigators found that 71 percent of the fibromyalgia patients also were suffering from major depression, as opposed to only 13 percent of the arthritis patients. There was also a significantly higher incidence of depression in the relatives of fibromyalgia patients than in the arthritis group. If the pain and disability of fibromyalgia were the cause of patients' depression, we would expect that the same would be true of the rheumatoid arthritis patients. Instead, the results are highly suggestive that either fibromyalgia is a manifestation of depression or that both fibromyalgia and depression are manifestations of some third process.

The cycle of fibromyalgia, sleep disturbance $\Rightarrow$ muscle tension $\Rightarrow$ muscle and joint pain $\Rightarrow$ fibromyalgia $\Rightarrow$ depression, is another example of a vicious circle, and the search for a single cause is futile. Does it begin with depression, with fibromyalgia, or with primary sleep disturbance? It seems only intuitive that people who live for 20 or 30 years in a state of hypervigilance, always in fight-or-flight mode, muscles always tense, will eventually begin to have aching muscles, tendinitis, backaches, and other symptoms that eventually develop into fibromyalgia. In any case, the use of tricyclic antidepressants has been proven effective. The treatment of symptomatic pain with Darvon, Percodan, or other opioids is quite common in medical practice, but obviously is contraindicated when so much overlap exists between this disease and depression.

Other Chronic Pain Syndromes

Scientific understanding of the phenomenon of pain, especially its psychological aspects, remains inadequate. We know that patients with chronic pain—temporomandibular joint syndrome, migraine, back pain, and pain caused by structural damage to the nerves—are more likely to suffer from depression than people without pain, but we don't know if the depression is a psychological effect of the pain (perhaps of the restriction of activity due to pain, perhaps due to learned helplessness, excessive self-focusing, etc.) or a physiological accompaniment to pain, or both. We know that when pain improves, depression improves. We know that the same neurotransmitters, serotonin and norepinephrine, that seem to be implicated in depression also play a critical role in pain modulation (Fields, 1987, 1991). A study of certain psychological symptoms manifested in chronic pain patients found that the patients scored significantly higher on all the symptoms (worthlessness, hopelessness, "everything an effort," guilt, self-blame, loneliness, disturbed sleep, worry, and low energy) but that "everything an effort," disturbed sleep, worry, and low energy were especially highly evident in the depressed patients (Von Korff & Simon, 1996). This may be evidence that the somatization defense works—that patients who somatize are somewhat protected from the guilt, self-blame, hopelessness, and loneliness of depression, but not protected from the physical manifestations of somatization—lack of energy, disturbed sleep, etc.

Surprisingly, the intensity of pain does not seem to be a predictor of depression, but interference with activities and diffusion of pain does. This finding suggests that the effect of pain on depression is indirect—that pain causes disability and worry which in themselves are depressing. Depressed people are not more likely than others to develop most pain symptoms (back pain, stomach pain, TMJ). But among both depressed people and those not depressed, one pain symptom increases risk for others.

Heart Disease

People with heart disease are more likely to have depression than the general population. People who have heart disease and depression are more likely to have future heart attacks and shortened life span than people with heart disease alone. Athough depression can be expected to reduce problem-solving ability and to interfere with compliance with treatment and rehabilitation, most evidence now indicates that depression is a separate independent risk factor in addition to contributing to these other risks (Frasure-Smith, Lespérance, Juneau, Talajic, & Bourassa, 1999). Older antidepressants can have toxic effects on the heart, while SSRIs and other newer medications appear to be safer. However, no long-term studies have been completed. Relief of depressive symptoms in patients with heart disease has been shown to improve quality of life and perhaps increase longevity. But depression is rarely diagnosed by cardiologists or primary care physicians. Even articles that recommend improved treatment of depression among heart patients argue that treatment may have deleterious effects if the patient finds the concept of depression disturbing (Musselman, Evans, & Nemeroff, 1998)—as if we can't treat the symptoms without naming the disease.

TEACHING SELF-CARE

Realistic Standards

One psychoanalytic view of depression is that it has to do with grief and loss; another is that it stems from failure to live up to one's ego ideal. While much of treatment should focus on helping the patient function more effectively, it's also true that depressed people tend to be perfectionistic, to expect more from themselves than they do from others. Thus, an important aspect of treatment is to help the patient learn to question his expectations, to evaluate himself more fairly.

Consumer culture tends to equate happiness with financial success. The depressed patient may believe that, in order to be happy or feel at peace, he must have a certain level of income. This is a myth.

> What matters more than absolute wealth is perceived wealth. Money is two steps removed from happiness: Actual income doesn't much influence happiness; how satisfied we are with our income does. If we're content with our income, regardless of how much it is, we're likely to say we're happy. Strangely, however, there is only a slight tendency for people who make lots of money to be more satisfied with what they make. . . . This implies two ways to be rich: one is to have great wealth. The other is to have few wants. (Myers, 1992, p. 39)

Once we're past a certain level of want where basic necessities are taken care of and we have a little leisure time, increased income has almost no relationship to increased happiness. Moreover, greater income doesn't noticeably influence satisfaction with marriage, family, friendships, or the self—all of which substantially influence our sense of well-being. If we are not subject to crushing poverty or discrimination, people of every income can experience about the same amount of joy in life.

It can be much easier to decrease want than to increase wealth, but it implies a deliberate rejection of consumer culture. Sometimes out of fear of imposing our values on others, we hold back from what might be a very helpful intervention. If we can help the patient sort out his priorities and spend more time and energy in activities that will take him closer to his long-term best interests, we should. I suggest that patients deliberately set aside time to identify what's truly important to them. They may make a list of ten things they feel make living worthwhile, then rank them in order of importance. Then I suggest that they set the list aside for a few weeks, do the same exercise to create a new list, then compare the two. After a few tries at this exercise the patient's core values begin to emerge.

The eye-opening part of the exercise for most patients is then to monitor how they spend their time; how much of their daily activities actually express their core values or take them closer to their goals. Most people are shocked to find out how much time they are wasting. The depressed patient may need reassurance that he is normal in this; but the lesson is to deliberately take time each day in activities that take one closer to goal attainment.

Prevention magazine conducted a study to determine what people identified as the top ten stressors in their lives (Davidson, 1997). The single greatest stressor was personal finances. In one year alone, the indebtedness of the average credit cardholder increased by 23 percent. The fact that everyone is doing it doesn't make it wise. Debt is a significant source of strain in everyone's life and one that certainly adds to depression.

I encourage patients for whom debt is a problem to take immediate steps to reverse the situation:

1. If you're in debt, stop all nonessential spending until you're out of debt.
2. When you're out of debt, start a forced savings plan.

Identifying Our Introjects

The automatic negative thoughts of depression, the voice that "shoulds all over" us (Ellis, 1994), can often be given a personality, a trick which helps us to objectify and develop distance from it. It's the depression talking; it's Mother, it's Dad. *Hi Dad, how are you doing, sorry can't stay, gotta go. Talk to you later.* The nagging voice, the belittling voice, the suspicious or jealous voice, the voice that tells us nothing is good enough. *Okay, I know, but just this moment I'm doing the laundry. I have to get this done right now, later on you can tell me what a loser I am.* We can help the patient get some power over these voices by rendering them a little absurd, like Woody Allen's hallucination in *New York Stories* of his mother in the sky, complaining about him to the whole neighborhood. *How do you picture your father when he talks to you like this? How is he dressed? Does he come into the room and sit down, or just stand there and humiliate you from the doorway?* These kinds of images can become a shared running joke in the therapy. We can also teach the patient to remember the teacher, the aunt, the big sister, the grandfather who provided support, love, and encouragement. We can go through a process of helping a client build a new internal boundary between what's me and what's not-me.

The Body

In the World Health Organization study of mental illness in primary care (Üstün & Von Korff, 1995), it was found that patients with major depression presented with psychological concerns only rarely. Most complained primarily of somatic symptoms (41 percent), pain (37 percent), and fatigue and sleep problems (12 percent) (Wittchen, Lieb, Wunderlich, & Schuster, 1999). Goldberg (1995) found that mixed anxiety-depression was the third most common presenting problem of patients in primary care, after upper respiratory infections and hypertension. Depression is among the most common reasons why people seek alternative therapies (Astin, 1998). No wonder; as Western medicine becomes more highly disease-focused, the patient who has vague complaints is likely to feel unwanted.

Depression is significantly associated with higher death rates following heart attack, for both sexes, controlling for all other health and social variables (Frasure-Smith et al., 1999). Depression is associated with increased mortality for the general hospital population, across all diagnostic groups, not only cardiac cases (Herrmann et al., 1998). Why depression has this effect is not known. Wulsin, Vaillant, and Wells (1999), carefully reviewing all the English-language studies published in the last 30 years, found that, as might be expected, higher rates of suicide, smoking, alcohol use, and generally poor physical health were associated with both depression and mortality, but did not seem to account for all the effect. It is possible that some underlying physiological mechanism—whether inborn or a response to stress—could result in greater risk for depression and for early death.

But it also seems quite likely that people with depression tend to die a little sooner because they don't practice good self-care. They don't eat right or exercise regularly; they don't know how to relax and play, how to take time out to de-stress themselves. I think that part of our responsibility to depressed patients is to inform them of these unpleasant facts and help them learn how to take better care of themselves. To the extent that the depressed patient's interest in alternative medicine helps attain this goal, it should be encouraged. Massage, meditation, relaxation therapy, acupuncture, and herbal medicine can all help the stressed-out patient learn vital relaxation skills. Proper nutrition is essential to good overall health and not as easy to achieve as we generally believe. As with anything else, self-care can be carried too far, so that the patient obsessively tries to control his environment without paying attention to the interpersonal and emotional sources of his stress. But in my experience, less harm has been done to depressed patients by practitioners of alternative medicine than by traditional medicine, which overprescribes opiates and surgery for psychosomatic pain, tranquilizers and sleeping pills for stress. A good massage, by contrast, never hurt anyone.

CHAPTER 13

Practice, Practice, Practice

I N A RECENT STUDY of 200 patients who had vague physical complaints but no identifiable disease, the reassurance of a diagnosis and treatment plan had a significant effect on recovery. Of those who were told that no serious illness was found and that they would soon be well, 64 percent recovered in two weeks; for those who were told that the cause of their symptoms was unclear, only 39 percent improved (Brown, 1998). Non-MD mental health professionals are likely to underestimate the power of the implicit reassurance that comes with the degrees on the wall, the nurses, the lab equipment in the office, and the prescription pad. But perhaps most important is the structure that a diagnosis and treatment plan provide. *All the vague and seemingly disconnected things that are bothering you make sense when you consider them as separate manifestations of depression. Try not to worry too much. We know how to treat this. I'm going to give you some suggestions.*

Depressed patients need a structure, a plan, a time frame. *This is how therapy works: We talk about feelings; we use the mood log; you need to report to me changes in your feelings, moods, behavior; you need to be honest with me about self-destructive behavior, etc. . . . . This is what you can expect from medication. . . . These are circumstances when you should call me. . . . This is how long it might take. . . . This is how we will deal with your insurance company. . . .*

The therapist's knowledge about depression and its effects can help the overwhelmed, confused, and despairing patient bring clarity and hope to his present condition. The mere act of asking intelligent questions that reveal a familiarity with the disease and suggest connections between seemingly random phenomena is in itself an educational process that can be quite helpful. The patient learns "that there is something 'normative' about [his] behavior even if it isn't 'normal' for him or her" (Schuchter et al., 1996, p. 84). As the patient begins to appreciate that there is a body of knowledge about his condition that can be helpful to him, he can become a student of his own disease.

TABLE 13.1
Aphorisms of Depression

Problems and symptoms are not the same.

Depression is a disease.

If I change what I do, I can change how I feel.

I need to reconnect with my emotional life.

I need to identify and correct self-destructive thinking
and behavior patterns.

I need to let my guard down.

I need to learn to take care of myself.

I need to practice detachment.

Change can come from anywhere.

There is a part of me that doesn't want to get well.

I am more than my depression.

Depression is a social problem.

Just as we do not recognize that the skills of depression are acquired behavior, we have trouble recognizing that we can learn new, more adaptive
skills. These will seem awkward at first, like trying anything new, but eventually they become integrated into the self. As we've said, we no longer have the
luxury of the years-long "middle phase" of treatment where the nondirective
therapist could count on the patient to learn new behavior through trial and
error. We owe it to our patients to provide direction and to give them a cognitive map of how they will be expected to recover. One of the best ways we
can help them is by reminding them to go to the psychic gym: that they are
developing new muscles, new coordination, and the way to do that is through
practice.

To help my patients understand how they can best help themselves, I often
provide them with a list of aphorisms about depression, which can serve as a
stimulus for thought and discussion (Table 13.1). These ideas are discussed in
more depth in the remainder of the chapter. I find that these flat assertions, presented as statements of fact, have a way of getting around defensiveness. The patient learns that these observations are manifestations of his condition, not weakness or lack of character on his part. He can become involved in the task of
identifying how these phenomena are manifested in his case, rather than feeling he is being assaulted piecemeal by the therapist who keeps unpleasantly
surprising him with new interpretations of his own behavior that he thought he
understood.

"PROBLEMS AND SYMPTOMS
ARE NOT THE SAME"

Some patients contact us in emotional distress, or because they are unable to sleep, or have intrusive thoughts of suicide, or other symptomatic manifestations of depression. Others are primarily troubled by problems in living—they aren't getting along with their spouse, they can't make decisions, their own bodies are in rebellion. Most people have a mixture of both kinds of troubles.

Likewise, most patients understand intellectually that they are unlikely to get lasting symptomatic relief without fixing the problems that are giving them stress, and also that their own symptoms are getting in the way of fixing their problems. So, although individual priorities vary widely, most people acknowledge that they need help that addresses both kinds of issues.

But this distinction is also a source of much resistance to making real change. The patient who is troubled primarily by symptoms is too likely to look for medication, or some advice or interpretation by the therapist, to be a magical cure that will require no effort on his behalf. *He wants to be changed.* The patient who is troubled mostly by problems is too likely to assume that if only circumstances in his life change, he can feel better without having to change himself.* *He wants others to change. Nobody wants to change himself.*

I find that attention to the tension arc between problems and symptoms keeps the patient off balance in a stimulating way that prevents him from taking a rigidly defended position. When he talks about his symptoms, I ask about his problems, and vice versa. I want to keep reminding him that the two are intimately related.

I also want to keep the focus on things the patient can do something about. When we talk about symptoms, I want to talk about self-control, self-care; in essence, we are turning the management of symptoms into problems. When we talk about problems, I want to reinforce the distinction between problems we can alter and problems we simply must accept. I want to keep reminding the patient who is too highly focused on symptoms that recovery from depression comes from taking charge of his own life; and the patient who is concerned about problems he can do nothing about that he needs to understand how his overconcern makes him symptomatic in ways he's probably unaware of.

"DEPRESSION IS A DISEASE"

Therapists who resist the disease model or who believe they can "cure" depression through perfect psychotherapy really need to have the facts of life

---

*While we should give the patient the benefit of the doubt and start with the assumption that he may be merely a victim of bad luck or circumstance, most often we find that long-standing depression has resulted in the patient's taking an active role in creating the troubling circumstances in his life, and he is likely to do so again unless something happens to break the pattern.

explained. The same applies to physicians who believe they can treat depression with a pill for a few months and make it go away. Patients who have one episode of major depression have a 50-50 chance of escaping another; patients who have two or three episodes are about 70 percent likely to have more; and patients who have more than three episodes are 90 percent likely to have additional episodes (Keller, Shapiro, Lavori, & Wolfe, 1982). In follow-up studies of 10 to 20 years, the majority of patients with depression have repeated hospitalizations or otherwise poor outcomes (Angst, 1999). We can give patients hope that by taking care of themselves they can be among the number who maintain recovery; but by not warning them of the odds we infantilize them and deprive them of knowledge they need in order to make good life decisions.

Schuchter and colleagues (1996) present a detailed model for applying the disease model for practice. I find it too limiting for all patients, but perfectly appropriate for many with depression. The authors acknowledge that depression is associated with regression in many areas of functioning, and argue that it can be helpful to the patient to contrast regressed functioning with the more adaptive and healthy functioning which he is capable of when not depressed. A tool such as Erikson's (1950) familiar hierarchy of developmental stages can help identify areas that do not immediately present themselves as issues. The point is not to expect that the patient can be cured of depression and therefore capable of healthy functioning permanently and consistently; but that he can strive for more adaptive functioning even during an episode, and this achievement can be a source of great pride and strength.

If depression is a disease, it is a very unique one, and the therapist and patient must communicate carefully and clearly about its nature. The primary benefits of the disease model are to help the patient recover from the self-blame that accompanies depression and to develop hope through recognition that the disease has a long course but does not mean never feeling well again. The risks are that it can reinforce passivity, hopelessness, and helplessness—the patient can conclude that only a miracle of science can save him. I emphasize to people that depression is a disease like alcoholism—the only real cure comes from changing our own behavior. We are certainly not to blame for being depressed, but unfortunately we are responsible for our own recovery. For patients who don't like the alcoholism analogy, I'll trot out examples of people who've been disabled in accidents. What happened to them is tragic and unfair, but they have no choice except to learn new skills in order to help themselves get through life. Once they do, their chances of having a happy and fulfilling life are no different than those of anyone else.

Another advantage of the disease model is that it helps the patient stay alert to recurrences. Despite our best efforts at teaching patients to identify symptoms early, depression remains able to sneak up and capture them. It may be useful for the patient to periodically do a self-assessment like the Beck Depression Inventory or a special adaptation of such an instrument geared to the patient's idiosyncratic presentation; or to enlist loved ones in identifying the prodromal indicators of the disease. An early warning system like this can help the patient prevent what might be a minor episode from turning into another trauma.

"IF I CHANGE WHAT I DO,
I CAN CHANGE HOW I FEEL"

"Move a muscle, change a thought" is an old Alcoholics Anonymous aphorism. It might be more appropriate to say "Change a feeling," but AA has historically tried to steer clear of emotional language. The point is that how we are feeling is directly affected by what we are doing. When I'm stuck at home, depressed and feeling worthless, unable to write the next sentence or accomplish anything constructive, if I can remember to go for a walk, listen to some music, or play with the dogs, my mood will often change. Sometimes the change is not enough to say that I'm not depressed anymore, but usually it frees me up from the anger and frustration and enables me to move on to something more productive, which can lead to further change, and eventually to a real lift from the depressed state.

Matthew was unhappy with a planned job change. He was the manager of a large family business and in the process of retirement. When I first saw him, his skin was an unhealthy gray and he looked exhausted.

He was referred by his physician because of "stress." He described poor sleep and a constant feeling of fatigue. He usually is in a sad mood and describes feeling detached, not caring about the things that usually are important to him. He says that this has been his state for some time, but things are particularly stressful at work right now. He works 60–70 hours a week, as he has always done, but he is turning over the day-to-day operations to a new generation in his family so that he can have time to devote to his other interests in life. This is a change he wants very much, but he's finding that it will be harder than he thought to give up the daily adrenaline rush that comes from being the center of a complex and changing operation. He's known for being able to absorb it all and do whatever there is that needs to be done, but within the past year he's really lost his temper a few times, lashing out at people who aren't pulling their weight. He is extremely embarrassed by these outbursts. He's also recently been feeling like he's kidding himself about his new interests, that they are really trivial and unimportant and he will live out his retirement in meaningless pursuits. He reports being withdrawn from his family, just wanting to be left alone to read or watch sitcoms.

After the second session I suggested that Matthew start using the mood journal. He turned out to be an observant reporter. He noticed that each day during the week, as he trained the two people who were to take over aspects of his job, he became depressed and agitated. He felt that despite their intelligence and experience, they were not "getting it"—making obvious errors in judgment. In typical depressed fashion, he blamed himself ("I must be a lousy teacher") and catastrophized ("This was a stupid idea, it'll never work, I'll be stuck in this job all my life"). He would either lose his temper and be ashamed of himself, or withdraw and sulk. He noticed this pattern on four successive days. On the fifth day when it started again Matthew excused himself and went for a walk. He deliberately challenged his assumptions, telling himself things like "I am a good teacher, they can get it, they have to do it their way, I have to let them make mistakes." He came back and went through the day's training without getting depressed or upset. His improved mood lasted through the day, and he noticed a change in the evening too. Trying to wrap Christmas presents and becoming all thumbs, he laughed at himself instead of getting angry or giving up. His wife noticed his improved mood and offered to help out. They put some music on, finished wrapping, and had a pleasant evening together—the first in several weeks.

We continued treatment with sessions every other week for about a year. Matthew was successful in transitioning to a new role in life that was much more rewarding for him, and he took action in helping other family members with problems of their own. He referred many times to what he had learned on the day he went for a walk. For him, it was a very important realization—the equivalent of a eureka experience—that what he did could change his mood. Going for a walk and rehearsing a different interaction helped him change his behavior, and that in turn improved his state of mind. We were careful to point out that there was no guarantee—he could not be sure that he could always change a mood—but knowing that it was at least sometimes possible was a revelation that he never forgot.

Some patients seem to be very impressed and hopeful at the news that psychotherapy can make changes in the brain that are visible by positron-emission tomography (PET scans; Schwartz et al., 1996) or changes in brain metabolic rate similar to those caused by antidepressant medication (Baxter et al., 1992). People seem willing to buy the idea that depression is a manifestation of a change in the brain that can be altered by medication. But most people seem to assume that while the brain can do bad things to us, we can't do good things to the brain. The idea that life experience can actually make a change in the way the brain functions is potentially full of power and meaning for depression; it will just take some concrete success experiences before the depressive can begin to believe it.

"I NEED TO RECONNECT WITH MY EMOTIONAL LIFE"

We want to make it explicit to patients that depression is partly the result of a misguided effort not to feel, and to remind them that emotions are nothing to fear. We take it as a working hypothesis that mood changes are typically caused by an effort not to feel an emotion, and we keep working on the mood journal as proof and explication of that hypothesis.

Patients are often confused by this proposition; they believe that they suffer from an excess of feeling, an excess of despair, anger, hopelessness. They fear that if they feel more, they will be unable to bear it. Without getting into hair-splitting, I try to point out that they are feeling depression, which is an illness, whereas emotions are natural and inevitable. Most will acknowledge the difference between, for instance, sadness and depression, recognizing that a good cry prompted by a sad movie or powerful music can lift a depressed mood. With practice, patients will learn that emotions not only don't have to be frightening, they also add spice and color to life. Unless the patient can reestablish contact with the emotional side of his nature, the anhedonia of depression will never lift.

A certain number of depressed patients will report that they feel equally depressed all the time, with no fluctuations in intensity. This is a defensive maneuver that can be hard to overcome in the initial stages; the patient may fear that if he admits to any relief at all from his suffering his pain may be dismissed, or that the therapist will use that information as ammunition against him somehow: *See, you're not really so depressed, are you?* A useful technique is to ask when the depression has been its absolute worst: *Are there times when you feel even worse than you do right now?* Once the patient has been able to acknowledge this, then you may begin to use the mood journal. You may be saying, in effect, *We understand that your depression is always 9.5 on a 10-point scale, but sometimes, apparently, it gets even worse than that. Let's see if we can gain some understanding of what makes it worse.* As time goes on with this kind of patient, we may need to address specifically the fear noted above: that he has been afraid we would minimize his suffering or use the mood journal as a trick to make him feel better. We may need to help him identify how these fears came about and how they constitute an obstacle for recovery.

Many more patients will report that they feel no emotions whatsoever. They experience depression as an endless, boring grayness. Though we may see this as denial, efforts to broach it directly are likely to fail. Again, the mood journal can be a very useful tool. The patient's individual language style may have to be taken into account. For instance, I seem to meet many patients who have an extreme aversion to the word "anger." They will say they felt frustrated, put down, rejected, disrespected, irritated, or upset, but never angry. Other patients who need to hold on to their depression at all costs will deny ever feeling happy or joyful or calm; instead they may acknowledge feeling less stressed, or a little more energetic, or that they managed to forget about things for a while.

"I NEED TO IDENTIFY AND CORRECT
SELF-DESTRUCTIVE THINKING AND
BEHAVIOR PATTERNS"

At every session, the therapist and patient should review the patient's progress in identifying and correcting these patterns. The therapist is deliberately trying to reinforce knowledge acquisition and habit strength on the patient's part. In effect, we want the patient to become a more objective observer of himself.

- *Perspective.* We assume that the patient sees the world through brown-colored glasses and needs to make a self-conscious effort to correct for his habitual cognitive distortions—to develop awareness of opportunities for joy, to train his eye to see more flowers and fewer weeds.
- *Assumptions.* The patient has built an assumptive world on the basis of his skewed perspective. He needs to develop and maintain awareness of his own particular destructive assumptions and either challenge them logically *(What's the basis for believing that?)* or test them empirically *(What if I act as if I am not helpless?)*.
- *Logical errors.* We want the patient to develop greater awareness of his own unique logical system that supports depression. When he comes in reporting that he noticed how he catastrophized a situation or took excessive responsibility, we want to acknowledge and affirm his developing self-awareness.
- *Distorted perception of the self.* People with depression need to practice paying attention to positive feedback, to question their assumptions about their own role in events (bad things are always my fault, good things are always dumb luck, etc.).
- *Automatic negative thoughts.* I find that many patients learn to take delight in spotting ANTS; once they learn to identify the process as something outside themselves, it becomes a sort of game to develop awareness of its many manifestations. Countering the thoughts with empirical questions or positive affirmations almost becomes secondary to the enjoyment of identifying the sneaky bastards at work.
- *Work habits.* Procrastination is one of the principal behavioral manifestations of depression. We want to continually reinforce the application of basic organizational skills like learning to reward the self for effective work, developing stimulus control over problem behaviors, and establishing priorities.
- *Assertiveness.* People with depression rarely have a clear idea of mutual rights and responsibilities in relationships, from highway driving to raising children to working with colleagues in an office. Active treatment of depression makes this deficit explicit, and reinforces the patient for learning and implementing assertive skills.

"I NEED TO LET MY GUARD DOWN"

A key element of depression is the fear of intimacy. Depressed people believe themselves to be deeply defective, and fear that if others knew them as they know themselves, they would be rejected and scorned. So they keep up a mask for the world, pretending to be happy when they're not, pretending to be competent when they feel like they're falling apart. At the end of the day, if they're successful at this all they get is the conviction that they can fool people successfully. It just reinforces the depression.

At the same time, they feel a desperate need for love, respect, and affirmation, but their pretense makes it impossible for them to believe that anyone can know or love their true selves. As the patient begins to let his guard down bit by bit he learns that others are not repulsed by his feelings. He begins to understand that he is not really so different from other people, that the crippling shame he feels about himself is far out of proportion to the reality of his "awful secrets."

The therapist needs to actively and directly identify that the fear of intimacy perpetuates depression and help the patient practice intimacy. This means identifying persons and situations in the patient's world that are relatively safe and trustworthy, and encouraging the patient to begin to let his guard down a little at a time. This takes practice, patience, and a forgiving attitude from both the patient and the therapist. The therapist will not be omniscient; some of the patient's forays into intimacy will not turn out well, and the patient will be hurt. It may be an opportunity for the patient to learn that the hurt of real rejection is no worse than the hurt of imagined rejection—but it will hurt, and the therapist and the patient must both trust each other.

At the same time, the therapist must do everything he can to ensure that the patient's efforts are successful. This can mean very detailed analysis of people in the patient's life, their actual behavior and their behavior as seen by the patient; of the patient's presentation of himself, his ability to size up a situation objectively, his ability to shoot himself in the foot. It means teaching the patient the distinctions between letting his guard down appropriately and spilling his emotions too freely. It means talking about small talk, helping the patient learn how people signal each other about what it is acceptable to talk about and what is not. In essence, it means being as wise about people and the world as possible and being willing to share that wisdom with the patient.

"I NEED TO LEARN TO TAKE
CARE OF MYSELF"

The continuing challenge for the depressed patient is to learn to treat himself as if he is worthy of respect and love. By stating the problem this way, we make it explicit that bad self-care perpetuates the depression. I have a list of areas of self-care (Table 13.2) that I have found to be problematic with most patients, and we go over this list periodically during the course of treatment. I encourage patients to add to this list as they identify particular areas where they neglect or abuse themselves. This exercise may sound simplistic or demeaning to therapists who practice from a different perspective; again, it's part of my approach

TABLE 13.2
Basics of Good Self-Care

Exercise moderately but regularly.

Eat healthy but delicious meals.

Regularize your sleep cycle.

Practice good personal hygiene.

Get help for painful conditions.

Don't drink to excess or abuse drugs.

Spend some time every day in play.

Develop recreational outlets that encourage creativity.

Avoid unstructured time.

Limit exposure to mass media.

Distance yourself from destructive situations or people.

Allow yourself to feel pride in your accomplishments.

Listen to compliments and expressions of affection.

Avoid depressed self-absorption.

Build and use a support system.

Pay more attention to small pleasures and sensations.

Challenge yourself.

---

to identify depression as an active agent—an enemy—and build an alliance with the patient against it. It's the depression, not the patient, that makes him not brush his teeth or watch too much television.

"I NEED TO PRACTICE DETACHMENT"

At the same time that depressives need to cultivate the ability to feel, they also need to learn how to detach from their emotions. Detachment implies recognizing and acknowledging feelings but exercising some conscious control over how much we let them affect us. It suggests a certain passive, observant attitude toward emotions: an understanding that our feelings come and go, that they are subject to distortion and contagion, but that they have limited impact on our core self.

Much of depression seems to come from an obsessive quality that won't let the patient detach from the immediate turmoil or problem he's faced with. Unable to stop, calm himself, and objectively assess the situation, he's stuck doing only more of the same kind of ineffective intervention that keeps getting him in trouble. Frantic to fix the engine, he tries to replace the bolts with a pair of pliers instead of going to get a wrench, and he ends up stripping the bolt head and skinning his knuckles.

The therapist needs to help the patient distinguish between what's really important and what merely feels urgent. *Will this really matter next week? Is this how I really want to spend my time? What about this problem is realistically within my power to address, and what do I just have to accept?* Detachment is a highly underrecognized skill; we have to help the patient learn to appreciate its value and help him practice its implementation.

"CHANGE CAN COME FROM ANYWHERE"

Depression is a vicious circle, a self-reinforcing cycle. As we've discussed, one of the great advantages of abandoning linear causality is the realization that a vicious circle can be broken at any point.

Most patients think about depression as having a single cause: their job, their spouse, their serotonin level, their difficulty sleeping. Discussion of the common sense model of depression can challenge that linear thinking without putting the patient on the defensive. If we say *No, it's not your job stress, it's your response to your job stress that's the problem,* we are likely to raise all the patient's defensive anxiety about change and being blamed. However, if we say *You're caught in a vicious circle that perpetuates itself; but it's possible that if we can just help you sleep better at night (or play with your kids more, or treat your wife better, or change some of your depressogenic assumptions), you won't feel the job stress as so overwhelming anymore,* the patient is more apt to give our suggestions a try.

Acceptance of this premise also gives the patient hope and engages his creativity. He may be able to see that, while the head-on efforts he's been putting into trying to control his problem have been getting nowhere, if he backs off, looks around and examines the whole system, there may be other, more indirect, approaches to the problem that can yield better results.

"THERE IS A PART OF ME THAT DOESN'T WANT TO GET WELL"

I think we might as well just state it at the beginning of treatment: Most people with depression want to feel better but are going to be afraid of doing some of the things necessary to feel better. The same skills of depression which ironically contribute to the existence of the problem will be activated even more strongly when we try to change the problem. Many patients will resent the idea that they have to change anything to get relief; after all, they certainly didn't wish this condition on themselves. Most patients will acknowledge that they sometimes have moments of sanctimonious self-satisfaction, as if they've earned the right to be depressed. Many feel comfortable with depression as a familiar and safe place of retreat and self-indulgence. Acceptance of a depressed state means that the patient has been able to give up trying for success and focus instead on preparing for future disappointments. These "resistances" should be presented as an expectable part of the syndrome of depression, which contribute significantly to the patient's guilt and self-blame.

Naming this resistance in a matter-of-fact, objective way at the beginning of treatment has enormous advantages over waiting until it gets manifested and then pointing it out to the patient. For one thing, the patient is alerted to the problem (and also warned that *we* are alerted to the problem) and will be more likely to notice and acknowledge it himself. We can positively reinforce such noticing on the patient's part, contributing to the overall tone of respect and collegiality we want to maintain. The patient's view of himself as an active and capable agent is reinforced. On the other hand, if we wait until the patient manifests resistance to change, and then pounce on it like a cat on a mouse, we only reinforce the patient's sense of guilt and inadequacy, and we make him defensive. He will want to argue with us, instead of considering that we may have a point.

We have to help the patient develop awareness of the advantages and disadvantages of the sick role. It can be comforting; it can elicit sympathy and pity, which can be effective ways of getting some of our needs met and provide a sense of emotional closeness and support. But it also reduces one's self-esteem and ability to function, and in the end it drives others away—pity is not love. The patient must develop an awareness of the paradoxes of the disease model of depression: It *is* a disease, but one in which we have to take responsibility for our own recovery.

"I AM MORE THAN MY DEPRESSION"

If we take too narrow a focus in the therapy, restricting our vision to the manifest problem areas in the patient's life, and then concentrate only on how he contributes to the problem, we unwittingly reinforce his negative world view— that life stinks and it's his fault. This is an easy trap for us to fall into because in many ways it seems respectful of what the patient wants and it also makes his managed care company happy.

We need a more complete relationship with the patient; we need to be interested in parts of his life that are not the direct focus of treatment, and we need to have a relationship that is characterized by genuine interest, humor, and warmth. We need to be ready to play with the patient when it's appropriate, to talk about mutual interests in a mutually respectful way, to let ourselves be known a little when it suits the therapeutic purpose. We need to practice phrasing our interventions in such a way that they give credit to the patient's strengths as well as exploring his weaknesses. The patient is all too ready to believe that depression is a trait he carries within himself that poisons all interactions all the time.

We need to continually point out that there are times when the patient functions more effectively than at other times, that when he isn't functioning at his best there are good reasons for it, and that understanding those reasons means that change is possible.

As soon as the worst depression begins to lift, the patient should be expected to stretch himself a little. *Do one difficult thing every day. Call a friend, volunteer, express an opinion, be generous, take a chance.* Depression is not only an illness, but a failure of creativity. We all share the problem of creating meaning in our lives. The patient needs to find ways to be fertile, to grow and produce, to have an impact, if he ever wants to be free of depression.

"DEPRESSION IS A SOCIAL PROBLEM"

It's extremely helpful for patients to realize that depression is not just a disease within themselves but a condition which is an intimate part of the social fabric of contemporary culture. Some patients know this already and want to set me up as the voice of convention so that they can argue with me that society has contributed to their depression. I see no value in trying to be a blank screen and disputing the subject; it's simply a statement of fact. I do not want to shift the responsibility for helping himself off the patient's shoulders but I do want to help him understand that it is not by any means all his fault. In doing so I emphasize four points:

- People with depression suffer from discrimination. The stereotype that depression is a sign of weakness is a lie, yet others use that stereotype to make the patient feel guilty and afraid of asserting his rights. Health insurance plans practice open discrimination by offering separate, more limited, benefit packages for mental illness. Discrimination in schools and workplaces against people with depression is the rule, not the exception.
- Depression is reinforced by contemporary culture. Mass culture makes values more shallow; beauty and financial success are prized more highly than honesty, dependability, intelligence, or self-sacrifice. Yet these are attributes which are distributed by luck or accident of birth more than by ability. When the depressed patient feels isolated socially or unsuccessful financially, not only do those states have their own inherent negative effects, in Western culture they imply a deep personal failure, an inadequacy of the self.
- Depression is an epidemic, at least in part because of cultural change that goes unacknowledged. We don't have a substitute yet for the family, but the family has fallen apart. Children lack the security they need to form stable attachments and develop self-esteem. We're all working many more hours and have less time available for our loved ones and ourselves, but the media ignore that fact. Our culture values competition

over cooperation. There is more than a shred of truth in depressive realism: Relationships are full of disappointment and conflict and people
are unhappier than ever. We need to make conscious and sustained efforts to rebuild a sense of community.

- Everyone needs help. Self-reliance is overrated. We rely on our connections with others to give us a good feeling about the self, to remind
us that we are real and that our lives have value and meaning. Yet from
John Wayne to Sigmund Freud we have been taught that autonomy is
the highest virtue, that intimacy implies dependency. No one can pull
himself out of depression by his own bootstraps.

CHAPTER 14
Prepare for Termination

A T THE END OF ACTIVE TREATMENT for depression, we find ourselves caught between the conflicting demands of two models. On the one hand, we argue that depression is all about failed grief, an incomplete mourning that the patient has incorporated into himself, and that the therapeutic task is to help the patient find a new ending. On the other hand, we argue that there is no ending; that depression is a chronic disease and our task is to help the patient learn to live with it. Yet there is an ending to the therapeutic relationship, and how we handle it has enormous implications for the overall success or failure of the therapy.

Most good therapists can help a patient recover from a single episode of depression, and medication can help sustain that recovery for a while. But given the high relapse rate of depression, we must prepare our patients for the likelihood that they will experience other episodes. We can help them keep on practicing the skills that will help prevent future episodes through ongoing homework, and make plans for how they can get help when they need it again. This is the time to teach patients that a relapse is not a personal failure but a reoccurrence of a disease, and getting help early in an episode is far preferable to hitting bottom again.

TEACH SELF-MONITORING SKILLS

In order to be prepared to take effective action when future episodes of depression threaten, it's essential that the patient learn some basic self-monitoring skills. Many patients may have a pattern of "predictable crises"—anniversaries of a loss, depressions coinciding with seasonal cycles. There are events that can be anticipated to cause stress—holidays, family gatherings. The patient can learn to prepare himself mentally and emotionally for such times: by maintaining positive social support, reviewing cognitive errors, practicing good self-care, detaching and reminding the self that the stress will pass, making a special effort to refrain from past mistakes like substance abuse or outbursts of rage. Some patients write a letter to themselves which they can reread when they are feeling under stress. *The Depression Workbook* (Copeland, 1992) is an excellent resource for such practical reminders.

Because future loss is inevitable, the patient must also learn to grieve. A cognitive understanding of the psychic utility of grief and its stages should be a prerequisite for termination. Any depressed patient should be well aware by the end of treatment that loss means vulnerability and the pressure to return to using the skills of depression to try to avoid pain. The patient should be encouraged to make a ritual of grief. In the case of public losses like a death, the patient should participate in all social aspects of mourning, even if it feels artificial or unnecessary. When a loss is more private or individual—the last child leaving the nest, the death of a beloved pet—the patient needs to make a deliberate effort to enlist friends and to share feelings. Even though a current loss may not feel significant at the time, it has the potential to reactivate feelings associated with past losses that can trigger another depressive episode.

The ending of the therapeutic alliance, even if we leave the door open for return, is an occasion for grief. It's important that the therapist help the patient feel and express the emotions that are appropriate to saying good-bye to a trusted friend. This may require some modeling and openness on the therapist's part. Of course, this is an occasion when grief is mixed with feelings like hope and pride, like a graduation. It's another time for the patient to experience the full range of emotions.

Patients also must learn the individual warning signs that presage another episode of depression. Feelings like the blues or the blahs are only to be expected and need not be a subject of concern unless they last too long; it is when we begin to act depressed and think depressed that we should take warning. Some people first act grouchy, some become hypersensitive to slights; some have trouble sleeping, some sleep too much; some can't get their work done, others can't stop working. These patterns can be highly idiosyncratic. If the patient can recognize depression in its early stages, he is more likely to be successful in arresting it.

Family members and loved ones can serve an important role in monitoring the patient's status. The patient can teach them what to do himself, or an "exit interview" with the therapist and family can be part of the termination process. Frequently, attentive others can pick up warning signs before the patient is aware that anything is wrong. My wife knows by my withdrawal and irritability when I have trouble brewing. Certain patients wear their depression in their eyes or in their posture. When family members understand that "it's the depression talking" and not a reproach against themselves, they are more likely to be able to express concern for the patient without arousing defensiveness. If the patient has made an explicit request that they do this as part of his self-monitoring, he has also made an agreement to listen and pay attention.

Members of my self-help group long ago drew up a list of "advance directives" describing how they want to be treated when an episode is developing, which they discuss with friends and family members. The directives proceed in steps, depending on the severity of the problem.

Stage 1: Leave me alone, give me a little extra space.

Stage 2: Try to be a little extra patient, kind, and attentive.

Stage 3: Insist that I get some help: contact my therapist, review my medication, go to a meeting, take a break.

Stage 4: Drive me to the hospital.

A contract like this goes a long way toward establishing a bond between the patient and those he loves, a sense that they are allies in a continuing struggle against depression.

The patient should also be encouraged to make bargains or contracts with himself, in case the mood becomes overwhelming—because by then, he will not be able to make well-informed decisions. *If I ever get close to hitting the kids, I will get help. If I ever lose control of myself while drinking, I'll go on the wagon. If I can't get out of bed in the morning, I'll call my therapist again. If I have suicidal thoughts again, I will call the hot line.*

The patient's continuing need for medication after psychotherapy has ended is a special area of concern. For most patients, there is good reason to continue medication long after symptoms have abated. FDA guidelines suggest six months without symptoms before medication is discontinued, but many patients and physicians prefer to keep up a maintenance dose as long as no ill effects are noted. On the other hand, many patients are anxious to get off medications as soon as possible—sometimes because the side effects are problematic, sometimes just because they feel ashamed of being on antidepressants.

We need to help our patients recognize that the desire to get off antidepressants too soon is often a lingering symptom of depression itself, more of the patient's self-blame and sense of inadequacy—*I shouldn't need this crutch. I should be able to do it myself.* Patients with other chronic diseases—diabetes, heart disease—who are dependent on medication may actively resent the inconvenience and side effects of the medication, but they rarely feel personally inadequate because they need it. If they tinker with the dose or stop taking it altogether we usually understand the behavior as self-destructive acting out. The same is true of people who stop taking a successful antidepressant medication against medical advice. To say otherwise is to buy into the belief that they are indeed inadequate for depending on the medication.

Many nonmedical therapists are working with patients who are being medicated by the family doctor. While this may be a sufficient arrangement if the therapist, physician, and patient are all observant and familiar with depression and the effects of medication, when the patient ends talk therapy it may not be enough. Part of the termination process should involve the patient in assessing the MD's availability and skill in monitoring medication and the patient's own ability to self-monitor and to ask for a medication review if necessary. Since too many patients have to hit bottom before asking for help, it may be far preferable to arrange for the patient to see a psychiatrist who will arrange for a regular half-hour assessment visit every three months than to depend on the family doctor who must squeeze his patients into ten-minute slots. The patient is likely to be too diffident about interrupting the doctor's busy schedule to communicate adequately about a deteriorating condition.

Depression is a chronic disease, and the patient should be prepared to devote some regular attention to mitigating its effects, just like the heart patient needs exercise. I would like very much to see a national network of self-help groups for depression, as widely used as AA, but that dream seems a long time in the future. In the meantime, it behooves the therapist and patient preparing for termination to develop a series of regular homework exercises for the patient to practice. The following checklist is a preliminary guideline, but the homework really must be tailored to the patient's individual needs.

- *Live with emotions.* On the assumption that depression is an effort not to feel, the patient is expected to sensitize himself to the experience of emotions through regular periods of reflection.
- *Learn detachment.* At the same time as the patient learns to experience emotions, he learns that he need not be controlled by them. Practice in self-discipline and relaxation techniques helps significantly.
- *Practice intimacy.* The patient needs to continue to self-consciously lower his guard and reveal more of himself in situations and with people he can trust.
- *Set priorities.* Make a grid: On the X axis try to rank things by their importance; on the Y axis, by their urgency. By attempting to get the important things done first, the patient ends up with fewer urgent things to do and a greater sense of self-worth.
- *Avoid, alter, accept.* These are the only three things we can do with adverse events. When things cannot be avoided or altered, they must be accepted. This is a hard lesson that we must continually practice.
- *Practice self-care.* The patient must learn to treat his body and mind as nonrenewable resources, to practice the basic elements of self-care.
- *Practice responsibility.* The patient should learn to hold himself accountable for his own happiness. This means being appropriately assertive and expecting responsibility from others.
- *Find community.* Depression thrives on isolation and finds belonging toxic. The patient must join in activities and memberships that provide meaning and identity.
- *Bibliotherapy.* We want the patient to feel empowered with the understanding that he has a disease that millions of others have had and about

which a great deal is known. Regular reading of good self-help literature is a significant aid in this process.

LEAVING THE DOOR OPEN

We need to help prepare the patient for the idea that he may need more therapy in the future, and that such a need is not a mark of failure:

> Therapy should not be regarded as a standardized treatment for a disease. It doesn't have a set course with standard phases: beginning, middle, and end. . . . Sometimes the analysis is a background support for living, functioning in a way that is analogous to the way religion functions in many people's lives. We don't think to ask people how long they believe it will be necessary for them to attend church or temple services. (Hoffman, 1998, p. 255)

And think of all the chronic physical diseases where there is no question or stigma attached to lifelong treatment, even when it can be very expensive: dialysis, emphysema, multiple sclerosis, Parkinson's. If we truly understand that depression is just as much a crippler as any of these conditions—if it is indeed the functional equivalent to blindness or paraplegia that the World Health Organization believes—how could we imagine that there is a stigma to needing some help with it from time to time?

Booster shots may be a good idea for depression. Future therapy may consist of regular, infrequent contact, or brief episodes of weekly sessions, or both. Reynolds and colleagues (1999) followed patients with recurrent depression for seven years after they had been stabilized by acute treatment. The subjects were randomly assigned to placebo, medication only, cognitive behavior therapy only, or medication and CBT. There was a highly significant effect for active treatment over placebo in preventing recurrence of future episodes, with the best outcome (80 percent without recurrence) in the combined treatment group. Instead of termination, we might schedule the patient to come in for a session at regular intervals such as every three or six months.

One of the most salient points to remember about depression is its momentum. Depression is much easier to stop before it gets bad. Once we have really begun to slide downhill, it takes tremendous energy, effort, and time to stop us. The patient who is feeling mildly depressed and considering calling his therapist for a booster needs to consider this fact.

Thus, it seems inevitable that the therapist should be open to a frank discussion of his future availability as part of the termination process. We should declare our interest in hearing from the patient, if we truly have any, and we should respond appropriately to communications such as the traditional holiday card or an occasional letter or e-mail. We should maintain a mailing list for the purpose of informing patients of important developments in our practice— retirement, change of address, etc. When we do retire, we should consider the impact on all the patients out there who maintain a relationship with us even if they never see us.

It's axiomatic that the therapeutic relationship doesn't end with the last scheduled appointment. We continue to exist as an object in the patient's mind long after the treatment is over. Even in the analytic literature, where a thorough termination process and "resolution" of the transference neurosis is expected, research consistently shows that transference persists beyond termination (Gabbard & Lester, 1995). Any thoughts we might have about a post-termination "real" relationship with the patient should be tempered by the knowledge that the patient will need us in the future, whether or not he actually consults us professionally. The patient will have a mental representation of us—hopefully, as someone who has affection and respect for him and is interested in his continued growth—that we should take pains to preserve.

LIVING WITH A CHRONIC DISEASE

For some patients, there is a sense of regret that accompanies recovery. Looking back on a lifetime of opportunities wasted, underachievement, and interpersonal misunderstandings can be very difficult. There can be pressure to make up for lost time. A grief process and the ability to live in the present are necessary.

For patients who have a long history of depression, a review of their past in the light of an understanding of the effects of depression can offer many benefits. Much of the blaming that has been integrated into the self—believing oneself to be lazy, oversensitive, inadequate, or wimpy—can be reinterpreted as manifestations of a disease over which the patient had little control. And perhaps parents and other authority figures can be let off the hook a little considering the likelihood that they never appreciated the diagnosis or its meaning; perhaps, given the inheritability of depression, the patient may realize that his parents were themselves depressed. But this is of secondary importance compared to the possibility that the patient can come to redefine himself as, for example, heroically struggling against a debilitating disease rather than lazy, inept, or cowardly.

The final message of the disease concept of depression that we want the patient to remember is one of empowerment. Not *I have this disease, and therefore I'm not responsible.* Instead, *I have this disease, and I'd better be responsible, because no one else is going to do it for me. I'd better learn about my disease. I'd better find the best therapists and doctors I can. I'd better help my family understand. I'd better understand how my own behavior contributes to the disease, and I'd better do all I can to learn better ways of going about life.*

ACCEPTANCE AND WISDOM

Depression is the result of zealous application of the skills of depression, habits that we think will keep us from pain but which only perpetuate the disease, defenses against the awareness of our needs. Genuine recovery from depression requires the development of more adaptive skills that permit us to accept what life has to offer and make the best of it. In my experience, the following are the most important of these skills.

Altruism

Altruism is the ability to identify my own needs in others and achieve fulfillment in helping others get their needs met. It is what makes being a parent such joyful and restorative work. It implies a shift in perspective, from being a needy taker to being a bountiful giver. People with depression believe themselves to be needy takers. The conscious and deliberate practice of altruism makes it difficult to sustain that belief.

Pride

Pride is what we're supposed to feel when we've accomplished something good, but the depressive is made uncomfortable by that feeling—it's destabilizing, threatening somehow. We need to deliberately practice feeling proud—we need to learn to sustain the feeling, like a singer practices to sustain a note. It's an exercise in preventing depression.

Humor

A patient had been making substantial progress in recovering from her bulimia. During a period of stress, she binged again. When I commented that she sounded a little disgusted with herself as she reported the incident, she laughed sardonically, "You think so?" She went on to make it clear that she had seen herself, as it were, from a different, detached perspective, hunched over the toilet bowl; she was starting to feel that she had more pride than to do that to herself. She was realizing that she binges when she feels depressed, and there are better things to do about feeling depressed. I commented, "This is how symptoms usually go away, not all at once. We stop for a while, and our perspective shifts. We see how ugly it looks, and it also loses some of its magic. It doesn't do what it used to for us."
"Like my ex-boyfriend," she replied.

Exactly. What a wonderful comment! Humor forces us to shift our perspective. It takes the conflict we are in, the quandary of feeling caught between a wish and a fear, the shame of finding ourselves doing the same old stupid thing again, and turns the situation on its head. It plays with reality, combines meanings, confuses characters, leads to new insights—like defining the boyfriend as a symptom. It doesn't solve the problem, but it temporarily robs it of its power; and while the problem is disarmed, we can approach it in newer, more creative, ways with the perspective that not everything is riding on this; life will give us other chances.

Detachment

People with depression spend far too much time and energy trying to control things that either can't be controlled at all or aren't really worth the struggle; they merely feel urgent at the time. The ability to achieve a slightly detached attitude, to step back from the obsessive struggle we find ourselves locked into and ask: *Is this really how I want to spend this day, my life?* — this ability can be cultivated. Activities like prayer, meditation, regular exercise, listening to music, intimate conversation — things that force us to stop, slow down, catch our breath, question our perspective — can help us learn the art of detachment.

Anticipation and Suppression

Anticipation means dealing with a problem in advance, a little at a time. Suppression means the conscious decision to delay an intervention, to let a situation simmer before we decide what to do. When we see a difficult situation on the horizon, we are wise to prepare for it, review the contingencies, and rehearse the possible courses of action until we feel we're as prepared as necessity dictates. When we *are* prepared, we must be able to tolerate delay until the situation unfolds. People with depression have felt powerless to anticipate and unable to suppress, but these are new skills that can be learned with practice.

The Full Range of Emotions

Depression is an effort not to feel. The patient has come to believe that certain feelings are unacceptable and have to be banished from awareness. But that effort robs life of meaning, because emotions are what give us meaning. Without grief, we cannot experience joy; without rage, we cannot love. Recovery from depression means recapturing the ability to feel.

Creativity

Depression is stagnation, creativity its antithesis. We all have the problem of creating meaning in our lives. Some do it through consciously "creative" pursuits like the arts; others do it through their homes, their work, their relationships. Creativity requires putting logic and emotion together with an element of play. The depressed patient should be sent on his way with the mission of creating his life.

ORGANIZING AND MAINTAINING
A SELF-HELP GROUP

I've found that maintaining a self-help group for people with depression is a sat-isfying and effective use of my professional time. With public awareness of de-pression rising, at the same time that limitations on mental health insurance benefits restrict more individuals to short-term or medication-only treatment, there is greater-than-ever need for ways to provide emotional support, educate about medication, teach cognitive restructuring, and other techniques to assist depressed patients in recovery. A self-help group can greatly assist a therapist in meeting these purposes.

The group is run as a community education program instead of a therapeu-tic group. I find that the time saved in not billing and not keeping clinical records, the ability to keep patients engaged who would otherwise drop out of individual therapy, plus the ability to informally monitor medication, makes it a cost-effective use of my time. The major distinction between this and other groups is that the therapist participates both as a leader and as a member of the group, being open within limits about his/her experience with depression. This gives the therapist a unique and effective standing in the group.

The group meets weekly for 75 minutes. There is no charge for participation. The group is advertised in the community and is open to all comers. I do reserve the right to insist that members seek additional treatment as a condition of atten-dance if they appear to be unable to benefit from the group or are in any way un-safe. The target population consists of individuals with major depression, dysthymic disorder, adjustment disorder with depression, or DDNOS. People with accompa-nying substance abuse are not excluded, but there is strong group pressure to mon-itor medication and control substance use. Individuals with personality or thought disorders which grossly affect self-control and self-disclosure will not benefit.

The group follows a set of core beliefs:

- Depression is a disease and, like heart disease or diabetes, self-care is essential to recovery.
- Depression is not an emotion. Emotions are self-limiting. We don't bounce back from depression.
- Depression affects every aspect of ourselves—our thinking, behavior, emotions, self-esteem, and relationships with others—but we can iden-tify and control or accept those effects.

We borrow deliberately from Alcoholics Anonymous in adopting a set of prin-ciples, discussion and application of which become the guidelines for recovery. These principles were explicated in *Undoing Depression*:

- Feel your feelings.
- Nothing comes out of the blue.

- Challenge depressed thinking.
- Establish priorities.
- Communicate directly.
- Take care of your self.
- Avoid unstructured time.
- Take, and expect, responsibility.
- Don't seek to avoid stress.
- Look for heroes.
- Be generous.
- Cultivate intimacy.
- Practice detachment.
- Get help when you need it.

The group also maintains a set of objectives, which give us structure as we try to help each other:

- Maintain a running list of quick "mood changers"—simple things to do when the blues are creeping up on you.
- Learn how and when to get professional help and how to communicate with professionals.
- Understand the effects of our depression on our families and help to teach them about the disease.
- Learn about stress and how to cope with it more effectively.
- Identify depressive thinking habits and behavior patterns and strategize more constructive alternatives.
- Understand depressive shame, guilt, and self-blame, and learn to cultivate feelings such as pride and joy.
- Minimize collateral damage.
- Provide emotional support as members go through difficult times.
- Understand the effects of antidepressant medications and other medications and drugs.

I have been conducting a group like this for about four years, both within an agency where I was employed and now in private practice, using facilities donated by the local hospital. In our very thinly populated area, I find that the census varies from as low as four members to as many as ten or twelve. No individual has stayed with the group since its inception, but many attend regularly for a year or longer. It becomes an important part of people's lives.

I practice a limited form of self-revelation in the group. I will use myself as an example and will talk about what's troubling me in the present when I think I know the solution, but will refrain from discussing areas where I'm feeling too confused or overwhelmed. In this sense the group is not a complete self-help resource for me, and I recognize that I have to get those needs met elsewhere. Yet the opportunity to chat casually with people about my own experience even at this limited level is very refreshing and satisfying for me. Group members have always respected any boundaries I put around my sharing.

In this group and through consultation with other self-help groups, I am constantly reminded of the isolation of depression and of the power of helping others. Everyone who comes says that the most palpable difference between the group and all other social interactions is that in the group you never have to pretend to feel good when you don't. Members quickly realize that this is one of the reasons why they feel so alone in their depression; their perception is that everyone else in the world is happy and effective, and something must be wrong with them for feeling otherwise.

The freedom to trade war stories about medication side effects, managed care, and crazy therapists—subjects that are highly taboo in any other setting—facilitates a powerful camaraderie, a bond of affection and respect, which makes each patient feel less isolated. The experience of seeing that people who look reasonably put together can feel exactly as horrible as you do, if not worse, also puts a kind of cognitive dissonance on the assumption that depression means one is bad or inadequate.

Most powerful of all is perhaps the opportunity to help others. Many members stay with the group long after their original crisis is past because they have the opportunity to see that their experience can have meaning for other people. To share that you've also contemplated suicide, that you've been in the hospital, that there have been many days when you couldn't get out of bed *and to see that the sharing helps someone else* gives new meaning to our own suffering. When we can give others hope, we have hope for ourselves.

References

Ablon, J. S., & Jones, E. E. (1999). Psychotherapy process in the NIMH treatment of depression collaborative research program. *Journal of Consulting and Clinical Psychology,* 67(1), 64–75.

Abraham, K. (1979). Notes on the psycho-analytical investigation and treatment of manic-depressive insanity and allied conditions. In *Selected papers of Karl Abraham, M. D.* (D. Bryan & A. Strachey, Trans.). New York: Brunner/Mazel. (Original work published 1927)

Abramson, L. Y., Seligman, M. E., & Teasdale, J. D. (1978). Learned helplessness in humans: Critique and reformulation. *Journal of Abnormal Psychology, 87,* 49–74.

Agency for Health Care Policy and Research. (1993). *Clinical practice guideline: Depression in primary care. Vol. 1. Detection and diagnosis.* Washington, DC: United States Department of Health and Human Services, Public Health Service.

Agency for Health Care Policy and Research. (1999, March). Treatment of depression: Newer pharmacotherapies [On-line]. Available: http://www.ahcpr.gov/clinic/deprsumm.htm

Alexander, F., & French, T. M. (1946). *Psychoanalytic therapy: Principles and application.* New York: Ronald Press.

Alloy, L. B. (Ed.). (1988). *Cognitive processes in depression.* New York: Guilford.

Alloy, L. B., & Abramson, L. Y. (1979). Judgment of contingency in depressed and nondepressed students: Sadder but wiser? *Journal of Experimental Psychology: General, 108,* 441–485.

Alloy, L. B., & Abramson, L. Y. (1988). Depressive realism: Four theoretical perspectives. In L. B. Alloy (Ed.), *Cognitive processes in depression* (pp. 223–265). New York: Guilford.

American Association of Suicidology. (1997). *Some facts about suicide and depression* [Brochure]. Washington, DC: Author.

American Psychiatric Association. (1994). *Diagnostic and statistical manual of mental disorders* (4th ed.). Washington, DC: Author.

Angst, J. (1999). Major depression in 1998: Are we providing optimal therapy? *Journal of Clinical Psychiatry, 60* (Suppl. 6), 5–9.

Anstett, P. (1997, March 4). The suicide machine: The failure of medicine. *Detroit Free Press* [On-line serial]. Available: http://www.freep.com/suicide/index2.htm

Antonuccio, D. O., Danton, W. G., DeNelsky, G. Y., Greenberg, R. P., & Gordon, J. S. (1999). Raising questions about antidepressants. *Psychotherapy and Psychosomatics, 68,* 3–14.

Appleby, L., Cooper, J., Amos, T., & Faragher, B. (1999). Psychological autopsy study of suicides by people aged under 35. *British Journal of Psychiatry, 175*, 168–174.

Arieti, S., & Bemporad, J. (1978). *Psychotherapy of severe and mild depression.* Northvale, NJ: Jason Aronson.

Aron, L. (1991). The patient's experience of the analyst's subjectivity. *Psychoanalytic Dialogues, 1*, 29–51.

Astin, J. (1998). Why patients use alternative medicine: Results of a national survey. *Journal of the American Medical Association, 279*, 1548–1553.

Balint, M. (1979). *The basic fault.* New York: Brunner/Mazel.

Basch, M. F. (1975). Toward a theory that encompasses depression: A revision of existing causal hypotheses in psychoanalysis. In E. J. Anthony & T. Benedek (Eds.), *Depression and human existence* (pp. 485–534). Boston: Little, Brown.

Basch, M. F. (1988). *Understanding psychotherapy: The science behind the art.* New York: Basic.

Bass, A. (1999, October 14). Drug companies enrich Brown professor. *Boston Globe*, p. A1.

Baxter, L. R., Schwartz., J. M., Bergman, K. S., Szuba, M. P., Guze, B. H., Mazziotta, J. C., Alazraki, A., Selin, C. E., Ferng, H. K., & Munford, P. (1992). Caudate glucose metabolism rate changes with both drug and behavior therapy for obsessive-compulsive disorder. *Archives of General Psychiatry, 49*, 681–689.

Bearden, C., Lavellen, N., Buysse, D., Karp, J. F., & Frank, E. (1996). Personality pathology and time to remission in depressed outpatients treated with interpersonal psychotherapy. *Journal of Personality Disorders, 10*(2), 164–173.

Beardslee, W. R., Versage, E. M., & Gladstone, T. R. G. (1998). Children of affectively ill parents: A review of the past ten years. *Journal of the American Academy of Child and Adolescent Psychiatry, 37*(11), 1134–1141.

Beck, A. T. (1967). *Depression: Clinical, experimental, and theoretical aspects.* New York: Harper & Row.

Beck, A. T. (1976). *Cognitive therapy and the emotional disorders.* New York: International Universities Press.

Beck, A. T., Rush, A. J., Shaw, B. F., & Emery, G. (1979). *Cognitive therapy of depression.* New York: Guilford.

Beck, A. T., Ward, C. H., Mendelson, M., Mock, J., & Erbaugh, J. (1961). An inventory for measuring depression. *Archives of General Psychiatry, 4*, 561–571.

Bell, D. S. (1994). *The doctor's guide to chronic fatigue syndrome.* Reading, MA: Addison-Wesley.

Bennett, M. J. (1996). Is psychotherapy ever medically necessary? *Psychiatric Services, 47*(9), 966–970.

Berger, D. M. (1987). *Clinical empathy.* New York: Jason Aronson.

Berman, R. M., & Charney, D. S. (1999). Models of antidepressant action. *Journal of Clinical Psychiatry, 60* (Suppl. 14), 16–20.

Bertelsen, A., Harvald, B., & Hauge, M. (1977). A Danish twin study of manic-depressive disorders. *British Journal of Psychiatry, 130*, 330–351.

Bibring, E. (1953). The mechanism of depression. In P. Greenacre (Ed.), *Affective disorders* (pp. 14–47). New York: International Universities Press.

Blackburn, I. M., Eunson, K. M., & Bishop, S. (1986). A two-year naturalistic follow-up of depressed patients treated with cognitive therapy, pharmacotherapy, and a combination of both. *Journal of Affective Disorders, 10*, 67–75.

Blatt, S. J. (1998). Contributions of psychoanalysis to the understanding and treatment of depression. *Journal of the American Psychoanalytic Association, 46*(3), 724–752.

Blatt, S. J., Sanislow, C. A., Zuroff, D. C., & Pilkonis, P. A. (1996) Characteristics of effective therapists: Further analyses of data from the NIMH Treatment of Depression Collaborative Research Program. *Journal of Consulting and Clinical Psychology, 64*(6), 1276–1284.

Blatt, S. J., Zuroff, D. C., Quinlan, D. M., & Pilkonis, P. (1996) Interpersonal factors in brief treatment of depression: Further analyses of the NIMH Treatment of Depression Collaborative Research Program. *Journal of Consulting and Clinical Psychology, 64*(1), 162–171.

Borenstein, D. (1996). Does managed care permit appropriate use of psychotherapy? *Psychiatric Services, 47*(9), 971–974.

Bourne, E. J. (1990). *The anxiety and phobia workbook.* Oakland, CA: New Harbinger.

Bower, S. (1975). *Assert yourself.* Boston: Addison-Wesley.

Bowlby, J. (1980). *Attachment and loss. Vol. 3: Loss: Sadness and depression.* New York: Basic.

Brandchaft, B., & Stolorow, R. D. (1984). The borderline concept: Pathological character or iatrogenic myth? In J. Lichtenberg, M. Bornstein, & D. Silver (Eds.), *Empathy I* (pp. 333–358). Hillsdale, NJ: Analytic Press.

Brody, J. E. (1998a, November 3). Keeping clinical depression out of the aging formula. *The New York Times*, p. F7.

Brody, J. E. (1998b, January 6). Trying to cope when a partner or a loved one is chronically depressed. *The New York Times*, p. F9.

Brody, J. E. (1999, March 11). When symptoms are obvious, but cause is not. *The New York Times*, p. C1.

Brown, G. W., & Harris, T. (1978). *Social origins of depression: A study of psychiatric disorder in women.* New York: Free Press.

Brown, W. (1994). Placebo as a treatment for depression. *Neuropsychopharmacology, 10*(4), 265–288.

Brown, W. (1998, January). The placebo effect. *Scientific American*, 90–95.

Buechler, S. K. (1995). Hope as inspiration in psychoanalysis. *Psychoanalytic Dialogues, 5*(1), 63–74.

Burns, D. (1999). *Feeling good: The new mood therapy* (Rev. ed.). New York: Avon Books.

Casement, P. J. (1990). The meeting of needs in psychoanalysis. *Psychoanalytic Inquiry 10*, 325–346.

Clements, M. (1993, October 31). What we say about mental illness. *Parade*, pp. 4–6.

Consumer Reports (1995, November). Mental health: Does therapy help? 734–739.

Copeland, M. E. (1992). *The depression workbook.* Oakland, CA: New Harbinger.

Coryell, W., Akiskal, H. S., Leon, A. C., Winokur, G., Maser, J. D., Mueller, T. I., & Keller, M. B. (1994). The time course of nonchronic major depressive disorder. *Archives of General Psychiatry, 51*, 405–410.

Coyne, J. (1999). Thinking interactionally about depression: A radical restatement. In T. Joiner & J. C. Coyne (Eds.), *The interactional nature of depression: Advances in interpersonal approaches* (pp. 365–392). Washington, DC: American Psychological Association.

Cronkite, K. (1994). *On the edge of darkness: Conversations about conquering depression.* New York: Dell.

Curren, J. (n.d.). Letter to Dr. Kevorkian [On-line]. Available: http://www.islandnet.com/deathnet/Currenletters.html.

Curtis, R. (1989). Choosing to suffer or to . . . ? Empirical studies and clinical theories of masochism. In R. Curtis (Ed.), *Self-defeating behaviors: Experimental research, clinical impressions, and practical implications* (pp. 189–214). New York: Plenum.

Cytryn, L., & McKnew, D. (1996). *Growing up sad: Childhood depression and its treatment.* New York: Norton.

Damasio, A. R. (1994). *Descartes' error: Emotion, reason, and the human brain.* New York: Grosset/Putnam.

Davanloo, H. (Ed.). (1978). *Basic principles and techniques in short-term dynamic psychotherapy.* New York: Spectrum.

Davidson, J. (1997). *The complete idiot's guide to managing stress.* New York: Alpha Books.

Deitz, J. (1989). The evolution of the self-psychological approach to depression. *American Journal of Psychotherapy, 43*(4), 494–505.

Deitz, J. (1991). The psychodynamics and psychotherapy of depression: Contrasting the self-psychological and the classical psychoanalytic approaches. *American Journal of Psychoanalysis, 51*(1), 61–70.

Dill, J. C., & Anderson, C. A. (1999). Loneliness, shyness, and depression: The etiology and interrelationships of everyday problems in living. In T. Joiner & J. C. Coyne (Eds.), *The interactional nature of depression: Advances in interpersonal approaches* (pp. 93–126). Washington, DC: American Psychological Association.

Dohrenwend, B. P., Levav, I., Shrout, P. E., Schwartz, S., Naveh, G., Link, B. G., Skodol, A. E., & Stueve, A. (1992, February 21). Socioeconomic status and psychiatric disorders: The causation-selection issue. *Science, 255,* 946–951.

Donner, S. (1985). The treatment process. In H. Jackson (Ed.), *Using self psychology in psychotherapy* (pp. 51–70). New York: Jason Aronson.

Druss, B. G., & Rosenheck, R. (1998). Mental disorders and access to medical care in the United States. *American Journal of Psychiatry, 155*(12), 1775–1777.

Druss, B. G., Schlesinger, M., Thomas, T., & Allen, H. (1999). Depressive symptoms and plan switching under managed care. *American Journal of Psychiatry, 156*(5), 697–701.

Eastman, C. I., Young, M. A., Fogg, L. F., Liu, L., & Meaden, P. M. (1998). Bright light treatment of winter depression: A placebo-controlled trial. *Archives of General Psychiatry, 55,* 883–889.

Eells, T. D. (1999). Psychotherapy versus medication for unipolar major depression. *Journal of Psychotherapy Practice and Research, 8*(2), 170–173.

Ehrenberg, D. (1992). *The intimate edge.* New York: Norton.

Ehrenreich, B. (1999, January). Nickel-and dimed: On (not) getting by in America. *Harper's Magazine, 298.*

Elkin, I., Shea, M. T., Watkins, J. T., Imber, S. D., Sotsky, S. M., Collins, J. F., Glass, D. R., Pilkonis, P. A., Leber, W. R., Dockerty, J. P., Fiester, S. J., & Parloff, M. B. (1989). NIMH treatment of depression collaborative research program: General effectiveness of treatments. *Archives of General Psychiatry, 46,* 971–982.

Ellis, A. (1994). *Reason and emotion in psychotherapy* (Rev. ed.). New York: Birch Lane Press.

Engel, G. L. (1977). The need for a new medical model: A challenge for biomedicine. *Science, 196,* 129–136.

Engel, G. L. (1980). The clinical application of the biopsychosocial model. *American Journal of Psychiatry, 137*(5), 535–544.

Erikson, E. (1950). *Childhood and society.* New York: Norton.

Evans, M. D., & Hollon, S. D. (1988). Patterns of personal and causal inference: Implications for the cognitive therapy of depression. In L. Alloy (Ed.), *Cognitive processes in depression* (pp. 344–378). New York: Guilford.

Evans, M. D., Hollon, S. D., DeRubeis, R. J., Piasecki, J. M., Grove, W. M., Garvey, M. F., & Tuason, V. B. (1992). Differential relapse following cognitive therapy and pharmacotherapy for depression. *Archives of General Psychiatry, 49,* 802–808.

Fava, G. A., Rafanelli, C., Grandi, S., Conti, S., & Belluardo, P. (1998). Prevention of recurrent depression with cognitive behavioral therapy. *Archives of General Psychiatry, 55,* 816–820.

Fawcett, J. (1998). What to do when the miracle doesn't happen. *Psychiatric Annals, 28*(2) 71–72.

Felitti, V. J., Anda, R. F., Nordenberg, D., Williamson, D. F., Spitz, A. M., Edwards, V., Koss, M. P., & Marks, J. S. (1998). The Adverse Childhood Experiences (ACE) study: Relationship of childhood abuse and household dysfunction to many of the leading causes of death in adults. *American Journal of Preventive Medicine, 14*(4), 245–258.

Fenichel, O. (1941). *Problems of psychoanalytic technique*. New York: Psychoanalytic Quarterly.

Fenichel, O. (1945). *The psychoanalytic theory of neurosis*. New York: Norton.

Fiedler, J. L., & Wight, J. (1989). *The medical offset effect and public health policy: Mental health industry in transition*. New York: Praeger.

Fields, H. L. (1987). *Pain*. New York: McGraw-Hill.

Fields, H. L. (1991). Depression and pain: A neurobiological model. *Neuropsychiatry, Neuropsychology, Behavior Neurology, 4*, 83–92.

Fonagy, P., Moran, G. S., Edgcumbe, R., Kennedy, H., & Target, M. (1993). The roles of mental representations and mental processes in therapeutic action. *Psychoanalytic Study of the Child*, 9–49.

Fox, M. (1998, October 4). With Prozac, the rose garden has hidden thorns. *The New York Times*, p. W3.

Frances, A., First, M. B., & Pincus, H. A. (1995). *DSM-IV Guidebook*. Washington, DC: American Psychiatric Press.

Frank, J. D. (1966). Treatment of the focal symptom: An adaptational approach. *American Journal of Psychotherapy, 20*, 564–575.

Frank, J. D. (1974). *Persuasion and healing: A comparative study of psychotherapy* (Rev. ed.). New York: Schocken Books.

Frasure-Smith, N., Lespérance, F., Juneau, M., Talajic, M., & Bourassa, M. G. (1999). Gender, depression, and one-year prognosis after myocardial infarction. *Psychosomatic Medicine, 61*, 26–37.

Freud, A. (1966). *The ego and the mechanisms of defense* (Rev. ed.). New York: International Universities Press. (Original work published 1937)

Freud, S. (1917). Mourning and melancholia. In J. Strachey (Ed. and Trans.), *The standard edition of the complete psychological works of Sigmund Freud* (Vol. 17). New York: Norton.

Gabbard, G. O., & Lester, E. P. (1995). *Boundaries and boundary violations in psychoanalysis*. New York: Basic.

Gill, M. M. (1983). The interpersonal paradigm and the degree of the therapist's involvement. *Contemporary Psychoanalysis 19* (Suppl.), 200–237.

Gill, M. M. (1994). *Psychoanalysis in transition*. Hillsdale, NJ: Analytic Press.

Gilligan, J. (1996). *Violence: Our deadly epidemic and its causes*. New York: Putnam's.

Gitlin, M. J. (1999). A psychiatrist's reaction to a patient's suicide. *American Journal of Psychiatry, 156*(10), 1630–1634.

Glenmullen, J. (2000). *Prozac backlash*. New York: Simon & Schuster.

Goldberg, A. (1998). Self psychology since Kohut. *Psychoanalytic Quarterly, 68*, 240–255.

Goldberg, D. (1996). A dimensional model for common mental disorders. *British Journal of Psychiatry, 168* (Suppl. 30), 44–49.

Goldberg, R. J. (1995). Diagnostic dilemmas created by patients with anxiety and depression. *American Journal of Medicine, 98*, 278.

Goldstein, E. G. (1997). To tell or not to tell: The disclosure of events in the therapist's life to the patient. *Clinical Social Work Journal, 25*(1), 41–57.

Goleman, D. (1996, January 24). Critics say managed-care savings are eroding mental care. *The New York Times*, p. C9.

Goozner, M. (1998, June 22). Are Americans working better—or just more? *Chicago Tribune*, p. A1.

Greenberg, P. E., Stiglin, L. E., Finkelstein, S. N., & Berndt, E. R. (1993). The economic burden of depression in 1990. *Journal of Clinical Psychiatry, 54*, 405–418.

Gustafson, J. P. (1986). *The complex secret of brief psychotherapy*. New York: Norton.

Gut, E. (1989). *Productive and unproductive depression: Success or failure of a vital process*. New York: Basic.

Guze, S. B., & Robins, E. (1970). Suicide and primary affective disorders. *British Journal of Psychiatry, 117*, 437–438.

Gyarfas, M. G. (1980). A systems approach to diagnosis. In J. Mishne (Ed.), *Psychotherapy and training in clinical social work.* New York: Gardner Press.

Haines, B. A., Metalsky, G. I., Cardamone, A. L., & Joiner, T., (1999). Interpersonal and cognitive pathways into the origins of attributional style: A developmental perspective. In T. Joiner & J. C. Coyne (Eds.), *The interactional nature of depression: Advances in interpersonal approaches* (pp. 65–92). Washington, DC: American Psychological Association.

Hallowell, E. M., & Ratey, J. J. (1994). *Driven to distraction.* New York: Pantheon.

Hammen, C. (1991). *Depression runs in families: The social context of risk and resilience in children of depressed mothers.* New York: Springer Verlag.

Hammen, C., Rudolph, K., Weisz, J, Rao, U., & Burge, D. (1999). The context of depression in clinic-referred youth: Neglected areas in treatment. *Journal of the American Academy of Child and Adolescent Psychiatry,* 38(1), 64–71.

Hankin, B. L., Abramson, L. Y., Moffitt, T. E., Silva, P. A., McGee, R., & Angell, K. A. (1998). Development of depression from preadolescence to young adulthood: Emerging gender differences in a 10-year longitudinal study. *Journal of Abnormal Psychology,* 107(1), 128–140.

Harris, T., Brown, G. W., & Robinson, R. (1999a). Befriending as an intervention for chronic depression among women in an inner city. I: Randomized controlled trial. *British Journal of Psychiatry, 174,* 219–224.

Harris, T., Brown, G. W., & Robinson, R. (1999b). Befriending as an intervention for chronic depression among women in an inner city. II: Role of fresh-start experiences and baseline psychosocial factors in remission from depression. *British Journal of Psychiatry,* 174, 225–232.

Hartlage, S., Arduino, K., & Alloy, L. (1998). Depressive personality characteristics: State dependent concomitants of depressive disorder and traits independent of current depression. *Journal of Abnormal Psychology,* 107(2), 349–354.

Haynal, A. (1985). *Depression and creativity.* New York: International Universities Press. (Original work published 1976)

Health Care Financing Administration. (1999, October). Draft for comments only: Local medical review policy for insight oriented, behavior modifying, and/or supportive psychotherapy. *Medicare Provider News, 52,* 46–50.

Hedges, L. (1992). *Interpreting the countertransference.* New York: Jason Aronson.

Herrmann, C., Brand-Driehorst, S., Kaminsky, B., Leibing, E., Staats, H., & Rueger, U. (1998). Diagnostic groups and depressed mood as predictors of 22-month mortality among medical inpatients. *Psychosomatic Medicine,* 60, 570–577.

Hirschfeld, R. M. A., Keller, M. B., Panico, S., Arons, B. S., Barlow, D., Davidoff, F., Endicott, J., Froom, J., Goldstein, M., Gorman, J. M., Guthrie, D., Barek, R., Maurer, T., Meyer, R., Phillips, K., Ross, J., Schwenk, T. L., Sharfstein, S. S., Thase, M. E., and Wyatt, R. J. (1997, January 22–29). The National Depressive and Manic-Depressive Association consensus statement on the undertreatment of depression. *Journal of the American Medical Association,* 277(4), 333–340.

Hoffman, I. Z. (1998). *Ritual and spontaneity in the psychoanalytic process.* Hillsdale, NJ: Analytic Press.

Hollon, S. D., DeRubeis, R. J., Evans, M. D., Wiemer, M. J., Garvey, M. J., Grove, W. M., & Tuason, V. B. (1992). Cognitive therapy and pharmacotherapy for depression: Singly and in combination. *Archives of General Psychiatry,* 49, 774–781.

Holmes, G. P., Kaplan, J. E., Gantz, N. M., Komaroff, A. L., Schonberger, L. B., Straus, S. E., Jones, J. F., Dubois, R. E., Cunningham-Rundles C., & Pahwa, S. (1988). Chronic fatigue syndrome: A working case definition. *Annals of Internal Medicine,* 108, 387.

Hudson, J. I., Hudson, M. S., Pliner, L. F., Goldenberg, D. L., & Pope, H. G. (1985). Fibromyalgia and major affective disorder: A controlled phenomenology and family history study. *American Journal of Psychiatry,* 142(4), 441–446.

Hyams, K. (1998). Developing case definitions for symptom-based conditions: The problem of specificity. *Epidemiologic Reviews, 20*(2), 148–156.

Jacobson, E. (1971). *Depression.* New York: International Universities Press.

Jacobson, N. S., & Gortner, E. T. (2000). Can depression be de-medicalized in the 21st century: Scientific revolutions, counter-revolutions, and the magnetic field of normal science. *Behaviour Research and Therapy, 38*, 103–117.

Jamison, K. R. (1999). *Night falls fast: Understanding suicide.* New York: Knopf.

Jenkins, J. H., & Schumacher, J. G. (1999). Family burden of schizophrenia and depressive illness. *British Journal of Psychiatry, 174*, 31–38.

Joffe, R., Segal, Z., & Singer, W. (1996). Change in thyroid hormone levels following response to cognitive therapy for major depression. *American Journal of Psychiatry, 153*, 411–413.

Johnston, S. H., & Farber, B. (1996). The maintenance of boundaries in psychotherapeutic practice. *Psychotherapy, 33*(3), 391–402.

Joiner, T., & Coyne, J. C. (Eds.). (1999). *The interactional nature of depression: Advances in interpersonal approaches.* Washington, DC: American Psychological Association.

Joiner, T., Coyne, J. C., & Blalock, J. (1999). On the interpersonal nature of depression: Overview and synthesis. In T. Joiner & J. C. Coyne (Eds.), *The interactional nature of depression: Advances in interpersonal approaches* (pp. 3–19). Washington, DC: American Psychological Association.

Jorge, C. M., & Goodnick, P. J. (1997). Chronic fatigue syndrome and depression: Biological differentiation and treatment. *Psychiatric Annals, 27*(5), 365–371.

Judd, L. I., Akiskal, H. S., Maser, J. D., Zeller, P. J., Endicott, J., Coryell, W., Paulus, M. P., Kunovac, J. L., Leon, A. C., Mueller, T. J., Rice, J. A., & Keller, M. B. (1998a). A prospective 12-year study of subsyndromal and syndromal depressive symptoms in unipolar major depressive disorders. *Archives of General Psychiatry, 55*, 694–700.

Judd, L. I., Akiskal, H. S., Maser, J. D., Zeller, P. J., Endicott, J., Coryell, W., Paulus, M. P., Kunovac, J. L., Leon, A. C., Mueller, T. J., Rice, J. A., & Keller, M. B. (1998b). Major depressive disorder: A prospective study of residual subthreshold depressive symptoms as predictor of rapid relapse. *Journal of Affective Disorders, 50*, 97–108.

Kaelber, C. T., Moul, D. E., & Farmer, M. E. (1995). Epidemiology of depression. In E. E. Beckham & W. R. Leber, *Handbook of depression* (2nd ed., pp. 3–35). New York: Guilford.

Karasu, T. B. (1993). Toward an integrative model. In M. Shachter (Ed.), *Psychotherapy and medication: A dynamic integration* (pp. 11–33). Northvale, NJ: Jason Aronson.

Karen, R. (1992, February). Shame. *The Atlantic Monthly*, 40–70.

Karp, D. (1996). *Speaking of sadness.* New York: Oxford.

Katon, W., Robinson, P., Von Korff, M., Lin, E., Bush, T., Ludman, E., Simon, G., and Walker, E. (1996). A multi-faceted intervention to improve treatment of depression in primary care. *Archives of General Psychiatry, 53*, 924–932.

Katon, W., Von Korff, M., Lin, E., Walker, E., Simon G. E., Bush, T., Robinson, P., & Russo, J. (1995). Collaborative management to achieve treatment guidelines: Impact on depression in primary care. *Journal of the American Medical Association, 273*, 1026–1031.

Keen, S. (1991). *Fire in the belly: On being a man.* New York: Bantam.

Keller, M. B., & Hanks, D. L. (1994). The natural history and heterogeneity of depressive disorders. *Journal of Clinical Psychiatry, 55* (Suppl. 9A), 25–31.

Keller, M. B., Hirschfeld, R. M., & Hanks, D. (1997). Double depression: A distinctive subtype of unipolar depression. *Journal of Affective Disorders, 45*, 65–73.

Keller, M. B., McCullough, J. P., Klein, D. N., Arnow, B., Dunner, D. L., Gelenberg, A. J., Markowitz, J. C., Nemeroff, C. B., Russell, J. M., Thase, M. E., Trivedi, M. H., &

Zajecka, J. (2000). A comparison of Nefazodone, the cognitive behavioral-analysis system of psychotherapy, and their combination for the treatment of chronic depression. *New England Journal of Medicine, 342*(20), 1462–1470.

Keller, M. B., Shapiro, R. W., Lavori, P. W., & Wolfe, N. (1982). Recovery in major depressive disorder: Analysis with the LIFE table and regression models. *Archives of General Psychiatry, 39*, 905–910.

Kendler, K. S., Karkowski, L. M., & Prescott, C. A. (1999). Causal relationship between stressful life events and the onset of major depression. *American Journal of Psychiatry, 156*(6), 837–841.

Kessler, R. C., McGonagle, K. A., Zhao, S., Nelson, C. B., Hughes, M., Eshleman, S., Wittchen, H.-U., & Kendler, K. S. (1994). Lifetime and 12-month prevalence of DSM-III-R psychiatric disorders in the United States: Results from the National Comorbidity Study. *Archives of General Psychiatry, 51*, 8–19.

Kessler, R. C., Nelson, C. B., McGonagle, K. A., Liu, J., Swartz, M., & Blazer, D. G. (1996). Comorbidity of DSM-III-R major depressive disorder in the general population: Results from the US National Comorbidity Study. *British Journal of Psychiatry, 18* (Suppl. 30), 17–30.

Kirkpatrick, D. D. (2000, May 15). Inside the happiness business. *New York Magazine*, pp. 36–43.

Klein, D. N., Norden, K. A., Ferro, T., Leader, J. B., Kasch, K. L., Klein, L. M., Schwartz, J. E., & Aronson, T. A. (1998). Thirty-month naturalistic follow-up study of early-onset dysthymic disorder: Course, diagnostic stability, and prediction of outcome. *Journal of Abnormal Psychology, 107*(2), 338–348.

Klein, D. N., & Shih, J. H. (1998). Depressive personality: Associations with DSM-III-R mood and personality disorders and negative and positive affectivity, 30-month stability, and prediction of course of Axis I depressive disorders. *Journal of Abnormal Psychology, 107*(2), 319–327.

Klein, D. F., & Wender, P. H. (1993). *Understanding depression: A complete guide to its diagnosis and treatment.* New York: Oxford University Press.

Klein, M. (1940). Mourning and its relation to manic-depressive states. In *Contributions to psychoanalysis, 1921–1945* (pp. 311–338). London: Hogarth.

Klerman, G. M. (1993). Treatment of depression. In M. Shachter (Ed.), *Psychotherapy and medication: A dynamic integration* (pp. 185–198). Northvale, NJ: Jason Aronson.

Klerman, G. M., Weissman, M. M., & Markowitz, J. C. (1994). Medication and psychotherapy. In E. Bergin & S. L. Garfield (Eds.), *Handbook of psychotherapy and behavior change* (pp. 734–782). New York: Wiley.

Klerman, G. M., Weissman, M. M., Rounsaville, B., & Chevron, E. S. (1984). *Interpersonal psychotherapy of depression.* New York: Basic.

Kohut, H. (1971). *The analysis of the self.* New York: International Universities Press.

Kohut, H. (1977). *The restoration of the self.* New York: International Universities Press.

Kohut, H. (1984). *How does analysis cure?* (A. A. Goldberg, Ed.). Chicago: University of Chicago Press.

Kovacs, M., Akiskal, H. S., Gatsonis, C., & Parrone, P. L. (1994). Childhood onset dysthymic disorder. *Archives of General Psychiatry, 51*, 365–374.

Kramer, P. (1993). *Listening to Prozac.* New York: Viking Penguin.

Kraut, R., Patterson, M., Lundmark, V., Kiesler, S., Mukopadhyay, T., & Scherlis, W. (1998). Internet paradox: A social technology that reduces social involvement and psychological well-being? *American Psychologist, 53*(9), 1017–1031.

Lake Snell Perry & Associates (1999, July 22). Presentation of findings from focus groups and a nationwide survey of adults. Presented to the Carter Center and the MacArthur Foundation Symposium on the Surgeon General's Report on Mental Health, Atlanta, GA.

Lane, T. J., Nance, P., & Matthews, D. A (1994). Reply to "chronic fatigue syndrome (CFS) and psychiatric disorders" [Letter to the editor]. *American Journal of Medicine, 94,* 485.

Langs, R. (1973). *The technique of psychoanalytic psychotherapy,* Vol. I. New York: Jason Aronson.

Lave, J. R., Frank, R. G., Schulberg, H. C., & Kamlet, M. S. (1998). Cost-effectiveness of treatments for major depression in primary care practice. *Archives of General Psychiatry,* 55, 645–651.

Lavori, P. W., Keller, M. B., Mueller, T. I., & Scheftner, W. (1994). Recurrence after recovery in unipolar MDD: An observational follow-up study of clinical predictors and somatic treatment as a mediating factor. *International Journal of Methods in Psychiatric Research, 4,* 211–229.

Leenaars, A. (1988). *Suicide notes.* New York: Human Sciences Press.

Leenaars, A. (1992). Suicide notes, communication, and ideation. In R. W. Maris, L. Berman, J. T. Maltsberger, & R. I. Yufit (Eds.), *Assessment and prediction of suicide* (pp. 337–361). New York: Guilford.

Lewinsohn, P. M. (1974). A behavioral approach to depression. In R. J. Friedman & M. M. Katz (Eds.), *The psychology of depression* (pp. 157–177). Washington, DC: Winston.

Lewinsohn, P. M., Hoberman, H., Teri, L., & Hautzinger, M. (1985). An integrated theory of depression. In S. Reiss & R. Bootzin (Eds.), *Theoretical issues in behavior therapy* (pp. 331–359). New York: Academic Press.

Lewinsohn, P. M., Mischel, W., Chaplin, W., & Barton, R. (1980). Social competence and depression: The role of illusory self-perceptions. *Journal of Abnormal Psychology, 89,* 203–212.

Lewinsohn, P. M., Roberts, R. E., Seeley, J. R., Rohde, P., Gotlib, I. H., & Hops, H. (1994). Adolescent psychopathology: II. Psychosocial risk factors for depression. *Journal of Abnormal Psychology, 103*(2), 302–315.

Lewis, H. B. (1987). Introduction: Shame—the 'sleeper' in psychopathology. In Lewis, H. B. (Ed.), *The role of shame in symptom formation* (pp. 1–33). Hillsdale, NJ: Lawrence Erlbaum.

Libet, J. M., & Lewinsohn, P. M. (1973). The concept of social skill with special reference to the behavior of depressed persons. *Journal of Consulting and Clinical Psychology, 40,* 304–312.

Lin, E. H. B., Simon, G., Katon, W. J., Russo, J. E., Von Korff, M., Bush, T. M., Ludman, E. J., & Walker, E. A. (1999). Can enhanced acute-phase treatment of depression improve long-term outcomes? A report of randomized trials in primary care. *American Journal of Psychiatry, 156*(4), 643–646.

Linehan, M. M. (1987). Dialectical behavior therapy for borderline personality disorder. *Bulletin of the Menninger Clinic, 51,* 261–276.

Loring, M., & Powell, B. (1988). Gender, race, and the DSM-III: A study of the objectivity of psychiatric diagnostic behavior. *Journal of Health and Social Behavior, 29,* 1–22.

Luborsky, L. (1984). *Principles of psychoanalytic therapy.* New York: Basic.

Luhrmann, T. M. (2000). *Of two minds: The growing disorder in American psychiatry.* New York: Knopf.

Lyoo, I. K., Gunderson, J. G., & Phillips, K. G. (1998). Personality dimensions associated with depressive personality disorder. *Journal of Personality Disorders, 12*(1), 46–55.

Magruder, K. M., & Norquist, G. S. (1999). Structural issues and policy in the primary care management of depression. *Journal of Clinical Psychiatry, 60* (Suppl. 7), 45–51.

Malan, D. H. (1976). *The frontier of brief psychotherapy.* New York: Plenum.

Mann, J. (1973). *Time-limited psychotherapy.* Cambridge: Harvard University Press.

Mann, J. (1981). The core of time-limited psychotherapy: Time and the central issue. In S. H. Budman (Ed.), *Forms of brief therapy* (pp. 24–44). New York: Guilford.

Manning, D. W., Markowitz, J. C., & Frances, J. (1992). A review of combined psychotherapy and pharmacotherapy in the treatment of depression. *Journal of Psychotherapy Practice and Research, 1*(2), 103–116.

Maris, R. W., Berman, A. L., Maltsberger, J. T., & Yufit, R. I. (Eds.). (1992). *Assessment and prediction of suicide.* New York: Guilford.

Martin, D. J., Abramson, L. Y., & Alloy, L. (1984). The illusion of control for self and others in depressed and nondepressed college students. *Journal of Personality and Social Psychology, 46,* 125–136.

McCullough, J. P. (2000). *Treatment for chronic depression: Cognitive behavioral analysis system of psychotherapy.* New York: Guilford.

McGrath, E., & Keita, G. P. (1990). *Women and depression: Risk factors and treatment issues. Final report of the American Psychological Association's National Task Force on Women and Depression.* Washington, DC: American Psychological Association.

Menaker, E. (1981). Self psychology illustrated on the issue of moral masochism: Clinical implications. *American Journal of Psychoanalysis, 41*(4), 297–305.

Miller, A. (1981). *The drama of the gifted child (Prisoners of childhood).* New York: Basic.

Millon, T., & Kotik-Harper, D. (1995). The relationship of depression to disorders of personality. In E. E. Beckham & W. R. Leber (Eds.), *Handbook of depression* (2nd ed., pp. 107–146). New York: Guilford.

Mitchell, S. (1993). *Hope and dread in psychoanalysis.* New York: Basic.

Moore, T. J. (1999, October 17). No prescription for happiness. *Boston Globe,* p. E1.

Morrison, A. L. (1997). Ten years of doing psychotherapy while living with a life-threatening illness: Self-disclosure and other ramifications. *Psychoanalytic Dialogues, 7*(2), 225–243.

Morrison, A. P. (1989). *Shame: The underside of narcissism.* Hillsdale, NJ: Analytic Press.

Morrison, A. P. (1999). Shame, on either side of defense. *Contemporary Psychoanalysis, 35*(1), 91–105.

Moss, G. R., & Boren, J. H. (1972). Depression as a model for behavioral analysis. *Comprehensive Psychiatry, 13,* 581.

Motto, J. A. (1992). An integrated approach to estimating suicide risk. In R. W. Maris, A. L. Berman, J. T. Maltsberger, & R. I. Yufit (Eds.), *Assessment and prediction of suicide* (pp. 625–639). New York: Guilford.

Murray, L., & Lopez, D. (1996). *The global burden of disease. A comprehensive assessment of mortality and disability from disease, injuries, and risk factors in 1990 and projected to 2020.* Boston: World Health Organization, World Bank, Harvard University.

Musselman, D. L., Evans, D. L., & Nemeroff, C. B. (1998). The relationship of depression to cardiovascular disease. *Archives of General Psychiatry, 55,* 580–592.

Musson, R. F., & Alloy, L. (1988). Depression and self-directed attention. In L. Alloy (Ed.), *Cognitive processes in depression* (pp. 193–220). New York: Guilford.

Myers, D. G. (1992). *The pursuit of happiness.* New York: Avon.

Nathanson, D. L. (1992). *Shame and pride: Affect, sex, and the birth of the self.* New York: Norton.

National Depressive and Manic-Depressive Association. (1999, November 30). Most patients report troublesome side effects, modest improvement using current antidepression treatments [Press release].

Nemeroff, C. B. (1998, June). The neurobiology of depression. *Scientific American,* 42–48.

Nesse, R. M. (2000). Is depression an adaptation? *Archives of General Psychiatry, 57*(1), 14–20.

The New York Times (1998, August 14). "One in 5 teenagers is armed, a survey finds." p. A13.

Nolen-Hoeksema, L. (1990). *Sex differences in depression.* Stanford, CA: Stanford University Press.

O'Connor, R. (1997). *Undoing depression: What therapy doesn't teach you and medication can't give you.* Boston: Little Brown.

Pajer, K. (1995). New strategies in the treatment of depression in women. *Journal of Clinical Psychiatry, 56* (Suppl. 2), 30–37.

Parsons, T. (1951). Illness and the role of the physician: A sociological perspective. *American Journal of Orthopsychiatry, 21,* 452–460.

Post, R. M., Roy-Byrne, P. P., & Uhde, T. W. (1988). Graphic representation of the life course of illness in patients with affective disorder. *American Journal of Psychiatry, 145,* 844–848.

Post, R. M., Uhde, T. W., Putnam, F. W., Ballenger, J. C., & Berrettini, W. H. (1982). Kindling and carbamazepine in affective illness. *Journal of Nervous and Mental Disease, 170*(12), 717–731.

Pyszczynski, T., & Greenberg, J. (1987). Self-regulatory perseveration and the depressive self-focusing style: A self-awareness theory of reactive depression. *Psychological Bulletin, 102*(1), 122–138.

Rado, S. (1994). The problem of melancholia. In W. Gaylin (Ed.), *Psychodynamic understanding of depression* (pp. 70–95). Northvale, NJ: Jason Aronson. (Original work published 1928)

Raphael, B. (1983). *The anatomy of bereavement.* New York: Jason Aronson.

Real, T. (1997). *I don't want to talk about it: Overcoming the secret legacy of male depression.* New York: Simon & Schuster.

Regier, D. A., Farmer, M. E., Rae, D. S., Locke, B. Z., Keith, S. J., Judd, L. L., & Goodwin, F. K. (1990). Comorbidity of mental disorders with alcohol and other drug abuse: Results from the Epidemiologic Catchment Area Study. *Journal of the American Medical Association, 264,* 2511–2518.

Reiser, D. E. (1986). Self psychology and the problem of suicide. In A. A. Goldberg (Ed.), *Progress in self psychology* (Vol. 2, pp. 227–241). New York: Guilford.

Renik, O. (1995). The ideal of the anonymous analyst and the problem of self-disclosure. *Psychoanalytic Quarterly, 64,* 466–495.

Reynolds, C. F., Frank, E., Perel, J. M., Imber, S. D., Cornes, C., Miller, M. D., Mazumdar, S., Houck, P. R., Dew, M. A., Stack, J. A., Pollock, B. G., & Kupfer, D. J. (1999). Nortriptyline and interpersonal psychotherapy as maintenance therapies for recurrent major depression: A randomized controlled trial in patients older than 59 years. *Journal of the American Medical Association, 281*(1), 39–45.

Robins, L. N., & Regier, D. (Eds.). (1991). *Psychiatric disorders in America: The Epidemiologic Catchment Area Study.* New York: Free Press.

Rosen, L. E., & Amador, X. F. (1996). *When someone you love is depressed: How to help your loved one without losing yourself.* New York: Fireside.

Rosenhan, D. L. (1973). On being sane in insane places. *Science, 179,* 250–258.

Rothberg, J. M., & Geer-Williams, C. (1992). A comparison and review of suicide prediction scales. In R. W. Maris, A. L. Berman, J. T. Maltsberger, & R. I. Yufit (Eds.), *Assessment and prediction of suicide* (pp. 202–217). New York: Guilford.

Rotundo, E. A. (1993). *American manhood: Transformations in masculinity from the revolution to the modern era.* New York: Basic.

Rubin, S. S. (1997). Self and object in the postmodern world. *Psychotherapy, 34*(1), 1–10.

Ruvelson, L. (1988). The empathic use of sarcasm: Humor in psychotherapy from a self psychological perspective. *Clinical Social Work Journal, 16*(3), 297–305.

Sacco, W. P., & Beck, A. T. (1995). Cognitive theory and therapy. In E. E. Beckham & W. R. Leber (Eds.), *Handbook of depression* (2nd ed., pp. 329–351). New York: Guilford.

Sadowski, H., Ugarte, B., Kolvin, I., Kaplan, C., & Barnes, J. (1999). Early family life disadvantages and major depression in adulthood. *British Journal of Psychiatry, 174,* 112–120.

Safran, J. D. (1984). Assessing the cognitive-interpersonal cycle. *Cognitive Therapy and Research, 8*(4), 333–348.

Sapolsky, R. M. (1998). *Why zebras don't get ulcers: An updated guide to stress, stress-related diseases, and coping* (Rev. ed.). New York: W. H. Freeman.

Schneidman, E. S. (1984). Aphorisms of suicide and some implications for psychotherapy. *American Journal of Psychotherapy, 38*(3), 319–328.

Schor, J. (1998). *The overspent American: Upscaling, downshifting, and the new consumer.* New York: Basic.

Schore, A. N. (1997). A century after Freud's Project: Is a rapprochement between psychoanalysis and neurobiology at hand? *Journal of the American Psychoanalytic Association, 45*(3), 807–840.

Schrof, J. M., & Schultz, S. (1999, March 8). Melancholy nation: Depression is on the rise, despite Prozac. But new drugs could offer help. *U.S. News,* 43–48.

Schuchter, S. R., Downs, N., & Zisook, S. (1996). *Biologically informed psychotherapy for depression.* New York: Guilford.

Schuyler, D. (1998). *Taming the tyrant: Treating adult depression.* New York: Norton.

Schwartz, J. M., Stoessel, P. W., Baxter, L. R., Martin, K. M., & Phelps, M. E. (1996). Systematic changes in cerebral glucose metabolic rate after successful behavior modification treatment of obsessive-compulsive disorder. *Archives of General Psychiatry, 53,* 109–113.

Seligman, M. (1975). *Helplessness: On development, depression, and death.* New York: W. H. Freeman.

Seligman, M. (1990). *Learned optimism.* New York: Pocket Books.

Seligman, M. (1994). *What you can change and what you can't.* New York: Fawcett.

Seligman, M. (1995). The effectiveness of psychotherapy: The *Consumer Reports* study. *American Psychologist, 50,* 965–974.

Sharpe, M. K., Hawton, K., Simkin, S., Surawy, C., Hackmann, A., Klimes, I., Peto, T., Warrell, D., & Seagroatt, V. (1996). Cognitive behaviour therapy for the chronic fatigue syndrome: A randomized clinical trial. *British Medical Journal, 312,* 22–26.

Shea, M. T., Elkin, I., Imber, S. D., Sotsky, S. M., Watkins, J. T., Collins, J. F., Pilkonis, P. A., Beckham, E., Glass, D. R., Dolan, R. T., & Parloff, M. B. (1992). Course of depressive symptoms over follow-up: Findings from the NIMH treatment of depression collaborative research program. *Archives of General Psychiatry, 49,* 782–787.

Shore, M. F. (1994, September). Narrowing prevention. *Readings: A Journal of Reviews and Commentary in Mental Health,* 13–17.

Showalter, E. (1997). *Hystories: Hysterical epidemics and modern media.* New York: Columbia University Press.

Silverstein, B. (1999). Gender difference in the prevalence of clinical depression: The role played by depression associated with somatic symptoms. *American Journal of Psychiatry, 156*(3), 480–482.

Silverstein, B., Caceres, J., Perdue, L., & Cimarolli, V. (1995). Gender differences in depressive symptomatology: The role played by "anxious somatic depression" associated with gender-related achievement concerns. *Sex Roles, 33,* 621–636.

Slaby, A., & Garfinkel, L. F. (1994). *No one saw my pain: Why teens kill themselves.* New York: Norton.

Slater, L. (1998). *Prozac diary.* New York: Random House.

Slusher, M. P., & Anderson, C. (1989). Belief perseverance and self-defeating behavior. In R. Curtis (Ed.), *Self-defeating behaviors: Experimental research, clinical impressions, and practical implications* (pp. 11–40). New York: Plenum.

Smith, M. (1985). *When I say no, I feel guilty.* New York: Bantam.

Snyder, M. L., & Frankel, A. (1989). Making things harder for yourself: Pride and joy. In R. Curtis (Ed.), *Self-defeating behaviors: Experimental research, clinical impressions, and practical implications* (pp. 131–157). New York: Plenum.

Solomon, D. A., Keller, M. B., Leon, A. C., Mueller, T. I., Lavori, P. W., Shea, M. T., Coryell, W., Warshaw, M., Turvey, C., Maser, J. D., & Endicott, J. (2000). Multiple recurrences of major depressive disorder. *American Journal of Psychiatry, 157*(2), 229–233.

Spitzer, R. L, Gibbon, M., Skodol, A. E., & First, M. B. (1994). *DSM-IV casebook.* Washington, DC: American Psychiatric Press.

Stader, S. R., & Hokanson, J. E. (1998). Psychosocial antecedents of depressive symptoms: An evaluation using daily experiences methodology. *Journal of Abnormal Psychology, 107*(1), 17–26.

Stevens, D. E., Merikangas, K. R., & Merikangas, J. R. (1995). Comorbidity of depression and other medical conditions. In E. E. Beckham & W. R. Leber (Eds.), *Handbook of depression* (2nd ed., pp. 147–199). New York: Guilford.

Stolorow, R. D., & Lachmann, F. M. (1980). *Psychoanalysis of developmental arrests: Theory and treatment.* Madison, CT: International Universities Press.

Strupp, H. H. (1997, January 11). Quoted in B. Bower, Uncovering traits of effective therapists. *Science News, 151,* 21.

Sturm, R. (1997). How expensive is unlimited mental health care coverage under managed care? *Journal of the American Medical Association, 278*(18), 1533–1537.

Styron, W. (1990). *Darkness visible: A memoir of madness.* New York: Random House.

Suomi, S. J. (1991). Primate separation models of affective disorders. In J. Madden (Ed.), *Neurobiology of learning, emotion, and affect* (pp. 195–214). New York: Raven Press.

Talbot, M. (2000, January 9). The placebo prescription. *The New York Times Magazine,* pp. 34–43.

Terman, M., Terman, J. S., & Ross, D. (1998). A controlled trial of timed bright light and negative air ionization for winter depression. *Archives of General Psychiatry, 55,* 875–882.

Thase, M. E. (1999). The long-term nature of depression. *Journal of Clinical Psychiatry, 60* (Suppl. 4), 3–35.

Thase, M. E., Greenhouse, J. B., Frank, E., Reynolds, C. F., Pilkonis, P. A., Hurley, K., Grochocinski, V., & Kupfer, D. J. (1997). Treatment of major depression with psychotherapy or psychotherapy-pharmacotherapy combinations. *Archives of General Psychiatry, 54,* 1009–1015.

Thase, M. E., & Howland, R. H. (1995). Biological processes in depression: An updated review and integration. In E. E. Beckham & W. R. Leber (Eds.), *Handbook of depression* (2nd ed., pp. 213–279). New York, Guilford.

Thompson, C. (2000). Effects of a clinical-practice guideline and practice-based education on detection and outcome of depression in primary care. *The Lancet, 355,* 180–191.

Thompson, K. (1991). *To be a man: In search of the deep masculine.* Los Angeles: Jeremy Tarcher.

Tomkins, S. S. (1962). *Affect/imagery/consciousness: Vol. 1. The positive affects.* New York: Springer.

Tomkins, S. S. (1963). *Affect/imagery/consciousness: Vol. 2. The negative affects.* New York: Springer.

U. S. Department of Health and Human Services. (1999). *Mental health: A report of the Surgeon General.* Rockville, MD: Author.

U. S. Public Health Service. (1999). *The Surgeon General's Call to Action to Prevent Suicide.* Washington, DC: U. S. Department of Health and Human Services.

Uncapher, H., & Areán, P. (2000). Physicians are less willing to treat suicidal ideation in older patients. *Journal of the American Geriatrics Society, 48,* 188–192.

Üstün, T. B., & Von Korff, M. (1995). Primary mental health services: Access and provision of care. In T. B. Üstün, & N. Sartorius (Eds.), *Mental illness in general health care: An international study* (pp. 347–360). Chichester, UK: Wiley.

Vaillant, G. E. (1993). *The wisdom of the ego.* Cambridge, MA: Harvard University Press.

von Bertalanffy, L. (1968). *General systems theory.* New York: George Braziller.

Von Korff, M., Katon, W., Bush, T., Lin, E. H. B., Simon, G. E., Saunders, K., Ludman, E., Walker, E., & Unutzer, J. (1998). Treatment costs, cost offset, and cost-effectiveness of collaborative management of depression. *Psychosomatic Medicine, 60,* 143–149.

Von Korff, M., & Simon, G. (1996). The relationship between pain and depression. *British Journal of Psychiatry, 168* (Suppl. 30), 101–108.

Wachtel, P. L. (1993). *Therapeutic communication: Knowing what to say when.* New York: Guilford.

Wachtel, P. L. (1994). Cyclical processes in personality and psychopathology. *Journal of Abnormal Psychology, 103*(1), 51–54.

Wachtel, P. L. (1997). *Psychoanalysis, behavior therapy, and the relational world.* Washington, DC: American Psychological Association.

Wallerstein, J. S., & Blakeslee, S. (1989). *Second chances: Men, women, and children a decade after divorce.* New York: Ticknor & Fields.

Warner, V., Weissman, M. M., Mufson, L., & Wickramaratne, P. J. (1999). Grandparents, parents, and grandchildren at high risk for depression: A three-generation study. *Journal of the American Academy of Child and Adolescent Psychiatry, 38*(3), 289–296.

Weiss, E. L., Longhurst, J. G., & Mazure, C. M. (1999). Childhood sexual abuse as a risk factor for depression in women: Psychosocial and neurobiological correlates. *American Journal of Psychiatry, 156*(6), 816–828.

Weissman, M. M., & Klerman, G. L. (1977). Sex differences and the epidemiology of depression. *Archives of General Psychiatry, 34,* 98–111.

Weissman, M. M., Warner, V., Wickramaratne, P., Moreau, D., & Olfson, M. (1997). Offspring of depressed parents: 10 years later. *Archives of General Psychiatry, 54,* 932–940.

Wells, K. B., Burnam, M. A., Rogers, W., Hays, R., & Camp, P. (1992). The course of depression in adult outpatients: Results from the medical outcomes study. *Archives of General Psychiatry, 49,* 788–794.

Wexler, B. E., & Chicchetti, D. (1992). The outpatient treatment of depression: Implications of outcome research for clinical practice. *Journal of Nervous and Mental Disease, 180*(5), 277–286.

White, M. T., & Weiner, M. (1986). *The theory and practice of self psychology.* New York: Brunner/Mazel.

Whybrow, P. (1997). *A mood apart: Depression, mania, and other afflictions of the self.* New York: Basic.

Winnicott, D. W. (1965). *The maturational processes and the facilitating environment: Studies in the theory of emotional development.* Madison, CT: International Universities Press.

Winnicott, D. W. (1971). *Playing and reality.* New York: Basic.

Wirz-Justice, A. (1998). Beginning to see the light. *Archives of General Psychiatry, 55,* 861–862.

Wittchen, H.-U., Lieb, R., Wunderlich, U., & Schuster, P. (1999). Comorbidity in primary care: Presentation and consequences. *Journal of Clinical Psychiatry, 60* (Suppl. 7), 29–36.

Wolf, E. (1979). Countertransference in disorders of the self. In L. Epstein & A. Feiner (Eds.), *Countertransference: The therapist's contribution to the therapeutic situation* (pp. 577–594). New York: Jason Aronson.

Wulsin, L. R., Vaillant, G. E., & Wells, E. (1999). A systematic review of the mortality of depression. *Psychosomatic Medicine, 61,* 6–17.

Yapko, M. D. (1997a). *Breaking the patterns of depression.* New York: Doubleday.

Yapko, M. D. (1997b, January/February). Stronger medicine. *Family Therapy Networker,* 43–47.

Zielbauer, P. (1999, March 26). A promising young man kills himself, and a small town is shaken. *The New York Times,* p. B1.

Zung, W. W. (1965). A self-rating depression scale. *Archives of General Psychiatry, 12,* 63–70.

Index